I0029480

DANGEROUS IDEAS

THE DAWSON CENTRE
COLLOQUIA 2015 AND 2016

DANGEROUS IDEAS

Proceedings of the first two Colloquia
Christopher Dawson Centre
2015 and 2016

**Edited by Michael Stokes
and David Daintree**

Connor Court Publishing

Connor Court Publishing Pty Ltd

Copyright © Michael Stokes and David Daintree 2017

ALL RIGHTS RESERVED. This book contains material protected under International and Federal Copyright Laws and Treaties. Any unauthorised reprint or use of this material is prohibited. No part of this book may be reproduced or transmitted in any form or by any means, electronic or mechanical, including photocopying, recording, or by any information storage and retrieval system without express written permission from the publisher.

PO Box 7257
Redlands Bay Qld 4165
sales@connorcourt.com
www.connorcourt.com

ISBN: 9781925501582

Cover by Maria Giordano

Painting: Dance by Henri Matisse, 1910.

Printed in Australia

CONTENTS

PART TWO – COLLOQUIUM 2016

GENERAL INTRODUCTION

David Daintree

"It is true that Christianity is not bound up with any particular race or culture. It is neither of the East or of the West, but has a universal mission to the human race as a whole …"

"Secularization of culture is seen in its most striking form in the Communist State, where alone as yet the elimination of religion has been carried to its logical conclusion. Nevertheless, the same tendency exists elsewhere; in fact, it permeates the whole outlook of modern civilization. The average man lives more totally in the State than in the past, and even when he is not consciously hostile to religion, he no longer conceives it as a vital activity which must hold its central place in human life and society."

– Christopher Dawson

"Bernard of Chartres used to say that we are like dwarves sitting on the shoulders of giants, for we see more and farther than they, not by the sharpness of our own eyesight or the loftiness of our bodies, but because we are raised up and lifted on high by their colossal greatness."

– John of Salisbury

Following his installation as Archbishop of Hobart on 17 September 2013 the Most Reverend Julian Porteous signaled a determination to advance the Catholic Intellectual Tradition within the Archdiocese and beyond. He took steps to establish the Christopher Dawson Centre for Cultural Studies, in honour of a man who is considered to have been the greatest English-speaking Catholic historian of the 20th century. Christopher Dawson (1889-1970) was brought up an Anglican, converted to Roman Catholicism in 1914, and is principally known for his powerful defence of the vital role of the Christian religion as a major strand of Western culture. The aim of the Centre named after him is "to promote awareness of the Catholic Intellectual Tradition and Cultural Patrimony as essential components of human civilisation". The new Centre was launched by the Hon Tim Fischer AO on Thursday 10 April 2014. Archbishop Porteous graciously asked me to be its first Director and himself agreed to be its Patron.

The Centre seeks to encourage critical reflection and research on the history, literature, philosophy and theology that characterise Christian civilisation and culture, in order to raise the profile of these vital disciplines in intellectual life and to reclaim the high ground. These humane studies remain an essential key to the full and mature understanding of the underlying currents of Australian life. In an age of multiculturalism it is more important than ever to maintain our sense of proportion and hold fast to that synthesis of Faith and Reason that has been gifted to the world by the Christian Tradition. The Centre's focus is cultural and historical. Its supporters represent a wide range of opinion but have in common a desire to preserve and reinforce the intellectual traditions and practices of the West.

Since its establishment in 2013, the Centre has taken a lead in cultural and political debate in Tasmania. It supports the rule of law, and representative democracy. Specific research areas include Christianity in Australia, the defence and promotion of Christian culture as a central component of education in Australia, and Democracy and Freedom in the West. The Centre is honoured to have the support of an International Advisory Board of first-rate scholars and thinkers, as well as a strong local Advisory Committee of distinguished Tasmanians. While our establishment arose under the protection of inspiration of the Catholic Church, we are proud and delighted to have among our Advisors, nationally and internationally, men and women representing different Christian traditions.

The CDC publishes a wide variety of research papers and supporting opinion pieces, runs short courses, and hosts an annual Colloquium on a subject of high topical significance. This volume contains the proceedings of the first two of our Colloquia, held in June 2015 and 2016.

THE CONTRIBUTORS

Rabbi Dr Shimon Cowen is the Founder and Director of the Institute for Judaism and Civilization. This Institute was established to explore the interface of Judaism together with the universal ethics at the root of the world religions with the arts, sciences and values of contemporary civilisation. His most recent book is *The Theory and Practice of Universal Ethics – the Noahide Laws.*

David Daintree is founding Director of the Christopher Dawson Centre and was President of Campion College Australia from 2008 to 2012. Previously he had been Principal of Jane Franklin Hall in the University of Tasmania and Rector of St John's College, University of Sydney.

Thomas V. Gourlay is the president and co-founder of the Christopher Dawson Society for Philosophy and Culture Inc., and the manager of Campus Ministry at the University of Notre Dame Australia. He holds a Bachelor of Education (BEd) and Master of Education (MEd) from the University of Notre Dame Australia, and has worked as a classroom teacher and faculty head of Religious Education in a number of Catholic secondary schools in Western Australia. Tom also earned a Masters of Theological Studies (MTS) through The John Paul II Institute for Marriage and Family Studies in Melbourne, Victoria. He has been published in *New Blackfriars*, *The Heythrop Journal*, and *Homiletic and Pastoral Review.* Tom and his wife Elizabeth live in Perth, Western Australia and have one child, with one on the way.

Nora Liassis is a UTAS graduate in Humanities and Education and an Associate Professor of English Literature, with a PhD in Romanticism from the University of Reading, UK. She was Dean of the School of Humanities & Social Sciences at European University Cyprus, Nicosia from 2007-2014. She lectures on

European literatures in various genres and teaches a forum on Medical Humanities. Nora is also Cyprus President of the Australian Alumni Association which she founded in the 1990s. Her research and publishing areas include: Byronism; Romanticism and the Near East; contemporary verse; religion and literature, literary translations and cultural studies. In 2001 she presented an address at Harvard University on cultural looting and desecration of Christian and Moslem religious sites in Cyprus post 1974. She was also active in the 2010 organisation of Pope Benedict's apostolic journey to Cyprus at "the crossroads of culture and religion" to honor Apostle Paul's 2000th anniversary. Her most recent book, *Aphrodite and Venus in Myth and Mimesis* (CSP) 2015 engages with 700 sources from mythology, European and world culture, and a significant expository chapter on counter-voices to paganism.

Campbell Markham was Moderator of the General Assembly of the Presbyterian Church of Tasmania 2015-16. His great passion is preaching Christ Crucified (1 Corinthians 2:2), and training and mentoring future pastors and preachers. Campbell is Convener of the Social Justice Commission of the PCT, and for many years he and his wife Amanda-Sue have actively opposed government marriage redefinition and pro-abortion legislation. He is currently translating Adolphe Monod's classic nineteenth century treatise on suffering, *Les Adieux*.

Philippa Martyr currently works for the WA Department of Health. She graduated from UWA with a PhD in history in 1994, and taught at the Tasmanian School of Nursing, University of Tasmania, for six years before moving to the UK to become a Visiting Scholar at Oxford Brookes University, and then a Visiting Research Fellow at the Wellcome Unit for the History of Medicine, Norwich. She is an Adjunct Senior Research Fellow with the School of Psychiatry and Clinical Neurosciences, University of Western Australia. Martyr is the author of *Paradise of Quacks: an Alternative His-*

tory of Medicine in Australia (Macleay Press, 2002). Her research has appeared in (among other places) *Social History of Medicine, International Journal of Mental Health Nursing, Australian Health Review, Health and History, Australasian Psychiatry,* the *Australian Dictionary of Biography,* and *Issues in Mental Health Nursing.* Her current research interests include mental health history, epidemiology, and service analysis and evaluation. Martyr also writes for fun, and has published religious and political commentary, poetry and short stories in journals such as *Quadrant, Connor Court Quarterly, AD2000, Fidelity,* and *Homiletic and Pastoral Review.*

Rocky Mimmo is a Sydney-based lawyer. He has a Masters Degree in International Law from the University of NSW. His postgraduate Masters studies included an emphasis on Human Rights Law. He is married with eight children. He has devoted his adult life to working on social issues and attempting to influence public decision-makers on critical moral social issues. On these social moral issues, Rocky works in the background in and around politics. Although not party politically aligned, he is well connected on both sides of politics at the Federal and State level. He has made a study of Discrimination Laws and their impact on religious liberty in public and social conduct and on cultural values. Rocky has made many submissions to Parliamentary Committees and published articles arguing the case for religious liberty and human rights.

After many years of involvement in the moral social issues and noticing the decline and deterioration of religious and cultural values, Rocky founded the Ambrose Centre For Religious Liberty in 2007. The Ambrose Centre was publicly launched in Sydney in April 2009. Rocky is also the human rights lawyer for the Canadian-based international organisation *Protection of Conscience Project.*

Mark Podesta was ordained a Priest for the Archdiocese of Sydney in 2007. He was appointed as Assistant Priest at the Parish of St Mark's Drummoyne from 2007 to 2009. Fr Podesta was the Official Media Spokesperson for World Youth Day Sydney in 2008, hosting all of the live broadcasts to an estimated audience of one billion people worldwide. In 2009, Cardinal Pell asked Fr Podesta to study canon law in Rome, and three years later, Fr Podesta graduated with a Licence in Canon Law from the Pontifical Gregorian University in 2012. Upon his return to Australia, he was appointed as Administrator of the Parish of St Patrick's Mortlake from 2012 to 2014. Fr Podesta was appointed Director of the Archdiocese of Sydney Tribunal Office in 2013, and the majority of his ministry until 2017 involved running this office which deals with the question of the validity or nullity of marriages which have ended in civil divorce. As well as this, Fr Podesta is a Judge of the Regional Tribunal of Sydney; he teaches Canon Law at the University of Notre Dame Australia-Sydney, and provides canonical advice to bishops and clergy in Australia. In addition, Fr Podesta has been a member of the Sydney Archdiocesan Commission for Ecumenism and Interfaith Relations since 2005, and most recently assisted in the Parishes of St Patrick's Summer Hill and St Thomas Beckett's Lewisham on weekends.

Julian Porteous was appointed the eleventh Archbishop of Hobart on 19 July 2013 by His Holiness Pope Francis. He was ordained a priest for the Archdiocese of Sydney on 7th September, 1974, and served as Priest in many parishes of the Archdiocese. Archbishop Porteous was appointed Rector of the Seminary of the Good Shepherd, Sydney, in January 2002 and served in this role until the end of 2008. Pope John Paul II named him Auxiliary Bishop of Sydney in July 2003. Archbishop Porteous is actively involved in evangelisation, particularly among young people, and has been involved with a number of new ecclesial movements. He promotes the role and work of the new ecclesial movements as a grace given to the Church in our time to renew the Catholic faith and promote the evangelising mission of the Church. Archbishop Porteous chose as his motto, *Gratia et Veritas* – "Grace and Truth", a reference to John 1:17. Archbishop Porteous has published the following books: *St Brendan's, a Journey: The Story of an Australian Catholic Parish 1898-1998* (1997); *The New Evangelisation, Developing Evangelical Preaching* (2008); *After the Heart of God: the Life and Ministry of Priests at the Beginning of the Third Millennium* (2009); *A New Wine & Fresh Skins: Ecclesial Movements in the Church* (2010); *Streams of Grace: Spiritual Movements that Shaped the Church* (2011); *Become what you are: Growing in Christian Character* (2012); *Manual of Minor Exorcisms* (2012) and *Prayers for those experiencing Spiritual Affliction* (2012).

Usman Rana was born to Ahmadi Muslim Parents in Lyallpur (Faisalabad), Pakistan. With his parents he moved to Germany as a Refugee at the age of four. Growing up in Germany he struggled to make sense of his parents' religion and culture and ended up a agnostic. At the age of 18, thoroughly German by this time in temperament and upbringing, he returned to Pakistan and found himself alone with an unfamiliar culture and language. It was then that he met a young woman who diverted him from his misery and isolation – and became his wife. Subsequently he reacquainted himself with the local language and culture, started his studies again and became an IT Network Engineer. Extremists and Radicals disrupted his happiness and he became a refugee again, arriving in Australia where he lived a year in both Sydney and Brisbane before moving to Tasmania and to become the first President of the Ahmadiyya Muslim Association in that state. The World Wide Ahmadiyya Muslim Community (www.alislam.org) is the fastest growing Muslim Community in the World, represented in over 200 countries with millions of members worldwide.

Karl Schmude has combined a career in university librarianship and freelance writing with a formative role in the development of a liberal arts tertiary college. He has a BA from Sydney University, a Diploma in Librarianship from the University of NSW, and a Master of Letters from the University of New England (UNE). Beginning at the NSW State Library in Sydney, he moved to Armidale NSW in 1970 where he worked in the UNE Library for thirty years, serving as University Librarian from 1984 to 2000. He is a Founding Fellow of Australia's first liberal arts college, Campion College Australia, and serves as a Trustee of its governing body. From 2000 to 2015, he was Executive Director of the Campion Foundation.

Most recently, he has been appointed as Chairman of the Board of St Albert's College, the Catholic residential college at the University of New England in Armidale. He has published extensively on subjects associated with religion, history, literature and education. His feature articles and book reviews have appeared in Australian newspapers and journals as well as international periodicals in the USA, Canada, the UK and South America. He has written biographical booklets on G.K. Chesterton and Hilaire Belloc, and most recently Christopher Dawson (published by the Christopher Dawson Centre for Cultural Studies in Hobart). He is President of the Australian Chesterton Society and a member of the Editorial Board of the international journal, *The Chesterton Review*.

Sarjit Alexander Sidhu (Alex) has a BA with honours in politics, a BCom and an MA, also in politics, from the University of Melbourne. He has also completed an MPhil in moral and political theology at the University of Oxford and is currently completing his DPhil, also in moral and political theology. His thesis focuses on human rights, democracy and Christianity.

Alex has worked in the financial sector, as a business consultant with Ernst and Young, and academia, working at the University of Melbourne and the John Paul II Institute for Studies on Marriage and the Family (Melbourne Campus) lecturing in the areas of politics, philosophy and theology. He is currently working for the

Catholic Archdiocese of Hobart as the Private Secretary to the Archbishop of Hobart.

Michael Stokes is currently an Adjunct Associate Professor at the Law School of the University of Notre Dame Australia and an Adjunct Senior Lecturer at the Law School of the University of Tasmania. He has expertise in Australian Constitutional Law, Administrative Law, Environmental Law and the philosophy of law. He is well known for public comments and media appearances with respect to constitutional and other legal issues and has given evidence to the parliament on matters as diverse as legislation with respect to pulp mills and same sex marriage and abortion. He has written widely on Australian Constitutional law, especially on constitutional interpretation and the philosophy of language and on Tasmanian environmental law. He has substantial editorial experience, just having resigned as editor of the *Australian Journal of Legal Philosophy*. Because of his religious affiliation (he is a Latter Day Saint), Michael's research interests are increasingly focused on issues of concern to religious groups, such as abortion law reform and freedom of conscience, abortion and homicide, same sex marriage and antidiscrimination law and theory. He is currently working on a law project with respect to judicial review of government action for the Tasmanian Law Reform Institute.

Brendan Triffett lectures in Ministry and Theology at the Hobart campus of Alphacrucis College. He received his PhD in philosophy at the University of Tasmania in 2011 and specialises in the interaction of metaphysics and theology. He has published in *The Heythrop Journal* and is intermittently working on a book that will explicate and critique the Trinitarian theology of Aquinas. Brendan also dabbles in composition at the piano and especially loves the work of Beethoven, Chopin and Sibelius.

Richard Umbers was born in Auckland, New Zealand. He originally studied management at the University of Waikato in

1989 but transferred to University of Sydney in 1992 to receive more intense formation at a Centre of Opus Dei in Chatswood, Sydney. He later qualified with a Bachelor of Economics from University of Sydney and a Masters of Management from the University of Waikato, New Zealand. Bishop Richard entered the Opus Dei Seminary of Cavabianca, Rome, in 1996 and studied at Santa Croce Pontifical University, Rome, achieving a Bachelor of Theology in 1999. Between 1999-2002, Bishop Richard studied at the University of Navarre, Spain, where he received a Doctorate in Philosophy. On 14 February 2002, he was ordained a deacon and later ordained a priest on 1 September 2002. Since 2003, Bishop Richard has worked pastorally as a School and University Chaplain at a number of NSW colleges and also tutored and lectured at the University of Notre Dame, Sydney, between 2006 and 2013. Bishop Richard was most recently a representative of the Archbishop on the Council of Priests of the Archdiocese of Sydney and a member representative for the Archdiocese to the St John of God Hospitals. Bishop Richard is widely published in the area of philosophy, regularly addresses gatherings of youth, has an interest in social media, and has a library of his own podcasts.

David van Gend is a GP and President of the Australian Marriage Forum (www.AustralianMarriage.org). His best-selling 2016 book, *Stealing From a Child: The Injustice of "Marriage Equality"*, was published by Connor Court.

Robert van Gend was awarded an Australian Student Prize in 2011 and graduated from Campion College, Sydney in 2014 with the College Medal for the Bachelor of Arts (Liberal Arts), majoring in Philosophy, History and Latin. His first year mathematics essay, "The Fibonacci Sequence and the Golden Ratio in Music", was published in the journal, *Notes on Number Theory and Discrete Mathematics.* In 2016, Robert helped found Augustine Academy, a liberal arts school for upper high school students, where he is the philosophy lecturer. He plays viola with the Australian Youth Orchestra and is currently writing a thesis on the mind-body problem for a Master of Philosophy degree at the University of Notre Dame, Sydney.

Haydn Walters is a science and medicine graduate from Oxford University, and has higher doctorates in both discipline areas. He did post-doctoral work at University of California in San Francisco in the early 1980s and had extensive social and professional contact there with gay men, and with their health issues. He was Foundation Professor of Respiratory Medicine at Monash University during the 1990s and during that period was Professor of Medicine and Associate Dean (Research) in the Faculty of Health at the University of Tasmania. Between 2010-2013, as Associate Dean, Mercy Professor and Head of the Melbourne Campus of the University Notre Dame Australia, he established a 'Catholic' clinical school in Melbourne. Since then he has been a Professorial Fellow at the Universities of Tasmania and Melbourne, a Senior Practitioner Fellow with the National Health and Medical Research Council and Director of the NHMRC's Centre of Research Excellence for Chronic Respiratory Disease and Lung Ageing in Tasmania.

Christine Wood is the Director of the Office of Evangelisation and Catechesis in the Archdiocese of Hobart where she forms missionary disciples for the new evangelisation. Dr Wood has taught Biblical, Moral and Systematic Theology at John Paul the Great Catholic University, San Diego, Catholic Distance University in West Virginia, and the University of Notre Dame, Fremantle, and is the President of the St. John Centre for Biblical Studies in Sydney. She received her Ph.D. in Systematic Theology from Marquette University, Milwaukee, with a dissertation entitled, "The Metaphysics and Intellective Psychology in the Natural Desire for Seeing God: Henri de Lubac and Neo-Scholasticism." She earned her MA in Theology, as well as a Certification in Catechetics, from Franciscan University of Steubenville.

Sophie York is the National spokeswoman for Marriage Alliance (www.marriagealliance.com.au), an independent, grassroots organisation which advocates the right of all Australians to freely support the legal definition of marriage in Australia remaining exclusively between one man and one woman. This organisation considers that such marriage has served Australian families, society and culture well. It also considers that whenever major societal structural change is contemplated, the rights and freedoms of all possibly affected by the change, must be debated, acknowledged and protected. Sophie is a barrister at the NSW Bar, who works as a lecturer in Jurisprudence at Sydney University. She is an Officer in the Royal Australian Naval Legal Reserves. She is also a Red Cross-trained Instructor in the Law of Armed Conflict (International Humanitarian Law – IHL). She is a published author, a Board member of Campion College, and chairs a Police Committee. She is married to a medical specialist and is a mother of four boys.

Benno Zuiddam is an extraordinary associate professor with the faculty of Theology of North West University (South Africa) and Greenwich School of Theology (UK), and associate of the Centre for Patristic Research (the Netherlands). Dr Zuiddam is a trained journalist and served on the state board of a Christian political party. He received his education at five universities in the Netherlands and South Africa: Amersfoort/Ede, Kampen, Utrecht, Bloemfontein and Potchefstroom. Professor Zuiddam presently combines his residence in Australia with a research appointment with North West University in South Africa. He also serves as postgraduate tutor with Greenwich School of Theology (UK) and with the Centre for Patristic Research (Free University & Tilburg University, the Netherlands). In 2014 Dr Zuiddam was nominated and elected as fellow of the South African Academy for Science and Art. He has published in the fields of Classical Studies, New Testament, Old Testament, Church History, Patristics and Art history. He authored two monographs: "Hope and Disillusionment," a basic introduction to the history of the Western Church; and "Holy Letters and Syllables," on the role of Scripture in the early Church. Benno is married to Anne-Marié and they have four children.

Colloquium 2015

The Religious View of History:
A Celebration of Dangerous Ideas

Edited by Michael Stokes

INTRODUCTION TO THE 2015 COLLOQUIUM

David Daintree

"I was ashamed that for so many years I had yelped, not against the Catholic faith, but against fables of human imagination. I had in fact been rash and wicked in condemning matters that I ought to have taught myself to understand."

– St Augustine, *Confessions* 6.3

"Some philosophers indeed have argued in the past that the burden of proof is on the atheist. I think the origins of the laws of nature and of life and the Universe point clearly to an intelligent Source. The burden of proof is on those who argue to the contrary."

– Anthony Flew

During the past 100 years atheism and agnosticism have progressively gained dominance in the intellectual life of the West and of nations aligned to the Western tradition. This shift in thinking has accelerated almost exponentially in the last few decades to the point at which perhaps most public intellectuals in the West (and those influenced by them) have no affiliation with any religion and no sympathy for the religious impulse in others. Atheism, or what amounts to atheism, has thus become the 'default position' of many if not most Western thinkers. It is a consoling thought to many in our world that humanity might have outgrown religion. The religious view of history is uncongenial to most of the people we all rub shoulders with every day.

It is thus hardly surprising that the "marriage debate" has been won by the same-sex side in 21 Western countries. People who

1

believe that marriage is merely a contract, albeit a loving one, between any two human beings, that it has no necessary connection with procreation, and that it can be terminated by a simple legal process, have no concept of what most of us would see as the sacramental or sacred dimension. Given their intellectual background, and their experience of life, one can hardly expect otherwise.

One of the thoughts that inspired our decision to host this colloquium, and to go as it were on the front foot against prevailing opinion, came from C.S Lewis:

> Then I read Chesterton's *Everlasting Man* and for the first time saw the whole Christian outline of history set out in a form that seemed to me to make sense ... Really, a young Atheist cannot guard his faith too carefully. Dangers lie in wait for him on every side.

The influence of Christianity on Western thought and Western spirituality has been revolutionary. The greatness of its triumph has paradoxically led to its invisibility: in this post-Christian age everybody accepts the basic principles of Christian morality (apart from the sexual ones!). But in accepting those principles they forget the theology that spawned them. Justice, mercy, humility, brotherly love, the equitable distribution of goods were generally not understood to be virtues in the pagan world. Christianity made them obligatory, part of the air we breathe – but who notices air? The missionaries are not remembered, or if they are remembered they are reviled. But the fruit they bore has been kept and claimed as the birthright of the secular world, though the planting has been forgotten.

We see something of this in a poem by William Blake –

> To Mercy, Pity, Peace, and Love
> All pray in their distress;
> And to these virtues of delight
> Return their thankfulness.

It's not really an atheistic poem, but it can be read as such. Blake appeals to the modern mind. The virtues he so admires can be tidily excised from their religious roots.

Christianity is not the only faith that is having a hard time in the modern world. I recently toured five predominantly Muslim countries in central Asia – Uzbekistan, Turkmenistan, Kazakhstan, Kyrgyzstan and Tajikistan. I met many good, sweet-natured and committed Muslim people who deeply regretted that ISIS had led so many of their young people astray – and even more regretted the aggressive secularism of their own governments. A young trainee guide of school age told me that if he were seen at Friday prayers he would be liable to expulsion from his state high school. We who are Christians in the West may occasionally feel that the state is against us. But some people in the world much harder row to hoe.

It is virtually impossible for ordinary people in western nations today to imagine the impact of hope on a people raised in hopelessness. Those in modern times who are most likely to have experienced this are the missionaries who brought both the religion and aspects of the culture of the West to peoples who had previously lived in relative deprivation. Missionaries nowadays have a poor reputation in 'progressive' circles, have been the butt of untold jokes, and have been despised as agents of imperialism, so that any claim that they have done good will be most unwelcome to many, but it is easily tested by reading the accounts of those who actually brought medical aid, essential food supplies or education to societies that had previously had restricted or no access to such things. One of the very few missionaries of whom nobody has been able to think of anything damning to say was Albert Schweitzer, whose experience as both a Christian missionary and a medical doctor has been well chronicled and stands as a ready testimony to the good effect of the missions on underprivileged people. St Peter Claver in Colombia and Father Damian of Molokai are other outstanding examples of that same good spirit. Closer to our own days Mother Teresa of Calcutta, lacking the protection that time and custom commonly bring, has been bitterly condemned by many who see Christian charity as a subterfuge for imperialism.

Let us be clear: *Mission* was an imperative of Christianity from the beginning. The modern leftist sceptic finds it insufferable that missionaries claimed to improve the lives and cultures of those they worked among, yet the work of Schweitzer and others makes clear the (to some) unpalatable truth that they did indeed bring great benefits. When we read of the mass conversions of tribes and nations to Christianity we take refuge in the thought that they took place under compulsion. But there is ample evidence that nations as well as individuals exercised free will under the influence of impassioned and dedicated apostles and evangelists. In an age of individualism such as our own it is hard to appreciate that sense of community that might induce a people to convert en masse, for we struggle to understand the bonds of loyalty that could unite people more 'primitive' than ourselves. But that such mass voluntary conversions took place in late antiquity and the Middle Ages is clear, and the fact that similar things happened in Africa and the South Pacific at the very threshold of modernity may be taken as confirmation that such movements are indeed possible. In such nations as Samoa we can recognize Christianity as a popular and voluntary commitment of the hearts and minds of the people.

It is as difficult for us now to appreciate the extraordinary radicalism of the Enlightenment and its effect on our temperament as it is to understand the reaction of pre-Christian Europe to the coming of the Gospel. A world of apparently changeless institutions, contentedly devoted to the memory of its ancestors, resistant to change (and seeing no reason to change) is utterly incomprehensible to us who are the inheritors of Enlightenment attitudes. Today a belief in and an addiction to the Enlightenment notion of human progress is the best hope of many in the modern world. We see it in the faith that many ordinary people place in Science, the great Deliverer that has all the answers and will someday heal all diseases and give us all full, long and healthy lives. The most dangerous idea of all is that Science, for all the benefits it has brought us, is just not up to the task.

We are all heirs to these movements and are profoundly influenced by them, even if we are not fully aware and are temperamentally averse to them. The part played by Christianity in patrimony of the West has been neither ancillary nor supplementary, but literally essential: Western civilisation has been Christian in its very essence. Those who would understand the West cannot sift the Christianity out of it.

1

REVELATION AND THE IDEOLOGICAL USURPATION OF TRUTH

Thomas V. Gourlay

ABSTRACT

When a reductive approach is taken to the notion of revelation itself the Gospel loses its evangelical potency. In a culture which has reduced truth to mere ideology a renewed patristic and personal notion of revelation serves as significant threat not only to agnostic and atheistic social structures, but also those who would seek to use the faith to serve as a foot-soldier in an unending series of battles in the continuing culture wars.

Analysing the contribution of the young Fr Joseph Ratzinger to the Vatican II document *Dei Verbum*, this paper will seek to show that the document, ratified by the Council Fathers, promotes a return to a patristic notion of revelation – that what is revealed by God rather than being a mere list of doctrines or intellectual propositions to which intellectual ascent must be given, is in fact God's very self in the person of Jesus Christ.

Using the subsequent work of Ratzinger, as both Prefect of the Congregation for the Doctrine of the Faith, and eventually as Pope Benedict XVI, as well as the insights of British cultural historian Christopher Dawson this paper will seek to show that, much more than being "an ethical choice or a lofty idea", the Christian faith, hinging on the historical reality of the Incarnation and the continued encounter with the person of Christ, cannot be reduced to mere politics or ideology, no matter how closely aligned to the Christian faith any particular ideology may seem.

Introduction

The whole modern world has divided itself into Conservatives and Progressives. The business of Progressives is to go on making mistakes. The business of the Conservatives is to prevent the mistakes from being corrected.[1]

In reality Christianity is not merely a moral ideal or set of ideas. It is a concrete reality. It is the spiritual order incarnated in a historical person and in a historical society. The spiritual order is just as real as the material order. The reason we do not see it is because we do not look at it. Our interests and our thoughts are elsewhere. A few exceptional men, mystics or philosophers, may find it possible to live habitually on a spiritual plane, but for the ordinary man it is a difficult atmosphere to breathe in. But it is the function of Christianity to bring the spiritual order into contact and relation with the world of man. It is, as it were, a bridge between the two worlds; it brings religion down into human life and it opens the door of the spiritual world to man.[2]

Being Christian is not the result of an ethical choice or a lofty idea, but the encounter with an event, a person, which gives life a new horizon and a decisive direction.[3]

One thing I am particularly conscious of in contemporary Catholic and broadly Christian circles that might describe themselves as "conservative", "orthodox" or simply "faithful", is the danger

---

[1] G.K. Chesterton, *Illustrated London News*, 19 April 1924.

[2] Christopher Dawson, *Christianity as the Soul of the West, The Modern Dilemma*, Sheed & Ward, 1932.

[3] Benedict XVI, *Deus Caritas Est: On Christian Love*, Strathfield, NSW: St Pauls Publications, 2006.

of getting "lost in the battle" in the midst of the ongoing and ever growing cultural crisis which we are experiencing. What I mean by "getting lost in the battle" is that one can be so absorbed in whatever major or minor skirmish of the culture war which is currently being waged that the deeper spiritual war, that war being fought for the souls of men and women, can be forgotten in the struggle for victory in one area of social reform or another.

The danger, as I see it, is that well-meaning Christians who have come to describe themselves as "social and economic conservatives" have fallen into a trap that has them creating ideologies out of certain elements of the Christian message, and substituting them for the Gospel as such. These efforts essentially reduce the faith to mere ethical and philosophical propositions that will either be used as a club, or defended to the death in the latest manifestation of the culture wars.

Exploring the early work of the young Fr Ratzinger on Revelation the following paper will point to a conception of Truth which overcomes the temptation to reduce the faith to a list of "ethical propositions" or "lofty ideals". Utilising the work of Dawson and others it will then outline a particularly Augustinian and evangelically more potent model of engaging in public discussion concerning the more neuralgic issues of our times.

Ratzinger and *Dei Verbum* – a personalistic notion of revelation

It is well known that in the years leading up the Vatican II Council (1962-1965), many of the brighter sparks in the Catholic theological world were becoming increasingly dissatisfied with the notion of revelation which was most commonly found in their seminary theological manuals.[4] As it was taught according to

---

[4] For a detailed analysis of some of the movements and major personalities see Fergus Kerr, *Twentieth Century Catholic Theologians: From Neoscholasticism to Nuptial Mysticism,* Blackwell Publishing, 2007.

the theory developed by Spanish Jesuit Francesco Suárez (1548-1617), revelation consisted of a series of intellectual propositions which required the intellectual assent of the believer.[5] This stood at odds with a deeper patristic notion of revelation which was being rediscovered through the work of a number of the ressourcement theologians, not least of whom was Fr Henri de Lubac SJ. De Lubac was to be a significant influence on the young Fr Ratzinger, who in his postdoctoral dissertation, or "Habilitationsschrift," challenged the prevailing notion of revelation at the time in a study of the theology of history and revelation as presented in the writings of St. Bonaventure.[6] In his memoirs he recounts that his studies up until that point in his life had led him to the conclusion that "Revelation now appeared no longer simply as a communication of truths to the intellect, but as a historical action of God, in which truth becomes gradually unveiled."

In this thesis, amongst other insights, the Suárezian notion of revelation was challenged, and what could be considered as a personalist understanding of God's self-revelation in history, is developed. He writes that, for Bonaventure, "'revelation' is synonymous with the spiritual understanding of Scripture; it consists in the God-given act of understanding, and not in the objective letter alone."[7] The work presses into the mystery of revelation according to St. Bonaventure, and makes a clear distinction between Revelation and Scripture. Ratzinger writes that:

> Bonaventure holds that the content of faith is found not
> only in the letter of Scripture, but in the spiritual meaning

---

[5] A great deal of work in unpicking this Suárezian notion of revelation is done by Jesuit scholar J. Montag, see J. Montag, "Revelation: The False Legacy of Suárez," in *Radical Orthodoxy: A New Theology*, ed. J. Milbank, C. Pickstock, and G. Ward (Oxon: Routledge, 1999).

[6] Josef Ratzinger, *The Theology of History in St. Bonaventure* trans. Zachary Hayes, Franciscan Herald Press, 1989.

[7] Ibid., 63.

lying behind the letter. Furthermore, we can see why it is that for Bonaventure, Scripture, simply as a written document, does not constitute revelation, whereas the understanding of Scripture, which arises in theology, can be called revelation, at least indirectly.[8]

This has tremendous impact not only on how the Scriptures themselves are read and studied, but for how the Christian conceives of truth itself. For if Jesus Christ, the very revelation of the Father and his love[9] is the way, the truth and the life [Jn 14:6] then the believer cannot conceive of truth as a list of propositions or ethical ideals distilled from the written Gospels as such. No, instead the believer has to assert with Pope Benedict XVI that

> [being] Christian is not the result of an ethical choice or a lofty idea, but the encounter with an event, a person, which gives life a new horizon and a decisive direction.[10]

A Dawsonian Synthesis

This notion of revelation as the historically incarnate second person of the Trinity was one clearly understood by British cultural historian Christopher Dawson (1889-1970). Dawson's obviously Augustinian view of the world and of history, and more particularly of the human person enabled him to see that the human person was created with the ability to perceive and receive revealed truth, and to respond to it. Dawson's writings exhibit a worldview which locates the 'restless heart' of Augustine as the real dynamic of world history. His awareness of Original Sin enabled him to see that, while the human person is an innately religious or worshipping being, that they in fact will at times direct their adoration, rightly due to their creator alone, towards things which are less worthy of said adoration.

---

[8] Ibid., 66.

[9] *Gaudium et Spes*, 22.

[10] Benedict XVI, op. cit., 1.

In his day this was being most concretely evidenced in the growth ideological movements which built on the radical rationalism of the Enlightenment. In 1928 Dawson wrote, "[i]t is true that there still exists a widespread prejudice against any religion which claims to rest on divine or supernatural revelation. The old 18th century ideal of a purely rational religion – a Religion without Revelation – has not lost its attractiveness to the modern world."[11] One might argue that this was even felt in certain theological circles of his day, in particularly rationalistic veins of Thomistic thought.

Dawson was quick to point out that the religious impulse in man had not and indeed could not have died. He writes, "[t]he fact that religion no longer finds a place in social life does not necessarily involve the disappearance of the religious instinct. If the latter is denied its normal expression, and driven back upon itself, it may easily become an anti-social force of explosive violence."[12] And that is what the 20th century witnessed.

The most deadly ideological movements of his day, namely National Socialism and Bolshevism, both employed significant religious characteristics. Dawson's critique of National Socialism is particularly telling on this point. For Dawson all ideology, including that of the modern liberal democracy, is rightly identified as anti-human by Dawson. More than merely denouncing evil as it was most explicitly manifest, Dawson's insight to the human person and the nature of truth as such saw him denounce the growth of ideology wherever he saw it. In an essay entitled "The Left-Right Fallacy" from 1946, Dawson writes damningly about the politicisation and ideologisation of almost everything. For Dawson all ideologising is totalitarian in nature. He writes, '[t]he tactics of to-

---

[11] Christopher Dawson, *Progress and Religion: An Historical Inquiry*, ed. Christina Scott and Don J. Briel, The Works of Christopher Dawson (Washington D.C.: Catholic Univeristy of America Press, 2001), 188.

[12] Ibid., 177.

talitarianism are to weld every difference of opinion and tradition and every conflict of economic interests into an absolute ideological opposition which disintegrates society into hostile factions bent on destroying one another.'[13]

Pointing to the rampant absurdity of the rapid growth in ideological positions in his own day Dawson wrote:

> For example, there are Liberals and Conservatives, there are Republicans and Monarchists, there are anti-clericals and clericals, there are Communists and Fascists, there are Socialists and Individualists, there are Semites and anti-Semites. All of these are different oppositions, which have no necessary connection with one another, yet all of them are brought under the Left-Right headings and thus forced into ideological alliances which may be unnecessary and absurd. Moreover, when you have got your opponents all neatly ticketed you can then repeat the same process on any section of them – dividing the Socialists into Socialists of the Left Center in Socialists of the Extreme Left, or the Liberals into Moderates or Progressives, so as to submit them to the same process of confusion and disintegration.[14]

For Christians to engage in such reductive activities would be abhorrent to Dawson. The truth, revealed to us as the person of Jesus cannot be made to fit into our neat ideological categories. The kind of ideologisation that Dawson demonstrates above does not allow for genuine dialogue to take place, nor does it allow for genuine truth to be sought. For Dawson, this simplification of complex philosophical ideas into colours (ie Red for Communist, Pink for Socialist etc) or just mere ideologically driven terms, as is still done still in the political sphere today, is counter-productive at best and absolutely destructive at worst. He writes:

---

[13] Christopher Dawson, "The Left-Right Fallacy," *The Catholic Mind*, April (1946).
[14] Ibid.

In this campaign of disintegration the Right-Left mythology is a perfect god-send to the forces of destruction. It provides them with a crude and simple but highly effective instrument which can be applied to almost any situation and by which any number of different issues can be merged together in a mass of confusion and ideological clap-trap.[15]

In our present cultural environment we see more and more the simplistic labeling of legitimate arguments as mere bigotry and subsequently dismissed as the voice of hatred. My reading of Dawson sees him cautioning against Christian involvement with such ideologically driven disputation. For Dawson any attempt to align the Christian faith with one or another ideology emerges only from a faith not adequately pervasive of the life of the people, of their culture. This is not to say that Christian persons, or indeed any person of good will cannot be involved in ongoing debate about social mores or public ethics, to the contrary they should be increasingly so. What it does mean however is that we cannot use the tactics of those who are promoting modes of life and social organization which are antithetical to human flourishing. Propaganda quite simply is not fitting for the human person, even if it is promoting a 'culture of life.'

For Dawson, the critique of ideology was, as I mentioned above, not limited to national socialism or communism. His critique of the modern liberal democratic state earned him the label of fascist in not a few magazine editorials and letters to the editor. But for Dawson, an ideological loyalty to the modern liberal demoncratic state would be equally reductive. For him, the point was not to find the best ideology, or the one which had most in common with the Christian worldview and throw all his support behind that. For him the ultimate measure of truth was Truth himself, and in assessing

---

[15] Ibid.

the validity of any mode of societal structure the ultimate end or *telos* of the human person, namely union with the Trinitarian God in heaven, must be held in view.

More than just a Dangerous Idea

The idea which I am presenting here as being particularly dangerous to the current atheistic order is unsurprisingly not in fact and idea at all, but rather a person – Truth Incarnate. The fact of this personal God who is Truth, who became incarnate and is active in history blows apart our pre-conceived notions and opens up "new horizions." Our continued efforts to live in relation with this Truth and to be conformed to it allows an openness and a freedom that quite simply cannot coincide with any attempt to further another ideology. Because of this we can say that individual experience has a value, and our engagement with others who perhaps might not share our values on life, marriage and the like can be strengthened by our willingness to engage with the experience of the other. When one can acknowledge that wherever there is truth it is the Lord's,[16] then and only then can a dialogue between person occur which is truly fruitful. This is far more than a mere assertion which would establish life for example as one ultimate good among other, incommensurate goods, such as knowledge, play, aesthetic experience, sociability or friendship, and religion. This has deeper roots in a theological anthropology that posits man's ultimate end in an eternal union with the Trinity itself.

I want to conclude with an example of a recent movement which I've had little to do with, but which I see as having real potential. A few years ago in Sydney at the Great Grace conference organized by the Archdiocese a lecture was presented by Dr Austen Ivereigh

---

[16] "Let every good and true Christian understand that wherever truth may be found, it belongs to his Master", Augustine, *On Christian Doctrine*, trans. D.W. Robertson (New York: Liberal Arts Press, 1958), II.18.28.

who spoke about the original impetus for the Catholic Voices group which he and other established. I wasn't at this conference, but had an opportunity to listen to a recording. In his presentation Ivereigh spoke of how the announcement of Pope Benedict XVI's UK visit in 2010 was being received rather negatively by a significantly vocal group. This group had established a website and were circulating a petition which would see the Pope's invitation to the UK revoked and his diplomatic credentials suspended. Along with this, they had written a long list of complaints which they saw as reasons for this, reasons including recent clerical sex abuse scandals, the Catholic Church's position on women clergy, same sex marriage, abortion euthanasia and the like.

For the Catholic Voices group, this list of concerns became something of an agenda or a program. Here they had a list of issues which were stumbling blocks to the faith, and the people who were voicing such concerns were genuine in their motivation for justice and truth. These neuralgic issues became not just battle lines upon which new battles in the culture wars were to be fought, but points of contact – opportunitites not just to share a Catholic of Christian perspective, but to speak the truth, a Truth which is Love Incarnate.

Rather than get buried in the temptation to dig in in a culture war scenario and attempt to defend a crumbling social order that is barely reminiscent of a Christendom that has long since crumbled, these issues became opportunities to invite others to "come and see" (Jn 1:46), to share with them the reasons for our hope (1 Pet 3:15).

Conclusion

In his 1959 work *The Movement of World Revolution,* Dawson wrote that, 'In the war of ideas, it is the crudest and the most simplified ideology that wins.'[17] I think all here can acknowledge that the truth of this can be seen most acutely in the blatant slogan-eering being bandied about in the campaigns around the Western world attempting to redefine marriage. Against this growing tide of popularism Christians, and indeed all men and women of good will need to engage with more than the buzzwords and emotional pro-paganda so readily used by others in the debate. What provides the strongest threat to the current atheistic social order is in fact noth-ing more than a Christianity which is radically free from ideology. Lewis' Screwtape was 'on the money' when we informed his dear nephew Wormwood of the impotency of any kind of "Christianity and ...". And I will leave you with his words:

> What we want, if men become Christians at all, is to keep them in the state of mind I call "Christianity And". You know – Christianity and the Crisis, Christianity and the New Psychology, Christianity and the New Order, Chris-tianity and Faith Healing, Christianity and Psychical Re-search, Christianity and Vegetarianism, Christianity and Spelling Reform. If they must be Christians let them at least be Christians with a difference. Substitute for the faith itself some Fashion with a Christian colouring.

---

[17] Christopher Dawson, *The Movement of World Revolution*, ed. Don J. Briel, The Works of Christopher Dawson (Washington D.C.: Catholic University of America Press, 2013), 74.

References

Augustine, *On Christian Doctrine*. Translated by D.W. Robertson, New York: Liberal Arts Press, 1958.

Benedict XVI. *Deus Caritas Est: On Christian Love*, Strathfield, NSW: St Pauls Publications, 2006.

Dawson, Christopher. "The Left-Right Fallacy", *The Catholic Mind*, April (1946).

Dawson, Christopher, *The Modern Dilemma: The Problem of European Unity*, Essays in Order no. 5, New York: Sheed and Ward, 1932.

——— *The Movement of World Revolution*, The Works of Christopher Dawson. edited by Don J. Briel Washington D.C.: Catholic University of America Press, 2013, 1959.

——— *Progress and Religion: An Historical Inquiry*, The Works of Christopher Dawson, edited by Christina Scott and Don J. Briel, Washington D.C.: Catholic University of America Press, 2001. 1929.

Kerr, Fergus, *Twentieth Century Catholic Theologians: From Neoscholasticism to Nuptial Mysticism*, Oxford: Blackwell Publishing, 2007.

Montag, John. "Revelation: The False Legacy of Suárez", In *Radical Orthodoxy: A New Theology*, edited by John Milbank, Catherine Pickstock and Graham Ward, Oxon: Routledge, 1999.

Ratzinger, Joseph. *The Theology of History in St. Bonaventure*, Translated by Zachary Hayes, Chicago, Ill: Franciscan Herald Press, 1989.

Vatican II, *Gaudium et Spes. Pastoral Constitution of the Church in the Modern World*, 1965.

2

CHRISTOPHER DAWSON'S RESPONSE TO CULTURE AND RELIGION IN CHRISTIAN LATIN POETRY

Nora Liassis

ABSTRACT

This paper proposes to review Dawson's illuminating but measured responses to the Latin writings of Christian poets of the fifth-sixth centuries and their literary visions for the religion of Jesus Christ. Their affinity with the State accommodated both the classic tradition and Christianity within formal advancement of Christian Latin hymnals and poetry and the consolidation of Latin as the language of western Christianity with the decline of Greek influence. The paper focuses selectively on meaningful poetic works by the foremost Prudentius Clemens from his perspective as life-long Christian, holding a dynamic vision for Christianity and a Christian Rome. His contemporary, Christian humanist poet Paulinus of Nola and the poet philosopher of scholastics Boethius compose innovative poetry promoting community worship and amalgam of Christianity with the classical tradition. The people's devoted favourite was Ambrose of Milan, and his glorious hymnals mark the beginning of Western Christian poetry. Within the varied Latin verse genres of Early Medievalism Christianity had become immersed in the culture of Latin as liturgical and literary language of the Church. Discussion evaluates Dawson's critical reception of such poetry, in transit from the classical to the medieval world. The poets' embrace of new literary forms paved the way for the innovative, rhythmical verse and dynamism of the Middle Ages which surpassed traditional classical models. The poetry of the Church was a resounding achievement in this era and the eras that followed, as Dawson's encompassing perspective acknowledges in his intellectual responses to poetic innovation. Such allegories, hymns and genres ultimately secured a dynamic literary transition and mimesis within a unified Christian vision for all the Roman peoples.

* * * * *

This notion of revelation as the historically incarnate second person of the Trinity was one clearly understood by British cultural historian Christopher Dawson (1889-1970). Dawson's obviously Augustinian view of the world and of history, and more particularly of the human person enabled him to see that the human person was created with the ability to perceive and receive revealed truth, and to respond to it. Dawson's writings exhibit a world view which locates the "restless heart" of Augustine as the real dynamic of world history. His awareness of Original Sin enabled him to see that, while the human person is an innately religious or worshipping being, that they in fact will at times direct their adoration, rightly due to their creator alone, towards things which are less worthy of said adoration.

In his day this was being most concretely evidenced in the growth of ideological movements which built on the radical rationalism of the Enlightenment. In 1928 Dawson wrote, "It is true that there still exists a widespread prejudice against any religion which claims to rest on divine or supernatural revelation. The old 18th century ideal of a purely rational religion – a Religion without Revelation – has not lost its attractiveness to the modern world."[1] One might argue

---

[1] Christopher Dawson, *Progress and Religion: An Historical Inquiry*, ed. C. Scott and D.J. Briel, *The Works of Christopher Dawson*, Catholic Univeristy of America Press, 2001, 188.

that this was even felt in certain theological circles of his day, in particularly rationalistic veins of Thomistic thought.

Dawson was quick to point out that the religious impulse in man had not and indeed could not have died. He writes, "[t]he fact that religion no longer finds a place in social life does not necessarily involve the disappearance of the religious instinct. If the latter is denied its normal expression, and driven back upon itself, it may easily become an anti-social force of explosive violence."[2] And that is what the 20th century witnessed.

The most deadly ideological movements of his day, namely National Socialism and Bolshevism, both employed significant religious characteristics. Dawson's critique of National Socialism is particularly telling on this point. For Dawson all ideology, including that of the modern liberal democracy, is rightly identified as anti-human by Dawson. More than merely denouncing evil as it was most explicitly manifest, Dawson's insight to the human person and the nature of truth as such saw him denounce the growth of ideology wherever he saw it. In an essay entitled "The Left-Right Fallacy" from 1946, Dawson writes damningly about theo politicisation and ideologisation of almost everything. For Dawson all ideologising is totalitarian in nature. He writes, "[t]he tactics of totalitarianism are to weld every difference of opinion and tradition and every conflict of economic interests into an absolute ideological opposition which disintegrates society into hostile factions bent on destroying one another."[3]

Pointing to the rampant absurdity of the rapid growth in ideological positions in his own day Dawson wrote:

> For example, there are Liberals and Conservatives, there
> are Republicans and Monarchists, there are anti-clericals

---

[2] Ibid 177.

[3] C. Dawson, "The Left-Right Fallacy," *The Catholic Mind*, April (1946).

and clericals, there are Communists and Fascists, there are Socialists and Individualists, there are Semites and anti-Semites. All of these are different oppositions, which have no necessary connection with one another, yet all of them are brought under the Left-Right headings and thus forced into ideological alliances which may be unnecessary and absurd. Moreover, when you have got your opponents all neatly ticketed you can then repeat the same process on any section of them – dividing the Socialists into Socialists of the Left Center in Socialists of the Extreme Left, or the Liberals into Moderates or Progressives, so as to submit them to the same process of confusion and disintegration.[4]

For Christians to engage in such reductive activities would be abhorrent to Dawson. The truth, revealed to us as the person of Jesus cannot be made to fit into our neat ideological categories. The kind of ideologisation that Dawson demonstrates above does not allow for genuine dialogue to take place, nor does it allow for genuine truth to be sought. For Dawson, this simplification of complex philosophical ideas into colours (ie Red for Communist, Pink for Socialist etc) or just mere ideologically driven terms, as is still done still in the political sphere today, is counter-productive at best and absolutely destructive at worst. He writes,

In this campaign of disintegration the Right-Left mythology is a perfect god-send to the forces of destruction. It provides them with a crude and simple but highly effective instrument which can be applied to almost any situation and by which any number of different issues can be merged together in a mass of confusion and ideological clap-trap.[5]

In our present cultural environment we see more and more the simplistic labeling of legitimate arguments as mere bigotry

---

[4] Ibid.
[5] Ibid.

and subsequently dismissed as the voice of hatred. My reading of Dawson sees him cautioning against Christian involvement with such ideologically driven disputation. For Dawson any attempt to align the Christian faith with one or another ideology emerges only from a faith not adequately pervasive of the life of the people, of their culture. This is not to say that Christian persons, or indeed any person of good will cannot be involved in ongoing debate about social mores or public ethics; on the contrary they should be increasingly so. What it does mean however is that we cannot use the tactics of those who are promoting modes of life and social organisation which are antithetical to human flourishing. Propaganda quite simply is not fitting for the human person, even if it is promoting a "culture of life."

For Dawson, the critique of ideology was, as I mentioned above, not limited to national socialism or communism. His critique of the modern liberal democratic state earned him the label of fascist in not a few magazine editorials and letters to the editor. But for Dawson, an ideological loyalty to the modern liberal demoncratic state would be equally reductive. For him, the point was not to find the best ideology, or the one which had most in common with the Christian world view and throw all his support behind that. For him the ultimate measure of truth was Truth himself, and in assessing the validity of any mode of societal structure the ultimate end or telos of the human person, namely union with the Trinitarian God in heaven, must be held in view.

More than just a Dangerous Idea

The idea which I am presenting here as being particularly dangerous to the current atheistic order is unsurprisingly not in fact and idea at all, but rather a person – Truth Incarnate. The fact of this personal God who is Truth, who became incarnate and is active in history blows apart our pre-conceived notions and opens up "'new horizons.'" Our continued efforts to live in relation with this Truth and to be conformed to it allows an openness and a freedom that quite simply cannot coincide with any attempt to further another ideology. Because of this we can say that individual experience has a value, and our engagement with others who perhaps might not share our values on life, marriage and the like can be strengthened by our willingness to engage with the experience of the other. When one can acknowledge that wherever there is truth it is the Lord's,[6] then and only then can a dialogue between persons occur which is truly fruitful. This is far more than a mere assertion which would establish life for example as one ultimate good among other, incommensurate goods, such as knowledge, play, aesthetic experience, sociability or friendship, and religion. This has deeper roots in a theological anthropology that posits man's ultimate end in an eternal union with the Trinity itself.

I want to conclude with an example of a recent movement which I've had little to do with, but which I see as having real potential. A few years ago in Sydney at the Great Grace conference organized by the Archdiocese a lecture was presented by Dr Austen Ivereigh who spoke about the original impetus for the Catholic Voices group which he and others established. I wasn't at this conference, but had an opportunity to listen to a recording. In his presentation Ivereigh spoke of how the announcement of Pope Benedict XVI's UK visit in 2010 was being received rather negatively by a significantly vocal group. This group had established a website and were circulating a petition which would see the Pope's invitation to the UK revoked and his diplomatic credentials suspended. Along with this, they had written a long list of complaints which they saw as reasons for this,

---

[6] "Let every good and true Christian understand that wherever truth may be found, it belongs to his Master", Augustine, *On Christian Doctrine*, trans. D. W. Robertson, Liberal Arts Press, 1958, II.18.28

reasons including recent clerical sex abuse scandals, the Catholic Church's position on women clergy, same sex marriage, abortion euthanasia and the like.

For the Catholic Voices group, this list of concerns became something of an agenda or a program. Here they had a list of issues which were stumbling blocks to the faith, and the people who were voicing such concerns were genuine in their motivation for justice and truth. These neuralgic issues became not just battle lines upon which new battles in the culture wars were to be fought, but points of contact – opportunities not just to share a Catholic or Christian perspective, but to speak the truth, a Truth which is Love Incarnate.

Rather than get buried in the temptation to dig in in a culture war scenario and attempt to defend a crumbling social order that is barely reminiscent of a Christendom that has long since crumbled, these issues became opportunities to invite others to "come and see",[7] to share with them the reasons for our hope.[8]

Conclusion

In his 1959 work *The Movement of World Revolution*, Dawson wrote that, "In the war of ideas, it is the crudest and the most simplified ideology that wins."[9] I think all here can acknowledge that the truth of this can be seen most acutely in the blatant sloganeering being bandied about in the campaigns around the Western world attempting to redefine marriage. Against this growing tide of popularism Christians, and indeed all men and women of good will need to engage with more than the buzzwords and emotional propaganda so readily used by others in the debate. What provides the strongest threat to the current atheistic social order is in fact noth-

---

[7] Jn 1:46.

[8] 1 Pet 3:15.

[9] C. Dawson, *The Movement of World Revolution*, ed. Don J. Briel, *The Works of Christopher Dawson*, Catholic University of America Press, 2013, 74.

ing more than a Christianity which is radically free from ideology. Lewis' Screwtape was 'on the money' when he informed his dear nephew Wormwood of the impotency of any kind of "Christianity and …". And I will leave you with his words:

> What we want, if men become Christians at all, is to keep them in the state of mind I call "Christianity And". You know – Christianity and the Crisis, Christianity and the New Psychology, Christianity and the New Order, Christianity and Faith Healing, Christianity and Psychical Research, Christianity and Vegetarianism, Christianity and Spelling Reform. If they must be Christians let them at least be Christians with a difference. Substitute for the faith itself some Fashion with a Christian colouring.

Christopher Dawson's response to Culture and Religion in Christian Latin Poetry

Dawson's analysis of Christian Latin poetry is related to his holistic approach towards religion, society and culture in general; –"a strong living culture has to have a strong living religion … they rise and fall together". Indeed nascent Christianity had embraced many poetic forms like the sacred songs or psalms used in worship, and obviously there was the exemplary Magnificat, an alluring literary text still evocative and workable for commentary, worship and mimesis. However, this essay examines more specifically Dawson's critiques of leading Christian Latin poets in the fourth to sixth centuries, with their orientation obviously distinct from that wider Latin literature expounded in the paganism of classical antiquity. Dawson had always advanced the interactive connection between religion and living culture, and civilisation and society. Before the mid-third century there was no definite trace of Latin Christian poetry since the first Christian literature in the West was written wholly in Greek with the majority of the Church at Rome composed of Greek-speaking Christians, Jewish in origin. Even so, the adoption of Latin was critical as the language of Western Christianity and the influence of the convert Tertullian, along with the language of Italy, Gaul and Spain advanced Latin as the Church's liturgical and literary language. Early hymnal poets of the fourth century consulted Latin students to decipher mythological and historical allusions and grammatical usage.

Latin fathers like Prudentius adapted Horace and Virgil as models, although the Vulgar Latin which advanced Church Latin was promoted by Caius Vettius Acquilinas Juvencus, a noble Spaniard and priest of Emperor Constantine. Juvencus argued comparatively that the continued success of Homer and classical poets surely validated even greater glory for worthy literature written on Jesus Christ.

Dawson, meanwhile, noted quite logically that one's culture is the key mechanism and interface for the motivation of those verbal and intellectual abilities that we humans possess, such as the rational skills of speech, authorship, or leadership qualities; all moulded by one's respective cultural exposure and nurture over time. Also of significance for Dawson are a people's interaction with poetry and their awareness and appreciation of gifted, inspirational poets in their midst who lay down literary and thus cultural traditions. On another level he also reiterated Christianity's rich practice of language through liturgy and urged the faithful to take a backward sociological glance at the one thousand years of medieval Christianity in order to better comprehend the historical roots of modern Europe.

The eastern term hymn or psalmody is quite loose in defining a song of praise to the Divine, adapted for communal singing and prayer in church. Roman liturgy had also introduced Breviary hymns and prayers for the canonical hours which were recited in divine office as short lyrical poems signifying hymns. The early Middle Ages would consolidate this genre within Christian liturgical history. Over time, Christian poets, applying classical form, moved away from the symbolism of pagan mythology and vernacular Christian poetry to embrace biblical allusions and Latin translations. *The Making of Europe*[10] promotes the contribution of the Classical-Christian and Anglo-Saxon poetic minds as it peruses the rise of nations and the progress of Christianity.

St Ambrose, Bishop of Milan 340-397 AD

Ambrose, the saintly, scholar bishop, statesman and preacher of Milan, son of a pagan and a lyrical Christian mother, was born in Roman Gaul. He consolidated the Church in the late Roman Empire and converted Augustine of Hippo. The very many hymns that he composed were widely known and treasured in most of the western hymnaries until they were integrated permanently into the Roman office. Augustine's Confession, for example, testifies to Ambrose's winning poetic impact through song during his own personal struggles on the path to self-recognition and his grieving over the devout Monica's demise:

> "What tears", he says, "did I shed over the hymns and canticles, when the sweet sound of the music of Thy Church thrilled my soul! As the music flowed into me, and the tears ran down, and there was gladness in those tears — for the bitterness of my sorrow could not be washed away from my heart "– but he remembered as he lay upon his bed, the verses of Ambrose.[11]

Augustine has been labelled, alternatively, for his embrace a new world order as a medieval man or someone representative of

---

[10] Christopher Dawson, *The Making of Europe 400-1000 AD. An Introduction to the History of European Unity.* London; Sheed and Ward, 1936.

[11] Augustine. *The Confessions*, 8. 12. 29 Quoted Karen Armstrong in *The Case for God*, 119

the classical tradition. However, Dawson views him as a man of his own age, namely that of the Christian Empire.

Ambrose's hymn "Deus creator omnium" – "Creator of the Earth and Sky" is one of four devout hymns that Augustine verifies as Ambrose's composition. Augustine also points out another positive aspect of hymnody in that the singing of hymns and psalms, as in the Eastern provinces, relieved the weary faithful of protracted nocturnal vigils and confessions. In this sense language, inevitably, became an imbedded theme when Ambrose's hymns and Augustine's treatise further enriched and vitalised Christian community practice in the west. In addition, Ambrose's introduction of antiphonal or responsorial singing registered a communal reciprocity that favoured turn-taking in the congregation and actually was adopted by later European composers like Bach and Mendelssohn.

The remarkable Cambridge Christian Latin scholar, the late Frederic Raby, notes that nearly all of the 40-41 hymns of Ambrose (or perhaps even more) are not exclusively part of the office of Roman secular clergy. Yet, taken together Ambrose of Milan should be regarded as the father of Catholic hymnody, because he created a school and tradition which found a permanent place in Church liturgy. The hymns of Ambrose in the rhythmical unit of the classical iambic Dimeter were written for congregational purposes and encouraged imitation. These enjoyed immense popularity, known collectively as the *Hymni Ambrosiani* thus denoting Ambrose's exclusive poetic form of liturgical hymnody by applying four verses of iambic demeter (a two-foot line) comprised of eight syllables.[12] Actually, St Hilary was the first hymnist in the west, but he adopted Eastern Church style during his sojourn in Asia Minor. Ironically, his banishment into exile by the Arian Emperor Constantius brought him into intimate relations with the

---

[12] Frederic Raby, *A History of Christian Latin Poetry from the Beginnings to the Close of the Middle Ages*. Oxford: Clarendon Press, 1953, 28-36.

richer culture and learning of the Greek churches, and there he must have conceived the idea of introducing a Latin hymnody into the West.[13] Ambrose though, was a realist on the function of hymns: "All strive to confess their faith and know how to declare in verse on the Father and the Son and the Holy Ghost." His hymns share verbal and technical correspondences as does the familiar hymn "Veni redemptor gentium" ("Come Redeemer of the Nations").

Another familiar text is the evening Compline hymn sung daily "Te Lucis ante terminum: "Now that the daylight fades away ..." which applies the metre and strophe typical of Ambrose. It remains one of his most beautiful hymns in the Roman office and reminds us of the early Christians' anxious wariness of menacing nocturnal forces:

> te lucis ante terminum,
> rerum creator, poscimus,
> ut solita clementia
> sis praesul et custodia.
> procul resident somnia
> Et noctium phantasmata
> hostemque nostrum comprime
> Ne polluantur corpora.[14]

Ambrose and his loyal followers at one point defied an imperial order to quit Milan. With the Basilica surrounded, he calms the faithful through hymn-singing until the blockade is lifted. In such a dynamic literary context, Dawson also credits the Church's expansive Christian community culture, in feeding the poor, and maintaining hospitals and orphanages in a dual sociological image of church and empire, even in distant Alexandria. More specifically,

---

[13] Ibid., 42-3.
[14] Ibid., 41

Dawson's tribute sums up, in his eloquent diction, the centrality of the Christian Ambrose:

In Saint Ambrose above all the Western church found a leader who could maintain the rites of the Church … but who was at the same time a loyal friend of the emperors and a devoted servant of the Empire. Ambrose was indeed a Roman of the Romans, born and trained in the tradition of imperial civil service, and he brought to the Church public spirit and devotion to duty but as an independent unity separated in culture and religion from the old Roman world. "But Ambrose stands midway between the old classical ideal of civic responsibility and the relations between Church and the State … midway between … civic responsibility and the mediaeval ideal of spiritual power. Ambrose has something of the Roman magistrate and something of the mediaeval pontiff."[15]

Christopher Dawson also credits Ambrose with development of Christian culture through hymns testifying to the enrichment of Christianity and creative praise of God in rhyme.[16] As the exponent of the first Christian state he had a far-reaching influence on the ideals of the western Church. With the schism of the Church Western Christianity had emerged as a distinct unity, separated in culture and religion from the old Roman world.[17]

Aurelius Prudentius Clemens 348-410 AD – fifth century

Dawson's works consistently espouse the intellectual dynamism of the Latin west. In this sense he could advance no greater exponent than the Spaniard Prudentius Clemens. "Yet the greatest of the Christian poets was Prudentius, whom Bentley termed 'the

---

[15] Dawson, op. cit., 43-4.

[16] Ibid., 36-47.

[17] Ibid., 43-4.

Christian Virgil and Horace.'"[18] Of all the Christian writers, Prudentius shows the fullest appreciation of the classical tradition in both literary and social aspects. Ambrose introduced hymn-singing to divine worship, but Prudentius was a more gifted and expansive poet in his political, religious and didactic verses. While he does represent, to a large degree, the values and politics of the new religion he also demonstrates, as does Christopher Dawson, an impressive concinnity aligned equally with a healthy respect for the power of poetry.

Roman historians (like Michael Grant) have noted that "… the most significant of Prudentius's works, historically, is the two-book poem "Against Symmachus/Contra Symmachum", an intellectual polemic against the pagan gods which urges a prominent pagan of the day, the City Prefect Symmachus, that despite due reverence of Rome's destiny, the famed pagan Altar of Victory must be expelled from the Senate House (Curia).[19] The attack on Symmachus begins when Prudentius's compelling logic refutes the habitual argument that old customs are truly worthy of reverence because our ancestors have bequeathed them to us. The poet though, facing an untenable situation, is quick to demonstrate another side of nationhood, namely that frivolous Rome had introduced new gods with each fresh victory and had not been at all faithful to Rome's past. While the opposing orator insists that Rome is ruled by her genius, Prudentius terms this at least "a variable genius since … Rome is the servant of Christ". Intense patriotism breaks forth as Prudentius celebrates the strength of Christian Rome to quell her enemies: certainly a necessary step for a peaceful union paving the way for wider Christianity as reflected in the concrete detail of his poem "Deus undique Gentes" – "God of the Gentiles", which

---

[18] Ibid.; R. Bentley, quoted Gerard O'Daly, Days linked by Song: *Prudentius' Cathemerinon* Oxford University Press, 2012, 220.

[19] See Michael Grant, *Greece and Rome*, London, Guild Publishing, 1986, 138.

acknowledges Christ's promotion of a unifying multinational Rome for the Roman provinces.[20]

The poem "Against Symmachus" is more specific in exposing the ornate female display of the golden statue of the goddess "Victory", featuring a palm and laurel wreath, both trophies from the Phyrric War (280-275 BC). Symmachus sought restoration of the ancient gods and the Altar in an on-going drama between Popes and those pagans like Julian the Apostate who had restored the altar to spite and to slight the Christian senators. Ambrose's letter of respect had cautioned the young Christian emperor Valentinian II, to defend his religion over pagan superstition, and furthermore wisely reminded the young ruler that the shimmering spectacle of the golden goddess statue was merely base metal within. Prudentius had so admired this communication that in the year 402 AD, he was challenged via Latin poetry to assume the Ambrosian task in arguments advancing patriotism, theology, didacticism, martyrology, and even one of the poet's favourite haunts, the early Christian art in the Roman catacombs; thereby addressing himself not so much to emperors as to the world stage at large: "Trouble no more the worshippers of Christ, O greatest of the Furies.", or "Heresy is disposed of by Faith". Prudentius was twenty-six years old when Ambrose was Bishop of Milan.[21]

Prudentius is also credited, more broadly, with his literary contribution to the stylistic and frequently over-wrought genre of allegory which flourished in the later Middle Ages. The "Pysychomachia" is an allegorical account of the tense battle for the 'soul' of man. This polemical poem presents the first poetical Christian allegory, an original creation, which caught the fancy of the Middle Ages, inspiring much mimesis in literature and art and strongly influencing Renaissance allegorical works. Epic combats

---

[20] Raby, op. cit., 66

[21] *Contra Symnachum*; Raby, op. cit., 62-9

occur between Virtues and Vices, and Christian Faith against Paganism with the combatants emulating the epic speech tradition. Another outcome demotes "Lust" consigned unsurprisingly to the abyss, as often seen in religious clashes of Renaissance literature where only the good and the worthy must surely win out. The poet's theme above is transparent in its metaphors and personification, unlike the more familiar typically veiled allegory.[22]

Rather different and more expansive and pragmatic, is Prudentius's' "Hymn X " for the "Burial of the Dead" in the volume *Cathemerion Liber*, a title signifying a poetic prayer for every day. Here the poet is genuinely concerned with Christian sentiments opposing the bereft and longing of even any one soul. This is an interesting and obviously sincere commentary on communal respect in terms of Christian dogma and decency. For example, particular care must be extended to the bones of the dead, as that same body will need to rise up with agility on judgment day. The first great Christian poet also traces such sentiment and practices as the importance of burial for securing entry into the home of the deceased. This, though is not in line with the classic mythologies' vast unknown land of the dead governed by a Dis or a Hades. In parallel, another concern in the poem for a Christian at least could be the destruction of the corpse by fire which would well hinder resurrection on the day of the Lord. Overall, we accept that burial dwells with the absent and the afterlife and could conclude that the Office of the Dead is one of the most venerable and ancient portions of the Breviary. Raby's summary argues that:

> It would be true, indeed, to say that the whole of the poetry of Prudentius is coloured by this doctrinal intention ... to reassure his Catholic readers of the doctrine of the ascension but not so intrusively as to undermine or distract from the beauty of the verse ...

---

[22] *Psychomachia*, Raby, op. cit., 61-6

Prudentius, says Raby is first a Catholic. And only in the second place a poet.

The "Hymn for Every Hour" in the same volume Cathemerion is composed in trochaic tetrameters. It moves with a solemn measure as the opening poem of the Hymns for the Christian's Day. This is a series of twelve typical hymns covering the cock-crow, mealtime fasting, and Holy days. The twelve-hour day was adopted by the Romans around 291 BC. Ambrose for one prayed seven times daily although fasting was initially for self-discipline, not penance but later served as constructive preparation for communion.

The translator of the Cathemerion, Martin Pope, notes that "The Hymn for all Hours" acknowledges Christ the King as the poet's Muse, "with his praise my lyre shall ring". However two stanzas on, the speaker utters a more profound statement of nomenclature, harmonised by the skilful syntax and internal rhyme in this renowned Christian "Hymn for all Hours" where Prudentius defines and combines a synthesis honouring the Christ of Theology; the Saviour sung by the prophets; and:

> Of the Father's heart begotten, ere the world from chaos rose,
>
> He is Alpha; from that Fountain all that is and has been flows,
>
> He is Omega, of all things yet to come the mystic Close.[23]

Dawson's helpful critique of the Cathemerinon verse collection notes that Christian poetry was learning to make use of the new 'mythology' which derived mostly from the lesser-known Old Testament Legends. The masters of Prudentius were the classical Roman poets, but their mythology was forbidden to a Christian singer. However Mythology and symbolism go hand in hand in the Cathemerinon. In fact one could say that the majority of emperors had a vested interest in perpetuating polytheism. One could also argue that the respective religions became aligned reciprocally in

---

[23] Ibid., 47.

terms of the non-Christian ... with "Christianity" the valid marker of nomenclature. The lengthy hymns are more appropriate for personal prayer but selections do appear in the Catholic hymnary's detailed index of hymns or hymnals. The subject matter is perhaps less appealing than Prudentius' masterful, gracious style: "Now and again, in reading them, we seem to breathe the air of an earlier time, when the faith was young and full of hope."[24]

In the approaching fall of the Western Empire the poet had divined with almost prophetic insight the significance of the changes that had come upon the ancient world. The new Christian Rome, whose advent Prudentius had hailed, was indeed destined to inherit and preserve the old ideal of Roman unity in a changed world. For it was to Rome that the new peoples came ...

Translation brings forth a mixed register, with different schemata, new language and if in the first or second person voice a poet creating a direct line of dialogue. A recent translation of Prudentius's Cathemerion was produced by the renowned classics translator, poet and novelist David R. Slavvitt, who applies an elegant but lighter touch than that of Prudentius to the Daily Round, accommodating the twelve hours, feasts and the fast days.

Prudentius' own perspective, as a public figure and life-long fourth century Christian Latin poet, obviously envisioned a Christian Rome's capacity for unity in civilisation, a timely outlook when in the fourth and fifth centuries the poetical tradition of the West merged with the nascent Christian culture. Dawson admires Prudentius' gifted intellect and poetic leanings and his embrace of Christian poetry, inspired through a dedicated faith in Christ. "Of all the Christian writers Prudentius shows the fullest appreciation of the classical tradition in both its literary and its social aspects".[25] He is certainly the most impressive of the early Christian verse-

---

[24] Ibid., 45.
[25] Dawson, op. cit., 58.

makers and directly significant to late Latin and early-medieval culture and religion.

Here Dawson summarises the Spaniard's classic contribution to culture and Christianity:

> And thus, although Prudentius had no more idea of the approaching fall of the western Empire than had Claudian or Namatian, he had divined with almost prophetic insight the true significance of the changes that had come upon the ancient world … Through all the chaos of the dark ages that were to follow, men cherished the memory of the universal peace of the Roman empire with its common religion, law, and culture; and the repeated efforts of the Middle Ages to return to the past and to recover this lost unity and civilisation, forward to the future prepared the way for the coming of a new European culture.[26]

One might add too, an affiliation and appraisal of the dynamic genre of Christian Latin poetry alongside such an historical achievement.[27]

Paulinus of Nola c. 355-c. 431AD

Christopher Dawson also notes early attempts in the West to produce Christian poetry on Biblical subjects drawn from passages by the great Roman poet Virgil:

> The Western poetical tradition was more accomplished than the East and during the fourth and fifth centuries this tradition was fully assimilated by the new Christian culture. One such outcome emerged with the ascetic conversion of a devout Lombardian Christian, Paulinus of Nola near Naples though born at Bordeaux. He was a genuine

---

[26] Ibid., 23-4.
[27] Ibid.

> Christian humanist ... not a great poet but a man of high
> culture. He popularised the ideals of the new Christianity
> among the educated classes in the Western provinces.[28]

He was engaged with poetry, and the missionary and political schemes of the Emperor Charles who appointed him grammar master in the Royal school. Paulinus later committed to an educated, ascetic life of exemplary tolerance under his inspirational guardian Saint Felix who is still fêted in Latin culture across the new worlds and the old.

Paulinus actually wrote the first poetic elegy on literary record. It was to comfort a Christian couple's loss of their young son, a longing well felt by Paulinas and his Spanish wife Theresa, also bereft of their only child. Paulinus's attempt at a wedding poem is, likewise, the first documented Christian epithalamium, composed for the nuptials of a local couple, Julianus and Titia. Unlike the earlier classical era mythology has no sanctioned place in this divergence from traditional pagan song. The sensual gods are absent from the bridal ceremony and their long-standing roles now submit to Christian virtues in Paulinus's Carmen 25 and his choice of an imagistic Christian framework to detract the audience from the old beliefs and worship. Despite the aesthetic rhythms of the poem it becomes apparent that the cadences of this verse can both augment or deflate its point of view. The epithalamium rebuts the traditional performance of pagan gods in match-making, vice and mischief. The strains from the pagan duo of Venus and Cupid are finally redundant and the laurels of this prototype Christian marriage are graced with "peace, modesty and piety", exemplified by "vergo puer Christi, virgo puella, dei". The young virgin mother Mary now embodies considerable cultural and didactic sway in an image far remote from classical hymnals to the gods. The reassuring motif of Christian marriage is bolstered by a respect for human dignity,

---

[28] Ibid., 58-9. Also Raby, op cit., 68-9.

and a spiritual fulfilment through sacrament, beyond struggle and stress. The coherence and the discourse of faith here advance a poetical mediation of a salvation working within a moral framework, uplifting human dignity.

Dawson actually finds common themes in the poems of Prudentius and Paulinus of Nola, "... demonstrating that the cult of the martyrs, which had its origin in the protest of the Christian mind ... had become transformed into a social institution and a manifestation of civic piety".[29] Patriotism, within the city state found a new cohesion through local cult saints ... in this case Saint Felix is honoured with a basilica as representative guardian of the city and its carnivals while he imparts a share in his glory through local worship practice, albeit one on a lesser scale than Rome's Peter and Paul, but nevertheless consolidated by an harmonious Christian community.

Boethius c. 480 -524 AD

Anicius Boethius, a sixth century Roman philosopher, and Consul in 510 AD was suspected of state treason, imprisoned, and brutally executed. It is generally believed that he was a Christian. Dawson describes him as:

> the last of the classics, – the first of the scholastics ... a great educator through whom the mediaeval West received its knowledge of Aristotelian logic and the rudiments of Greek mathematics. His tragic death put an end to his philosophical translation ... but in compensation it gave the world The Consolation of Philosophy ... a masterpiece which in spite of its deliberate reticence, is a perfect expression of the union of the Christian spirit with the classical poetic tradition.[30]

---

[29] Dawson, op. cit., 59.
[30] Ibid., 65.

For Boethius, as a philosopher-Christian, the burning questions of the day were ... still those of the debate of the first Christian centuries about the nature of "God". Within its context the Philosophy is a book with concrete detail but a heavy imprint and its sensory images are both thought provoking and poignant while exposing the rhetorical dimension of verse.

The translator, Victor Watts perceives similarities between pagan philosophers who upheld the mortality of the soul and eternal happiness, and those adhering to Christian thought. He argues that Christianity itself was a philosophy, evident from "Boethius's embrace of the composition of the treatise when returning to philosophy under political incarceration and despair."[31] Evans also notes a challenge to Christian scholars because the decision to record probably indicates a Christian Boethius when he wrote the ecological tractates ... But it is Philosophia, his guide, who brings him a consolation which depends ultimately upon his resignation and an intellectual grasp of what had before seemed a random and disorderly sequence of catastrophes.[32] Raby sums up: "The fundamental aim of the work is to make the language of philosophy approach as close as possible to the meaning of faith".[33] It was translated into several vernaculars in the same period. One observes that memory and emotion are powerfully combined in a poem with detailed sensory images. Here, despite his own unjust fate this verse extract of Boethius from Book I pays admiration to the creator of the universe which can interact as either Christian or Classical. The lines, though, suggest that Boethius's reference to celestial landscapes is more than mere description:

---

[31] Boethius, *The Consolation of Philosophy*, translated with an Introduction by Victor Watts, London, Penguin 1999, 3.
[32] G.R. Evans, *Philosophy and Theology in the Middle Ages*, Routledge, London, 1993, 5.
[33] Raby, op. cit., 112.

Creator of the starry heavens,

Lord on thy everlasting throne,

Thy power turns the moving sky

And makes the stars obey fixed laws. . . .

Corrupted men sit throned on high;

By strange reversal wickedness

Down treads the necks of holy men.

Heap condemnation on the just;…

Of this great work is man so mean

A part by fortune to be tossed?

Lord hold the rushing waves in check

Make stable all the lands of earth …[34]

In comparison Emperor Marcus Aurelius (121-180AD) touched on similar philosophical issues like those of Prudentius and Boethius in his own *Meditations*. The volume engages with philosophy, religious exercises, moral virtue and humanism as in this reflection on the soul of man:

3.2 What a noble thing is the soul ready for its release from the body if now must be the time, and prepared for whatever follows – extinction, dispersal, or survival! But this readiness must come from a specific decision: not in mere revolt, like the Christians, but thought full, dignified and – if others are to believe it – undramatic.

4. … have I done something for the common good? Then I too have benefited. Have this thought always ready to hand; and no stopping.[35]

---

[34] Boethius, op, cit., Book IV, 15-16. Translated with an Introduction by Victor Watts, London, Penguin, 1990, IV, 15-16.

[35] Marcus Aurelius, *Meditations*. Translated with Notes by Martin Hammond, London, Penguin books 2006, 106.

For most of the poets discussed in this essay the looming concept of the promise of one's salvation is worked through in this world rather than the next.

Faltonia Betitia Proba (c. 306- c. 353)

Classical women composing poetry in Latin or Greek in the first century amounted to twenty-nine female classical poets, but only sixteen are extant and others often fragmentary as is the case with Faltonia Proba and her Cento. Like other Christian poets she reflects a personal vision of her adopted Christianity and comments on spiritual and prophetic visions and motifs for herself as a convert from paganism.

She was indeed a singular female author among the Christian Latin poetry under review. Faltonia Proba was a fourth century Latin poet who was one of the first ancient writers to model her Christian verses on the pagan Virgil's classical works. She termed herself a "prophet". Her husband Adelphius was a prefect of Rome around 351 AD and he and their large family also converted. She had a special softness for the Saint Anastasia and is buried at her church in Rome. Proba literally unravelled the Latin poet Virgil's epic poems and merged them into Virgil's verses, which were assembled and labelled as a pedagogical model known from her given title as "Proba's Purpose".

The classical Homeric-style Cento was adopted by this convert daughter of a pagan Roman Consul. The Cento as a poetic form is best described as a patchwork literary composition uplifting lines from other sources to simulate a verse collage. As such her linguistic methodology re-assembled a close-reading of Virgil's classical texts in her seven-hundred line poem honouring the Christian context of the life of Jesus of Nazareth, whose creation of the seasons emulates the gifted Virgil's Georgics. There were other

Centos, by the Christian rhetorician Marius Victorinus for instance around 300 AD who composed in hexameters but lacked Proba's fidelity to her Virgilian source text. Proba was the first Christian poet to apply the Cento to focus exclusively on Genesis in her epic poem, "Virgilianus de Laudibus Christi", which concluded with the Coming of the Holy Spirit. "And so neatly was it done that a person unacquainted with this work would easily believe Virgil to have been both prophet and evangelist".[36]

Proba composed a workable didactic pattern for children to be taught their religious history and rhyme although the poem is not merely pedagogical. Centos require some technical skill in handling of metre and verb form. Proba, accordingly, has been classified as perhaps the most influential Christian Latin poet of Late Antiquity on the cusp of the Middle Ages. That she achieved her pedagogical goal, despite hostility to her Christian themes in an anti-Christian era, is partly attributed to her own respected status and enthusiasm, but also her appeal to school children through that perennial crowd pleaser, a captivating story with a mobile cast of varied personalities and dramatic events. Even so, in the preface "Proba's Purpose" she does not shirk from her proselytising mission, and writes assertively in the first person to castigate hypocrisy, duplicity and pietism and, in particular, false leaders who have violated vows of peace in their blood-thirsty desires to rule:

> Once I wrote of leaders violating sacred tracts,
>
> Of those who cling to their terrible thirst for power;
>
> Of so many slaughters, the cruel campaign, of Kings …
>
> Now, all-powerful God, take, I pray, my sacred song, …
>
> that I, Proba, the prophet, might reveal its secrets.

---

[36] Giovanni Boccaccio, *Famous Women*. Translated by Virginia Brown. The Tatti Renaissance Library, Harvard and Cambridge University Press 2003, 202-4.

Now I spurn the nectar of Olympus, find no joy

in calling down the Muses from their high mountain
haunts; ...

be at my side, Lord, set my thoughts straight,

as I tell how Virgil sang the offices of Christ.[37]

It was customary for women classical poets to name themselves
outright as a confident belief in their textual skills. Proba though also
used the labels vatis and prophet to suggest her divinely inspired
poetry. She refers to her own Christian baptism as "Libation of
the Light", a caption quite suggestive of a meaningful coherence
of transcendence and faith. After all poetry gives knowledge of
ourselves in relation to the world. The reference above to Virgil
"song of Christ" was a common belief in early Christianity, drawn
from Virgil's Eclogue 4, telling of the birth of a child who would
return the world to its former paradise.

Originality, it seems was not highly prized back then. St. Jerome
(c. 331-c.420), with his austere, intellectual religious drive both
resisted and decried the dangers of pagan texts, and belittled the
Cento poetic genre as merely "pieces of literature", even though
Virgil had drawn heavily from Homer's epic compositions.
Dawson, rightly, promotes St. Jerome as "the unsurpassed master
of Latin among the Fathers of the Church". The renowned ascetic,
and multi-lingual translator, after five years in Syria, was now
engrossed in his Bethlehem cave, ruling the monastery, when
Proba came on pilgrimage to Jerusalem. Derogatory of her literary
skills, he corresponded with Paulinus of Nola, informing him that
"an old chatterbox ('garrulosa anus') in Jerusalem wanted to teach
scriptures before understanding them. Consequently Pope Gelasius
(492-496 AD) declared Proba's *De Laudibus Christi* an apocryphal

---

[37] *Proba, the Prophet,* translated by Josephine Balmer, 112-3; *Classical
Women Poets,* Bloodaxe Books, 1996, 122-3

text, with public readings forbidden. During the Middle Ages, though, her intriguing Cento resonated as a dynamic educational tool in a convergence of literature, learning and language. Giovanni Boccaccio in the renaissance era included Proba in his volume Famous Women for her quick-witted perception that the Roman poet Virgil's poems could serve as an appropriated "base model" for the history of both the Old and New Testaments and the history of culture, pedagogy and religion among the Roman peoples. A comparative image of Proba's abilities is reflected in two familiar Renaissance sketches of her, one instructing the Globe of the whole wide world, and the other keeping good company with her numerous books; poetic images no doubt which exhibit the driven vitality of those well-read converts who had embraced and fostered Christian scholarship and had so much to offer.

The poetry of the Christian Church was an invaluable and spontaneous structured initiative of early Western Christianity, whose multiple achievements persisted for over a whole millennium and extended in time to the Christian states of the West. The poetic genres embodied in church practice were variously, classical models, Western and Eastern hymnody, and much later the vernacular literary styles of contemporary society. The vast spiritual body of Christian Poetry extended gradually to Christian lands. Whether it be Saint Patrick's hymns and Old Irish poetry or Dante's rich tripartite vision in the iconic Divine Comedy, Christian poetry has recorded man's need for belief, consolation and redemption, expressed through the power of devout human emotion, and often amazing depths of faith and yearning. All of which, within the broader context of Christopher Dawson's erudition, certainly lay claim to our own philosophical, literary and cultural imaginations alongside the progress of the image of Christian Latin Poetry as partly sketched in this essay.

References

Armstrong, Karen, *The Case for God –What Religion Really Means*, London, Vintage Books, 2010.

Augustine of Hippo. *The Confessions*, translated and edited by Philip Burton, with an introduction by Robin Lane Fox, London 2007

Auerelius, Marcus, *Meditations*. Translated with Notes by Martin Hammond, London, Penguin books 2006.

Boccaccio, Giovanni, *Famous Women*, Translated by Virginia Brown. The I.Tatti Renaissance Library, Harvard University Press, Cambridge Massachusetts, London, England, 2003.

Boethius, *The Consolation of Philosophy*, Translated with an Introduction by Victor Watts, London: Penguin, 1999.

Clark, Elizabeth Ann, "Jesus the Hero in the Virgilian cento of Faltonia Betitia Proba". Byzantine Studies Conference, University of Trieste, 2006.

Dawson, Christopher, *The Making of Europe 400-1000 AD. An Introduction to the History of European Unity.* London; Sheed and Ward, 1936.

*Early Christian Women writers; the Interesting Lives and Works of Faltomia Betitia Proba and Athenais-Eudocia.*Scientific Coordinator Professor Sylvie Hauser-Boral, University of Bucharest, 2008. online.

Evans, G.R., *Philosophy in the Middle Ages*, Routledge: London and New York, 1993.

Grant, Michael (Ed.), *Greece and Rome – The Birth of Civilization*, MacGregor, Robert R., *The Last Stand of Polytheism: The Altar of Victory*, Rice University, Houston, April, 2003.

Newman, Cardinal John Henry, *The Church of the Fathers*, With an Introduction and Notes by Francis McGrath. Gracewing and Notre Dame Press, Herefordshire, 2002.

Plant, Michael I, *Women Writers of Ancient Greece and Rome: An Anthology*, University of Oklahoma Press, 2004.

"Proba, the Prophet", translated by Josephine Balmer, *Classical Women Poets*, Bloodaxe books, Newcastle upon Tyne, 1996.

Prudentius, Aurelius Clemens, *The Hymns of Prudentius*, Translated by Martin Pope, London, J.M. Dent, 1905

Raby, F.J.E., *A History of Christian Latin Poetry from the Beginnings to the Close of the Middle Ages*, Oxford: Clarendon Press, 1953.

Rivers, Isabel, *Classical and Christian Ideas in English Renaissance Poetry*, London and New York, Routledge 2007.

Slavitt, David R., translator, *Hymns of Prudentius, The Cathemerinon, or the Daily Round*, Baltimore: Johns Hopkins University Press, 1996.

Trout, Dennis E., *Paulinas of Nola: Life, Letters and Poems. Transformation of the Classical Heritage*, Los Angeles: University of California Press, 1999.

Ward, Father Leo, *Christopher Dawson on Education*, Notre Dame University Press, Indiana,Falls, 1973.

3

THE CHURCH'S DISTURBING HIGHER ALLEGIANCE TO CHRIST: THE PROMISE OF FREEDOM FOR ALL

Campbell Markham

ABSTRACT

Christians have always sought to obey the civil authorities (Rom 13:1-7), but pledge ultimate loyalty to Jesus Christ (Phil 2:9-10). Totalitarian governments and atheistic world views are threatened to the core by the Christian's higher allegiance, and frequently attempt to coerce conformity by persecution. Thus Christians holding to God's plan for marriage and family are being punished today by the academy, the media, and even civil powers. Likewise, Chinese Christians have lived under brutal totalitarian repression for well over a century, and Christians in Imperial Rome were frequently ordered, under threat of death, to confess *Caesar est Dominus*. Such persecution was explicitly promised by Christ (Mat 5:10-12). Where human decrees contradict the law of Christ, Christians have reluctantly resorted to civil disobedience: πειθαρχεῖν δεῖ θεῷ μᾶλλον ἢ ἀνθρώποις (Acts 5:29), which acts were prefigured by faithful Jews of the old covenant (Daniel 3-6, 1 Maccabees). The Church's brave and principled allegiance to Christ under persecution intensifies the threat to the atheist world view. The atheist-materialist world view, however, enslaves humanity: to the pitiless and arbitrary rule of 'might is right' now, and hopeless nihilistic extinction at death. The Church's 'dangerous' higher allegiance and brave loyalty to God points a godless world from heartless nihilism to the gracious and purposeful rule of Christ.

* * * * *

Seventy-one year-old pensioner Bryan Barkley was a British Red Cross volunteer for over twenty years. In October 2014 he was dismissed.[38] How does an elderly *volunteer* get himself dismissed from the Red Cross? Did he embezzle funds? Did he attack a client?

His offence was this: He protested against the British same-sex 'marriage' bill in front of his local cathedral. His open, Christian, and biblical allegiance to the God-given institution of marriage was so obnoxious and disturbing to his society, that he was debarred from even giving his time to community service.

The Church's allegiance to Jesus has always disturbed a world that does not, as John's Gospel says, *recognise him* nor *accept him*. And disturbance has inevitably attracted ostracism, fines, abuse, coercion, and forced re-education, or "sensitivity training" as it is now put. And in not a few cases in the history of the church, this Christ-caused upset has even brought death to his followers.

However, it is precisely when the Church adheres to Christ in the teeth of this hostility, that the world sees the promise of freedom in the Great Saviour who stands gloriously above the suffocating materialistic atheism of our age. Let's look at this step by step.

God's people have always sought to obey the civil authorities.

The Hebrew prophets taught that kings and empires were appointed by Yahweh's hand. Thus Daniel foresaw the succession of power from Babylon to Persia to Greece to Rome passing entirely under the decree of the Lord.

Because the Church knew this – that the Sovereign Lord decides who rules and when – its earliest writings urged its people to obey

---

[38] *Daily Mail* (Australia), 1 November 2014.

the civil authorities. Thus Peter's first epistle coordinates fearing God with honouring the βασιλευς, the king or emperor.[1] It is arresting that the βασιλευς was for Peter the unspeakable Nero,[2] who, Tacitus records, burned Christians alive in his garden "to illuminate the night when daylight failed."[3] God's people were to "honour" even a monster like that. Why? Because the Lord had appointed him to that position of power.

Paul likewise commanded Christians in Rome, also enduring Nero's megalomania, to "obey the governing authorities, because there is no authority except from God ... And this is why you should pay taxes, too, because the authorities are all serving God as his agents."[4] The logic is inexorable. If God is omnipotent, then no human power exists apart from his ordination. Every earthly ruler is a kind of puppet ruler under God. To rebel against the king, is to rebel against the power behind the throne.

So Justin Martyr in the second century urged Christians to pray for their rulers, that God "would bless them with length of days and a quiet reign, a well-established family, a stout army, a faithful senate, an honest people, and a peaceful world, and whatever else either prince or people can wish for."[5]

The Church's *ultimate* loyalty to the Highest Power was never in question.

When earthly kings forget the King of kings, the second Psalm teaches that Yahweh laughs, for ultimately His Son will "break them with an iron sceptre."[6] (One thinks of the mace in our lower

---

[1] 1 Peter 2:17.

[2] Βασιλευς, "the possessor of the highest office in a political realm", BDAG, 169.

[3] Tacitus, *Annals*, 15.44.6.

[4] Rom 13:1, 6.

[5] Justin Martyr, *Apology,* 30.4-5.

[6] Psalm 2:9.

houses of parliament: both symbol and weapon.) And Paul taught in Philippians 2 that "God exalted him to the highest place, and gave him the name that is above every name, that at the name of Jesus every knee should bow, in heaven and on earth and under the earth."[7] For Peter, Jesus' rule is absolute and comprehensive: He is "at God's right hand, with angels, ruling forces, and powers subject to him."[8] And in the Apocalypse John sees Jesus seated on a throne above every other throne, and indeed above the entire created order.[9]

The second coming, the consummation of Christ's rule

The Apostles taught, however, that the consummation of Christ's rule is delayed until his Parousia, his second coming and final judgement. Until that day the world will rebel against God's Anointed King. And until that day "the ruler of this world" will continue to obfuscate and lead astray and spoil God's good order.[10]

And so although Christians honoured the civil authorities as God's regents, this never meant holding that governing authorities would rule with holy perfection, nor that they would never forget the source and purpose of their power, nor indeed that they would never abuse their power. So the Sanhedrin and Governor Pilate condemned Jesus, a manifestly good and innocent man, in an astonishingly grotesque act of injustice.

The Christian duty to obey Christ would clash with the Christian duty to obey the governing authorities

It was inevitable then that the Christian duty to obey Christ would clash with the Christian duty to obey the governing authorities – marred to a greater or lesser degree by ignorance, foolishness,

[7] Phil 2: 9-10.
[8] 1 Pet 3:22.
[9] Rev 4:2-6.
[10] ὁ του κοσμου ἄρχων. Jn 14:30.

impotence, and atheism – whenever the governing authorities commanded something in opposition to Christ's will.

Acts 4 is the first recorded example of this. The Sanhedrin commanded the disciples "on no account to make statements or to teach in the name of Jesus" (verse 18), which directly contradicted the Lord's Great Commission to teach the nations about Him.[11] And so Peter and John replied: "You must judge whether in God's eyes it is right to listen to you and not to God. We cannot stop proclaiming what we have seen and heard."[12]

They obeyed Christ, disobeyed the Sanhedrin, and went out and preached again. And so they were hauled before the High Priest for a second interview: "We gave you a strong warning", he said, "not to preach in this name, and what have you done?" The Apostles' reply was axiomatic: πειθαρχειν δεῖ θεῷ μαλλον ἡ ἀνθρωποις. "It is necessary to obey God rather than man."

They beat them, of course. But they rejoiced, as Luke puts it, that they "had the honour of suffering humiliation for the sake of the name", and "went on ceaselessly proclaiming the good news of Christ Jesus."[13]

This set the course of Christ's Church, sailing forward into a Christ-dishonouring world until he returns.

Christians will conscientiously obey earthly authorities, inasmuch as this does not contradict our ultimate allegiance to Christ; in which case we will disobey the earthly authority, and submit to their penalty: not merely with patience, but even with the joy of experiencing the persecution that our Lord himself experienced.[14]

---

[11] Mat 28:20.
[12] Acts 4:19-20.
[13] Ibid., 5:40-42.
[14] Mat 5:10-12, 1 Pet 4:13.

Let us survey some examples of how this has played out:

From 27 BC Octavian collected ever more illustrious titles for himself: *Augustus*, "Illustrious One", *Princeps* "First Head", *Imperator Caesar Divi Filius*, "Commander Caesar, son of the deified one", *Pontifex Maximus*, "Greatest High Priest", and *Pater Patriae*, "Father of the country." Thereafter, by supposed apotheosis, every emperor was counted among the pantheon.

The Empire would tolerate a very broad array of local customs and religious practices among its conquered subjects, just so long as they confessed *Caesar est Dominus*, and *only* Caesar. Refusal was treason, the worst possible crime in the eyes of the Empire. And so a collision between the Church and the might of Rome was inevitable.

Thus Dio Cassius wrote that in the late first century that Domitian exiled and executed Christians on "a charge of atheism."[15] And Pliny, Roman Governor in Bithynia, writing to Trajan in AD 112, likewise described how he forced Christians to recite "a prayer to the gods at my dictation", to make "supplication with incense and wine" to a statue of Trajan and "images of the gods", and "moreover [to] curse Christ – things which (so it is said) those who are Christians cannot be made to do."[16] Trajan's reply urged that only the one who "denies himself to be a Christian, and makes the fact plain by his action, that is, by worshipping our gods, shall obtain pardon."[17]

As Polycarp, the hoary disciple of the Apostle John, stood in the stadium before his executioners and a jeering crowd, the proconsul urged, "Swear, and I release you; *curse Christ*." And Polycarp confessed, "Eighty-six years I have served him, and he

---

[15] Dio Cassius, *Epitome*, 67.14.

[16] Pliny, Ep 10.96.5.

[17] Ibid., 10. 97.

has done me no wrong: how then can I blaspheme my King who saved me?"

Pagan totalitarianism could not tolerate the Christians' higher allegiance to Christ. But every true μαρτυς stood firm unto death.

The persecution was not just pagan. Justin reported that even the Jewish rebel Barcochba, in the fourth decade of the second century, commanded that Christians "be led to cruel punishments, unless they would deny Jesus Christ."[18]

Atheist totalitarianism has been no more flexible. In 1792, upon the declaration of the First French Republic, a Culte de la Raison was violently enforced. Church lands were confiscated, symbols of worship were banned and destroyed, and bishops and priests were bound to swear an oath of fidelity to the new atheist order.

On 21 October 1793, a law was enacted subjecting prêtres réfractaires and their protectors to exile or death. Hundreds of priests and nuns were executed for "treason" and "separatism." Three weeks later, on 10 November 1793, the madness culminated with the worship of the Goddess "Reason" in the freshly vandalised Cathedral of Notre Dame.

A century later Vladimir Lenin agreed with Karl Marx that "religion is the opiate of the people."[19] "This saying ... is the cornerstone of the entire ideology of Marxism about religion. All modern religions and churches ... are always considered by Marxism as the organs of bourgeois reaction, used for the protection of the exploitation and the stupefaction of the working class." Although religion was never officially outlawed in Soviet Russia, from 1917 relentless purges saw millions of professing Christians sent to the

---

[18] Justin Martyr, op. cit., 1.31.
[19] Karl Marx, *A Contribution to the Critique of Hegel's Philosophy of Right*, "Introduction", 1844.

Gulags, psychiatric hospitals, and firing squads for their real or perceived resistance to the rule of the State.[20]

In the 21st century the Christian's higher allegiance to Christ continues to enrage the totalitarian mindset. Before our very eyes we watch the raven-garbed murderers of Islamic State forcing Christians to convert, to forsake property, or to die.

In late 2014, twenty-one Coptic Christians, labourers from Egypt, were captured by Islamists in the city of Sirte, in Libya. No doubt they were given the ultimatum given to every captured infidel: "Convert or die." But they did not turn from Christ, and on 15 February 2015 they were led to a Mediterranean beach and beheaded *en masse*. The leader of the execution squad was proud to be "chopping off the heads that carry the Cross delusion." And as they died they called upon the name of Jesus.

Sadly, but not surprisingly, Barak Obama wouldn't refer to these men as Christians, but called them instead "Egyptian nationals." And so he ignored the very stated reason for their deaths, and papered-over their brave witness to Christ.[21]

And so the 'Land of the Free' ramps up its own opposition against Christians. In 2006 photographer Elaine Huguenin refused to photograph, because of her Christian beliefs, a lesbian commitment ceremony. In 2012 she was found guilty of discrimination and ordered to pay $6,700 in legal fees to the complainants. In 2011 Massachusetts Catholic Charities were ordered to accept homosexual couples as candidates for adoption. They refused and thought it better to close its adoption arm than to disobey Christ.

In February 2013 Aaron and Melissa Klein refused to bake a

---

[20] Dimitry V. Pospielovsky. "A History of Soviet Atheism in Theory, and Practice, and the Believer." *A History of Marxist-Leninist Atheism and Soviet Anti-Religious Policies*, Volume 1. New York: St Martin's Press (1987).

[21] "Statement by the Press Secretary on the Murder of Egyptian Citizens", The White House, 15 February 2015.

cake for a lesbian 'wedding', because it would violate their faith. In 2014 the Oregon Bureau of Labor and Industries ruled that they had broken anti-discrimination laws, and fined them $135,000. The Obama National healthcare program mandates that companies fund their employees' contraception, abortion drugs, and sterilisation. The prosecutors will be busy, as Christians obey God rather than man.

Right now in Australia the "Safe Schools" program is educating our children about the goodness of homosexual behaviour, and the badness of disagreeing with it. It urges students to "call out" those who demur as "homophobes", to intimidate them into conformity. Listen to how a Safe Schools information booklet teaches our high-school children to treat those who disagree with the new values:

> Being labelled a "homophobe" (someone who is homo-phobic) isn't a nice title to have, and isn't something most people want to be known as. Responding with "stop being a homophobe" or "you're being transphobic" can make the person aware that their actions aren't OK.[22]

And as a pastor I know that many of my young people are ostracised and abused for not going along with the crowd: For obeying God rather than man.

Two thousand years of church history teach that totalitarian governments and atheistic worldviews are threatened to the core by the Christian's higher allegiance, and frequently attempt to coerce conformity, or at least silence, by persecution. But the Christian cannot ultimately be gagged or coerced to follow the pattern of this world, for we "must obey God rather than man."

But here is the remarkable thing: the Christian's patient response to persecution wins admiration for the Gospel. In the book of Daniel; Shadrach, Meshach, and Abednego refused to

---

[22] *Stand Out* booklet, Safe Schools Coalition, 17.

bow down to the 90 foot golden statue of Nebuchadnezzar. And they were threatened:

> Now when you hear the sound of the horn, flute, zither, lyre, harp, pipes and all kinds of music, if you are ready to fall down and worship the image I made, very good. But if you do not worship it, you will be thrown immediately into a blazing furnace. Then what god will be able to rescue you from my hand?[23]

Shadrach, Meshach and Abednego replied to the king:

> O Nebuchadnezzar, we do not need to defend ourselves before you in this matter. If we are thrown into the blazing furnace, the God we serve is able to save us from it, and he will rescue us from your hand, O king. But even if he does not, we want you to know, O king, that we will not serve your gods or worship the image of gold you have set up.

And so they were thrown into the furnace, and were saved by the mysterious fourth person, "a son of the gods."[24] How did Nebuchadnezzar respond?

> Praise be to the God of Shadrach, Meshach and Abednego, who has sent his angel and rescued his servants! They trusted in him and defied the king's command and were willing to give up their lives rather than serve or worship any god except their own God.[25]

Some 600 years later, who can doubt that the brave and patient death of Stephen, the first Christian martyr, had a profound impact on the Pharisee Saul, and that this was a key moment on the road to his conversion. For it was the converted Paul who later wrote: "If your enemy is hungry, feed him; if he is thirsty, give him something

---

[23] Dan. 3:15-18.
[24] Ibid., 3:25.
[25] Dan. 3:28

to drink. In doing this, you will heap burning coals on his head. Do not be overcome by evil, but overcome evil with good."[26]

The second century Epistle to Diognetus asks, "[Do you not see Christians] flung to the wild beasts, to make them deny their Lord, and yet unconquered? Do you not see that the more of them are punished *the more their numbers increase?*"[27]

And Justin said, "Though we are beheaded, and crucified, and exposed to beasts and chains and fire and all other forms of torture, it is plain that we do not forsake the confession of our faith, but the more things of this kind happen to us so much the more are there *many others who become believers and truly religious through the name of Jesus.*"[28]

The suppression of Iranian Christians is brutal. And yet an Iranian man came to our church three years ago begging to be shown how to become a Christian. When we tried to buy him a Bible in Farsi there was not a single one to found in Australia. Why? They had sold out! I phoned my friend Samuel Green, an expert on Islam, and he said: "Hundreds of Iranians are converting to Christianity. Iranian churches are growing rapidly."

The Chinese Government has done nothing but suppress the Christian Church. In 1952 all 10,000 foreign missionaries were expelled. In 1966 the Cultural Revolution was launched: Churches were closed, Bibles were banned, and Chinese pastors were imprisoned in their hundreds. And the Church has done nothing but flourish.[29] It is estimated that there were 1.5 million Christians

---

[26] Romans 12:20-21.

[27] 7:7-9.

[28] *Dialogue with Trypho*, 100, 3-4.

[29] Bob Davey's book *The Power to Save* (Darlington: Evangelical Press, 2011) does an excellent job of summarising mission to China over the past two centuries.

in China in 1971. Today conservative estimates put the number at more than 67 million.[30]

Apparently, attacking the Church is like attacking the Hydra. When you cut off one head, two appear. You cut off those two, now there are four! Tertullian summed it all up with the timeless aphorism, "The blood of the martyrs is the seed of the church."[31]

8) The suppression of Christians is intended to crush the church by frightening others away from it. But it has had precisely the opposite effect. Why? Because the patient martyr points to the truth of Christ. The martyrs' cheerfulness and calm in the grip of ridicule and injustice and agony is a powerful witnesses to their convictions.

It is a powerful witness to their belief in the *Parousia*, the coming of Christ who will inaugurate the New Heaven and the New Earth, where there will be no more tears, no more sickness, no more death. It is a powerful witness to their belief in the Final Judgement, when all wrongs will be righted, when every crime will be punished, and every good deed rewarded.

Faithful persecuted Christians will accept ridicule with patience. They will accept prosecution and fines with patience. They will accept imprisonment with patience. They will accept death with patience, and even with a species of joy. Because they know the promised blessing of Christ for His persecuted:

> Blessed are you when people insult you, persecute you and falsely say all kinds of evil against you because of me. Rejoice and be glad, because great is your reward in heaven, for in the same way they persecuted the prophets who were before you.[32]

---

[30] "Risen Again: China's Underground Churches", *Time Magazine*, 21 October 2014.

[31] Tertullian, *Apologeticus*, ch. 50.

[32] Matt. 5:11-12.

"If you are insulted for bearing Christ's name, blessed are you, for on you rests the Spirit of glory and of God."[33]

The Christian can rejoice when they are persecuted for Christ's sake, because they have the Spirit of God. But for Peter the promised Spirit is given for far more than the Christian's comfort, for he is the "Spirit of glory."[34] If God's glory is the manifestation of his attributes and character, then when a Christian bears persecution patiently, the Spirit of Glory manifests the love and mercy of God to all within the sufferer's orbit.

A corrupted text claims that when Polycarp was martyred, the executioner pierced his burning body with a dagger, "And there came forth a dove, and a great quantity of blood, so that the fire was extinguished; and all the people wondered that there should be such a difference between the unbelievers and the elect."[35] The dove of course is a symbol of the Holy Spirit, and so the corrupted legend points to Peter's great truth: that on the patient persecuted rests the Spirit of Glory. When Christ's own suffer, the Spirit is preaching. He is proclaiming: "Look! There is something beyond this life! There is life beyond the grave for all those who put their trust in Jesus!" Patient suffering therefore points to the promise of freedom for all who will kiss the Son. "How blessed are all who take refuge in him!"

The case of sacked Red Cross volunteer, 71-year-old Bryan Barkley, is mild, but typical of the time between Jesus' ascension and *parousia*. The laws of Christ and the laws of man will collide. And when this happens the Christian will say: *We must obey God rather than man!*

This disturbs a godless world. And it will respond with ridicule,

---

[33] 1 Peter 4:14.

[34] το της δοξης και το του θεου πνευμα.

[35] *Martydom of Polycarp*, ch. 16.

ostracism, prosecution, fines, imprisonment, and even death. But as Christ's people patiently and even joyfully suffer the consequences, the Spirit of Glory will manifest the truth, and point the persecutor to the Eternal King, and the New Heaven and the New Earth that are found in Him.

Whether on the scaffold, or before the Oregon Bureau of Labor and Industries, the Church's "dangerous" and disturbing higher allegiance and brave loyalty to Christ points a godless world from heartless atheism and materialism, to the gracious and purposeful rule of Christ, and even to His gift of salvation.

4

TRACTION OR FRICTION: THE CHURCH AND THE WORLD

Philippa Martyr

ABSTRACT

The Second Vatican Council sought, among other things, to improve the quality of the Church's engagement with the modern world. This is a perfectly Christian goal, but its success or failure depends on how Christians understand the Church-world relationship in the first place. By exploring how the Church functions in the world, and its mission in terms of the world, we can see how misunderstanding this relationship impedes the divine traction – meant to draw the world forward – and turns it instead to friction, which damages both the Church and the world.

* * * * *

This talk emerged out of two provocations. The first was when I attended the excellent Campion College symposiums in 2012. I heard Professor Francesca Murphy give a presentation on a concept which she had been mulling over for some time, namely: has Christianity had a "Christianising" effect on other world religions, since it came into the world? I immediately responded to this idea with an enormous Yes, because my mind had run along the same tracks, although not with such clarity.

The Redemption has, I believe, worked like a sort of bath fizzer in the world; as it expands and explodes, it permeates everything in creation, so much so that you can no longer separate it out. We cannot go back to an "unredeemed" world now, any more than early Christians who changed their minds could "reverse" their baptism by pagan rituals. So how could this central explosive event not also affect the ongoing development of other religions in the world, especially those which preceded Christianity, such as Judaism, Buddhism and Hinduism?

The second provocation was when I was asked to respond to an article submitted to *Connor Court Quarterly*, originally called "The Catholic Church and the Republic of Modernity" by Elena Douglas, which was eventually published as "Letter to a New World Pope". I read this article, which was full of sweet reasoning and pleasant moderation. It proposed an agenda which no right-thinking person could possibly want to disagree with. It was really more in sorrow than in anger that the author was writing, hoping to help us poor unreconstructed self-absorbed Promethean neo-Pelagians into the Church of the 21st century.[36]

On my first reading of this article, I am not ashamed to tell you that I had an experience quite similar to that of Jill and Eustace in *The Silver Chair*, when the witch throws the powder on the fire and begins thrumming the mandolin. Thrum, thrum, thrum, and repeating soothing nostrums, and the children begin to fall under the spell of the words and the atmosphere. So I thought that if someone as notoriously hard-headed as me was thinking, "Hmm, yes, this is actually quite reasonable", then goodness knows what this article would do to much nicer and less cynical people.

---

[36] Douglas also published her article on the ABC Religion and Ethics website, where it remains to this day. Elena Douglas, "The Catholic Church and the Republic of Modernity: Challenges for Pope Francis", ABC Religion and Ethics, 8 April 2013, www.abc.net.au/religion/articles/2013/04/08/3732311. htm – accessed 4 August 2015. I have not made any online comments on this article. I am indebted to Fr John Zuhlsdorf for his repeated use of the phrase "self-absorbed Promethean neo-Pelagian", even though it originated with Pope Francis in *Evangelii Gaudium*, s. 94.

So I decided to invoke the Puddleglum response and put my foot on the fire, and use the pain and the foul smell to wake me and everyone else up. My eventual published response to this article, called "Letter to a New World Pope – II", was very blunt, but hopefully not uncharitable.[1] I was primarily writing to remind myself of why I am a Christian, and what a wonderful thing that is to be, and what a terrifying, tremendous thing the Church really is, and how selling it down the river to a transient thing called "the republic of Modernity" is a terrible mistake.

In my article, I made the following points:

> The Church is not some kind of cultural heritage precinct which exists to preserve lovely art and music.
>
> It is not the Church's job to engage with modernity because modernity has something to offer the Church. It's the Church's job to engage with the World in order to save it.
>
> It is the perennial task of the Church to engage with the World, because that's why the Church exists – to save the World.
>
> However, engaging with the World is a tricky process, and if the Church goes about it in the wrong way, we end up with nothing but trouble, and no one gets saved.

Elena Douglas talked about something she called the Republic of Modernity, which she seemed to think was a very fine and splendid thing, but all it made me think of were guillotines and blasphemous movies and death camps, and I said that in the article as well.

So these provocations got me thinking about why and how we can get things so wrong, and I think it is because many good

---

[1] Philippa Martyr, "Letter to a New World Pope – II", *Connor Court Quarterly*, 3(7): 13-20.

Christians do not understand the relationship between the Church and the World in the first place. This includes me, so I have been doing some thinking since then, and I have tried here to explain what I think the relationship might look like.

The imagery that helps me to explain things is that of wheels – possibly wheels within wheels. In fact, I would go so far as to draw on the wheel imagery that you find in the first chapter of Ezekiel. If you are not familiar with this, Ezekiel sees heaven, and he sees winged seraphim, but also cherubim, who move with four enormous wheels, called ophanim in Hebrew. These wheels turn in every direction, moved by the cherubim, and they have eyes all over them, and there are four of them. Four is the traditional Judeo-Christian number of creation. The number 4 always refers to all that is created; of man in his relation to the created world. It is the number of things that have a beginning, and which have material completeness. Hence it is the "world" number.

How do these wheels possibly represent the relationship between the Church and the World? The early Christians said, "The world was created for the sake of the Church."[2] The Church is the goal of all things in the World. Clement of Alexandria says, "Just as God's will is creation and is called 'the world,' so his intention is the salvation of men, and it is called 'the Church'".[3]

Wheels are also a useful image to me because I find I can best explain how I see the relationship between the Church and the World in terms of mechanics. Traction is the process of a force moving or transmitting power across another surface. One of the things traction needs to move an object is an element of friction, which is that resistance that happens when you try to move something across something else.

---

[2] *Catechism of the Catholic Church*, 760.
[3] Ibid.

It's not strange to use mechanics to describe this, even though we are used to using organic language where the Church is concerned, because as in nature, so in grace, and mechanical laws are just as natural as organic laws.

I think this relationship of traction and friction is what we see happening between the Church and the World. The Church is hugely dynamic, and by contrast the World is actually quite static. I think that the Church is the moving force, and the World is the surface across which it is moving, and as it moves, it changes and actually improves the surface across which it is moving. The trouble is that people like Elena Douglas believe that the World is doing the prime moving, and the Church is resisting like a monolith that needs to be dragged forward, and that the World can improve the Church by dragging it along and forcing it to conform to the World's current standards.

So how can we get this engagement wrong, on a small or a large scale? One of the examples of the Church's over-engagement with the World I used in my response to Douglas was the Spanish Inquisition. In its day, the secular Inquisition in Spain was the very cutting edge of modernity – in 1478 the "modern age" was just beginning; the nation state was in its infancy, but it was very clearly the political way of the future. What better form of aggiornamento for the Church than to engage in this process? And yet today, this looks unspeakable and incomprehensible. It was a misuse of that divine authority and that impetus, because forced conversions are not what God wants from His children.

Not everyone is happy talking about the Inquisition, so other examples I used were the Byzantine Empire, Gallicanism in France, and the Reformation in England. All these are examples of where the Church over-engaged with the World. And the Church came off second-best, and people suffered, and the wonderful forward movement of the Church sank instead into the mire of the World. The World did not benefit, and neither did the Church.

How do I know this conclusively? I am only able to speculate, because I know God can always bring good out of bad. But I remember reading a wonderful counterfactual history – just a few paragraphs at the end of an article – which postulated a Renaissance England after the victory of the Spanish Armada, blossoming with art, music, learning and leading the civilised world, and producing incidentally a Catholic North America.[4] When I tell Protestant friends about this, they are outraged, because they cannot imagine the Armada victory ever being a good thing. We will never know, because obviously this victory did not take place. But we can speculate.

The Church is like a chariot of fire that moves forward all the time. Chesterton describes it very well: "the heavenly chariot flies thundering through the ages, the dull heresies sprawling and prostrate, the wild truth reeling but erect".[5] The opharim are traditionally believed to be the wheels under God's throne that keep it moving about. As the Church moves forward, it draws the World forward with it. But over-engagement with the World quickly creates high levels of friction, and this damages both the Church and the World.

It is a well-known principle in the spiritual life that if you are not going forward, you are actually going backwards. We stop; the mechanics seize up, and then we begin to drift backwards. We all know this stuck, paralysed feeling in the Church, especially with the more egregious examples of "modern" liturgies with draped fabrics and earthenware. I think you see the same damaging friction and eventual stasis at work in religious orders that lost large numbers

---

[4] I have never been able to trace this piece since, although I have been provided with two leads on this, neither of which is the article in question.

[5] G.K. Chesterton, *Orthodoxy*, chapter 8, "The Romance of Orthodoxy".

during the 1960s and 1970s. It is because they over-engaged with the World and became secularised, and thus lost that divine traction that would have kept them truly moving forward, and always responding and reforming internally when they needed it.

I once saw a wonderful real life example of this forward movement. During World Youth Day in Sydney, a huge procession of Catholics was happening through the city, and a group of protestors decided to jeer at them and throw condoms. I watched footage of this, and what I saw was a procession that simply kept moving past a fixed group of protestors, held behind a barrier. They could throw all the condoms they liked, but that procession was not stopping. It was moving forward, and the protestors were being left behind because they were stuck in the one place.

And I thought, "That's it right there – that's the Church, moving forward all the time." This is all very Christopher Dawson-like in sentiment, as he says much the same thing in his book *Progress and Religion*.[6] If you are a fan of Rodney Stark's books, he believes that everything that is authentically modern and positive in human history has been brought about by Christianity.[7] Decent social and legal treatment of women, basic capitalism, and the scientific method are three examples of huge improvements in our lives which the Church has brought to the World through this process of traction, of drawing the World forward.

However, C.S. Lewis warns us in *The Screwtape Letters* of the danger of using Christianity simply or principally as a form of social improvement, and he is absolutely right.[8] What you have to do instead is to get your Christianity right, and then you will absolutely want to draw the World forward into the light with you.

---

[6] Christopher Dawson, *Progress and Religion*, Catholic University of America Press, 2001.

[7] For example, Rodney Stark, *The Victory of Reason*, Random House, 2006.

[8] C.S. Lewis, *The Screwtape Letters*, ch. 25.

The interface where this traction and friction takes place is, of course, us. And inside us, we have the same wheels within wheels that we see outside of us. This is the place where the Church engages with the World, one soul at a time, one person to one person. It is as individual and as collective as that. It really takes place at three levels – inside us, in our relations with others, and then at the broader institutional level.

What you cannot do is opt out of the process altogether. Even the eremitical life or the enclosed religious life is oriented towards saving the World and drawing it forward. I suppose that the opposite problem might be under-engagement with the World, but that tends to take the form of strange little cults which try to live separatist lives. These have a way of going horribly wrong, because those in them become separated from the Church. The Church is not designed to withdraw from the World; it has to stay engaged in that process of drawing the World forward.

If you as an individual are living your Christian life to the full, you will be drawn forward into a future full of life and promise and hope, and you will draw others along with you. But if you as an individual Christian become bogged down in the World, you will slow down and then start going backwards. You will become fossilised in your own particular time and space, and you will be unable to move from this spot, because you have lost the impetus and dynamism of the Church.

So this analogy of traction and friction as a way of describing the relationship between the Church and the World should reassure us that when this relationship is painful, it may be because it is actually working properly. You need that element of friction to draw the object forward using traction. We should also be able to renew our belief in the genuine gifts that the Church has to offer the World, and continue to offer them ourselves to others, in and out of season.

5

WELCOME TO THE NEW HOLLYWOOD

Rocky Mimmo

ABSTRACT

The modern world is throwing up ideas and concepts that are having a radical effect on the organisational structure of society. Thankfully, this is mainly limited to the Western world.

The breakdown of the family, which is obvious to most commentators, is at least part due to the sexual revolution that dates back to the early 1960s. The increasing recognition of homosexuality is changing social norms, including attitude to marriage. Similarly, the lower birth rate and the popularity of living together outside of marriage is moving the organisational structure away from the family unit and toward the individual.

Such developments are not without consequences. Courts in the West have ruled that the sexual activity of a homosexual oriented person should be accepted as part of the orientation. Thus, it becomes unlawful to discriminate between the provision of a service between a heterosexual and a homosexual couple. Marriage is being viewed as nothing more than a sexual relationship, hence children become an appendix to the relationship not integral to it.

Cultural values are determined by a relativism anchored on personal whims and gratification; guidance on morals is no longer set by religious leaders but by celebrities and the media.

Beliefs, once informed by religion, are now determined by

secular imperatives. Ideology and climate change have been held to be beliefs equal in standing and weight to religion.

Discrimination laws are written within human rights language and interpreted so as to favour the rights of the individual and to trump religious liberty.

These are not merely dangerous ideas but amount to the spreading of an anti-religious secularism.

* * * * *

The modern world is throwing up ideas and concepts that are causing a radical shift in the organisational structure of society. Thankfully, this is mainly limited to the Western world.

The breakdown of the family is at least in part due to the sexual revolution that began in the early 1960s. Sophisticated forms of contraception have encouraged sexual promiscuity, weakened fidelity and made long-term marriage less secure.[9]

The increasing recognition of homosexuality is changing social norms, including attitudes to marriage. Similarly, the lower birth rate and the popularity of couples living together outside of marriage, is moving the organisational structure away from the family unit and in favour of the individual.

Such developments do not occur in isolation. Courts in the West have accepted that the sexual activity of a homosexual-oriented person should be accepted as part of that orientation. Thus, it becomes unlawful to discriminate in the provision of goods and services between a married heterosexual couple and a homosexual couple.

The meaning of marriage is becoming irrelevant as it is seen more as a sexual relationship: the definition of family is accepted

---

[9] See Mary Eberstadt, *Adam and Eve After the Pill*, Ignatius Press, San Francisco, 2012, in particular chs. 3 and 5.

to mean any couple in a committed relationship. Furthermore, the relationship itself need not be geared towards the founding of a family. Hence, children become an appendage to the relationship, not integral to it.

Cultural values are determined by a relativism anchored in personal whims and gratification; parliaments and courts allegedly reflect community values as religious voices become increasingly isolated. Guidance on morals is no longer given by religious leaders but set by celebrities and the cult of popularism.

Beliefs, once informed by religion, are now determined by secular imperatives. Political ideology and climate change have been held to be beliefs equal in standing and weight to religious beliefs.

Discrimination laws are written to reflect human rights and interpreted to favour the rights of the individual; they trump religious liberty whenever the rights are in contest.

These are not merely dangerous ideas; they amount to the spreading of an anti-religious secularism which once would have been called an alternative ideology.

Professor Marcello Pera, lecturer in Philosophy, author and former President of the Italian Senate, explained the situation in Europe this way:

It is a battle on all fronts, from politics to science, from law to custom, in which religious traditions that baptised Europe and fostered her for centuries are now being accused of threatening the secular state, obstructing social co-existence, and hindering scientific research. Europe hides its Christian symbols and discourages the use of religious greetings such as Merry Christmas and Happy Easter because it does not wish to offend non-believers or members of other religions.[1]

---

[1] Marcello Pera, *Why We Should Call Ourselves Christians,* 23.

It is best if we avoid delusion and realistically examine where we who are religious believers stand in the scheme of things. It is helpful to accept the true position: our opportunity to influence the political order is not wide. Too often well-intentioned Christian spokespersons believe they are in a strong position to negotiate political outcomes when in fact they are forced to concede defeat rather than merely limiting a worse outcome. They fail to understand the force of popular sentiment.

The Western world has embraced a secularism devoid of religious morality. It has, in the words of Professor Pera, "disowned its origins". Like Pontius Pilate when he asked Jesus Christ: "What is truth?" without waiting for an answer; truth is no longer important. It is the here and now that matters: it is the relativism of the day. It is the by-product of the sexual revolution which has pervaded our moral compass and affected every corner of our lives.

It is worth reflecting on who we are and what we believe. To this end, I wish to address three matters: the nature of religious liberty; some recent decisions of courts and tribunals; the present and future challenges.

What is Religious Liberty?

To fully appreciate the concept of religious liberty we should consider what the word religion means and the force it is capable of exerting. Remember that many people have given their lives in defence of their belief in religion. Many Buddhist Monks heroically stood in defiance of the ruling authorities in Burma and Tibet and lost their lives in doing so. Many thousands of Christians likewise have been put to death in Northern Africa, in ISIS controlled lands, in Pakistan and in South East Asia.

In the celebrated *Scientology case*,[2] decided by the High Court of Australia, the joint judgment of Mason ACJ and Brennan J is still widely cited. The relevant part says:

> ... for purposes of the law the criteria of religion are twofold. Firstly, a belief in a Supernatural Being, Thing or Principle; and secondly, acceptance of canons of conduct in order to give effect to that belief, though canons of conduct which offend against the ordinary laws are outside the area of any immunity.

It is clear that a belief without canons of conduct is insufficient to satisfy the criteria of religion. Once we accept a belief it is necessary that we conduct ourselves in a manner consistent with what that belief would expect of us. There needs to be demands on how we live our lives; on how we behave in our homes, in our place of work, in the marketplace and how we respond to threats to our religion.

The Constitutional Court of South Africa also gave an insight into how religion is viewed. In the matter of *Christian Education of South Africa v Minister of Education*,[3] the court said:

> Yet freedom of religion goes beyond protecting the inviolability of the individual conscience. For many believers, their relationship with God or Creator is central to all their activities. It concerns their capacity to relate in an intensely meaningful fashion to their sense of themselves, their community and their universe. ... Religious belief has the capacity to awaken concepts of self-worth and human dignity which forms the cornerstone of human rights.[4]

---

[2] *The Church of the New Faith v The Commissioner for Pay-Roll Tax*, 154 CLR 120.
[3] CCT 4/00, 18 August 2000.
[4] Sach at par. 36.

The teachings of the Catholic Church are consistent with both matters mentioned above. In 1998 the late Pope, now St John Paul II, wrote in his great Encyclical, *Fides et Ratio*:

> ... fundamental questions which pervade human life: Who am I? Where have I come from and where am I going? Why is there evil? What is there after life?... They are questions which have their common source in the quest for meaning which has always compelled the human heart ...[5]

Similarly, the Second Vatican Council document, *Humanae Dignitas*, proclaimed by Pope Pius VI in December 1965, was a Declaration on Religious Freedom. It said:

> ... all are bound to seek the truth and to hold fast to it ... the human person has a right to religious freedom ... and all ... are to be immune from coercion ... of any human power ... and no one is to be forced to act in a manner contrary to their own beliefs, whether privately or publicly whether alone or in association with others, within due limits.[6]

Unremarkably, the teachings of the Catholic Church are one with the two illustrations of what courts have commented upon in matters of religion. Religion is identified by a belief in an external force which is outside this world and that belief has a force (its canons) which directs you to perform certain acts. Religious liberty is therefore a search for truth.

Recent Decisions of Courts and Tribunals

In recent times we have seen increasingly adverse decisions from Courts and Tribunals. In addition, legal academics are arguing that religion has no role in public policy and should be restricted to the private sphere.

---

[5] *Fides et Ratio*, par. 1.

[6] Ibid., par. 2.

In what is called the Cobaw case, the Victorian Supreme Court of Appeal held that the Exclusive Brethren had no right to deny a request for use of the Resort Centre at Phillip Island to a homosexual support group, which came under the acronym of Cobaw.[7] The request was for use and accommodation. The Exclusive Brethren organisation's stated belief was that sex was a function within marriage and thus could not facilitate the use of their centre by a homosexual support group. The Court held that the Christian Brethren could not manifest their Christian beliefs by rejecting the group. The Court further held that the Resort Centre was not conducted for religious purposes. Religious purposes was one of the grounds for Incorporation and contained within the Articles of Incorporation of the Resort Centre. The Court of Appeal did not regard this as a persuasive argument.

In another case, the Queensland Anti-Discrimination Tribunal[8] held that the St. Vincent de Paul Society, although acknowledged to be identified with the Catholic Church and inspired by Catholic teachings, was not an organisation acting for religious purposes . The Tribunal held that a rule of the Society requiring a Catholic only to hold the position of 'Captain' for a region was discriminatory and could not stand. Part of the Captain's role was to recite prayers prior to a meeting; however, the Tribunal did not think this was sufficient reason to disallow non-Catholics from holding the position of Captain. The Tribunal commented that there was no reason why a non-Catholic could not hold the position and in all likelihood do an equally good job.

In 2012 a prominent group of Academic law professors and

---

[7] *Christian Youth Camps Limited and Mark Rowe v Cobaw Community Health Services Limited and Victorian Equal Opportunity and Human Rights Commission* [2014] VSCA 75.

[8] *Walsh v St Vincent de Paul Society Queensland No. 2* QADT32 (12 December 2008).

lecturers made a submission to the Federal Parliamentary Inquiry on the merging of all Commonwealth Discrimination Acts that Religious Institutions should have no privileges in discrimination law. They said that religious institutions and individuals should enjoy no immunities, privileges or greater rights than others in the community in the delivery of goods and services nor be allowed to employ persons only of their own faith within their institutions.[9]

In 2008 Carolyn Evans, the Dean of Law at Melbourne University wrote in the *Harvard International Law Journal*:

> There is an increasingly powerful movement to subject religion to the full scope of discrimination laws, with some scholars now suggesting that even core religious practices, such as ordination of clergy, can be regulated in the name of equality.[10]

Presently, the Victorian Government has a Bill before the Victorian Parliament to restrict the right of religious schools in employing persons of their own faith unless they teach core subjects – like Religion.

One of the last pieces of legislation which the Gillard Government approved in 2013 was to amend the *Sex Discrimination Act*. It introduced several measures. One was to insert rights for persons claiming Gender Identity not to be discriminated against. Gender Identity was defined to include "appearance and mannerisms".

Another amendment was to remove the right of Home Care Centres run by religious organisations to determine the type of accommodation upon admission. The amendment took away the right of discretion for such Home Care Centres to offer two single rooms to a same-sex couple seeking accommodation. Now, given

---

[9] Discrimination Law Experts Group Submission, *Human Rights and Anti-Discrimination Bi*ll, 29 December 2012, see 27-29.

[10] *Harvard ITJ Online*, vol. 49, April 2008, 41.

the amendment, these Home Care Centres are compelled to provide a same-sex couple accommodation with a double bed regardless of the teaching of that Centre's religious beliefs. The Government justified the amendment because government funding was provided to the Home Care Centre. Such a precedent may be used in future for religious run schools and welfare agencies to conform with government policy and not the teachings of their faith.

3. Present and Future Challenges

This brings me to the issue of the public debate on same-sex marriage.

Put aside your own views on this question for a moment. Allow me to say the whole campaign by Marriage Equality is run on a deception, albeit a very clever one.

There appear to be three limbs to their campaign; removal of discrimination, equality in marriage and human rights.

Firstly, the campaign relies heavily on removing discrimination. However, should same-sex marriage come about then there will be not one relief from discrimination for the homosexual couple: the law already provides equal rights to a homosexual couple. From access to the Family Court, to taxation laws, to welfare laws, to superannuation laws: there is no longer a distinction.

Secondly, the word "equality" has been invoked to suggest somehow homosexual persons are not equal. This is a lie. The only thing that changes in the event of same-sex marriage is that marriage will mean something different to what has been understood since Aristotle; that is, what was understood as marriage required a union of a man and woman. Joining a man and man or a woman and a woman does not establish equality: it merely changes the meaning of marriage. The redefinition of marriage would not come with the presumption of monogamy as exists in a traditional heterosexual marriage. The marriage equality campaigners consistently refuse to commit to monogamy in their sexual union. The union becomes one of desire not a union for procreative mates as a same-sex couple do not engage in a procreative sexual union. The biological coupling of the unions is so diametrically different that it defies logic, appearance, form and manner. How can an apple and an orange be equal in taste and appearance? Deception can only achieve it.

Thirdly, the claim that allowing homosexual couples to marry is a Human Right. The European Court of Human Rights which is regularly quoted as an authority within human rights jurisprudence has ruled, on two separate occasions in two separates cases, there is no human right for same-sex marriage.[11] There exists no Article or paragraph in any International Human Rights Instrument which states a human right for homosexual couples to marry.

Should we get same-sex marriage then everything changes. Unless existing laws are changed, then under existing Discrimination Laws in Australia, all schools, including faith-based schools, will be forbidden to teach that marriage is a union of man and woman only. It is doubtful that clergy will be permitted to preach on marriage as their Church teaches. Those involved in the distribution of goods and services will be prevented from acting on conscientious beliefs. These are not alarmist predictions but what is evident in Canada, in the United Kingdom, some parts of Europe and starting to surface in the United States .

Once the foundational grounding of procreative activity to affirm a marriage is abolished then all other unions have equal claims to marriage by weight of the changed definition. In logic and in reason, if marriage only requires a committed couple expressing their love of each other, within a sexual relationship, why cannot an equal expression of love, in all likelihood genuine love, between

---

[11] *Schalk and Kopf v Austria*; *Hamalainen v Finland* [2014] ECHR 787.

a consensual sexual relationships between a threesome not have equal value? Indeed, why would not a caring and sympathetic public, after years of argument and public campaigning over 5-10 years or so, not favourably consent to a further change in the definition of marriage from two people to three people. Two people brought together in a loving union of desire have no monopoly nor mandate to prevent an expanded loving union of desire. If three people in a loving, caring and consensual relationship campaigned on "love", why would not a disengaged society lean the same way as it has towards same-sex marriage.

It is patently clear that having created a new foothold on a wider meaning of equality and given the increased exposure of transgenderism in the United States and England, an emerging campaign for which we need to prepare, is that of transgender equality. Such campaigning has already surfaced in England. Same-sex marriage is only the beginning.

So, we might ask ourselves why religious liberty is important. A simple glance at the facts will assist in giving the answer to this question. Over 25% of Australians identify as Catholics. There are over 1,300 Catholic parishes in Australia where more than 600,000 parishioners worship each Sunday. The St Vincent de Paul Society has 40,000 members and volunteers helping people in need across Australia. There are in excess of 700,000 students in over 1,700 schools taught by over 55,000 teachers. In healthcare, Catholic Agencies provide more than 9,000 hospital beds and over 1,900 residential aged care beds. Catholic Social Welfare is the largest welfare provider outside of Government with more than 60 member organisations employing over 10,000 staff and volunteers providing a huge range of services. If such a significant body cannot be allowed to have a public voice in social and public policy making, then democracy is indeed a system dominated by the anti-religious elitist. Welcome to the new Hollywood!

6

THE CONTRIBUTION OF THE CHRISTIAN CONCEPT OF MARRIAGE TO WESTERN CIVILISATION

Julian Porteous

ABSTRACT

This paper will examine the impact the Christian conception of marriage made to the status and treatment of women and children in ancient Roman society. In contemporary western society there is little appreciation of the role the Church played in improving and elevating the status and treatment of women and children in society. By looking at the reality of daily life in pre-Christian western society we can get a better sense of the dangers involved in abandoning the heritage bequeathed to our society from its Christian roots.

* * * * *

1. A question often discussed these days is: how did Christianity manage to capture the Roman Empire? How did a tiny persecuted religion from isolated part of the Roman Empire succeed in becoming the established religion of the Empire in a relatively short span of time?

For the first three hundred years of its existence Christianity suffered from periodic and sometimes extremely harsh persecution. On occasions Christians were convenient political scapegoats, as in the case of the Emperor Nero blaming Christians for the fire which destroyed much of the city of Rome. At other times they were persecuted because of false rumours that they took part in secret rites of incest (agape meals seen as love feasts) and cannibalism (receiving the body and blood of Christ). Mostly it was because they would not accept sacrifice to Roman gods. They were seen as subversive to the State.

Yet Christianity continued to spread among the ordinary people right across the vast Roman Empire. It spread more by the influence of ordinary Christians upon their neighbours, than by some planned program of evangelisation. While there were some extraordinary itinerant preachers like Paul of Tarsus, it was the fact that ordinary Christians stood out in their local communities as people of quiet yet strong personal convictions about personal salvation, eternal life and forgiveness. They were also notable for their charity towards the poor, and not only among their own.

When the Emperor Julian sought to restore paganism he complained that Christianity "has been specially advanced through the loving service rendered to strangers and through their care of the burial of the dead". "It is a scandal", he said, "that there is not a single Jew who is a beggar and the [Christians] care not only for their own poor but for ours as well; while those who belong to us look in vain for the help we should render them".[12]

Christianity had an extraordinary influence upon Roman society and proved to be attractive to many ordinary citizens. The Christian apologist, Justin Martyr, wrote to the Emperor Antoninus in an effort to express some of the defining characteristics of the Christians. He said:

> We formerly rejoiced in uncleanness of life, but now love
> only chastity; before we used the magic arts, but now

---

[12] Julian the Apostate, *Letter to Arsacius*, Letters.

dedicate ourselves to the true and unbegotten God; before we loved money and possessions more than anything, but now we share what we have and to everyone who is in need; before we hated one another and killed one another and would not eat with another race, but now since the manifestation of Christ, we have come to a common life and pray for our enemies and try to win over those who hate us with just cause.[13]

It was not the doctrinal teaching that enabled Christianity to spread but the witness of changed lives. It was the sheer goodness of the Christians that was so disarming.

2. The Roman view of life, marriage and family

These new attitudes to life and living found expression in approaches to marriage and family. The second century pagan writer Celsus was critical of Christianity claiming it to be a religion of women, slaves and children. He touched upon an important point about the appeal of Christianity to women.[14]

Roman society limited marriage to free citizens. Slaves and non-Romans were not allowed to be married. Further, the Roman understanding of marriage was that a woman was bound to a man, but a man simply had a wife. He was under no obligation to remain sexually faithful to his wife. Indeed there was no formal act of marriage. Those who were living together were considered married. If they separated then the union ceased to exist. In Roman society a man could marry a child bride against her will, sometimes as young as eleven or twelve years old.

The law of *Patria Potestas* meant that the male had full legal authority over his household, including his wife. Women were

---

[13] Justin Martyr, *First Apology*, ch. 29.
[14] See Thomas Taylor, *Arguments of Celsus, Porphory, And the Emperor Julian*, Kindle Edition, retrieved from Amazon.com.au

dependent on the husband to gain the status of being married. The word for marriage, *matrimonium*, is derived from the Latin word, *mater*, mother. Marriage was about a woman becoming a mother.

3. The Christian alternative

In this social context Christianity offered women a freedom and dignity they had not known. It proposed that there was a mutuality in marriage. Men were to be prepared to love their wives as Christ loved the Church.[1] (Eph 5:25) A husband was expected to have a sacrificial love for his wife. He was expected to be sexually faithful. Marriage was to be monogamous.

This was a radical new way of seeing marriage. It was a liberation for women, but also ensured a stronger environment for the raising of children.

Further to this Roman society approved of infanticide. It was legally approved and even encouraged by philosophers, among them Cicero. The historian Plutarch said that the Carthaginians "offered up their own children, and those who had no children would buy little ones from poor people and cut their throats as if they were so many lambs or young birds; meanwhile the mothers stood by without a tear or moan."[2]

It seems so foreign to our sensibilities today but even the usually high principled philosopher Seneca said, "We drown children at birth who are weakly and abnormal."[3] Female children were particularly vulnerable. It was not uncommon for even wealthy families to have only one daughter.

Christians from the outset vigorously opposed infanticide. Every life, they understood, had value. The apologist Justin Martyr stated,

---

[1] Eph 5:25.

[2] Plutarch, *Moralia*, 2.17.

[3] Seneca, *De Ira*, 1.15.

"We have been taught that it is wicked to expose even newly-born children."[4]) For mothers who had borne these infants this message was embraced with gratitude.

Christians viewed marriage very differently. Christians believed that all people – and not just Roman citizens – were entitled to be married. In the early communities there were a number of slaves who embraced the new faith. They were treated as brothers and sisters in line with apostolic teaching. There is no longer slave or free, all were equal in Christ.[5]

Sexual fidelity was strongly promoted among the Christians. This was a clear teaching in the Christian New Testament writings. The Lord taught definitively on the subject of divorce, saying that it was not in the plan of God for humanity.[6] St Paul taught similarly in his letter to the Corinthians: "To the married I give this command (not I, but the Lord): A wife must not separate from her husband. But if she does, she must remain unmarried or else be reconciled to her husband. And a husband must not divorce his wife.[7] This stance was particularly attractive to women as it provided them with a security that they previously did not possess.

It seems that in early centuries Christians sought the blessing of God upon their marriages. They were placed under God. Even though formal wedding ceremonies only developed in later centuries, in the ninth century in the East and later in the West, still Christians were deeply aware of the teaching of the Lord about the indissolubility of marriage. They understood from the biblical texts that marriage was to be a profound inter-personal union. They

---

[4] Justin Martyr, op. cit., ch. 27.

[5] Gal 3:28.

[6] Matt 19:8.

[7] I Cor 7:10 -11.

were aware that God wanted to bless and support their marriage and family life.

The Christian witness to the sacredness of marriage, family and human life was very appealing to women. Female converts were ideally placed to pass on their faith to their children and as St Peter recommended their witness could win over their husbands to the Christian faith: "Wives, in the same way submit yourselves to your own husbands so that, if any of them do not believe the word, they may be won over without words by the behaviour of their wives."[8] It is not surprising to note that women were very prominent in the early Church and wealthy women became great benefactors of Christianity.

The biblical view of husbands and wives as equal partners caused a sea change in marriage. Christian women started marrying later, and while many cultural norms still limited the freedom of women to choose their husband they did sense a greater freedom. The greater marital freedom that Christianity gave women eventually gained wide appeal.

4. Influence on legislation

When Christianity became the established religion in the Roman Empire Christian leaders were able to exercise influence over the rule of the Emperors. Thus after his conversion, the Emperor Constantine enacted two measures addressing the problem of infanticide. Firstly he arranged for the provision of funds out of the imperial treasury for parents over-burdened with children and gave all the rights of property of exposed infants to those who saved and supported them. Finally the Emperor Valentinian (364-375), who was a Christian, outlawed the practice of infanticide in the Roman Empire.

---

[8] I Pet 3:1.

The whole social environment began to change as Roman Emperors also gave funds to the churches to support the poor, the widow and orphans. Christianity was changing the entire social system for better. Christianity continues to help improve the social environment. It has been at the forefront of practical charity, in particular the provision of education and in the improvement in the quality of law. It has fostered in the arts the pursuit of beauty and has even been a key promoter of scientific advancement.

5. Marriage as a Sacrament

Another important advance that Christianity offered to the status and stability of marriage was to recognise that marriage was more than just a human institution reliant upon the human capacity for it to flourish. For Christians marriage had a sacral dimension. Marriage drew the Christian into a union which was blessed by God. As St Augustine stated:

> Among all people and all men the good that is secured by marriage consists in the offspring and in the chastity of married fidelity; but, in the case of God's people [the Christians], it consists moreover in the holiness of the sacrament, by reason of which it is forbidden, even after a separation has taken place, to marry another as long as the first partner lives.[9]

St. Ambrose of Milan speaks of marriage as being sanctified by the blessing of a priest.[10] This teaching raises marriage to a dignity which strengthens its status not only in the eyes of the Church but also in eyes of society. It is to be held in high esteem. Couples themselves are invited to view their union as a means of grace and as a sacred vocation. They are inspired to live their union at the spiritual as well as physical and emotional level.

---

[9] St Augustine, *The Good of Marriage*, ch. 24.
[10] St Ambrose, *Epistle xix to Vigilius*, in Migne, P. L., XVI, 984.

The understanding of marriage as a sacrament further strengthens the notion that marriage involves far more than just human capacity for fidelity. Pope Francis spoke of marriage as an "icon of the Trinity" and had this to say about fidelity:

> The plan inherent in marriage is truly wonderful! It is expressed in the simplicity, and also the fragility, of the human condition. We are well aware of the many difficulties and trials there may be in the life of a married couple ... The important thing is to keep alive the link with God, which is at the basis of the matrimonial bond. When a husband prays for his wife, and a wife for her husband, the bond remains strong; each one prays for the other. It is true that married life has many difficulties: work, there isn't enough money, there are problems with the children ... and often the husband and wife become irritable and argue amongst themselves. There are always arguments in marriages, and at times even plates are thrown. But we must not be sad about this: this is the human condition.[11]

Catholic Theology speaks of marriage as an ontological reality, that is, it penetrates the very being of the two people involved. This is inspired in part by the teaching of the Book of Genesis, emphatically endorsed by the Lord, that the two become one. As the Lord said, "they are no longer two but one".[12] There is a change in their ontological state.

Christianity has a most exalted view of the dignity of the married state and invites societies to embrace this vision as a way of further enhancing the standing of marriage in the society.

---

[11] Pope Francis, "Marriage, the heart of God's loving plan for humanity", Wednesday Audience, 2 April 2014.

[12] Matt 19:6.

6. Christian understanding of marriage

Western Civilisation has inherited of the core elements of this Christian understanding of marriage. Christian thought and practice has enhanced what is naturally evident about the meaning of marriage. However, voices are being raised which challenge this understanding of marriage and threaten to undermine marriage in our society. Marriage already faces many challenges and is in a weakened state. To redefine marriage to include couples of the same sex as is currently being proposed in a number of western nations, would seriously undermine marriage and encouraging a return to a more pagan outlook and practice. Our society needs to strive to strengthen the dignity and stability of the marriage union, not weaken it.

Of course, the Christian view of marriage is inspired by Scriptural teaching. We do as Jesus himself did and base our understanding on the teaching of the Book of Genesis. Here we find divine wisdom and discover the intentions of the Creator. The key elements to the nature of marriage as evident to human wisdom are made explicit in the Scriptural revelation.

The teaching of the first book of the Bible states the obvious truth that human life is to be lived in marriage partnership. The Book of Genesis explains that God created man and woman with marriage in mind. Marriage was to be the complementary union of a man and a woman – sexually, physically, emotionally and spiritually. This is an extraordinarily strong and profoundly intimate union, so much so that the two become one, as the Scripture teaches. Masculinity and femininity are designed in such a way that they are a mutual completion of the other. Man – or masculinity – and woman – or femininity – need each other. The Book of Genesis simply says that it is not good for the man to be alone. A man by himself – a woman by herself – is not complete.

Then the instruction is given – "go and multiply and fill the earth". Once this powerful union between a man and a woman is established, the couple can generate new life and multiply – the two are to increase exponentially over time. This union ensures that the child also benefits from the contribution of the man – the father – and the woman – the mother. Each has a unique and complementary contribution to make to either the son or the daughter of the union.

I recall once passing a church and seeing on the billboard outside the image of an open book – the Bible. Underneath it was written: "For best results follow the Maker's instructions". This has particular significance when it comes to considering the plan of God for marriage and family. God's designs we know are wise, provident and fruitful.

7. Argument for marriage from reason

However, in our engagement with society we cannot argue the case for marriage and family by turning to the authority and wisdom of Sacred Scripture alone. This revelation assists us as Christians in our own understanding, but we cannot base our presentation of the truth about marriage and family on this authority. We know that we cannot say, "Scripture teaches ..." It will not wash in public debate.

We have to argue the case for marriage and family on the basis of rational argument. This argument flows from common human experience and observation and can be backed up by facts and research. The revelation of the truth of human nature given in Sacred Scripture accords with natural reason. There is one truth, not two truths. The truth found in Revelation of course always provides an authoritative guide for the Christian, the right use of human reason working on the basis of experience and observation will necessarily be in accord with Revelation. Faith and reason are not opposed, but are actually complementary. As Christians, sociological data and appeal to the deepest levels of our humanity will accord with what we know through faith.

The true knowledge of human nature is possible through the use of reason working from experience and observation, what is referred to as "natural reasoning". St Paul in his Letter to the Romans argues as much: "... pagans who never heard of the Law but are led by reason to do what the Law commands, may not actually 'possess' the Law but they can be said to 'be' the Law. They can point to the substance of Law engraved on their hearts."[13]

8. Marriage, family and human flourishing

What our society has gained from its Christian heritage does provide the foundation for human flourishing. The empirical evidence in support of marriage understood in the traditional Christian sense is abundantly clear. Stable marriage unions have significant influence on general social wellbeing not only of individuals but for society as a whole. Strong marriages and families support economic well-being, enhance personal safety and security, foster personal happiness and encourage flourishing communities. Healthy families reduce social security demands on governments.

Healthy marriages and families, thus, are a social good. Marriage offers men and women a path for their personal human development in that it encourages a mutual and complete giving of self. Within the covenant of fidelity – a solemn vow to be faithful "in good times and in bad" – their human dignity is elevated and they create a human environment which fosters their personal flourishing. Such a family environment ensures that children have the best opportunity to be nourished in such a way that they, in their turn, will be able develop similar life-giving family environments.

---

[13] Rom 2:14-16.

9. Human sexuality

Christianity has a clear understanding of the nature of human sexuality and its place in God's plan for human life. Pope John Paul II further enriched this understanding through a special series of teaching he gave during his Wednesday audience which have come to be known as the "Theology of the Body".

It is clear that there are movements in contemporary society that radically distort the true nature and beauty of human sexuality. This is the case when it is presented simply in terms of pleasure. Here human sexuality is viewed as existing only for individual self-gratification. This is based on a false philosophical anthropology and has radically undermined the importance of marriage for both human flourishing and for the good of society. Human sexuality, to be realised in its fullness, in its most complete and fulfilling way, in the way in which it was designed, requires monogamous life-long commitment of sexual fidelity between a man and a woman.

We will only effectively strengthen marriages and families in society if there is a right understanding of human sexuality. A distorted view of human sexuality fundamentally undermines marriage, for at the heart of marriage is the highest expression of human sexuality.

A crucial way in which we can strengthen marriage is therefore by showing young people that the only appropriate physical expression of human sexual intimacy is marriage. Any physical expression of human sexual intimacy outside of marriage is a fundamental attack on human flourishing and can only result in the loss of genuine human happiness.

The very nature of human sexual intimacy is procreative. The sexual organs themselves are primarily designed for reproduction, so that there is no way in which they can be viewed as anything other than inherently generative. They, of course, also provide the possibility of pleasure, but this is not their sole function. This fact is almost completely, and perhaps deliberately, ignored in the popular culture.

Sadly we see that sexual intimacy is portrayed solely in terms of pleasure and self-gratification. We need to make society aware that there are serious moral obligations involved in the exercise of sexual intimacy, obligations to the person with whom we share this intimacy and the new human life that might come into existence as a result of this intimacy. Sexual intimacy is never an individual act of self-gratification or pleasure, it is by its very nature a relational-generative act of the highest order. It is never 'casual' but rather involves the most fundamental aspect of our human nature: a sharing of one's own body and an invitation to new life. It is only through Christian teaching that we can ultimately grasp the full meaning and beauty of human sexuality.

10. The contribution of the Christian conception of marriage to Western civilisation

Christianity has made a major contribution to the conception of marriage in Western Civilisation. This understanding born of Divine Revelation and the use of natural reason has forged societies which enable people to truly flourish as human beings. To abandon the Christian understanding will set marriages and families adrift, and the ones who will suffer most will be the children.

We need to courageously proclaim that the Christian teaching on marriage and family needs to be upheld and continue as the solid foundation to our society.

7

THE REVOLUTION OF RELIGION: THE DANGEROUS IDEAS OF CHRISTOPHER DAWSON

Karl Schmude

ABSTRACT

This paper looks at the revolutionary nature of religious ideas, and specifically those of Christianity, as explored by Christopher Dawson and applied to modern secularist culture. It discusses the impact of religion as a spiritual power that challenges the conventional social and political order, touching the minds and hearts of individuals as well as the collective life of a culture, and providing a new centre of purpose and stability. It considers Dawson's belief that the organised exclusion of religion that is modern secularism has a deadening effect on a culture, encouraging social conformity and depriving citizens of ultimate meaning and hope.

* * * * *

1. Introduction

My purpose in this paper is to explore Christopher Dawson's ideas on religion and culture, which I've characterised in the sub-title as 'dangerous', in the context of the main theme of this Dawson Centre Colloquium.

The linking of 'Dawson' and 'danger' may at first seem a singular and even strange one. In appearance and manner, Dawson came across as anything but "dangerous". He was the essence of the conservative gentleman – one might say, very much the "unmenacing man": quiet, reserved, living the life largely of a reclusive scholar; physically frail, suffering from poor eyesight as well as from bouts of depression during his long life; and capable of enjoying private conversation but not at home in a public setting. When he went to America in the late 1950s to take up a Chair at Harvard University, he gave guest lectures at various institutions. In New Orleans, a former student of his at Oxford, Fr C.J. McNaspy SJ, urged the organisers of his lecture to fix the microphone as close to his mouth as possible without his swallowing it! Dawson was, as Fr McNaspy commented to me, "always better to read than to listen to".[14]

But Dawson's delicate appearance and mild manner belied the power and impact of his ideas. If he seemed to be conservative and contained in manner, his ideas were revolutionary in their potential. He revealed an extraordinary – and, I think, unrivalled – penetration of the connections between the mysteries of religious faith and the realities of cultural life. He recognised the profound and pervasive links between religion and culture, and he showed in a wide array of historical studies, particularly in relation to Europe but also to other cultures, how central the concept of religion has been in human history, and how profoundly the lived experience of religious faith has influenced the course of cultures throughout the ages.

If I may offer an aside for a moment, I think Christopher Dawson highlights a difficulty in present-day discourse – which relates to the work of the Christopher Dawson Centre and our colloquium – and that is, how inadequate are the terms of intellectual description we commonly hear – "conservative", "progressive", "traditional",

---

[14] Private letter, C.J. McNaspy to author, 7 June 1972.

"liberal", and so on. I think they have become hopelessly confused and distinctly unhelpful – mixed up with assumptions about freedom and progress and liberation and enlightenment, which are rarely unpacked in the interests of intellectual clarity. There are all kinds of things that conservatives don't want to conserve – and all kinds of things that liberals are no longer liberal about. So the terms are increasingly misleading, and don't apply descriptively – even though they continue to be used pejoratively.

Let me turn now to the title of this paper, "The Revolution of Religion." The common – and conventional – attitude is that religion is anything but revolutionary; that it is, in fact, staid and boring, or more negatively, oppressive and abusive. Christopher Dawson, of course, took a distinctly different view, seeing religion in human history as immensely alive and creative; dynamic and liberating. Consider his picture of the roots of Western European culture in the Middle Ages:

The centre of the common culture [of Europe] lay north of the Alps in the area between the Rhine, the Rhone, and the Loire, and it was in this centre that the creative movements of medieval culture had their origin. In the eighth and ninth centuries it was the centre of the Carolingian empire and the Carolingian culture. In the tenth and eleventh centuries it was the source of the movement of monastic and ecclesiastical reform which had its centre in Lorraine and Burgundy, and it was the alliance of these two movements with the Papacy which determined the form of medieval Christendom and the character of its culture. So, too, in the following period this area was the source of the Crusading movement and of the Cistercian reform, and the centre of the university movement, of the scholastic philosophy, and of Gothic architecture and art.[1]

In visualising this sketch of the cultural importance and impact

---

[1] Christopher Dawson, *The Movement of World Revolution* Sheed & Ward, 1959, 30-1.

of religion, one can appreciate the comment of the English author and actor, Robert Speaight, who said that, when reading Dawson, "the centuries lie before you like a map".[2]

Dawson recognised the creative function of religion. As he unfolded in the first of his Gifford Lectures (at the University of Edinburgh in 1947), religion is an energiser and life giver. It inspires people with purpose and hope:

> In all ages the first creative works of a culture are due to a religious inspiration and dedicated to a religious end. The temples of the gods are the most enduring works of man. Religion stands at the threshold of all the great literatures of the world. Philosophy is its offspring and is a child which constantly returns to its parent.[3]

Religion is, therefore, an agent of change. It has revolutionary effects. Yet Dawson also saw the conservative function of religion. It has been, as he noted in the Gifford lectures, "the guardian of tradition, the preserver of the moral law, the educator and the teacher of wisdom".[4]

This conservative function is reflected in the root meaning of the word, "religion", from the Latin word for "binding". As the English priest-scholar Ronald Knox once explained, religion is something that binds a person – binds him to God. On that account, it ties him down and restrains him. It invokes the sanction of a higher power to commit a person to a higher ideal and prevent his lapsing from that ideal.[5] From such binding, from such a fundamental loyalty, comes a paradox that is severely alien – and seriously objectionable

---

[2] Robert Speaight, *The Property Basket: Recollections of a Divided Life,* Collins & Harvill Press, 1970, 218.

[3] Christopher Dawson, *Religion and Culture. Gifford Lectures: Delivered in the University of Edinburgh in the year 1947,* Sheed & Ward, 1948, 50.

[4] Ibid., 50-1.

[5] Ronald Knox, *Caliban in Grub Street*, Sheed & Ward, 1930, 37.

– to the contemporary mind. It is that religion – as a "binding" devotion – leads to true freedom, and true creativity.

There is a second paradox – and that is, that the concept of "revolution" is not simply an act of overthrowing but rather of "restoring". The word "revolution" has, of course, undergone a change of meaning. Prior to the French Revolution, as the American literary editor Gregory Wolfe has pointed out, the word meant "come full circle", as a wheel is rotated until it returns to its original position – so, a restoration of order and equilibrium.[6] In this sense religion is "revolutionary", in that it seeks to restore a condition that has been lost – a condition of abandoned innocence calling for reconciliation.

These paradoxes – of "religion" as "binding" and of "revolution" as "restoring" – are brought out very clearly in the writings of G.K. Chesterton. In his inimitable style – he was a journalist all his life – Chesterton pointed out on many occasions (and, most notably, in the chapter called "The Eternal Revolution" in his book, *Orthodoxy*) that religion, and in particular Christianity, is truly progressive because it induces people to persevere and be devoted and faithful. As he put it: "I could never conceive or tolerate any Utopia which did not leave to me the liberty for which I chiefly care, the liberty to bind myself."[7]

More than a century ago, Chesterton realised that the tendency to abolish all permanent bonds and loyalties would not bring the social paradise of freedom but rather the social nightmare of devaluing and trivialising human life and experience: "All my modern utopian friends look at each other rather doubtfully, for their ultimate hope is the dissolution of all special ties."[8]

---

[6] *Image*, No. 81, Summer 2014, 4.
[7] G.K. Chesterton, *Orthodoxy*, John Lane, The Bodley Head, 2008, 225.
[8] Ibid., 227.

Similarly, Chesterton believed that the basis of so-called "progressive" thought was faulty, in that it tended to presume that progress was inevitable and irreversible. It is prone to believe that things are improving over time. But Chesterton argued the opposite:

> [T]he only real reason for being a progressive is that things actually tend to grow worse. The corruption in things is not only the best argument for being progressive; it is also the only argument against being conservative ... [for] all conservatism is based upon the idea that if you leave things alone you leave them as they are. But you do not. If you leave a thing alone you leave it to a torrent of change. If you leave a white post alone it will soon be a black post. If you particularly want it to be white you must always be painting it again; that is, you must be always having a revolution. Briefly, if you want the old white post you must have a new white post.[9]

So, even to ensure continuity, Chesterton argued, one has to be revolutionary. He recognised the restorative intention of "revolution" – that it is continually striving to put things back in place; to recover a lost condition. For this reason, religion has been the most revolutionary force in the human heart – and in history.

Revolutions, of course, have usually been associated with destruction, and even violence. We think of events like the French and American Revolutions, and the many Communist revolutions of the past century. Let me propose that religion, while revolutionary, is not destructive, except when it assumes a political character and comes to serve a political cause – as in the case of the Catholic IRA in northern Ireland, liberation theology in Latin America, or Islamist terrorism in the Middle East and elsewhere.

But religion is destructive of one thing – namely, the ego and

---

[9] Ibid., 210-1.

the ever-present human temptation to create idols. We think of Les Murray's powerful lines in his poem, "Church", contrasting Christianity with the false objects of faith founded on self-worship:

> the true God gives his flesh and blood.
> Idols demand yours off you.[10]

Religion challenges the ego and the human tendency to build and worship idols, or false gods. And it recognises that breaking away from idols is painful. In this respect, a phrase of the American Catholic writer, Flannery O'Connor, is telling. O'Connor spoke of "the violence of love" – and commented that, in the Christian understanding, grace produces healing – but, before it heals, it cuts with the sword Christ said He came to bring.[11]

If we are inclined to doubt – or don't feel we can argue convincingly – that religion is a revolutionary force of profound power and appeal, then we might contemplate the impact of various ideologies that have each adored a golden calf and functioned as a substitute religion over the past century – notably, Communism with its worship of class, and Nazism with its worship of race.

In Dawson's mind, Communism was remarkably like a religious faith:

> ... Russian Communism does resemble a religion in many respects. Its attitude ... [is that] of a believer in the gospel of salvation; Lenin is more than a political hero, he is the canonised saint of Communism ...; and the Communist ethic is religious in its absoluteness and its unlimited claims to the spiritual allegiance of its followers.[12]

---

[10] Les Murray, "Church," in *The Biplane Houses*, Black Inc, 2006.
[11] Flannery O'Connor, *The Habit of Being: Letters Edited*, with an Introduction by Sally Fitzgerald, Farrar, Straus, Giroux, 1979, 411.
[12] C. Dawson, *Religion and the Modern State*, Sheed & Ward, 1936, 58.

Such fervent political movements have the force of religion in terms of ultimate loyalties, but they nonetheless operate at an earthly level only and do not really correspond to any genuine transcendental reality. They do not appeal to what Dawson called "a higher and more universal range of reality than the finite and temporal world to which the state and the economic order belong."[13]

In one of his first books, *Progress and Religion*, Dawson noted:

> Every living culture must possess some spiritual dynamic, which provides the energy necessary for that sustained social effort which is civilisation. Normally this dynamic is suppled by a religion, but in exceptional circumstances the religious impulse may disguise itself under philosophical or political forms ...

Moreover, the fact that religion no longer finds a place in social life does not necessarily involve the disappearance of the religious instinct. If the latter is denied its normal expression, and driven back upon itself, it may easily become an anti-social force of explosive violence.[14]

In our time, we have witnessed a new substitute religion in the form of an anti-religion – a new idol that has all the hallmarks of religion and yet is opposed to the very idea of religion. I'm referring to the huge surge of secularism in present-day society.

Secularism has developed from a social condition into a cultural and political ideology – from a situation in which the presence of religion has been quietly understood and practically accepted into one that increasingly excludes religion – and is determined to banish it as socially backward, personally crippling and politically dangerous.

---

[13] C. Dawson, *Religion and the Rise of Western Culture. Gifford lectures: Delivered in the University of Edinburgh 1948-1949,* Sheed & Ward, 1950, 7.
[14] C. Dawson, *Progress and Religion: An Historical Enquiry,* Sheed & Ward, 1929, viii, 228.

Now, it may reasonably be argued that this anti-religious shift in the form of an ideology is not new – that it springs from the 18th century rationalist Enlightenment. Yet at that stage, the warning signs of where an anti-religious ideology might lead were not fully recognised. In his later writings, most notably his 1961 work entitled *The Crisis of Western Education*, Christopher Dawson argued that the hopes of the Enlightenment in France were consumed by the savagery that took place at the time of the French Revolution:

There has never been a society that was more civilised in the humanist sense than the French society of the Enlightenment, nor one more completely convinced of the powers of reason and science to solve all the problems of life and to create a completely rational culture, based on a firm foundation of science and philosophy. Yet when this society ... had the opportunity to put their ideas into practice in the first years of the French Revolution, they failed disastrously and were themselves destroyed, almost to a man, by the eruption of the irrational forces that they had released.[15]

In another work, *The Gods of Revolution*, which did not appear until after Dawson's death in 1970, he offered a number of vital insights into the relationship between ideology and action. He argued that it was the intellectual revolution of the French Enlightenment that paved the way for the political revolution, and that the political upheaval could not have taken place without the preceding intellectual revolution. He noted the inherent contradiction between the liberal theory of the French Revolution and the realities of the revolutionary situation as it unfolded in the late 18th century; and he emphasised the extent to which an all-encompassing ideology inspired the mass executions known as the Reign of Terror, which was not confined to those identified as traitors but rapidly spread to great numbers of bystanders – people who were judged as indifferent and

---

[15] C. Dawson, *The Crisis of Western Education,* Sheed & Ward, 1961), 192.

condemned for not actively working for the new order of a regenerated humanity.[16] Dawson himself saw the blending of intellectual and political revolution in 18th century France as a prefigurement of totalitarian movements in the 20th century.[17]

How does this historical background relate to the rise of modern secularism? I think that it might shed light on the ways in which a prevailing ideology that seeks to banish religion can become perverted and engulfed by totalitarian zeal. In a series of lectures delivered at Cambridge on Christianity and culture, just before World War II, T.S. Eliot quotes Christopher Dawson (whom he held in very high regard) on the rise of what Dawson called "a kind of totalitarian democracy". Eliot himself commented:

> That Liberalism may be a tendency towards something very different from itself, is a possibility in its nature. For it is something which tends to release energy rather than accumulate it, to relax, rather than to fortify. It is a movement not so much defined by its end, as by its starting point; away from, rather than towards, something definite … By destroying traditional social habits of the people, by dissolving their natural collective consciousness into individual constituents, by licensing the opinions of the most foolish, by substituting instruction for education, by encouraging cleverness rather than wisdom, the upstart rather than the qualified, by fostering a notion of getting on to which the alternative is a hopeless apathy, Liberalism can prepare the way for that which is its own negation: the artificial, mechanised or brutalised control which is a desperate remedy for its chaos.[18]

---

[16] C. Dawson, *The Gods of Revolution,* Sidgwick & Jackson, 1972, 94.

[17] C. Dawson, *Beyond Politics,* Sheed & Ward, 1939), 71.

[18] T.S. Eliot, *Christianity and Culture. The Idea of a Christian Society and Notes Towards a Definition of Culture*, Harcourt, Brace & World, 2008; orig. ed. 1940, 12.

Let me mention two dimensions of present-day secularism which Dawson identified, and which mark a clear difference from the secularising tendencies of 18th century France. The first is the unitary nature of present-day culture, dominated as it is by technology and conditioned by communications media. Dawson countered the idea that modern culture is pluralistic in character, as is often assumed. On the contrary, he contended, it is "more unitary, more uniform and more highly centralised and organised than any culture that the world has known hitherto".[19]

Dawson saw the universal nature of contemporary education as being a major cause of this condition. It is very largely funded and controlled by the state and, to that extent, secularist in its assumptions and values, and "it brings the whole of the younger generation under the same influences and ideas during the most impressionable period of their lives".[20]

Dawson was, of course, offering these comments decades before the rise of the internet and of social media, and the ways in which these channels of communication actually convey and confirm certain perceptions and assessments more rapidly and excitedly than ever before.

A basic reason for the unitary nature of modern culture – and what Dawson saw as its totalitarian tendencies – is the rise of mass consciousness. As early as 1939, he argued that the liberal ideology of the modern democratic State disguises its totalitarian character. The essence of the totalitarian regime, he believed, was to be found not in dictatorship – and in 1939, there was the dual menace of Communism and Nazism – but in mass consciousness and mass organisation. It was this condition at the level of ordinary life which Dawson saw as leading to the removal of religion from public and

---

[19] Dawson, op. cit., n. 16, 146.
[20] Ibid., 146.

cultural life. While he acknowledged that the dictator State, with its "militant mass consciousness" and "ideological fanaticism", was more menacing than the liberal democracies, for in the democracies, minorities still had legal rights and the survival of a liberal ideology continued to favour religious and other freedoms, he perceived the same fundamental psychological problem in both cases – and that is, "how the individual and the minority is to resist the pressure of mass opinion and mass emotion, and how it is possible to reconcile spiritual freedom and personal responsibility with the mechanised existence of a unit in the economic machine".[21]

He noted a critical difference between the well-off and ordinary people:

> No doubt the rich man, the scientist and the politician enjoy much more freedom under a parliamentary government than under a dictatorship, but the average man and woman, and still more the average boy and girl, are no more their own masters in the one than in the other. Their minds are moulded and their opinions are formed insensibly by the mass suggestion and mass propaganda of the press, the radio and the cinema. [What would he have said of the vast explosion of communications media in our time!] And the only difference is that the fascist and communist States attempt to direct this propaganda in accordance with their respective ideologies, whereas in the democracies it is a soulless force which is inspired purely by the motive of profit.[22]

To highlight a second dimension of the secularism of contemporary culture which Dawson identified – and that is, its artificial character, which he believed is unlike anything experienced in previous ages:

---

[21] Ibid., n. 18, 77.
[22] Ibid., 68, 76-7.

Our modern Western secularised culture is a kind of hothouse growth. On the one hand, man is sheltered from the direct impact of reality, while on the other he is subjected to a growing pressure which makes for social conformity. He seldom has to think for himself or make vital decisions. His whole life is spent inside highly organised artificial units – factory, trade union, office, civil service, party – and his success or failure depends on his relations with this organisation. If the Church were one of these compulsory organisations modern man would be religious, but since it is voluntary, and makes demands on his spare time, it is felt to be superfluous and unnecessary.

How are Christians to overcome this difficulty? The answer is not an easy one, for the problem of the conversion of the sub-religious is not unlike the problem of the education of the subnormal. The only real solution is to change the cultural environment which has made it possible for this unnatural state of things to develop. For the sub-religious is also in a certain sense the subhuman, and the fact that apparently healthy and normal individuals can become dehumanised in this way shows that there is something seriously wrong in the society and culture that have made them what they are.[23]

Yet while culture and society are unitary, Dawson noted that religion was pluralistic, and the capacity of any particular faith, even one that has been numerically significant in Western society such as Catholicism, to "stand out against the pervasive and overwhelming pressure of the 'common way of life',"[24] was extremely limited.

I think there continues to be value in Dawson's reflections on the way in which the French Revolution consumed the hopes of the rationalist Enlightenment and exposed them as illusions.

---

[23] Dawson, op. cit., n. 16, 173.

[24] Ibid., 146.

And Dawson's insights may serve as a pointer to the final fate of secularism, however dominant it currently seems to be. For any philosophy that does not address the spiritual needs and concerns of people, and fails to satisfy the deepest longings of the human heart, cannot finally hold sway in a society, despite its apparent dominance and irresistibility.

The key feature of a secularist society is that, despite its appearance of openness, it is actually a closed world which lacks any access to transcendental realities – except false ones. The contribution of religion – and for Dawson, in particular Christianity – is not merely the addition of a religious element to the culture, but rather a prising open of this closed, self-absorbed world, so that human society is invested with a new spiritual purpose and vitality that is capable of transcending the conflicting interests of individual and class and race.

Let me conclude with a reflection of G.K. Chesterton's on why religion is so revolutionary – and so "dangerous". (If I am quoting Chesterton so much today, it's not only because he said a great deal worth quoting, but he also harboured a deep respect for Christopher Dawson and could express in an arresting way many of the insights which Dawson presented learnedly and at length in his many historical studies.)

In his major work, *Orthodoxy*, Chesterton ruminated on the common criticism of Christianity that, historically, it was so obsessed by seemingly small issues of theology. He spoke of "the earthquakes of emotion about a gesture or a word". Why bother, when it was "only a matter of an inch". But Chesterton responded: "… an inch is everything when you are balancing". And he argued that "balance" was at the heart of Christianity:

> The Church could not afford to swerve a hair's breath on some thing if she was to continue her great and daring

experiment of the irregular equilibrium. Once let one idea become less powerful and some other idea would become too powerful. It was no flock of sheep the Christian shepherd was leading, but a herd of bulls and tigers, of terrible ideals and devouring doctrines, each one of them strong enough to turn to a false religion and lay waste the world.

Remember that the Church went in specifically for dangerous ideas; she was a lion tamer. The idea of birth through a Holy Spirit, of the death of a divine being, of the forgiveness of sins, or the fulfilment of prophecies, are ideas which, any one can see, need but a touch to turn them into something blasphemous or ferocious.

... if some small mistake were made in doctrine, huge blunders might be made in human happiness ... Doctrines had to be defined within strict limits, even in order that man might enjoy general human liberties. The Church had to be careful, if only that the world might be careless.[25]

I think this sums up, in a provocative and popular way, the "revolution of religion", and why Dawson's ideas on the impact of religion on culture in history are so "dangerous".

---

[25] G.K. Chesterton, op. cit., n. 8, 182-3.

8

CHRISTIANITY AND THE LIBERAL TRADITION, FRIENDS OR FOES?

Alex Sidhu

ABSTRACT

This paper will examine the claim that with the Second Vatican Council the Catholic Church finally embraced political liberalism. It will outline some of the difficulties with this claim and seek to offer a counter-narrative which holds Christianity to be the basis of a true political theory of liberation.

* * * * *

There continues to be much debate over the relationship between Christianity and liberalism, both liberal political structures and liberal political theory. This is particularly true of Catholicism. From consistent explicit criticism and condemnation of so-called liberal social and political movements which advocated freedom of conscience, speech and religion, and mass democracy prior to the 20th century, reading the documents of the Second Vatican Council, one cannot help but be struck by what seems at first glance at least to be a virtual about face on these matters, if not an open embrace of liberal political theory.

Indeed a theorist no less than the standing of John Rawls argues in his work *The Law of Peoples*, that "Catholicism as a result of Vatican II, in particular the recognition of the right to religious freedom as based in the dignity of the person" is more or less compatible with his own political liberalism.[1]

It is not possible in this short paper to adequately capture the full complexity of the relationship between Christianity and liberalism. In part this is due to the many different ways in which the term liberalism is understood and used in different western societies, within both popular and academic contexts.

For my part I use and employ the term liberalism to denote political theories which hold the fundamental or ultimate political value to be some conception of autonomy, liberty and/or equality. For me, when all is said and done, what distinguishes a liberal theory from a Catholic political theory is that the liberal theory (of democracy) holds to some understanding of autonomy and/or equality as the most fundamental political value, whereas for the Christian this will be their commitment to God. For the Christian the ultimate political value is the transcendent truth, who is God, a Trinity of persons who has outlined His plan for humanity in the moral and divine law. The liberal, by definition, cannot hold this foundational political commitment without ceasing to be a liberal. A liberal democracy would therefore, on this understanding, be a democracy that embodies some form of liberal theory, rather than simply any democracy that recognises certain personal rights and freedoms, and other limitations on power. Liberalism is best understood not as a political system with a particular structure, but a political structure that embodies a particular political theory.

It is also important to distinguish between actual political orders and political theories. We often hear of Australia or other Western nations being described as liberal democracies. This confuses the issue. The political order we have in Australia and indeed those in other western societies are not the embodiment of a single

---

[1] John Rawls, *The Law of Peoples*, Harvard University Press 2001, 126-7.

unified political theory (liberalism), rather they are the outcome of a complex history of bargaining, political compromise and both pragmatic and prudential judgement influenced by a range of different philosophical and theological ideas. The Australian political system is not a purely liberal system of government.

In this paper I want to suggest that Christianity – in particular referring to my own tradition, the Catholic tradition – is not compatible with liberal political theory, focusing in particular on anti-perfectionist liberal political theory (a type of liberalism that seeks to remain neutral on fundamental metaphysical and theological matters).

I want to outline and address two key difficulties in very basic terms.

First, I want to offer a critique of the liberal anti-perfectionist claim to neutrality between rival conceptions of the good.

Second, I want to expose the truth claims of so-called anti-perfectionist liberal theory, which are supposed to be neutral between rival metaphysical and theological truth claims. Far from simply being about autonomy and or equality, in this theory we can find the outlines of a very controversial conception of the person and the nature of human existence.

One of the themes of this colloquium is "a celebration of dangerous ideas". Christianity, I would contend is – from the point of view of the dominant mind-set in contemporary society – a dangerous idea. Dangerous because increasingly Christians and indeed Christianity itself, are viewed as 'harmful' to society. Simply to express Christian teaching and ideas in public on such subjects as human sexuality and marriage in the current climate is viewed as "able or likely to cause harm or injury" to a range of individuals. Indeed, one not need look further than the Tasmanian context to find such an example of this. Rodney Croome, the national director of Australian Marriage Equality, recently charged that the distribution of the Australian Bishops Pastoral letter on Marriage to Catholics, titled "Don't Mess with Marriage" was likely to cause 'harm', and therefore we might say is 'dangerous' particularly to those experiencing same-sex attraction or being raised in same-sex households. He condemned Archbishop Julian Porteous, the Catholic Archbishop of Hobart, for having the temerity to distribute this pastoral letter to parents with children in Catholic schools. In other words he condemned a Catholic Archbishop for merely seeking to inform those within the Catholic community of Catholic teaching on marriage and sexuality.

How have we come to this point, where a Catholic Archbishop is accused of potentially harming people in promoting Catholic teaching?

As Archbishop Julian has noted in response to this attack, in an age that is increasingly emotivist and subjectivist, to believe in and make a claim to objective truth is viewed as a form of intolerance, or bigotry towards others: it is to presume to judge other views as wrong. Truth it is argued, or the claim to truth, is harmful, or dangerous. Yet should we be surprised at this trend in western society?

John Rawls, perhaps the most influential political philosopher of the 20th century, based his entire political theory around the notion of the truth being fundamentally dangerous to the stability of modern western societies.

To call Rawls a liberal is somewhat of a misnomer, for at the core of Rawls' political philosophy is not so much a fundamental commitment to liberty but to stability. Rawls was concerned with the problem of pluralism or conflict between rival conceptions of the good and the danger this posed to the ongoing stability and peacefulness of contemporary Western political orders.

Rather than seek some actual common ground or workable modus vivendi between rival parties, in his work *A Theory of Justice* Rawls sought to the move beyond claims to truth and instead develop principles of justice for the governing of society based on, or which could be justified by appeal to, an ideal decision procedure, instead of some particular claim to the true human good. He sought to devise a decision procedure to provide the basis for principles for the governing of society which all (reasonable) individuals might affirm, regardless of their differences. Realising some years later that there was a problem with the textual presentation of the argument – which meant that it could be viewed as relying on a comprehensive truth claim – Rawls sought to re-cast his theory in explicitly 'political' terms so that he could remain on the surface, philosophically or theologically speaking. The result was his work *Political Liberalism*, based for the most part on a collection of essays he had previously published to address this weakness he had identified with his argument.

Rawls was not concerned with liberty or freedom of the individual as such, rather these were only useful to the extent that they provided the best way to achieve long-term social and political stability. He believed that only societies in which individuals have a sense of freedom, and justice are likely to be socially and politically stable in the long term.

Liberalism itself is really the attempt to address the problem of social and political pluralism. It seeks to provide a way of structuring and governing society that all might be willing to accept despite their particular metaphysical or theological commitments. In this why all liberals are ultimately concerned about the problem of stability.

In this Rawls and liberalism more generally are the product of modern political philosophy, arguably the father of which is Thomas Hobbes. It was Hobbes who was first to clearly state that the central political concern or focus must be to ensure the stability of society in the face of rival interests. For Hobbes this was best achieved through the Leviathan, through force. Rawls seeks to better realise the Hobbesian desire for political stability not through overt force but instead by the appeal to apparently neutral political principles which can unite all people regardless of their particular conception of the good.

What these modern theorist such as Hobbes, Locke and Rawls share in common is the rejection of claims to objective truth in politics. Politics, it is argued, should not be about the seeking to realise what is good and true, rather they maintain that it ultimately should be about stability.

Claims to objective truth, it is held, are fundamentally dangerous to the stability and well-being of human societies. They are dangerous because they do not admit of compromise. That consummate European politician Pontius Pilate was the very embodiment of this mind-set, indeed given the opportunity to stare Truth in the face, he asked, "Quid est veritas": "Truth, what is that?" Pilate, like the modern politician, was faced with social unrest and instability, so Truth itself was sacrificed by Pilate for the sake of political stability. We know however that God used the sinfulness of man to achieve reconciliation between God and humanity, for it was through the sinfulness of man, the weakness of Pilate, that Christ was put to death.

Authentic Christianity, properly understood, however is far from being able or likely to cause harm or injury. It is in fact the opposite of a dangerous idea. Christianity, far from being an idea, is a way, or for Christians more precisely it is the way to true human fulfilment and happiness.

The denial of objective truth, or the ability to know such truth, particularly in politics, is in fact the most dangerous idea we confront. If the political order is not based on the true understanding of the human person there is a potential for great evil and suffering to occur, as has been witnessed in the 20th century. What has allowed theorists to deny engaging the question of truth in politics is the further claim that is it possible to engage in politics in such a way so as to remain neutral between metaphysical and theological truth claims.

We regularly hear in the popular media that Christians, or indeed any person with strongly held religious beliefs, ought not seek to impose their religious views on others through government or legislation. That the state or government can and should remain neutral on theological or metaphysical truth claims. The religious believer should 'take off' or 'put aside' these beliefs before entering debate within the public realm. This has been a central claim of those referred to as "anti-perfectionist liberals", such as John Rawls.

The work of the Thomist philosophy Alasdair MacIntyre is helpful in exposing the problem with this claim to neutrality. MacIntyre notes that the notion that one can remain neutral between rival conceptions of the good ultimately has its basis within the discredited epistemology of the Enlightenment. He critiques two assumptions in particular.

First is the notion that reason and understanding are "independent of ... social and cultural particularities" and that these particularities are merely the "accidental clothing of reason in particular times and places".[2] Second, and following from the first, is the presupposition of universal conceptual fixedness, the belief that:

> all rational persons conceptualise data in one and the same way and that therefore any attentive and honest observer, unblinded and undistracted by the prejudices of prior

---

[2] Alasdair MacIntyre, *Whose Justice? Which Rationality?*, 6.

commitment to belief, would report the same data, the same facts, but also that it is the data thus reported and characterised which provide enquiry with its subject matter.[3]

Conceptual fixedness

The problem with this presupposition according to MacIntyre is that there is no simply given, neutral, natural or impartial way of conceptualising and characterising reality, particularly human actions and the social and political world. Rather, we are confronted with equally ultimate rival ways of conceiving and understanding how things are. Not only do we lack a universal rational standard to which appeal can be made to resolve our moral and political disagreements, more importantly we lack a given, natural or more basic way of conceiving and conceptualising how things are. MacIntyre maintains that theorists such as Thomas Kuhn and Gaston Bachelard have taught us that,

> relative to any particular type of enquiry, there are always at least two modes of conceptualising and characterising the data which constitute its subject matter, a pretheoretical (although not of course preconceptual) prior-to-enquiry mode and a mode internal to that particular type of enquiry which already presupposes one theoretical or doctrinal stance and commitment rather than another.[4]

MacIntyre cites Kuhn's example of a stone swinging from a line to make his point, "those innocent of enquiry see and report a stone swinging from a line, a theoretically committed Aristotelian will observe an instance of constrained natural motion, an adherent of Galileo a pendulum". The criteria for identifying everyday objects and persons are pretheoretical, "so that we are able to assert that it is one and the same swinging stone which is observed by both

---

[3] Alasdair MacIntyre, *Three Rival Versions of Moral Enquiry*, 17.
[4] Ibid.

Aristotelian and Galilean physicists". But, argues MacIntyre, "there is no way of identifying, characterising, or classifying that particular datum in a way relevant to the purposes of theoretical enquiry except in terms of some prior theoretical or doctrinal commitment".[5] What is true in the case of physical enquiry, MacIntyre argues, "holds also for theological and moral enquiry".[6]

In attempting to resolve disagreement between those inhabiting rival moral and political standpoints we lack the ability to appeal to some more basic way of viewing and understanding reality.[7] We are always already making sense of reality, in particular human action and the social and political order, through some particular way of conceiving and understanding and cannot engage in enquiry without some prior theoretical or doctrinal commitment. This means that there can be no stripping away of bias and prejudice to reveal a true, natural, objective and impartial way of conceiving, characterising and understanding how things are, as the theorists of modernity, particularly the enlightenment theorists, believe.[8]

---

[5] Ibid.

[6] Ibid.

[7] Incommensurability and translatability between rival conceptual schemes is an important matter, particularly whether it is possible to fully and authentically understand a rival conceptual scheme if there is no common standard to which appeal can be made. MacIntyre argues that in order to authentically understand a rival conception scheme we must treat it like learning a foreign language.

[8] "From the seventeenth century onwards it was commonplace that whereas the scholastics had allowed themselves to be deceived about the character of the facts of the natural and social world by interposing an Aristotelian interpretation between themselves and experienced reality, we moderns – this is, we seventeenth-century and eighteenth century moderns – had stripped away interpretation and theory and confronted fact and experience just as they are. It was precisely in virtue of this that those moderns proclaimed and named themselves the Enlightenment, and understood the medieval past by contrast as the Dark Ages. What Aristotle obscured, they see." Alasdair MacIntyre, *After Virtue: A Study in Moral Theory*, 2nd ed., University of Notre Dame Press, 1984, 81.

For there is no more basic materialist or physicalist way of conceiving that is less controversial than other philosophical ways of conceiving. They are equally ultimate and equally controversial. There is no neutral or impartial ground upon which one can stand and see how things really are and act as neutral adjudicator. It is therefore not a matter of deciding whether to theorise through a particular theoretical standpoint or not, rather it is a matter of one's self-awareness of the theoretical standpoint through which one is always already ineliminably conducting enquiries, Aristotelian, Augustinian, Thomist, Humean, Kantian, Hegelian, Marxist, Husserlian, liberal, analytic, phenomenological or existentialist etc, or some combination of several different standpoints. For example, with regard to the moral and political reality: "Where Aristotle's formulations are in terms of arche, techne, psyche, logos, ergon, praxis, pathos, arête, and polis, Hume's deploy impression, idea, passions calm and violent, nature, artifice, virtue, society, and government."[9]

The disagreement between those affirming rival conceptions of the good is therefore vastly more significant and complex than a disagreement concerning the nature of the human good. For the disagreement between rival standpoints extends to how we actually conceptualise, conceive and characterise the moral and political matters in dispute, and more generally human action and social and political order. In other words, "systematic disagreement upon fundamental issues extends to disagreement over how such disagreements are to be formulated and characterised".[10]

With regard to human reason, MacIntyre argues that as there is no absolute way of conceiving and understanding, everything must emerge from history, from some specific social and cultural context. Moral and political enquiry, indeed reason itself, are "tradition-

---

[9] MacIntyre, op. cit., n. 2, 378.
[10] Ibid., n. 3, 13.

constituted and tradition-constitutive".[11] Reasoning always already takes place within some particular context, within some particular theoretical framework, and on the basis of some particular way of understanding. There is no pure reason that comes from nowhere; rather reason is always already situated in some particular context.

History is not simply peripheral or ancillary, some distinct academic field of enquiry, rather we are the very outcome of history, and while there are of course rival histories and narratives, there is as yet no neutral, independent or non-historically situated standard to which appeal can be made. MacIntyre employs the concept of 'tradition' to capture the necessarily social and historically situated nature of our particular way of conceiving and understanding. To "appeal to tradition is to insist that we cannot adequately identify either our own commitments or those of others in the argumentative conflicts of the present except by situating them within those histories which made them what they have become".[12] Whether we recognised it or not we are inescapably the "bearers of tradition", whether we realise it or not we are necessarily situated within a particular narrative or overall context.[13] The particular theoretical framework or conceptual scheme we inhabit is therefore also situated within some broader history or tradition, according to MacIntyre.[14]

For MacIntyre it is not a matter of being faced with the choice of whether to live our lives within a particular tradition or not, or the choice of whether to theorise within a particular tradition or

---

[11] Ibid., n. 2, 9.

[12] Ibid., 13.

[13] The concept of "tradition" in MacIntyre's work has a very particular meaning. A "tradition" is a movement of thought with overall continuity. See op. cit., n. 2.

[14] The idea of our beliefs being the embodiment of some background understanding is a theme in the work of a number of important thinkers, in particular Martin Heidegger, Michael Polanyi, Hans Georg Gadamer, Charles Taylor, Richard Rorty, and Stanley Fish.

not. Rather we are confronted with the choice of self-awareness or ignorance: the choice of becoming aware about exactly what tradition through which one is always already inescapably living and always already inescapably theorising and enquiring, or remaining entrapped in ignorance.[15, 16]

Truth in theorising – no escaping unqualified claims to truth

The further important point which we can distil from MacIntyre's work that is the culmination of these two points is the non-avoidability of truth-claiming in moral and political argument and theorising. While, as far as we can ascertain, we have no neutral or independent standard to which appeal can be made to resolve disagreement, the further insight MacIntyre contributes is that in theorising and arguing we cannot escape necessarily making and relying on claims to objective truth, or what is "unqualifiedly true".[17] In advancing a particular moral or political claim we are ineliminably advancing a particular claim concerning how things are. We advance such a claim or undertake such theorising on the basis of things being the way in which we conceive and understand them to be and not otherwise. If things are other than we conceive

---

[15] MacIntyre, as he explains, draws particularly upon the work of Giambattista Vico, Georg Friedrich Hegel, Friedrich Nietzsche, R.G. Collingwood and Hans Georg Gadamer in his critique of modernity. The central problem with the Enlightenment for these thinkers is the attempted flight from history and context to the absolute universal. In their own distinctive ways Vico, Hegel and Nietzsche argue that human beings are necessarily always already context or history-bound; if the universal can be approached it is only as always already context-bound. See op. cit., n. 2.

[16] There is no absolute historicism where history is the only standard; rather the point is to recognise that our understanding is inescapably historically conditioned.

[17] A. MacIntyre, "Moral Pluralism Without Moral Relativism", in K. Brinkmann (ed.), *Ethics*, Bowling Green, Bowling Green State University 1999, 3.

and understand them to be then the claim or theorising would not make sense and would be without grounds. As MacIntyre puts it, "[w]hat is being claimed on behalf of each particular moral standpoint in its conflicts with its rivals is that its distinctive account of the nature, status and content of morality … is true".[18] And it is because we believe our understanding is unqualifiedly true that we advance particular moral and political claims over opposing claims. MacIntyre further argues, "conceptions of justice and of practical rationality generally and characteristically confront us as closely related aspects of some larger, more or less well-articulated, overall view of human life and of its place in nature".[19] One only continues to actively maintain one's particular moral and political position on the basis that one's particular way of conceiving and understanding human nature, action and the moral and political order is true, in that it is not affected by distortion and misrepresentation.[20]

There is no way to avoid relying on some particular fundamental truth claim in living our daily lives, some particular claim about the nature and purpose of human existence. It is simply a matter of what belief we are relying on, and how consistent and well-

---

[18] A. MacIntyre, "Moral Relativism, Truth and Justification", in L. Gormally (ed.), *Moral Truth and Moral Tradition*, Four Courts Press, 8.

[19] Ibid., n. 2, 389.

[20] The question of truth is complex and it is not possible to undertake an exhaustive discussion of rival theories of truth. The basic problem this thesis seeks to highlight is that truth claiming is inescapable. Milbank and Pickstock speak of this as the "meta-assertion of truth" which involves the belief that our particular way of understanding "is how things are" as opposed to another way. Truth in this sense is presupposed as a good. People do not want to be living their lives according to a false understanding of how things are. It is not important that we are unable to establish how things are absolutely; what is important is that we cannot but live according to some particular way of conceiving and understanding and therefore are confronted with the decision to which understanding we ought to give our allegiance. See John Milbank and Catherine Pickstock, *Truth in Aquinas*, Routledge, 2001, 3.

developed this understanding is. If Christianity is not informing political decision making and policy development it will be some other fundamental commitment, most likely hostile to the Christian understanding of reality and the human person.

We need to therefore ensure that Christians are not silenced in the social and political arena because they hold so-called religious beliefs. Everyone holds and lives their life on the basis of some fundamental or ultimate beliefs. We need to bring these to the fore in public policy debates. We need to unearth the presuppositions of those who do not publicly express their commitment to any particular belief system to ensure that it is clear they are necessarily imposing their fundamental beliefs on others when they advocate particular policy.

The truth is not dangerous to politics, rather what is dangerous is to try and hide the fact that all of us operate from some fundamental set of values or belief system about the nature and purpose of human existence, that we all operate on the basis of some particular hierarchy of values. What is dangerous and injurious to society is not to expose these unavoidable truth claims. Those who do not express religious views in the social and political order are not somehow neutral with regard to metaphysical and theological commitments. They are always already unavoidably committed to some fundamental set of values whether they realise this or not.

The second feature I want to focus on is the vision of the human person and human existence we find at the heart of the modern, liberal, social contract theory approach. In the attempt to move beyond the inherent limitations of human knowledge and understanding, the modern tradition formalises a dualistic understanding of reality (the seeds of which can already be found in the work of late medieval nominalism), an attempted cleaving apart of the orders of nature and supernature, that has a fundamental

121

impact on our understanding of the nature of things, in particular our relationship to the Divine.

I want to use the work of The Radical Orthodoxy theorists, particularly Catherine Pickstock to develop this point. According to the Radical Orthodoxy theorists, modernity and the logic inherent in the works of the modern thinkers, is best understood as anti-theology that is ultimately nihilistic. Pickstock speaks of modernity as "the emergence of the unliturgical world" whose "ideal course involves the eradication of the unknown, the choreography of 'spontaneity', and the anticipation of all eventualities via a textual calculus of the 'real'." What she means by this is that modernity involved the attempt to achieve absolute certainty in knowing in order to overcome all elements of disorder in human nature and indeed nature itself, and in some sense achieve a divine perspective of things through purely human effort.

The belief of the 'modern' thinkers, according to the Radical Orthodoxy position, was that critical or scientific human reason unaided could understand more accurately the nature of our situation, specifically the nature of human existence, than theology could through divine revelation. In other words, that human reason alone could establish an absolute foundation for human knowing without recourse to God. (This understanding was based on the presuppositions already discussed which MacIntyre critiques.) This was combined with the idea that somehow nature, in particular the human person, is self-sufficient and independent from God and can know all of reality accurately and with absolute certainty without the need for God. As opposed to the understanding that nature and all creation has been created by God through Jesus Christ and radically dependent on Him for continued existence, and therefore only knowable through Him.

The Radical Orthodoxy position views this understanding not simply as a radical rejection of Christianity but as essentially nihilistic. It argues that the attempt by these thinkers to "treat worldly phenomena such as language, knowledge, the body ... apart from God ... [in order] to safeguard their worldliness, in fact, to the contrary, it is to make this worldliness dissolve".[21] For "without an appeal to eternal stability, one has to define a purely immanent security", yet this immanent security in the form of an "immanent static schema or mathesis" can only be "grounded in nothing" and one must assume "that this essential structure is only an illusion thrown up by the void".[22] In rejecting God as the ground of all things, the modern project, in practical terms, sought to gain control over reality through a "project of mathesis or of 'spatialising' knowledge, that is to say, of mapping all knowledge onto a manipulable grid."[23] The problem is that in trying to grasp absolutely all knowledge in this way, there can be no assurance of achieving anything but subjective assertion. There is no eternal ground to which appeal can be made, only human subjectivity.

Radical Orthodoxy, on the contrary, employs a theological framework of "'participation' as developed by Plato and reworked by Christianity", as "any alternative configuration perforce reserves a territory independent of God" and hence "literally grounded in nothing".[24] With this framework of participation there is an acceptance,

> with postmodernism, [of] the indeterminacy of all our knowledge and experience of the selfhood, ... [yet] it construes this shifting flux as a sign of our dependency on a transcendent source which 'gives' all reality as a mystery, rather than as adducing our suspension over the void.[25]

---

[21] John Milbank et al., *Radical Orthodoxy*, Routledge, 1999, 3.

[22] Ibid.

[23] Catherine Pickstock, *The After Writing: The Liturgical Consummation of Philosophy*, xii.

[24] Milbank, et al., op. cit., n. 21, 3.

[25] Pickstock, op. cit., n. 23, xii.

There is no claim to absolute knowledge or to represent reality in its fullness; truth is regarded as unchanging, eternal but yet not "graspable" and immanently "available". Pickstock, in her own theological project, has attempted to show "how philosophy itself, in its Platonic guise, did not assume, as has been thought, a primacy of metaphysical presence, but rather, a primacy of liturgical theory and practice."[26] According to Pickstock, Platonic philosophy did not seek or claim absolute metaphysical certainty or "a metaphysics of presence". Instead it was about leading a liturgical life in worshiping God through the denial of radical human autonomy and self-sufficiency.

The social and political works of the modern thinkers, particularly the social contract theorists, Hobbes, Locke and Rousseau, are necessarily premised upon an anti-'participation' theology. This is manifest in their work, specifically in seeking to base their political theories in a supposedly more basic, natural, or primal understanding of human beings than that found in Christian Scripture. It is also evident in their reduction of Christianity to 'religion', or the creation of 'religion' as a purely private and inward matter to replace authentic publicly embodied Christianity, where Christian faith is to have no role or consideration in governing the society except as a means of producing and maintaining social unity and obedience to the state.[27] Rawls seeks to avoid all this controversy and disagreement by a "method of avoidance", where he does not explicitly approach politics or the question of justice on the basis of some comprehensive or controversial doctrine, but instead on the basis of particular modern ideas dominant in the prevailing public political culture. Yet from the Radical Orthodoxy position, Rawls's "method of avoidance" (an attempt to avoid metaphysical and theological commitments in politics)

---

[26] Ibid.

[27] See W.T. Cavanaugh, *Theopolitical Imagination,* Bloomsbury, 2003.

already indicates its fundamental rejection of Christianity and the theological framework of participation in its stated attempt to remain neutral towards God.

As already mentioned, the most fundamental concern in Rawls' "political liberalism" is that of conflict. For Rawls, politics and justice are to be understood in terms of fundamental conflict over scarce resources requiring an absolute and definitive solution. This way of viewing politics and justice, however, is not neutral, impartial, more basic or natural. It is a highly distinctive conception of politics which rejects the Christian understanding of human existence as one of "original peace" for what Milbank describes as one of "original violence".[28] According to Milbank this belief of "original violence" in the context of modern politics is that there is "only [chaotic conflict] … which cannot be tamed by an opposing transcendent principle, but can only be immanently controlled by subjecting it to rules and giving irresistible power to those rules in the form of market economics and sovereign politics".[29] This logic is embodied in "political liberalism". The original political problem for Rawls is that of original conflict or "original violence"; there is nothing more important or crucial to understanding human beings with regard to politics than conflict and the need to resolve conflict. In this way, Rawls' approach to the question of politics and justice necessarily favours one particular story of human existence over others, in particular the Christian understanding. According to Milbank, "Christianity … recognises no original violence. It construes the infinite not as chaos, but as a harmonic peace which is beyond the circumscribing power of any totalising reason."[30]

From the Christian perspective the notion of "original violence" is a rejection of humanity created in the Imago Dei where "original"

---

[28] John Milbank, *Theology and Social Theory*, 5.

[29] Ibid.

[30] Ibid.

harmony and integrity between the relationship of God to man, between human beings, within human nature, and between man and nature was lost through original sin, bringing about what is an unnatural state of conflict and disunity in the whole of creation. What in the Christian understanding is unnatural and foreign to humanity's true nature is in Rawls made the most basic feature. There is no further or higher truth for Rawls that must be considered, there is only conflict and the need to overcome this conflict, nothing matters more. The Christian theological anthropology of Imago Dei is replaced by what is now considered the most important way of understanding the person with regard to political matters: the person as 'free' and 'equal' will presupposed to nothing but base self-interest. The most basic and primary feature of politics and justice for Rawls is therefore one of original conflict between rival 'free' and 'equal' wills, each seeking to gain more of what they desire according to their desire or conception of what is good for them.

Eternal salvation through Jesus Christ is no longer the most important consideration in all decision making for Christians on fundamental political matters. This is to be replaced with salvation through the Rawlsian state. In developing "political liberalism" Rawls therefore develops a counter soteriology to Christianity: a competing story of salvation. Both have the same goal: "the salvation of humankind from the divisions that plague us".[31] Rawls argues that we must give our highest allegiance on fundamental political questions to achievement of earthly stability in the form of the demands of reasonableness, reciprocity and public reason; the Catholic Church, in contrast, argues that our highest political allegiance must ultimately be to God and His vision for human happiness and fulfilment, and that true and lasting peace will only be realised by the second coming of Jesus Christ.

---

[31] Cavanaugh, op. cit., 9.

Rawls' work, whether intended or not, is therefore premised on the argument that the most important consideration on fundamental political matters is political stability and not eternal salvation. For Rawls it is the salvation offered by the nation state that is politically more important than the eternal salvation offered by Jesus Christ.

In seeking to achieve perpetual peace through purely human structures, instead of recognising that true peace can only be realised through the Divine, Rawls is implicated in what Pickstock has referred to as "necrophilia", the love of dead things. In prioritising the concern for purely earthly peace over that of the life to come, Rawls gives up a lasting or eternal peace for a "pseudo-eternity of merely spatial permanence which, unlike genuine eternity, is exhaustively available to human gaze".[32] Rawls advocates that we go after what for him appears more real and permanent, rather than what is actually lasting and permanent, eternal life in the Holy Trinity. The problem is that in going after what appears more real and tangible, Rawls is actually grasping after what is dead or dying. In preferring the finite over the infinite Rawls is preferring dead things over what is truly living.

A true Christian politics

The question of an authentic Christian political approach is complex and beyond the scope of this paper, yet the Radical Orthodoxy approach provides some basic guidelines. It establishes that there can be no compromise with any form of theoretic liberalism such as Rawls's "political liberalism", or any approach that does not recognise God as the ultimate source of all that is. As Milbank observes, "[i]f theology no longer seeks to position, qualify or criticise other discourses, then it is inevitable that these discourse will position theology: for the necessity of an ultimate organising

---

[32] Pickstock, op. cit., n. 23, 104.

logic … cannot be wished away."[33] There is no neutral way of approaching fundamental political questions. If the Christian does not approach these questions on the basis of a Christian theological framework, it will on the basis of some other theoretical framework.

Theorising about politics is of course different from actual political practice where political structures are the outcome of complex historical processes of conflict, disagreement and compromise, and not the embodiment of a single well-developed theory. Yet the same basic approach applies. Political structures that embody a non-Christian theological framework(s) are to be treated as imperfect and tolerated rather than embraced because they are the embodiment of the rejection of Christianity. Social and political orders that embody such an understanding are accepted as a reality that one cannot avoid but must seek to resist, in the same way as one would seek to resist the ideology of totalitarian systems. What is central for the Christian is that there is no permanent or lasting home on earth and no political theory or structure that they can finally embrace as their own. The only true political community is the Kingdom of God, which is not realisable through human effort on earth in its fullness, but something that will only arrive with the second coming of Jesus Christ.

---

[33] Milbank, op. cit., n. 28, 1.

9

CHRISTIANITY, DISCRIMINATION AND SAME-SEX MARRIAGE – THE MORAL AND POLITICAL CHALLENGE

Michael Stokes

ABSTRACT

The anti-discrimination movement presents a moral challenge to some traditional institutions supported by many, but not all religions. The institutions under challenge on the grounds that they are unfairly discriminatory include the idea that marriage is between a man and a woman and the idea that inherent differences between men and women ought to be reflected in the social roles which they play, such as those of husband and wife and mother and father. The challenge is a moral challenge because it appeals to widely accepted ideals such as equality and justice in its support. In fact, the arguments are essentially similar to those used to challenge discrimination against blacks and other ethnic minorities. The paper considers possible responses to the challenge and concludes that the only successful answer is to accept that the onus is on those who argue for different legal and social responses to for example, same sex relationships and heterosexual relationships to prove that they have good reason for doing so. Different treatment is not discrimination if there is good reason for it. That requires that we do the social science necessary to prove the case.[34]

[34] ‌‌‌‌‌‌‌ M Phil (Oxon) LL B (Utas), Adjunct Senior Lecturer Law School,

1. Equality, Christianity and the same sex marriage debate.

Christianity is one of the sources of the idea that in some fundamental sense all humans are equal. Peter learnt that God is no respecter of persons in the events leading to the baptism of Cornelius and the acceptance of non-Jews into the early Christian church.[1] Paul stressed the equal worth of all in the eyes of God regardless of gender, ethnic origins and status by stating that there is neither Jew nor Greek, bond nor free, nor male nor female in Christ.[2] In the 20th century, Christians such as the Rev Martin Luther King and Bishop Tutu played leading roles in the struggles against racial discrimination and apartheid.

Many in the gay lobby see the gay movement as an extension of these struggles for equality and against discrimination. But many Christians find themselves on the other side of the fence – in opposition to the gay lobby on issues such as same sex marriage and adoption by same sex couples.

Because of the fundamental equality of all people in the eyes of God, Christians need strong reasons to oppose claims to equal treatment. The basic reason why many Christians are opposed to same sex marriage is that they regard marriage as a divinely ordained union between a man and a woman for life. In their view there is no divine sanction for same sex marriage so that it is wrong for the state to permit it. Many are also concerned that legalising same sex marriage will add to the legitimacy and frequency of practices such as surrogacy, artificial insemination and adoption by same sex couples which they oppose for reasons which are beyond the scope of this paper.

Because so many people are opposed to religious arguments

University of Tasmania.

[1] Acts 10 and 11.

[2] Gal 3:28.

being used as a basis for public policy, some Christians have been relying on other, non-religious justifications for opposing same sex marriage. The paper argues that most of the arguments which they have used are not good arguments, leaving them open to charges of prejudice.

In these circumstances, it is tempting to adopt the position that the state should not regulate marriage at all but should confine itself to regulating significant relationships, leaving churches and civil celebrants to determine whom they will marry. Although the proposal does end the spectre of state-endorsed same sex marriage, it suggests that the state has no interest in promoting the most stable form of family, that based on a marriage between a man and a woman. As in my opinion the State has an interest in promoting marriage between a man and a woman, this position, despite its attractions should not be adopted.

The paper concludes that Christians opposed in principle to same sex marriage must not be afraid to adopt the religious argument against it. At the same time, they need to defend the propriety of relying on religious arguments in public debates. In time, the debate over the propriety of using religious arguments in public debates may be seen as more important than the debate over same sex marriage.

2. The issues in the Australian same sex marriage debate

In some jurisdictions, the major issue is whether the state should recognise and protect same sex relationships. That issue has already been determined in Australia, where a range of significant relationships other than marriage, including but not limited to same sex relationships, are given legal recognition and protection under Relationship Acts. The degree of recognition and protection given is similar to that given to marriage under the *Marriage Act,* so state recognition and protection of same sex relationships is not an issue.

Nor is any issue of liberty in the sense of freedom from constraint involved. Not being able to marry does not impose significant constraints on gays in the sense that they are free to form same sex relationships and families and legally they can have children, although for biological reasons those children will not be the children of both parents. There is of course some limitation on their positive freedom, that is their capacity to do some legal acts. They cannot marry and in some jurisdictions they may not have the capacity to adopt children or to access fertility treatment. But the latter two limitations on capacity are not dependent on their being able to marry and can be removed whether or not they are permitted to marry. Many legal disabilities flowing from their incapacity to marry have been removed. For example, in Tasmania the rules relating to inheritance on intestacy and for making a claim to family maintenance on an estate are now the same as for married couples.[3] Where disabilities still exist, they can be removed whether or not same sex marriage is legalised.

There are two key points at issue in Australia. The first concerns the essential nature of marriage. Many opponents of same sex marriage oppose it on the ground that marriage is essentially a union between a man and a woman, so that same sex relationships cannot be marriages. This argument is not an argument about the meaning or definition of the word marriage but about the essential nature of the phenomenon itself. So if it is correct, the argument would hold good even if the meaning of the word changed to include same sex relationships. If that happened, the word marriage would cease to refer to the phenomenon itself, but would refer to a broader class

---

3 *Testator's Family Maintenance Act 1912* (Tas) sections 2 and 3A, *Intestacy Act 2010* (Tas) section 6.

of phenomena which included same sex marriage. If we did not develop another word to refer to the phenomenon we now refer to as marriage, we would have difficulty talking about it. But that would not change the nature of the phenomenon.

On the other hand, those who support same sex marriage see marriage as a manmade institution which we can change to meet human needs and aspirations. They argue that the state is free to determine who may marry. As marriage is designed as a celebration of love and as a way of gaining legal recognition for a long term, even life long commitment, same sex couples should be permitted to marry. To refuse to permit them to marry is to discriminate unfairly against them and to refuse to accept that their long-term relationships are as valuable and as worthy of respect as are long-term heterosexual relationships.

The second point at issue relates to the nature of families and the rights of children. Some opponents of same sex marriage argue that allowing same sex marriage is not in the best interests of children and that therefore it should not be permitted. There are a number of issues here relating to the impact of same sex couples on the children they raise and relating to practices such as surrogacy which may receive a boost from the legalisation of same sex marriage. They are beyond the scope of this paper.

3. The religious argument against same sex marriage and its place in public debate

The religious argument is a natural law argument, claiming that marriage has essential features which are natural in that humans cannot change them. Putting it simply, the religious argument, widely accepted in the Judaeo-Christian tradition, is that God ordained marriage as a relationship between a man and a woman for life to the exclusion of all others. As marriage is a divinely established institution, it is sacred. Given the commandment to multiply and replenish the earth,[4] its sanctity is in part dependent on the ability of the parties to it, a man and a woman, to procreate and raise children. However, its sanctity is not completely dependent on the parties having that ability. A marriage between a man and a woman who are unable to have children is equally sacred. As marriage is sacred, humans do not have the right or the power to change it. Instead, we should accept God's wisdom and subject ourselves to God's will on the issue. This argument asserts that same sex relationships lack an essential feature of marriage in that they are not a relationship between a man and a woman and that therefore it is wrong to recognise them as marriages.

Sceptics will object to this argument on the grounds that the argument assumes the existence of God and claims that we know God's will with respect to questions such as same sex marriage. As we cannot be certain of the existence of God or of God's will with respect to any question, we should not attempt to base public policy on God's will. It is too speculative and we risk imposing our own prejudices and values on God, thus attempting to make them unchallengeable. However, it is not clear that secular arguments based on the assumptions such as that man is the measure of all things have stronger foundations. Both the religious and the secular position are rational and are based on coherent views about the relationship between humanity, God and the universe. Neither is demonstrably true in any scientific sense. We can use either in an attempt to give a degree of objectivity to our own beliefs and prejudices which they do not deserve. It would be wrong to reject either or both as a permissible basis for public policy arguments because of their lack of certainty. As all moral arguments are based on some unprovable, metaphysical assumptions about human nature and the place of humanity in the universe, the alternative is nihilism in which public policy is determined by power rather than by moral argument.

---

[4] Genesis 1:28.

The idea that religious doctrines and beliefs should be excluded from public debate is often based on a false understanding of the secular state and of the implications of the separation of church and state. Neither the ideal of the secular state nor the separation of church and state require that religious ideas be excluded from public debate. The separation of church and state requires two things, that there be no official state religion and that the institutions of church and state be legally separate from each other, so that church institutions and officers are not required by law to perform state functions and vice versa. The separation of church and state does not require that religious doctrines and beliefs be excluded from public debate.

It may be objected that if religious ideals and doctrines may be used in public debate, it may lead to the adoption of policies whose sole justification is religious. Once the state becomes the enforcer of religious doctrines, the separation of church and state is at an end. It is possible to imagine extreme cases in which state enforcement of religious doctrines would end the separation of church and state. For example, if the state forced every one to take the sacrament according to the rites of a particular church and to adhere to the beliefs of that church on pain of imprisonment, the separation of church and state would be at an end. But the way to prevent something like that happening is to adopt a robust guarantee of freedom of religion and conscience, not to ban religious ideas and doctrine from public debate. A robust guarantee of freedom of conscience has two advantages over banning religious ideas from public debate; it does not require major limitations on freedom of speech and it protects the freedom of conscience of every one, both religious and secular.

Subject to limits necessary to protect freedom of conscience, there is no reason why the state should not base legislation on religious beliefs alone. Let us assume that the only basis for refusing to allow same sex marriage is the religious doctrine that God ordained marriage as a sacred union between male and female. There is no reason why that doctrine should not provide some justification for state legislation limiting marriage to a union between a man and a woman any more than there is any reason why secular doctrines of the autonomy of the individual should not provide some justification for legislation permitting a woman to have an abortion. As noted above, both are rational and both are based on coherent views about the relationship between humanity, God and the universe. Neither is demonstrably true in any scientific sense. Both may lead to legislation which persons who do not hold the relevant religious or secular beliefs may reject as immoral. But that is not a reason for rejecting either view as unable to provide some justification for the legislation in question.

In a well-governed state there are three barriers to the imposition of abhorrent secular doctrines on religious people and abhorrent religious doctrines on secularist people. Firstly, the doctrines need to have a degree of popular support. If they do not have that, they are unlikely to have government support or be accepted in parliament as a justification for legislation. That makes it unlikely that extreme ideas, whether religious or secular, will become the basis of legislation. Secondly, in a well-governed society, people respect the views of those with whom they disagree. Even if they believe that the other's views are profoundly wrong, they respect that they are held sincerely and that the holders of such views should not be forced to act inconsistently with them. Thirdly, there needs to be a robust guarantee of freedom of conscience which can be invoked by persons forced to act in breach of strongly held beliefs, whether religious or secular.

These barriers and protections make it unnecessary to exclude religious ideas and doctrines from public debate in a secular state. Instead, openly religious arguments must be permitted in public debate. To rule them out is to make secularism the official state ideology, as Marxism was the official ideology of the Soviet Union. In the Soviet Union, policy arguments which could not be framed in Marxist Leninist terms could not be put. Similarly, in a state with a secular ideology, policy arguments which cannot be framed in secular terms are excluded from all public debates. That is not justified by any doctrine of separation of church and state or of the secular state.

In conclusion, there is no good reason for excluding arguments based on a religious view of marriage as a sacred relationship between a man and a woman, ordained of God, from debates about same sex marriage. However, in the current clime, these arguments may not have too much traction. In particular, they may not appeal to anyone who does not already accept them. Many will see them as an attempt to give ancient Jewish prejudices found in the Bible the status of God's will. Hence, although reasonable arguments, they may not win the public debate.

4. Non-religious arguments for opposing same-sex marriage.

Because of a growing reluctance to allow religious arguments in public debate, many religious opponents of same sex marriage have tended to rely on other arguments. Some of these arguments are bad and their users open themselves up to charges of prejudice and bigotry.

There has been a reluctance to recognise, apart from the religious objection, the strength of the gay case. The arguments for same sex marriage parallel, with some key differences, the arguments for no discrimination against blacks and other ethnic groups. A major difference is that blacks were discriminated against because of the colour of their skin, a characteristic over which they had no control, while gays have been discriminated against because of their behaviour in having gay sex and in entering same sex relationships, something over which they have control. The gay lobby have sought to minimise the difference by arguing that gays are born, not made, that being gay is a characteristic over which the gay has no more control than does a black over the colour of their skin. If that is the case, it is arguable that it is wrong to discriminate against them on the basis of controllable behaviours which result from an uncontrollable characteristic where those behaviours do not cause harm to others.

I will not evaluate the claim that being gay is a characteristic over which a person has no control in this paper. It is an important claim, because if true, it changes the nature of the argument for gay marriage and gay adoption. If true, the argument for gay marriage can be based on the principle that it is wrong to discriminate against a group of people because of a characteristic which is part of their nature in the sense that, like their skin colour, they cannot change it. On the other hand, if it is false, the arguments for gay marriage must be based on personal autonomy, on the claim that it is wrong to prevent a person marrying the person of their choice without good reason. That claim is weaker because although autonomy is important, it may give way to other important principles.

The case for gay adoption is also stronger if being gay is a characteristic over which the gay has no control. It is natural to desire children. If gays have a characteristic over which they have no control which makes it difficult for them to have children of their own they may be deserving of our empathy and assistance in becoming parents. Their claim on our compassion and assistance does not trump all other considerations. For example, if it is not in the best interests of the child to be adopted by gay parents that may trump any claim to assistance which the gay may have.

If being gay is a choice rather than an innate characteristic, gays do not have a claim on our compassion or to our assistance. But there may be other arguments which support their right to adopt, such as the argument that all other things being equal, they should not be ruled out simply because they are of the same sex.

Although the issue of whether being gay is a choice or an innate characteristic over which a person has no control is important for the debates about gay marriage and gay adoption, this paper does not take a position on it because many of the arguments against gay marriage can be evaluated without taking a stand on that issue. Where the issue is important to the evaluation of an argument, I will point that out and examine the consequences for the argument of gayness being a choice rather than being innate.

Many of the gay arguments parallel arguments used in the debates about freeing the slaves and ending apartheid and other forms of racial discrimination. Some of the opposing arguments which Christians have used parallel arguments used by the opponents of freeing slaves and of desegregation and apartheid. They were rightly rejected in the arguments about slavery and racial discrimination and should be rejected in these debates. Others have no parallels in the arguments about slavery and racial discrimination. I have not sourced the arguments which the paper examines or attributed them to any author because they are arguments which I have heard used in public debate and discussion. It is as important that these arguments, as well as the arguments which are found in the literature, are soundly based because these are the arguments which are likely to influence the ordinary person.

4.1. Refusing to allow same sex marriage is not discriminatory because marriage has always been heterosexual. It is not discriminatory to continue a practice which is ancient and almost universal.

The parallel argument that slavery is justified because it is a widespread and ancient institution was rejected in the argument to free the slaves. It would have been wrong to accept it in the debate about slavery and it is equally wrong to accept it in current debates about marriage. The fact that an institution is ancient does not justify it. At the most, all we can say is that ancient and widespread institutions may have advantages and benefits which are not immediately apparent. But we cannot assume that that justifies discrimination if we are unable to identify those advantages. Even if we could identify the benefits, they may not be sufficiently great to justify discrimination.

4.2. Marriage by definition means a relationship between persons of the opposite sex, and the State cannot change that.

This is a definitional argument – the word marriage simply refers to a class of heterosexual relationship so that it is a misuse of language to use the term marriage to refer to a same sex relationship. If it is accepted, it gives us a reason for rejecting the gay lobby's claims without considering their moral merits. The argument fails for two reasons. Firstly, the meaning of words changes. It is arguable that the meaning of the term marriage changed fundamentally in the last century. At the beginning of the century marriage was a relationship entered into for life in that normally it was only ended by the death of one of the parties. Although available on very narrow grounds, divorce was rare. There were only a few hundred divorces and 2,375 divorcees in Australia in 1901, the first year in which statistics were kept for the whole country.[5]

By the year 2000, marriage was no longer for life in the same sense. Although most couples entering upon marriage hoped and intended that it would last for life, divorce had become so easy to obtain and so common that a marriage was terminable at the will of one party regardless of the wishes of the other. In 2014 there were 46,498 divorces in Australia. Hence marriage in 2000 was not

---

[5] Australian Bureau of Statistics *A Snapshot of Australia, 1901* Table 4 Registered Marital Status 1901. (Australian Bureau of Statistics Website www.abs.gov.au, 5 May 2016)

for life in the same sense as it was in 1900 in that it could and did often end before the death of one of the parties. It is possible and perhaps not unlikely that persons living in 1900 would not accept that a relationship which is as easily ended as a marriage is today is properly described as a marriage. They may well argue that such a relationship does not fall within the meaning of the term marriage as properly understood.

We would not accept their claim because for us such relationships are clearly marriages. Both may be right because the meaning of the term marriage may have changed over the years, meaning in 1900 a relationship which usually only ended at the death of one of the parties and meaning today a relationship entered into with the intention that it last for life but terminable at the will of one of the parties. If the meaning of marriage can change in this fundamental way, there is no reason why it could not change to include same sex relationships.

More importantly, language use and word meaning reflects current attitudes and prejudices. As a result, some words, such as nigger, are discriminatory on their face and need to be 'rescued' or dropped from our vocabulary. The gay lobby could argue, in response to the claim that marriage by definition refers to a class of heterosexual relationships and that therefore it is a misuse of the term to apply it to same sex relationships, that current usage reflects current discriminatory practices against same sex couples. Hence, the term should be extended to same sex relationships so as to remove the discriminatory elements from its meaning. If that cannot be done, it should be dropped from our vocabulary like the term nigger because of its inherently discriminatory and offensive connotations. The implication is that marriage should be abolished as essentially discriminatory so that no one should be able to marry.

4.3. If parliament is able to extend marriage to include same sex relationships, it will be able to make any change to the law of marriage which it chooses.

This is a good argument if we accept the religious objection to same sex marriage or some other natural law argument supporting the view that the essential nature of marriage is fixed and cannot be changed by human action. But it depends upon the natural law position that the powers which parliament can rightfully exercise are limited by the natural law. If we do not accept the natural law position, there can be no objection to parliament's changing the law of marriage as it sees fit. (Apart from the constitutional objection that the Commonwealth parliament has limited powers and may not be able use the marriage power to make any and every possible change to the law of marriage.) Parliament has already made major changes to the law of marriage in the *Family Law Act,* which changed marriage from a relationship entered into for life to one terminable at the will of one of the parties.[6]

Arguably, this change, which has affected a very large percentage of the population, is of much greater significance than the legalisation of same sex marriage, which is likely to affect far fewer people. Few doubt that the *Family Law Act* made fundamental changes to the institution of marriage by introducing no fault divorce and by making the fault of the parties irrelevant to property and custody issues. By comparison the gay lobby may argue that they are not asking for fundamental change – only a minor change to the rules about who can marry, affecting few people.

---

[6] The sole ground for divorce under the *Family Law Act* is the irretrievable breakdown of the marriage as evidenced by separation for at least one year; *Family Law Act 1975* (Com) section 48. This effectively permits one party to a marriage to divorce the other without the other's consent, as if one party decides that the marriage has irretrievably broken down and leaves, there is nothing the other party can do to prevent the resulting separation and divorce.

It may be objected that the real significance of the proposal to permit same sex marriage is symbolic, changing the public perception of the nature of marriage and of families, rather than its likely impact on people. But the same could be said of the *Family Law Act*. Before that Act was passed a party to a marriage could and often did put an effective end to that marriage unilaterally by leaving the other party. Actions for the restitution of conjugal rights, although possible, were very rare and were considered anachronistic in the sense that it was considered wrong to force a person to perform their marriage vows. At the same time, the view that a marriage should only be ended if one party was found guilty of a major breach of the marriage covenant was losing ground. No fault grounds such as separation for a period such as five years, and manipulation of the fault system, for example, by colluding in manufacturing or providing evidence of adultery were becoming more common and more accepted.

But the *Family Law Act* was a watershed, symbolically endorsing such behaviour by allowing a party to terminate a marriage unilaterally in law as well as in fact and by making it easier for a party to do so. Its endorsement of such behaviour may have had a greater effect than any of the legal changes which it introduced by encouraging people who were unhappily married to leave. It also changed attitudes towards adultery and other breaches of the marriage covenant by making them irrelevant to custody and property issues. As a result it changed public perceptions about the nature of marriage in fundamental ways. Hence, even if we accept that the major significance of permitting same sex marriage is symbolic, changing perceptions of the nature of marriage and of families, its symbolic significance is much less than that of the *Family Law Act,* which changed marriage from a relationship entered into for life to one terminable at the will of one of the parties.

The fundamental changes which parliament has made to the law of marriage have had an impact on social attitudes. To the extent that these changes are inconsistent with the Christian conception of marriage as a divinely ordained union for life, from the natural law perspective parliament had no right to make them. But if we do not accept the Christian conception or some other natural law position, parliament is entitled to make changes to the law of marriage as it sees fit.

4.4. Adopting same sex marriage commits us to permitting polygamy and incest

This argument fails if being gay is an innate characteristic rather than a choice. If that is the case, the argument for allowing gays to marry is based on fairness; it is unfair to discriminate against a group of people on the basis of innate characteristics over which they have no control. That argument does not provide an argument for allowing siblings to marry or for permitting polygamy. Polygamy and incest are not the result of uncontrollable innate characteristics but are the result of choices.

On the other hand, if being gay is not innate but is a choice, the argument has some merit. If being gay is a choice, the argument for gay marriage becomes one based on the value of autonomy, that is the value of respecting people's autonomous choice of life partners. Similar arguments based on the importance of respecting people's autonomous choice of life partners can be made for allowing polygamy and permitting incest. However, supporters of gay marriage on the grounds of autonomy are not necessarily committed to permitting incest or polygamy because there may be other arguments against permitting them which outweigh the arguments for permitting them based on autonomy.

4.5. Gays should establish their own institutions, their own form of relationships, rather than asking to be allowed to marry.

This argument is only consistent with requirements of fairness and equal treatment if we assume that to deny gays access to marriage but to allow them separate institutions is to treat them as equals. To this extent, it parallels the *Plessey v Ferguson* argument that giving blacks separate institutions could be consistent with the requirements of equal treatment.[7] That argument was used to justify segregation of blacks in the US. It was rejected in *Brown v Board of Education*[8] because separate by its very nature was unequal, especially when the group treated separately were historically subjected to discrimination. Given the context, separate meant unequal.

Gays may argue that like Afro-Americans, they have been subject to discrimination over a long period of time and that therefore, regardless of the position if they had not been discriminated against, separate treatment in their case is necessarily unequal treatment. This is a strong argument, making it difficult to defend the position that gays should be denied access to marriage but should be encouraged to develop their own alternatives to it.

4.6. The begetting of children is of the essence of marriage. As same sex couples cannot beget children they should not be permitted to marry.

The claim that the begetting of children is of the essence of marriage is reasonable because for most of human history, the begetting of children was one of the purposes of marriage and was a natural consequence of marriage in that most married couples had children. However even if we concede that the begetting of children is of the essence of marriage, the argument fails because

---

[7] 163 U.S. 537 (1896).

[8] 347 U.S. 483 (1954).

heterosexual couples who by reason of age or for other reasons cannot have children are allowed to marry. Their incapacity to have children is not a bar to their marriage so it should not be a bar to same sex marriage.

Heterosexual couples who are incapable for one reason or another of having children have always been permitted to marry because marriage has always had purposes other than the begetting of children. These purposes include companionship and committing to sharing our life with a person whom we love. As heterosexual couples are permitted to marry for these purposes, all other things being equal, same sex couples should be permitted to do so too.

It may seem that marriage between a heterosexual couple who are incapable of having children can be distinguished on a number of grounds from same sex marriage. Firstly, the former does not offend against the principle that marriage is a relationship between a man and a woman, whereas the latter does. But this argument depends upon a natural law view of marriage as necessarily a relationship between a man and a woman. If we do not accept the natural law position, it provides no independent support for the view that it is fair to permit heterosexual couples who cannot have children to marry while not permitting gay couples so to do.

Secondly, there are costs involved in not permitting heterosexual couples who are incapable of having children to marry which are not involved in the prohibition of same sex marriage. It may not be clear whether a heterosexual couple is capable of having children and it would be expensive and a gross violation of the right to privacy to make them prove their fertility before permitting them to marry. Some of the problems could be solved by refusing to allow women who are too old to have children to marry. For administrative convenience we could adopt a set age such as sixty. However, such a proposal would cause great distress to older couples who lose the right to marry, especially to those who believe that marriage is the only permissible form of sexual relationship. Besides, such a proposal raises other issues of discrimination. It may treat older women differently from older men, because, unlike older women, men may retain the ability to father children into old age.

None of these arguments provide good reasons for discriminating between infertile heterosexual couples and same sex couples. Instead, they suggest that it is more reasonable to permit same sex couples to marry than to prohibit marriage between infertile heterosexual couples.

4.7. The biological argument

The biological argument is an argument that something about the biology of humans brings males and females together in long lasting, even life long relationships. One suggested biological feature is that human young are so dependent on adults for such a long time that it takes more than one adult to nurture them properly. Hence men and women are biologically conditioned to form long-term relationships to ensure that men take responsibility for their children. The tendency to form long-term relationships for the benefit of their children may be the biological basis of marriage. Because of its importance, marriage is given a special status and surrounded by a web of custom and practice.

The problem with the biological argument is that although it demonstrates the importance of long term male female bonding, it does not show why, when same sex couples form similar long term relationships, they should not be given the same status. If gays form long term bonds with persons of the same sex, the biological argument suggests no good reason why those relationships should not be treated in the same manner as long term heterosexual relationships, that is as marriages. There may not be the same biological imperative for these relationships in that they are not needed to ensure that fathers accept responsibility for their children. But not all marriages are based on this biological imperative because heterosexual couples who are incapable of children because of age or other factors are permitted to marry. So it is arguable that the lack of this biological imperative to form long lasting relationships should not, on grounds of fairness, be a bar to same sex marriage.

4.8. Conclusion

Few of the arguments for opposing legalising same sex marriage considered above, other than the religious argument, can be accepted. Some, such as the appeal to the long standing practice of heterosexual marriage as justifying the ban on same sex marriage and the argument that same sex couples should develop their own institutions rather than seek to marry discriminate against same sex couples and cannot be accepted. Similar arguments were used to justify slavery and racial segregation and were rightly rejected. They cannot be accepted here.

Other arguments discriminate more subtly against same sex couples but should be rejected for that reason. The most popular of these arguments is the argument that procreation is of the essence of marriage and as same sex couples cannot procreate, they should not be permitted to marry. The argument is discriminatory because heterosexual couples, who for one reason or another are unable to procreate are permitted to marry. All other things being equal, same sex couples should not be denied the same privilege.

The proposal to permit same sex marriage is likely to be accepted. Leaving aside its impact on children, which is not considered in this paper, the only strong, acceptable arguments against the proposal are the religious, natural law argument that marriage is a divinely ordained relationship between a man and a woman and similar natural law arguments. These arguments are not likely to appeal to those who are not of a religious persuasion. This raises the issue of how religious people should best act to defend the religious view of marriage as a union between a man and a woman for life to the exclusion of all others.

5. Should Christians advocate that the state cease to regulate marriage?

A position which initially appears attractive for Christian opponents of gay marriage is to argue that the State abandon regulating marriage, in particular that it abandon determining who can and cannot marry. Instead, it should recognise and regulate all significant relationships on the same basis. In Australia, the States have already enacted legislation, the Relationship Acts, recognising and regulating significant relationships, including gay relationships. If the above proposal were accepted, the Commonwealth would repeal the *Marriage Act,* so that the State Relationships Acts were left to regulate marriages as well as other significant relationships.

The result of such a proposal would be to strip marriage of all legal consequences. It would then become a purely private matter between the parties, who would be free to choose the type of ceremony they wanted and the type of commitment they wanted to make to each other to celebrate their relationship. If the parties wanted a religious marriage, they would be free to go to the church of their choice for that service. As the religious marriage would have no legal consequences, each Church would be free to perform marriages on its own terms, setting the qualifications for marriage according to its own doctrine.

The advantage for Christians of such an approach is that if the state has no interest in marriage except as a significant relationship, churches need have no concern about who can enter state sanctioned relationships. Most churches have no objections to the state recognising gay relationships as significant relationships, only to the state recognising such relationships as marriages. Besides, such an approach seems consistent with separation of Church and State. The State inherited control of marriage when it took over many functions of the Church in the Reformation. Because marriage was traditionally of interest to the Church, churches have retained an interest in the matter, being authorised by the State to perform and register marriages and having an interest in who should and should not be allowed to marry. If the State ceased to regulate marriage except as a significant relationship, it would lead to greater separation between Church and State, so that marriage in church would have no civil consequences, leaving churches to determine for themselves who they would marry. This of course, would not rule out secular marriages. Again, secular celebrants would be free to determine for themselves who they were willing to marry.

Although it appears attractive, this argument should be rejected. It assumes that the only State interest in marriage, as in other significant relationships, is in ensuring the welfare of the children of the relationship and a just distribution of property in the event of a split. This assumes no state interest in trying to ensure stable family relationships. If the State has an interest in stable families, it has an interest in encouraging marriage which is the most stable family form. So the position that the state interest should be limited to an interest in significant relationships is a strange position for Christians, who believe the family is the basic and probably the most important unit in society, to adopt.

6. Defending the Christian conception of marriage

Same sex marriage is inconsistent with the Christian conception of marriage as the divinely sanctioned union of one man and one woman for life to the exclusion of all others. Although in my opinion it is not as big a threat to the Christian conception of marriage as is the epidemic of divorce, Christians may feel that as a matter of conscience they are obligated to oppose it. That is not likely to be a popular stand. However, Christians should not be tempted to rely on bad non-religious arguments in order to comply with the popular prejudice against using religious arguments in public debates. To rely on bad arguments is to fail the moral challenge posed by the same sex marriage debate and is likely to discredit the Christian stand. Reliance on bad arguments may lead to Christians being labeled as prejudiced and bigoted and deservedly so.

Instead, Christian opponents of same sex marriage must not be afraid to rely on the religious, natural law arguments against allowing same sex marriage. These arguments are principled and meet the moral challenge posed by the same sex marriage debate. In putting them, Christians need to defend the relevance of religious arguments to public debate. That argument is as important as the argument over same sex marriage and may in the end have a greater impact on the future of society.

10

IN WHAT SORT OF DARKNESS?
A CLARIFICATION OF THE CHRISTIAN UNDERSTANDING OF THE ACT OF FAITH IN RESPONSE TO ATHEIST MISUNDERSTANDINGS

Brendan Triffett

ABSTRACT

Is the act of faith a decision with no basis whatsoever in evidence or reason, a leap of trust made in absolute darkness? Or is faith another kind of knowing, a special way in which one experiences something (God)? That is, does faith perhaps involve some sort of rapport between the believer and God, who is indeed 'given', though in some invisible manner? Another question: Do believers understand their faith as affirming the existence of God when there is absolutely no experience, absolutely no good reason to do so? Contemporary atheists seem to think that this is essentially what faith is. 'Faith' for them is an act of sheer belief, where this belief does not correspond to anything in reality. The epistemology (theory of knowledge) assumed by the atheist critique is as follows. A belief is true on the condition that there really is something 'out there' that corresponds to it. Thus, there is nothing in the intentional act itself – the act in which I affirm the existence of something – that makes that intellectual act either true or false. So on the side of the subject who has the belief, there is no structural difference between a belief that is true and a belief that is false. But this epistemology is an inappropriate model for belief in God. There is a long tradition for which the human person's act of faith is a participation in God's revelation and presence. If this is what Christians claim their faith is like, perhaps contemporary atheists have missed the point when they reject Christian faith. In exploring this hypothesis I will draw on Eckhart, von Balthasar and Jean-Luc Marion.

* * * * *

1. Introduction

Someday I'd like to write a short book that challenges what I call the doctrine of blind faith:

> T1 Whether or not God exists, faith or belief in God is completely blind.

It is my contention that the doctrine of blind faith is based on a misunderstanding of what faith is, and how believers experience and live out their faith. What do I mean by blind faith? I hope the following fictional story will help.

Imagine that you were born and raised in a relatively primitive society. The society is completely self-contained. The land which this society inhabits is surrounded by an impenetrable dome. Let's suppose that the dome also extends so far down that nobody can dig under it. There is absolutely no way of knowing what might be on the other side of the dome, if indeed there is anything at all. As far as anyone knows, there is no way of breaching the dome from the inside. As far as anyone knows, nothing on the outside of the dome has ever made its presence known to the people inside the dome. All sorts of legends have been written about the Other Side. These have been handed down from generation to generation. But there is no way of testing whether any of these legends are true. For the sake of argument, let's agree that there is no way of deducing what things might be like on the Other Side based on how things are on the inside, using the methods of science, or philosophy, or whatever. Now suppose that one day, you read one of these legends and decide that it is true. For the sake of argument, let's agree that you are not gifted with clairvoyance or supernatural inspiration or anything like that. You go to your family and assert in their presence, excitedly, that there truly is an Other Side, that there are other lands and other beings on the other side of the dome. You go on to give detailed descriptions of what those lands and beings are like. You end by saying that the greatest of the beings on the Other Side is an immortal shape-shifting beast called Og.

The purpose of this story, which is loosely inspired by the 1998 film, *The Truman Show*, is to illustrate what I mean by a completely blind belief. The person who affirms the existence of Og does so from a place that is closed in on itself phenomenologically. Nothing "from the outside" can manifest itself to the inside of that enclosure - or at least, nothing *does* manifest itself to the inside. My purpose here is not to claim that it is possible to have a completely blind belief in God. My purpose, rather, is to explain what completely blind belief in God would be like if it did occur. Here is my working definition:

> T2 A completely blind belief is a belief that (1) reaches out from the believing subject to some supposedly transcendent object (2) in the absence of any manifestation that reaches from the object to the believing subject.[1]

In short, a completely blind belief is a belief that is *not called forth* by the object of belief, either immediately or through mediating signs. For a Christian, by contrast, true belief in God is a

---

[1] I mean "object" in a fairly broad sense – that which is intended, referred to or signified. I am not suggesting that God is an "object" in the narrower sense – a discrete entity that is able to be fully comprehended.

response to a *prior divine call*. "You did not choose me, but I chose you," says Jesus to his followers (Jn 15:16, NIV).[2]

It is often said that a believer's faith in God is utterly irrational, or completely unwarranted, because it is by nature totally blind. In this essay I offer a few preliminary thoughts on how a (philosophically-inclined) believer in God might respond to this accusation. I attend to the believer's epistemological relation to the God he believes in. My contention is that the atheist typically misunderstands this epistemological relation.

There is a reason for this misunderstanding. Atheists (and agnostics too) assume that the physical universe is completely closed in on itself, perfectly self-contained.[3] This pattern of thought first began to play a significant role in the history of Western thought with the advent of deism, which arose alongside the scientific revolution in the 17th century.[4] For the deists, God set up the machinery of the universe and then left it to operate on its own. Deists do not believe in the intimate involvement of God in nature, nor do they believe that God intervenes in history and reveals himself personally to mankind.[5] The natural

---

[2] For the purpose of this short essay it will be sufficient to note the contrast between a belief that is *not* called forth by the object of belief, and a belief that *is* called forth by the object of belief. There is far more that could be said about faith from a theological point-of-view. The theme of the call and the response is central to the "theological turn" in phenomenology. See, e.g., Jean-Luc Marion, *Being Given: Toward a Phenomenology of Givenness*, trans. Jeffrey L. Kosky (Stanford, CA: Stanford University Press, 2002), esp. §28.

[3] And not only atheist and agnostics. At certain moments even self-confessing Christians can labour under this paradigm without thinking.

[4] That is not to say that it was historically impossible for anyone to be an atheist until after deism had arisen (my thanks to Informal for pointing this out to me). Indeed, "disbelief in the supernatural is as old as the hills." Tim Whitmarsh, *Battling the Gods: Atheism in the Ancient Word* (New York, NY: Alfred A. Knopf, 2015), 4.

[5] To be sure, there are/were different kinds of deist. See the next note.

world, then, is phenomenologically self-enclosed. There are no divine self-manifestations that irrupt into the realm of the natural universe.

Naturalism took this view one step further and did away with the Creator. This is understandable, since a Creator who is not needed to sustain the existence of creatures, and who is not personally involved in the drama of human history, is a completely irrelevant figure anyway. I will speak of naturalism more in a moment. My point for now is this. The idea that the physical universe is closed in on itself, both metaphysically and phenomenologically, is an idea that in a certain sense "begins" with deism and finds its logical conclusion in atheism.[6]

For all intents and purposes, the agnostic is in the same boat as the atheist. They both deny that the presence of God is made known in nature and in history. From their point of view, a believer's belief in God is completely blind, even if it were granted that God exists. They assume that a Christian's belief in God (1) reaches out from himself to a supposedly transcendent object (2) in the absence of any manifestation that reaches from the object to himself.

As I have already indicated, in order to correct this misunderstanding of the nature of faith we would do well to reflect on the theme of the call and the response.[7] We would also do well to return to the reflections of Hans Urs von Balthasar, who says that we should not emphasise the absence of God so strongly that faith is reduced to a blind leap made by a desolate will. He calls for a counterbalance to the emphases found in the writings of Martin Luther and Søren Kierkegaard. A proper understanding of faith, he

---

[6] For discussion and references on deism and naturalism see James W. Sire, *The Universe Next Door: A Worldview Catalog*, 5th ed. (Downers Grove, Ill.: IVP Academic, 2009), §§3-4.

[7] See note 2.

says, should incorporate *pistis*, belief and *gnosis*, contemplation.[8] However, I only have space to explore one aspect of what would be a more thorough exploration of the nature of faith.

2. Naturalism and Empiricism

There are actually many different types of atheism. There is the atheism of the communist, and the atheism of the existentialist. There is the atheism of the Earth-worshipping environmentalist, and the atheism of the self-serving tycoon. But the type of atheism I want to look at here is different again. This type is marked by an exaggerated confidence in science. This is the atheism that says: *I do not believe in God since there is no empirical evidence for his existence.* Now implicit in this statement is the following claim: *Since belief in God is not supported by any physically observable fact or set of facts, it must be an utterly blind leap of faith.* In other words,

> T3 Given that there is no empirical evidence for God, to
> believe in God is to harbour a belief that is not informed
> by anything real "out there".

This is the claim that I will be challenging below. But in order to get to that point, I will need to say a little about naturalism and empiricism. Naturalism is the belief that the physical universe is all that there is. On this view, there is no such thing as God or angels or the immortal soul. There was no divine act of creation. There are no supernatural interventions. The universe is a self-contained system of natural causes and natural effects.[9] All events can be explained in terms of physical processes alone, at least in principle.

---

[8] Hans Urs von Balthasar, *The Glory of the Lord: A Theological Aesthetics*, ed. Joseph Fessio and John Riches, trans. Erasmo Leiva-Merikakis, Vol. 1: Seeing the Form (Edinburgh: T&T Clark, 1982), 131-40.

[9] Some naturalists say that there are many universes, but that doesn't concern us here.

Such processes involve physical matter, physical energy and the laws that govern causation.

Naturalists will admit that certain phenomena cannot yet be explained in terms of known physical processes. But they deny that these phenomena are manifestations of something divine or spiritual. The reason why these unusual phenomena[10] cannot be explained is simply that the sciences have not yet been perfected. Scientists are still discovering the laws of nature and struggling to understand them. So someone can be a naturalist and concede that scientists do not have everything worked out. That most infamous of naturalists, Richard Dawkins, admits that we are currently unable to explain exactly how life came to be out of non-living materials.

For naturalists, typically, science is the exemplary form of knowledge, since it is the most certain form of knowledge. "Science" here means the *physical* sciences such as physics, biology, chemistry and astronomy. (The Latin form of the word, *scientia,* had a broader meaning in medieval times, as does *Wissenschaft* in modern German.) For naturalists, typically, empirical evidence is the epistemological bedrock on which all reasonable assertions are founded. Empirical evidence is evidence delivered to sensuous perception under appropriate experimental conditions.

Empiricism is the notion that empirical evidence is the bedrock on which all reasonable assertions are founded. Given the historical link between naturalism and an exaggerated confidence in science, one can be forgiven for thinking that naturalism always implies empiricism. But things aren't that simple. For one might be a naturalist without being a *strict* empiricist. In the following section I outline two ways in which a naturalist might fail to be a strict empiricist. The first way involves *a priori* truths. The second way

---

[10] Such as this relatively recent miracle (or phenomenon, to use a more neutral word) of the dancing sun at Divine Mercy Hills in the Philippines. See www.youtube.com/watch?v=yF0_ysUivxE

involves moral truths (there is significant overlap between the two, but that does not matter).

3. Qualified Empiricism

Most philosophers will admit that there are *a priori* truths – truths that we recognise without relying on external observation and experiment. As an example of an *a priori* truth consider this principle: a physical whole is necessarily larger than its parts. Or consider the principle of non-contradiction: it is impossible for a (non-microscopic)[11] being to be X and not X at the same time and in the same respect. We do not need to survey every object in the universe in order to realise that it is impossible for a part to be greater than the whole of which it is a part. Nor do we need to set up a scientific experiment in order to see that the principle of non-contradiction is true. Indeed, not only is empirical evidence unnecessary here, it is also insufficient. No matter how much empirical data one gathers together, one can never arrive at a logically necessary truth just by considering that data. For logical necessity cannot be observed; it is not a physical property. Now to say that there are *a priori* truths does not yet amount to saying that God exists or that we have an immaterial soul. True, many philosophers *have* argued that our intuition of necessary truths points to the existence both of an eternal God and of the soul made in his image. Nevertheless, there are plenty of naturalists around today who would admit that there are *a priori* truths. These philosophers see no contradiction between their admission of *a priori* truths and their naturalistic atheism. They see themselves as

---

[11] If I am not mistaken, some interpretations of quantum mechanics allow a sub-atomic particle to be X and not X at the same time and in the same respect. I avoid this potential difficulty by restricting the rule to non-microscopic entities. In the latter category are included spiritual entities and macroscopic entities (anything material that is not microscopic).

naturalists but not as empiricists in the strict sense, for they hold that some reasonable assertions, such as those that involve logical necessity, are *not* founded on physical evidence.

Now to the second way in which a naturalist might fail to be a strict empiricist. There are a few contemporary philosophers who wax lyrical about higher ideals and "transcendent" values, even while remaining atheists. Here in Australia, for example, we have Raimond Gaita and John Armstrong.[12] On their view, human beings can recognise objective moral truths, even though these truths cannot be verified empirically. So while the intrinsic value of a person can be "seen", in an intuition that compels us to act ethically with that person, the intrinsic value of the person does not show up in the physical world in the way that velocity, weight and colour do. There are moral truths – it is wrong to torture a child, justice is to be pursued, and so on – and these moral truths can be recognised in some non-empirical way.[13]

To be sure, neither Gaita nor Armstrong would say that our recognition of intrinsic value and moral truth can be *divorced* from sensual perception. If I am not mistaken, they would say that our intuition of ethical values and principles is similar to our recognition of beauty. Our experience of beauty is tied up with our bodily experience of the physical world, but that is not to say that beauty is a physical property that can be measured using scientific

---

[12] See, for example, Raimond Gaita, *Good and Evil: An Absolute Conception*, Revised edition (London & New York: Routledge, 2004). For evidence of Armstrong's belief in "transcendent" ideals one need only read his views on "spiritual prosperity" in *In Search of Civilization: Remaking a Tarnished Idea* (Minneapolis, MN: Graywolf Press, 2009). Gaita and Armstrong might not be entirely comfortable with the "atheist" label. However, the label is true enough, and I am not claiming that either is a militant atheist.

[13] For a helpful overview of moral epistemology see Richmond Campbell, "Moral Epistemology", *The Stanford Encyclopedia of Philosophy* (Winter 2015 Edition), Edward N. Zalta (ed.), URL = http://plato.stanford.edu/archives/win2015/entries/moral-epistemology/

means. Likewise with intrinsic value and moral truth. These are not empirically verifiable quantities. Yet it is only through our sensuous involvement with the physical world that we come to recognise the intrinsic value of the human person and come to understand moral truth.

Now someone like Augustine would say that the human body manifests the reality of the human spirit, that the universe reflects divine order, and that our intuition of goodness and beauty in the world is a certain foretaste of divine goodness and beauty. By contrast, Gaita and Armstrong, being atheists, would maintain that the natural world is closed in on itself both metaphysically and phenomenologically. The world is closed in on itself *metaphysically*, since it is not sustained by some divine First Cause. The world is closed in on itself *phenomenologically*, since there is no God, and therefore no divine goodness and beauty that might be participated in and reflected in the world. Our response to "divine" goodness and beauty is not called forth by some divinity who transcends the natural world while being reflected in it. Rather, the "divine" is our label for the sacral dimension of natural reality, for the wondrous beauty experienced in the world around us.

Another example of this way of thinking is found in the work of the philosopher and novelist Iris Murdoch. She speaks of moral Ideals and of the Good (with a capital "G"), while denying the existence of God. On her view, enlightened persons recognise Platonic ideals and live by them.[14] Yet these ideals do not reside in some heaven, nor are they received in some immaterial soul. For ease of reference, this quasi-Platonic sort of naturalism - the naturalism associated with Iris Murdoch, Raimond Gaita and John Armstrong - will be called "soft" naturalism.

---

[14] See, for example, Iris Murdoch, *Metaphysics as a Guide to Morals* (London: Penguin Books, 1993).

To summarise this section, soft naturalists cannot be strict empiricists, since they believe in ethical principles, and perhaps also aesthetic values, that are given to human consciousness is a non-empirical way. And naturalists who believe in *a priori* truths are not strict empiricists either.

4. Responding to the Soft Naturalist

Details aside, the soft naturalist has everything right except his naturalism. He is right to believe in the "intrinsic value" or "preciousness" of human beings.[15] He is right to say that our belief in the intrinsic value of persons is not based on empirical evidence. And he is right to maintain that our belief in the intrinsic value of persons is informed by reality. Let's focus now on this third claim.

Whenever we act in a way that is truly ethical, our actions are informed by reality, by how things are at some fundamental level, by some deep and unchanging order of things (this is what I mean by "moral realism"). If, on the contrary, our moral beliefs (qua *moral* beliefs) were never informed by reality, then our ethical responses to people would never be "true" responses at all. No action would be ethically better or worse than any other, objectively speaking. There would be nothing profoundly "fitting" and good about taking care of a vulnerable child compared with exploiting that child, for example. Moral *nihilism* would be true instead. In such a world people might be able to have substantial moral commitments; they need not be avowed moral nihilists. They might be able to evaluate the moral beliefs and actions of others from their own moral standpoint. But none of these evaluations could be true or false, properly speaking. The evaluative ranking of

---

[15] I prefer "intrinsic value" to "preciousness"; Gaita adopts the latter term. On intrinsic value, see the introductory study by John F. Crosby and the first chapter in Dietrich von Hildebrand, *The Nature of Love*, trans. John F. Crosby and John Henry Crosby (South Bend, IN: St. Augustine's Press, 2009).

different attitudes and ways of life would be merely perspectival. From the perspective of someone pursuing *this* way of life with *this* hierarchy of values, or with *this* set of moral commitments, actions could be judged as morally "good" or "bad", ethically "fitting" or "unfitting". But these judgements could never be genuinely *authoritative*; they would merely be expressions of emotion, preference and/or approval (or disapproval), either at an individual level or at a collective level. This meta-ethical theory is called "moral cognitivism".[16] But against this view, it must be said that there are genuinely authoritative judgements which carry the authority of *objective* truth – which testify to *how reality is* at a fundamental level. This type of judgement is authoritative precisely because Reality – the objective moral order – speaks for itself in and through the particular judgement made by a particular person.

To repeat, moral nihilism is the view that there is no moral (or amoral) stance which is to be commended over any other, absolutely speaking. There may be viewpoints from which to evaluate other moral stances, but no objective moral order that could make any of these evaluations true (wholly or partially) or false (wholly or partially). But this goes against our deepest ethical intuitions. When we express horror and outrage over heinous crimes against humanity, we instinctively recognise that what has been violated is some unchanging moral order. This moral order has a transcendent character and is responded to as such; it is *not* reducible to some evaluative attitude, either individually or collectively. It would not do justice to our moral experience to say that the horror and outrage spoken of above are nothing more than expressions of one

---

[16] See Mark van Roojen, "Moral non-cognitivism vs. Non-cognitivism", *The Stanford Encyclopedia of Philosophy* (Fall 2015 Edition), Edward N. Zalta (ed.), URL = http://plato.stanford.edu/archives/fall2015/entries/moral-cognitivism/. Thanks to Michael Stokes for pointing me toward this theory.

evaluative perspective (individual or collective) amongst others – as if this evaluative response (horror and outrage at the Jewish Holocaust, for example) were no more true and fitting, absolutely speaking, than indifference or amusement. Since moral nihilism is false, and since moral non-cognitivism is a species of moral nihilism (in the sense of "moral nihilism" defined above), it must be that some actions are truly ethical, and that these actions are truly ethical insofar as they accord with a true vision of reality.

I would argue, then, that reality itself has a moral dimension, a radiant depth that calls forth our ethical responsibility. It is reality itself – reality in its moral dimension and radiant depth – that informs our thinking and doing whenever we are truly ethical.[17] But to repeat, this true vision of reality is not gained through empirical means. The "reality" to which moral beliefs should conform is an objective moral order rather an empirically verifiable set of facts. Such facts are no doubt *relevant* to our moral judgements, but they only ever gain their moral significance in view of a moral order which cannot be verified through empirical means.

The soft naturalist agrees to all of this. He maintains that our belief in the intrinsic value of persons is informed by reality even though it is not grounded in empirical evidence. He is therefore committed to T4:

T4 A belief need not be grounded in empirical evidence in order to be informed by reality.

---

[17] In other words, truth is inseparable from goodness and beauty. Here I am influenced by von Balthasar and the *Communio* circle of theologians, and also by John Milbank. For the latter's view of truth (as distinguished from that of Aquinas!) see John Milbank and Catherine Pickstock, *Truth in Aquinas* (New York, NY: Routledge, 2001). For references to von Balthasar on the transcendentals (esp. truth, goodness and beauty) see David C. Schindler, "Beauty and the Analogy of Truth: On the Order of the Transcendentals in Hans Urs Von Balthasar's *Trilogy*," *American Catholic Philosophical Quarterly* 85, no. 2 (2011): 297-321.

Now recall T3, the claim that I want to challenge:

T3 Given that there is no empirical evidence for God, to believe in God is to harbour a belief that is not informed by anything real "out there".

T3 relies on the claim that

T5 A belief must be grounded in empirical evidence in order to be informed by reality.

The soft naturalist must reject T5, since it contradicts T4. For this reason, the soft naturalist cannot use T3 as an argument against believing in God, at least not consistently. Since he claims that some of our moral beliefs are informed by reality without being empirically verifiable, he must allow that belief in God might be informed by reality without being empirically verifiable.

5. Responding to the Militant Atheist

That's all well and good, I hear you say. But how might an intelligent believer in God respond to T3 when it comes from the mouth of a hardened naturalist like Richard Dawkins? One method is as follows. First, force your atheist interlocutor to choose between moral nihilism and moral realism (that these are the only two options was shown in the previous section). Now the vast majority of people, atheists included, will want to say that there *is* something evil about torturing innocent children for the fun of it. Therefore they will be forced to reject nihilism, which will lead them to agree to moral realism. On this view (moral realism), to feel repulsed by the idea of someone torturing innocent children, as most people would be, is to be attuned to reality. Not to feel repulsed is to be out of touch with reality. There is something ethically significant about reality itself that imposes certain courses of action on our will. There are objective moral principles, and these are not of our own making – not even unconsciously or collectively.

Let's assume that you've gotten your atheist interlocutor to the point of realising that moral realism must be true. (There is no guarantee of this, of course. If a naturalist is not a soft naturalist, then chances are, he has put his faith in science. And it seems that most people who put their faith in science are mentally retarded when it comes to philosophy. They confuse physics with metaphysics, the study of being as being. I haven't worked out whether the obsession with science causes the philosophical retardation, or whether the philosophical retardation causes the obsession with science. More experiments need to be done.) Once you've gotten your interlocutor to this point, your next step is to ask him which empirical facts he relies on when he makes his basic ethical judgements. How exactly does he *know* that innocent children should not be tortured for the fun of it? He might reply by saying that it is an objective fact that children, as human beings, have a highly developed brain and central nervous system, that they are self-conscious, that they have deep feelings and emotions, and so on. Your response should be as follows: So you believe that a being with these particular properties (consciousness, sensitivity, affectivity, and so on) should *never* be treated in that way – not even in cultures where torturing someone for the fun of it is considered acceptable and apparently serves some social function. So how, exactly, might this morally significant belief of yours be empirically verified? Let's assume that your interlocutor is intellectually humble and honest (there is no guarantee of this either). Your humble interlocutor, having realised that there is no way of verifying his moral beliefs using science, should now admit that a belief need *not* be grounded in empirical evidence in order to be informed by reality. If prodded a little more he should say: Yes, I suppose it *is* conceivable that your belief in God *is* informed by reality, even though its validity cannot be empirically tested.

But as already indicated, things may not go to plan. Your

interlocutor may prefer to bite the bullet and embrace nihilism, rather than go along with your reasoning. If that situation should arise, your tactical response is simple. Point out that a nihilist like himself cannot expect to be taken seriously when he exhorts others to be as rational as he is. For if he expects his exhortations to be taken seriously, then he is not being consistent in his nihilism. And by being inconsistent he ironically fails to live up to the very standards of rationality that he exhorts others to live by. If his rationalistic ravings also include the claim that religion is the root of all evil, repeat the same point – it is inconsistent, and therefore irrational, for a nihilist like himself to take the high moral ground against anything.

I should warn you. All of this reasoning will fluster your atheist interlocutor terribly. It does not lead to a conclusion that he can easily accept. He wants to present himself as a respectable humanist – one who believes in justice and human rights and basic decency. He also wants to hold up scientific method as the key to all knowledge, and therefore as the key to human liberation. He would exalt rational man as the one who holds the key – the key that unlocks minds from the oppressive grip of superstition. But your own reasoning has shown him that he cannot do both of these at once. If he embraces nihilism, then he cannot present himself as a humanist. He cannot win favour by exuding humanistic optimism. But if he admits that there are objective moral principles, he must now give an account of how he *knows* these principles (before you came along he was able to keep this problem tucked away – or else his philosophical retardation prevented him from noticing the problem in the first place). And since he cannot see how moral principles might be verified through empirical means, he can no longer hold up scientific method as the key to all knowledge.

Don't be surprised if your atheist interlocutor tries to save face in a desperate measure. He may broaden his foundation and admit that *reason* is the key to knowledge and liberation, rather than the scientific method as such. This will allow him to include moral principles in his system of thought, while still giving science a special place. But if you push him any further he will simply dig his heels in. He will make his final appeal to "what any reason person would think." *Any reasonable person can see that it is wrong to torture an innocent child. Any reasonable person can see that belief in God is unreasonable.* If you ask him one more time why belief in God is unreasonable, his answer will amount to this: *because no-one who is reasonable believes in God.* In other words: *Atheists are in, believers are out. We have determined that belief in God has no place in our community, and that is that. Atheism is necessary for being included in our community of enlightened men, and belief in God is sufficient for being excluded.*

So often all this talk of enlightened "reason" comes down to just that: a sheer act of will. One group of men staking out the boundaries of their exclusive in-group by a collective decree in order to define themselves against others. *We are reasonable people, because we do not believe in God. You are not reasonable people, because you still do.* All their reasoning begins and ends there, in an arbitrary act of self-determination. The ground of their reasoning is nothing but will. A sheer willing that wills to believe that it is the clarity of pure reason rather than the darkness of sheer will. If through reason you attempt to shatter the delusion, you invoke the wrath of the will that wants to keep the delusion alive.

If what I have said above is true, then rationalistic atheism turns out to be supremely irrational, inasmuch as it is voluntaristic – based on an ungrounded act of will. But belief in God need not be voluntaristic at all – not if it is the proportionate response of the spirit to the self-manifestation of God. Thus the tables are turned, and the atheist's accusation turns back on the atheist himself.

11

A HISTORY OF MARRIAGE: NATURE, CULTURE AND THE PRESENT CRISIS

David Van Gend

ABSTRACT

Marriage, throughout human history, is an institution given by nature and strengthened by culture. The father of modern anthropology, Claude Levi-Strauss, called marriage "a social institution with a biological foundation". He notes that throughout recorded history the human family is "based on a union, more or less durable, but socially approved, of two individuals of opposite sexes who establish a household and bear and raise children." All our marriage laws and customs exist to reinforce this biological foundation, helping bind a man to his mate for the sake of social stability and for the sake of any child they might create.

"This triangle of truisms, father, mother and child, cannot be destroyed," said G.K. Chesterton; "it can only destroy those civilisations which disregard it."

At this point in history, the destroyers are at the gates. Powerful forces in the decadent West seek to establish "homosexual marriage" in law and so abolish a child's birthright to both a mother and a father; to forcibly normalise homosexual behaviour in culture and in the education of children; to suppress religious freedom with the full weight of anti-discrimination law.

Introduction

Marriage is a man-woman thing in culture because the 'breeding pair' is a male-female thing in nature. Only man and woman can create a child; only man and woman can give that child a mother and a father. So-called same-sex 'marriage' has no foundation in nature: it cannot create a child; it cannot give a child both a mother and a father. In fact same-sex 'marriage' makes it impossible for a child to have both a mother and a father, and that is an injustice against the child.

Same-sex couples, who make up 1% of all couples, are free to live as they choose, but they are not free to redefine marriage for all of us. They need to find a different word for their relationship, because it is not marriage.

That is the short version of "A history of marriage: nature, culture and the present crisis", and that should settle the matter. But it will not, and we are all now facing the long version: our federal government has decided to give the entire nation a vote, sometime after the next election, on whether to redefine marriage to include adults of the same sex.

Redefining marriage is a dangerous idea. It redefines everything from parenting and kinship bonds to sexual morality and acceptable religious doctrine. And according to G.K. Chesterton, it is a terminally dangerous idea, because, "This triangle of truisms, father, mother and child, cannot be destroyed; it can only destroy those civilisations which disregard it."

The destroyers are at the gates, and to resist them we must do two things: first, reassert the truth of marriage, and second, convince our fellow Australians of the harms of homosexual 'marriage' – specifically:

> That it will force future children to miss out on either a mother or a father;

That it will impose radical homosexual education on all of our children;

That it will intimidate conscientious objectors with the big stick of anti-discrimination law;

That it will mess with much more than marriage: it will radically deconstruct the bonds of parenting and kinship and the very notion of male and female.

The Truth of Marriage

At a public meeting here in Hobart three weeks ago, the question before us was "What defines marriage?" The answer, in my view, is that Nature ultimately defines marriage; the great natural force that brings male and female together to create new life – that is the foundation of marriage. Marriage is not a social or religious invention; it is a social and religious recognition of pre-existing biological reality: male, female, offspring. The father of modern anthropology, Claude Levi-Strauss, defined marriage as "a social institution with a biological foundation".[1] All of our marriage laws and customs exist to reinforce this biological foundation, helping bind a man to his mate for the sake of social stability and, above all, for the sake of any child they might create.

Not all marriages do create children – but typically they do, and the institution exists for the typical case. Married couples who cannot have children are still fully married because they fulfil the twin criteria of marriage: they bring together the two halves of nature, male and female, in a 'one-flesh' union; and they are still able to give a child, albeit an adopted child, the mother and father relationship a child needs. A homosexual couple does not bring together the two halves of nature in a one-flesh union, and

---

[1] Claude Levi-Strauss, "Introduction," in Andre Burguiere et al. (eds.), 1 *A History of the Family: Distant Worlds, Ancient Worlds* 5 (1996)

cannot give a child, even an adopted child, the mother and father relationship a child needs. They do not meet nature's job description for marriage.

This is not a religious argument. The atheist philosopher Bertrand Russell understood the child-centred basis for marriage. He wrote in his 1929 book *Marriage & Morals*:

> It is through children alone that sexual relations become of importance to society, and worthy to be taken cognizance of by a legal institution.[2]

Homosexual relationships obviously cannot create children, so society has no institutional interest in regulating such friendships. They are of importance to the individuals involved, and demand neighbourly civility, but such relationships are not marriage.

Surveying all of human history and culture, Levi-Strauss concluded that the family is "based on a union, more or less durable, but socially approved, of two individuals of opposite sexes who establish a household and bear and raise children."[3]

In the same way, the Chief Justice of the US Supreme Court, John Roberts, recognised the timeless structure and purpose of marriage in his dissenting judgement in the 2015 same-sex marriage case: "Marriage ... arose in the nature of things to meet a vital need: ensuring that children are conceived by a mother and father committed to raising them in the stable conditions of a lifelong relationship."[4]

Go as far back in written history as it is possible to go and you will find marriage between male and female as the natural

---

[2] Bertrand Russell, *Marriage and Morals* (London: Allen & Unwin, 1929), 96.
[3] Claude Levi-Strauss, *The View from Afar*, (The University of Chicago Press: Chicago, 1992) 40-1.
[4] Supreme Court of the USA, Obergefell v Hodges, March 2015 at http://www.supremecourt.gov/opinions/14pdf/14-556_3204.pdf

and necessary basis of family and society. Ancient legal codes of Hammurabi and King Dadusha in Babylon four thousand years ago specify social conditions for valid marriage similar to our own, including the need for a formal contract, a public ceremony and even obtaining consent from the in-laws.

If King Dadusha had been a guest at the Royal Wedding of Kate and Will he would have understood the Bishop of London's exposition, from the 1662 *Book of Common Prayer*, of why we have the institution of marriage:

> First, (marriage) was ordained for the increase of mankind...
> Secondly, it was ordained in order that the natural instincts and affections should be hallowed and directed aright...
> Thirdly, it was ordained for the mutual society, help, and comfort that the one ought to have of the other.

Note that the Bishop's basic rationale is anthropological, not theological: marriage exists to nurture a new generation, to discipline the feral instincts of males to constructive ends, and to be what John Locke called "the First Society" of husband and wife, mother, father and child.

What King Dadusha would not have understood, nor any other King or philosopher in the last four thousand years, is that two gentlemen sitting in the pews at the Royal Wedding, Sir Elton John and his partner David Furnish, would soon thereafter have their homosexual relationship elevated by English law to "the honourable estate of marriage". Homosexual and bisexual relationships are recorded in history but there has never been an institution of homosexual marriage, since it would serve no vital social purpose.

The ancient Greeks indulged homosexual relations but never confused that with the necessary life-task of marriage and family. As early as Homer we find the word *gamos* to describe the honoured relationship between man and woman that we recognise as monogamous marriage, centred on the *oikos* or family home. The Romans gave us the word "matrimony", made up of *mater* meaning mother, and *monium* meaning state or condition – matrimony is the institution built around motherhood.

As a rare aberration that proves the rule, the ancient Romans did record one case of homosexual 'marriage' in the year 64 AD, but that was the Emperor Nero – whom the contemporary historian Tacitus described as "corrupted by every lust, natural and unnatural".[5] Even that historian of decadent Rome had trouble concealing his disgust: "The emperor, in the presence of witnesses, put on the bridal veil. Dowry, marriage bed, wedding torches, all were there. Indeed everything was public which even in a natural union is veiled by night." I have not seen that historic gay wedding, that imperial affirmation that "love is love", celebrated in any TV ads for Marriage Equality.

So the truth about marriage is that it is given by nature and affirmed by every culture, because man and woman are uniquely empowered to nurture new life. This triangle of truisms, father, mother and child, is the "natural and fundamental group unit of society", as the Universal Declaration of Human Rights puts it, and no politician or plebiscite has the authority to repeal what is natural and fundamental to society.[6]

The first harm: instituting motherless and fatherless families as an ideal in law

The greatest harm of homosexual 'marriage' is that it forces future children to miss out on either their mother or their father. Same-sex marriage means same-sex parenting, because marriage is a compound right under Article 16 of the Universal Declaration of

---

[5] Tacitus, *Annals* XV, 37-41. https://facultystaff.richmond.edu/~wstevens/history331texts/tacitus3.html

[6] *Universal Declaration of Human Rights*, Article 16.

Human Rights: "the right to marry and to found a family". Therefore homosexual marriage involves both the legal recognition of an exclusive relationship and the right to form a family by adoption or artificial reproduction – but any child created within that 'marriage' would necessarily miss out on either her mother or her father.

Of course, there are already tragic situations where a child misses out on her mum or her dad, such as the death or desertion of a parent, but that is not something we would ever wish upon a child, and it is not something a government should ever impose upon a child. Legalising same-sex marriage would impose that deprivation on any child created within such an institution.

There are already situations where broken families reform as a homosexual household and nothing can or should be done about that. What we must not allow, however, is the situation where government facilitates the deliberate creation of motherless or fatherless families. A law establishing the institution of same-sex 'marriage' would be an act of premeditated injustice against future children.

Some people also raise the scenario of an abusive mother and father and argue that it is better for a child to have two loving same-sex carers than a dysfunctional pair of biological parents – yet neither option gives a child what she needs. We must reject both, restraining parents who would inflict abuse while also restraining governments who would inflict laws that institutionalise the motherless or fatherless child.

Senator Penny Wong and others insist that because some same-sex couples already obtain children by adoption or surrogacy, nothing is going to change with same-sex 'marriage'. That is not correct. A number of states rightly prohibit same-sex couples from adopting or creating a child by surrogacy, but a federal law for same-sex 'marriage' would overrule any state prohibitions on same-sex parenting. Such a law would become the nationwide, permanent violation of a child's right, where possible, to be raised by both mother and father.

Society is faced with an inescapable choice. As Australian ethicist Professor Margaret Somerville observes, the question of same-sex marriage "forces us to choose between giving priority to children's rights or to homosexual adults' claims."[7] Importantly, when we asked 1200 Australians in our Galaxy poll to choose between these conflicting priorities, they chose by a margin of three to one to give priority to the rights of the child to have both a mother and a father over the rights of two men to marry and start a family.[8] In the media, however, the rights of homosexual adults always take priority. Our aim in the Australian Marriage Forum has been to counter that bias and create a more child-centred public debate.

We say that a child has the right to look up and see the only two faces on earth that reflect her own: the woman and the man who together gave her existence. A little girl should not have to look up and see two "married men" posing as her parents. Neither man can be a mother to her; they cannot guide her as a mother would when she is growing from girl to woman nor model for her the complex relationship of husband and wife. Likewise, any boy needs his father's companionship and example to help him become a man; no matter how competent and caring a lesbian partner may be, she cannot be a dad to a little boy.

This is so self-evident that the advocates for same-sex 'marriage' have gone to extraordinary lengths to claim that gender doesn't matter for parenting, that a mother is nothing special and

---

[7] Margaret Somerville, "It's all about the children, not selfish adults," *The Australian*, 23 July 2011, www.theaustralian.com.au/opinion/its-all-about-the-children-not-selfish-adults/story-e6frg6zo-1226099613917

[8] "New Galaxy Poll for AMF: reframes the same-sex marriage debate," Australian Marriage Forum, http://australianmarriage.org/new-galaxy-poll-for-amf-reframes-the-same-sex-marriage-debate/

a father is dispensable. We all know their bland assurances that science shows there is no difference in outcomes for kids raised by homosexual couples. Such claims are not credible, either on the social science or on the testimony of adults who were raised by lesbian couples.

Heather Barwick is one such adult and she wrote in March 2015: "A lot of us, a lot of your kids, are hurting. My father's absence created a huge hole in me, and I ached every day for a dad. Same-sex marriage and parenting withholds either a mother or father from a child while telling him or her that it doesn't matter. That it's all the same. But it's not."[9]

Another example, Millie Fontana, a young Melbourne woman, said: "There's all this talk about equality for women, for gay people, for everybody, but where's the equality for children when it comes to this? I am in a position to explain to you the kind of damage it does to a child."[10]

And another, Katy Faust, who appeared on the ABC's *Q&A* in August 2015, wrote: "Our cultural narrative becomes one that tells children they have no right to the natural family structure or their biological parents, but that children simply exist for the satisfaction of adult desires."[11]

As far as the scientific evidence goes, sociologist David Popenoe states the obvious: "Few propositions have more empirical support in the social sciences than this one: Compared to all other family

---

[9] Heather Barwick, "Dear gay community, your kids are hurting," *The Federalist*, 17 March 2015, http://thefederalist.com/2015/03/17/dear-gay-community-your-kids-are-hurting/

[10] "The real issue with same-sex parenting from a child's perspective," YouTube video, posted by "Millie Fontana," 9 March 2015, https://youtube/FCrzKsrZ1eg

[11] Katy Faust, Amicus Curiae brief, US Court of Appeal of the Fifth Circuit, August 2014 https://www.scribd.com/doc/240312274/Katy-Faust-Amicus-Briefs

forms, families headed by married, biological parents are best for children." That is the settled science of forty years of research, and therefore any law that deliberately deprives a child of one or other married biological parent is, statistically speaking, disadvantaging the child.

Running counter to this established finding, a number of recent studies claim that children of lesbian couples do as well as, or better than, children of married biological parents. Note that there are no significant studies of the outcomes for children raised by two men – and yet this absence of research does not stop advocates waving their hands and claiming that kids do fine in all same-sex households.

These lesbian studies are deeply flawed by a biased self-selection process, too small a sample size to be significant, no control group to exclude confounding factors, and so on.[12] They are useful for newspaper headlines that impress impressionable people but are no scientific basis for public policy. Nevertheless, they have achieved their political goal of muddying the waters and establishing the folk myth that kids do just as well with same-sex couples.

There are only eight studies in this entire field that meet the gold-standard criteria of random sample selection and statistically adequate sample size; of those eight studies there are four that find detrimental effects for children in same-sex households and four that find "no difference".[13] Significantly, the four "no difference" studies were later found to suffer from major corruption in their

---

[12] L. Marks, "Same-sex parenting and children's outcomes: A closer examination of the American psychological association's brief on lesbian and gay parenting," *Social Science Research* 41, no. 4, (2012): 735-51. www.sciencedirect.com/science/article/pii/S0049089X12000580

[13] American College of Pediatricians et al, Amici Curiae brief, Supreme Court of the USA, April 2015, www.supremecourt.gov/ObergefellHodges/AmicusBriefs/14-556_American_College_of_Pediatricians.pdf

database, and once the corrupted data was corrected their finding of "no difference" no longer applied.

The most recent, and largest, peer-reviewed study (Sullins 2015) finds that children raised in same-sex households have four times the rate of significant emotional problems compared to children raised by their married biological parents.[14] Of course, the ideological assault on the paper and the author has been intense, but the study stands – and while it stands, no lawmaker should vote for a structure of same-sex 'marriage' and parenting that has been found to be detrimental to children.

Having mentioned the social science, I don't think it should be the deciding factor. No social science can answer the question that must be asked: the question of the fundamental injustice and primal harm to a child from wilfully depriving her of a mother or a father. Take the analogy of children forcibly adopted from their teenage mothers, a government policy until the 1970s for which our leaders apologised in 2013. Just because a social science study might show that such children are doing very well at school a decade later, competing well in sport and apparently well integrated with their peers – does that say anything about the injustice done to them at the start, by wrongfully removing them from their mother?

The same applies to future children deprived of a mother through government-approved homosexual marriage and adoption. Even if some future research were to claim that they turn out just fine years later, according to the crude measurements of social science, nothing would make up for the primal harm done to the inner life of those children.

In 2013, Prime Minister Julia Gillard delivered the national

---

[14] D.P. Sullins, "Emotional Problems among Children with Same-Sex Parents: Difference by Definition," *British Journal of Education, Society and Behavioural Science* 7, no. 2 (2015): 99-120, http://papers.ssrn.com/sol3/Papers.cfm?abstract_id=2500537

apology for forced adoption and spoke movingly of how government policy had broken "the most primal and sacred bond there is: the bond between a mother and her baby".[15] Do we never learn? We are now being asked to establish another policy, homosexual 'marriage' and parenting, that will, once again, break the primal and sacred bond between a mother and her baby. It will create a 'motherless generation' to whom some future Prime Minister will have to give another heartfelt national apology.

The second harm: imposing homosexual education on all of our children

If the law of the land says same-sex 'marriage' is normal and right, schools will be required to teach that same-sex behaviour is normal and right. Children will have to be taught that the sexual behaviour of two men is no different to the relationship of the child's mother and father in marriage – and parents will have no say.

We have seen this happen overseas. After the courts in Massachusetts legalised homosexual marriage in 2003, school libraries had to stock same-sex literature;[16] primary children were given homosexual stories like *King & King*[17]; some high school students were even given an explicit manual of homosexual advocacy entitled *Queer in the 21st Century*.[18]

---

[15] D. Wroe, "Amid the madness, Gillard shines with mother apology," *The Sydney Morning Herald,* 22 March 2013, www.smh.com.au/federal-politics/political-news/amid-the-madness-gillard-shines-with-mother-apology-20130321-2gixj.html

[16] "PARENTS OUTRAGED: Second-grade teacher (in David Parker's school!) reads 'modern fairy tale' to class on homosexual romance and marriage!" Mass Resistance, 19 April 2006, www.massresistance.org/docs/issues/king_and_king/index.html

[17] L. De Haan and S. Nijland, *King & King* (Berkely: Tricycle Press, 2002).

[18] *Queer in the 21st Century* at www.massresistance.org/docs/issues/black_book/black_book_inside.html

Robb and Robin Wirthlin were parents of a primary school child in Massachusetts when the change came in. They tell us:

> After Massachusetts legalised gay marriage, our son came home and told us the school taught him that boys can marry other boys. He's in second grade! We tried to stop public schools teaching them about gay marriage, but the courts said we had no right to object or pull them out of class.[19]

This conquest of the curriculum and usurping of parental influence over the moral education of their child is, in my view, a major cultural goal of the homosexual movement. In Australia, under the federally funded "Safe Schools" program, you can read at page 10 of the 2014 booklet, *OMG I'm Queer*, the following instruction for your child (and I leave out the most explicit passage): "I'm bisexual, so I ended up thinking of myself as having two virginities, my first time with a chick and my first time with a dude."[20] Yes, parents can object now and tell the Coalition Government to stop funding Labor's "Safe Schools" program – but parents will be sidelined and treated as bigots if they object to such material once homosexual 'marriage' becomes the law of the land.

It is worth considering the three major arguments that justify these programs in our schools, since they are the same three arguments that are used to justify same-sex 'marriage'.

1. To combat bullying

The first argument is that there is apparently a plague of gay-based bullying in our schools, and the best way to reduce that

---

[19] "Yes on 8 TV Ad: Everything To Do With Schools," YouTube video, posted by "VoteYesonProp8," 20 October 2008, https://youtube/7352ZVMKBQM

[20] Scott, *OMG I'm Queer*, uncensored 2014 version available, for example, at Golden Grove High School website http://www.goldengrovehs.sa.edu.au/our-school/learner-support/access-centre-counseling-service.html and document at http://www.goldengrovehs.sa.edu.au/images/PDFS/OMG%20Im%20Queer.pdf

bullying is to celebrate homosexuality in the curriculum and affirm same-sex 'marriage' in our laws. That is a doubtful proposition. In one large study comparing a thousand homosexual and heterosexual adults, published in the *British Journal of Psychiatry* in 2003, the researchers found no increase whatsoever in bullying of gay men compared to heterosexual men, whether at school or subsequently, whether verbally or physically.[21] The researchers noted, "Reports that gay and lesbian people are vulnerable to such experiences because of their sexuality are often taken at face value".

There are many reasons to be bullied at school – for being too smart, too dumb; too fat, too weak; or for being "gay" even when you are not gay. That is something many young people go through, and the claim that homosexual people suffer disproportionate bullying appears to be "taken at face value".

It is important to address all bullying in schools but an alleged plague of gay-based bullying should not be used to impose radicalised sex-education on all children.

2. *To combat suicide and depression*

The second justification is that if we do not celebrate homosexuality in schools and celebrate same-sex 'marriage' in our culture, we are culpable for depression and even suicide in young same-sex attracted people. That is an increasingly common argument – and it is outrageous.

On 12 August 2015, Sky News presenter Peter van Onselen suggested to the Hon Bruce Billson, Federal Minister for Small Business, that the Coalition would have blood on its hands because of its decision not to hold an immediate parliamentary vote

---

[21] M. King et al., "Mental Health and Quality of Life of Gay Men and Lesbians in England and Wales," *British Journal of Psychiatry* 183, no.6 (2003): 552-8, http://bjp.rcpsych.org/content/183/6/552.full, Table 4.

on same-sex 'marriage' but to defer the decision to a national plebiscite in a year or two. He said:

> Can you first just explain to me why it is an acceptable thing, the number of young Australians who are homosexual that will commit suicide between now and when the government finally gets its act together to have a plebiscite on this issue?[22]

On the same day in the *Sydney Morning Herald*, Justin Koonin, convenor of the NSW Gay and Lesbian Rights Lobby, specified our full-page ad in *The Australian*[23] as "toxic" and an example of the "bigoted opinions that we know cause harm to same-sex attracted and gender diverse young people".[24] In an earlier report about our television ad aired during Mardi Gras in March 2015,[25] the director of Australian Marriage Equality, Rodney Croome, said our ad was "actually harming the many Australian children being raised by same-sex couples".[26]

Do you see how this game works? If anyone makes the case for keeping marriage between man and woman, the mere act of raising

---

[22] "Interview with Peter Van Onselen, Sky News, Canberra," Australian Government Treasury, 12 August 2015, http://bfb.ministers.treasury.gov.au/transcript/095-2015/

[23] AMF newspaper ad in *The Australian*, 10 August 2015, "Its.Not.Marriage." http://australianmarriage.org/wp-content/uploads/AMF_Australian.jpg

[24] M. Koziol, "Same-sex marriage: LGBTI advocates fear harm from plebiscite," *SMH*, 15 August 2015, http://www.smh.com.au/national/samesex-marriage-lgbti-advocates-fear-harm-from-plebiscite-20150812-gixdri.html

[25] "Marriage Equality? What about equality for kids?" – Australian Marriage Forum – March 2015 – YT," YouTube video, posted by "Australian Marriage Forum," 6 March 2015, https://youtu.be/s80wL5al5NA

[26] M. Whitbourn, "Backlash after anti-marriage equality ad debuts on Mardi Gras night," *The Sydney Morning Herald*, 8 March 2015, 2016, http://www.smh.com.au/entertainment/tv-and-radio/backlash-after-antimarriage-equality-ad-debuts-on-mardi-gras-night-20150308-13y8yi.html

such an argument is "actually harming" children. There is only one solution: shut up and agree with Rodney and Mr Koonin. Breathing a word makes us culpable for depression and even death in young people.

Can the gay lobby not see their argument for the emotional blackmail it is, and the most uncivil insult to their fellow citizens who are simply defending the law of the land? Nobody denies that same-sex attracted people suffer disproportionately from depression and emotional distress, but never once, in my experience as a GP, has a patient's depression or distress been due to the "bigoted opinions" of straight society. It has always been due to something private and personal: perhaps the trauma of domestic violence from a lesbian partner, or self-disgust at their own compulsive sexual behaviour, or unresolved rage at childhood sexual abuse, or the spiritual grief of holding values that conflict with their unwanted sexual impulses – this is what drives their depression and distress, not whether or not there are laws out there for gay marriage.

We also know that gay people have close to double the rate of substance abuse, both alcohol or drugs, compared to the heterosexual population and that this is associated with increased depression and suicide.[27] The previously mentioned study in the *British Journal of Psychiatry* cautioned:

> It may be that prejudice in society against gay men and lesbians leads to greater psychological distress … Conversely, gay men and lesbians may have lifestyles that make them vulnerable to psychological disorder. Such lifestyles may include increased use of drugs and alcohol.[28]

---

[27] *2010 National Drug Strategy Household Survey report* (Australian Institute of Health and Welfare, 2011), http://www.aihw.gov.au/WorkArea/DownloadAsset.aspx?id=1073742131

[28] King, "Mental Health and Quality of Life of Gay Men and Lesbians," op. cit.

In Canada, where gay marriage was legalised in 2005, homosexual lobbyists in 2009 still cited drug and alcohol abuse as much higher amongst gays.[29] Changing the *Marriage Act* had not changed the dangers of the gay lifestyle.

It trivialises a homosexual person's suffering to blame it primarily on the external environment. The associated claim that we must legalise same-sex marriage or be culpable for gay suicide is political blackmail. One does not overturn the foundational institution of society, with all the harm that entails, as an act of psychological therapy for some depressed citizens. There are less destructive ways to help.

3. To do justice to people who are "born that way"

The final argument for affirming homosexuality in the curriculum and in our marriage laws is a powerful claim of justice: that gay people are simply born that way, so natural justice demands they should have equal marriage rights. This moral argument has great influence on public thinking, but it is false and needs to be refuted.

"If God made them that way", asked a female Anglican priest of my acquaintance, "how can we deny them their fulfilment as sexual beings?" Or as Lady Gaga put it in her same-sex anthem, "Born This Way": "It doesn't matter if you love him or capital H-I-M ... 'cause God makes no mistakes'."

On the contrary, all our lives are marred with mistakes of both nature and nurture, and we have to adapt. For some sexually confused people who suffer unwanted homosexual impulses, their capacity to adapt depends on realising that they are not in fact "born that way". No science supports the "born that way" theory. The American Psychiatric Association says: "the causes of sexual

---

[29] Human Rights Complaint against the Government of Canada, February 2009, http://web.archive.org/web/20090521102049/http://www.xtra.ca/BinaryContent/pdf/human%20rights%20complaint.pdf

orientation (whether homosexual or heterosexual) are not known at this time and likely are multifactorial including biological and behavioral roots which may vary between different individuals and may even vary over time."[30] Even the avowedly pro-gay American Psychological Association states: "No findings have emerged that permit scientists to conclude that sexual orientation is determined by any particular factor or factors."[31]

The director of the Human Genome Project, Francis Collins, notes that "sexual orientation is genetically influenced but not hardwired by DNA, and whatever genes are involved represent predispositions, not predeterminations."[32] There is no justification, then, for claiming gay people are "born that way". As studies of identical twins conclusively demonstrate, there is no simplistic gay gene.[33]

In the same way, psychological mechanisms are not sufficient to explain every case. All one can conclude is that the phenomenon is multi-factorial in origin, with predisposing and precipitating factors; a deeply ingrained but potentially modifiable psychological condition, not an innate identity.[34]

---

[30] "Position Statement on Issues Related to Homosexuality", American Psychiatric Association, December 2013, 2016, www.psychiatry.org/File%20 Library/About-APA/Organization-Documents-Policies/Policies/Position-2013-Homosexuality.pdf

[31] "Sexual Orientation & Homosexuality," American Psychological Association, www.apa.org/topics/lgbt/orientation.aspx

[32] D. Byrd, "'Homosexuality Is Not Hardwired,' Concludes Head of The Human Genome Project," *Life Site News*, 20 March 2007, www.lifesitenews. com/news/homosexuality-is-not-hardwired-concludes-head-of-the-human-genome-project

[33] "Identical Twin Studies Demonstrate Homosexuality is Not Genetic," NARTH Institute, www.narth.com/#!gay---born-that-way/cm6x

[34] See also the summary of adolescent fluidity of sexual orientation: "Adolescents, Therapeutic Choice and Scientific Integrity," American College of Pediatricians, 13 February 2014, www.acpeds.org/adolescents-therapeutic-choice-and-scientific-integrity

Senators at the May 2012 enquiry into the Marriage Equality Amendment Bill heard from a man who had been actively homosexual for most of his adult life but is now married with three children.[35] More recently, the high-profile founder of Young Gay America, Michael Glatze, left the gay world and married his girlfriend. In an interview he said, "When you leave homosexuality, there's a sense of growing up. There is a sense of leaving adolescence behind, of becoming whole."[36]

Such men are not meant to exist under the "born that way" theory. They incur the wrath of the homosexual movement for showing that they are neither born that way nor obliged to stay that way; they demonstrate that change along a spectrum is possible for some people, to some extent.

Consider the clinical findings of spontaneous change in sexual orientation: a large study in 2007 by Savin-Williams found that three-quarters of adolescents who had some initial homosexual attraction between the ages of 17-21 changed to experience only heterosexual attraction.[37] Another large study of some 14,000 young people by Ott and Corliss in 2010 found that two thirds of

---

[35] Official Committee Hansard, "Legal and Constitutional Affairs Legislation Committee on the Marriage Equality Amendment Bill 2010," Senate of the Parliament of Australia, 4 May 2012, http://parlinfo.aph.gov.au/parlInfo/search/display/display.w3p;query=Id%3A%22committees%2Fcommsen%2Fc8e9db57-3acd-4c0f-a11a-96077dfac944%2F0000%22

[36] "Interview With Former Gay Activist, Michael Glatze," Joseph Nicolosi website, February 2014, http://www.josephnicolosi.com/interview-with-former-gay-acti/

[37] R.C. Savin-Williams and G.L. Ream, "Prevalence and Stability of Sexual Orientation Components During Adolescence and Young Adulthood," *Archives of Sexual Behavior* 36, no.3 (2007): 385-94, http://link.springer.com/article/10.1007/s10508-006-9088-5. Note: for the drift from same-sex to opposite-sex attraction see Table 2 (Wave 1 to Wave 3, 71.7% male, 55.3% female) and for behaviour see Table 3 (Wave 1 to Wave 3, 71.6% male, 76.8% female).

those who thought they might be homosexual eventually became exclusively heterosexual.[38]

What these studies show is that most sexual confusion in adolescence clears away if left to itself.[39] A policy to "celebrate gay identity" among confused adolescents would encourage some young men to "come out" prematurely at school when, left alone, most would get over their confusion and avoid the grave physical and emotional harm of a homosexual lifestyle.

In my view, these three arguments for imposing homosexual education on all school children and for affirming same-sex marriage in our laws are scientifically spurious and morally misguided. None of them justify letting gay activists usurp the role of parents in determining the moral education of their children.

The third harm: suppressing conscientious and religious freedom

A law for homosexual 'marriage' will silence conscientious and religious objectors with the big stick of anti-discrimination law. In a graduation address at Campion College in 2011 while Dr Daintree was President, the former Prime Minister John Howard said:

> Changing the definition of marriage, which has lasted for time immemorial, is not an exercise in human rights and equality; it is an exercise in de-authorising the Judaeo-Christian influence in our society, and any who pretend otherwise are deluding themselves.[40]

---

[38] M.Q. Ott, H.L. Corliss, et al., "Stability and Change in Self-Reported Sexual Orientation Identity in Young People: Application of Mobility Metrics," *Archives of Sexual Behavior* 40, No. 3 (June 2011): 519-32, http://link.springer.com/article/10.1007%2Fs10508-010-9691-3

[39] For more recent clinical information, see L. Mayer and P. McHugh, "Sexuality and Gender: Findings from the Biological, Psychological and Social Sciences", *The New Atlantis*, 19 August 2016, especially page 25 and following, http://www.thenewatlantis.com/docLib/20160819_TNA50SexualityandGender.pdf

[40] "'Values in Western Civilisation' – the Hon. John Howard," Campion College graduation address, December 2011, http://www.campion.edu.au/values-in-western-civilisation-the-hon-john-howard/

Canadian Queen's Counsel, Barbara Findlay, declared, "The legal struggle for queer rights will one day be a showdown between freedom of religion versus sexual orientation". Consider a local showdown. We all know how Rodney Croome, the head of the gay lobby group Australian Marriage Equality, took offence at the recent Pastoral Letter by Australia's Catholic Bishops entitled "Don't Mess with Marriage".[41] This booklet conveyed traditional Catholic teaching on marriage to students in Catholic schools; but that was unacceptable to the gay lobby. Croome said in a Media Release in June: "I urge everyone who finds [the Catholic booklet] offensive and inappropriate, including teachers, parents and students, to complain to the Anti-Discrimination Commissioner."[42] In response, a transgender Tasmanian Greens candidate has reported Hobart's Archbishop Julian Porteous to the Anti-Discrimination Commission.

Significantly, the Pastoral Letter included this passage: "People who adhere to the perennial and natural definition of marriage will be characterised as old-fashioned, even bigots, who must answer to the law." As columnist Angela Shanahan wrote about this, "Since when has teaching your children what you and most of the world's population believe to be right, been a thought crime?"[43]

And this is happening while we have no law for same-sex marriage! What level of intimidation might the church expect once

---

[41] Australian Catholic Bishops Conference, *Don't Mess With Marriage* (2015), http://sydneycatholic.org/pdf/DMM-booklet_web.pdf

[42] "Media Release: Church school marriage booklet likely violates anti-bias law," Australian Marriage Equality, 24 June 2015, http://www.australianmarriageequality.org/2015/06/24/media-release-church-school-marriage-booklet-likely-violates-anti-bias-law/

[43] Angela Shanahan, "Gay marriage leaves Catholic schools under threat," *The Australian*, 4 July 2015, http://www.theaustralian.com.au/opinion/columnists/angela-shanahan/gay-marriage-leaves-catholic-schools-under-threat/news-story/c13f232f45b5cf15e196d288ccc500ec

homosexual 'marriage' is the law of the land? "For if men do these things when the wood is green, what will they do when the wood is dry?"[44]

Overseas, under laws for same-sex 'marriage', Catholic adoption agencies in a number of US states and in the UK have had to close when compelled by authorities to place children equally with homosexual couples.[45] A judgement of the European Court of Human Rights found that if same-sex marriage is legal in a member state, then any church that refuses to marry same-sex couples would be guilty of discrimination.[46] There should be no pretence in our Parliament that churches can be guaranteed lasting exemption from the law of homosexual marriage.

Equally, the individual will be given no exemption from holding approved opinions on homosexual marriage and parenting. David Blankenhorn observed,

> Once this proposed reform became law, even to say the words out loud in public – "Every child needs a father and a mother" – would probably be viewed as explicitly divisive and discriminatory, possibly even as hate speech.[47]

Consider the hounding and sacking of the head of Mozilla, Brendan Eich, for daring to give a donation to a political campaign defending natural marriage.[48] Or consider Mrs Stutzman, a florist

---

[44] Luke 23:31.

[45] Catholic Charities reference at http://www.weeklystandard.com/Content/ Public/Articles/000/000/012/191kgwgh.asp

[46] European Court of Human Rights ruling – reference at www.sconews. co.uk/news/17511/same-sex-'marriage'-is-not-a-human-right/

[47] D. Blankenhorn, *The Future of Marriage*, (New York: Encounter Books, 2007).

[48] B. O'Neill, "Same-sex marriage: coercion dolled up as human rights," *Spiked*, 30 April 2014, http://www.spiked-online.com/newsite/article/same- sex-marriage-coercion-dolled-up-as-civil-rights/14967#.V3mEQSN96Cc

in Washington State when the new gay 'marriage' laws came in. She gently explained to a long-term customer that she could give him flowers for any other occasion, but could not violate her faith by decorating a same-sex 'wedding'. She was prosecuted by the Attorney General, vilified in social media and swamped with hate mail. The legal expenses and toxic publicity may well cost this gentle Christian grandmother her florist business.[49]

"Won't somebody please think of the bakers", is the mocking line from gay activists. But it is no joke for father of five, Aaron Klein of Oregon, who was fined $135,000 and lost his livelihood as a baker, just because a lesbian couple demanded he bake them a wedding cake and he, in good conscience, declined.[50] Senator Wong, in her recent National Press Club debate, said that lesbian couples would simply avoid bakers who did not want to bake them a cake, but of course the opposite is true: the whole objective is to identify those bakers, or florists, or photographers, or wedding venue proprietors who are not compliant with the gay agenda and force them to comply – or break them.[51]

And in case we think the conservative side of politics will stand firmly against such intimidation, we read this month that a British 'Conservative' MP is calling for Christian teachers to be prosecuted under laws being proposed to curb jihadist hate-speech:

> New banning orders intended to clamp down on terrorist propagandists should be used against Christian teachers

---

[49] "The Barronelle Stutzman Story," YouTube video, posted by "Alliance Defending Freedom," 16 March 2014, https://youtu.be/MDETkcCw63c

[50] K. Harkness, "State Says Bakers Should Pay $135,000 for Refusing to Bake Cake for Same-Sex Wedding," *The Daily Signal*, 24 April 2015, http://dailysignal.com/2015/04/24/state-says-bakers-should-pay-135000-for-refusing-to-bake-cake-for-same-sex-wedding/

[51] "Gay marriage debate: Penny Wong vs Cory Bernardi," YouTube video, 29 July 2015, www.youtube.com/watch?v=Vyqz5tuPhIw

who teach children that gay marriage is "wrong", a Tory MP, Mark Spencer, has said.[52]

What more chilling example could there be of the intention of the elite to silence unacceptable views on homosexuality? As everyone's favourite Marxist, Brendan O'Neill, wrote this week,

Through gay marriage, the state — in the shape of the courts, the policing of "hate speech" and the restructuring of moral education in schools — is exercising greater control over what can be thought and said about human relationships.[53]

Any law normalising homosexual marriage will be a truncheon in the fist of the thought police, enforcing approved opinion on sexuality via their "human rights" commissions. It will be a major cultural triumph for advocates of state authority over individual conscience; it will be a major step in "de-authorising the Judaeo-Christian influence in our society" – and any who pretend otherwise are deluding themselves.

The fourth harm: the deconstruction of marriage and kinship

The final harm of homosexual 'marriage' is that it will not end there. Its perverse logic will work its way through ever more transgressive distortions of marriage, parenting, kinship and gender. First, the logic of gay 'marriage' must lead to group 'marriage'. Lord Daniel Brennan, former Chair of the Bar Association in the UK, wrote in March 2012:

After all, if you can abolish the most important pre-condition of marriage – namely that it requires a person

---

[52] J. Bingham, "MP: use anti-terror powers on Christian teachers who say gay marriage is 'wrong'," *The Telegraph*, 3 August 2015, www.telegraph.co.uk/news/politics/11780517/MP-use-anti-terror-powers-on-Christian-teachers-who-say-gay-marriage-is-wrong.html

[53] Brendan O'Neill, "Here's my beef with gay marriage," *Catallaxy Files,* 24 August 2015, http://catallaxyfiles.com/2015/08/24/guest-post-brendan-oneill-heres-my-beef-with-gay-marriage/

of each sex – why should you be able to retain other pre-conditions, such as limiting it to only two people?[54]

And in June this year, Chief Justice John Roberts of the US Supreme Court said in his dissenting ruling on same-sex marriage, "It is striking how much of the majority's reasoning would apply with equal force to the claim of a fundamental right to plural marriage."[55]

Last year, the *New York Post* featured three women in wedding dresses under the heading, "Married lesbian throuple expecting first child"[56] while in February this year the same paper introduced us to "the world's first gay married trio" in Thailand.[57] On the subject of throuples and beyond, Australian polyamorist Rachelle White told radio 6PR, "I do think we need to address same-sex marriage before we do move forward and look at polyamorous marriage." [58]

And why not? For if marriage is only about love and commitment, then on what logical grounds can we deny 'marriage equality' to three or four loving and committed adults who want society to honour their relationship? Love is love is love ... and love knows no boundaries ...

In this brave new boundary-free world, even incestuous couples have a case for marriage equality. In April 2012 an incestu-

---

[54] D. Brennan, "Gay marriage: eight centuries of law obliterated overnight," *The Telegraph*, 13 March 2012, http://www.telegraph.co.uk/women/sex/9140790/Gay-marriage-Eight-centuries-of-law-obliterated-overnight.html

[55] Supreme Court of the USA, *Obergefell v Hodges*, op. cit.

[56] D.K. Li, "Married lesbian threesome expecting first child," *New York Post*, 23 April 2014, http://nypost.com/2014/04/23/married-lesbian-threesome-expecting-first-child/

[57] F. Haque, "Meet the 'world's first' gay married throuple'," *New York Post*, 27 February 2015, http://nypost.com/2015/02/27/thai-throuple-believed-to-be-worlds-first-gay-married-trio/

[58] Rachelle White, Interview on Perth radio *6PR*, 5 May 2012.

ous relationship came to the European Court of Human Rights. Patrick Stuebing from Leipzig argued that he and his sister had the right to a "family life".[59] The case had inspired calls to legalise familial sexual relations. The ECHR refused, saying it was necessary for "the protection of marriage and the family" to punish incestuous relationships. That's nice, but for how long will courts uphold this quaint notion of "the protection of marriage and the family" once homosexual 'marriage' has breached the levee of sexual taboo that alone protects the natural order of marriage and family life?

Beyond the extension of gay 'marriage' to group 'marriage' or worse, the destructiveness of this revolution goes well beyond marriage itself to the broader bonds of blood and belonging. It is not just that the words "husband" and "wife" will have no place in a genderless Marriage Act; the words "mother" and "father" will also have to go from various documents such as passports or birth certificates. And as in Canada, the traditional legal term "natural parent" would be replaced by the soulless Big Government term "legal parent".[60] Under a law for same-sex 'marriage' the relationship of all parents with all children will be redefined and degraded; the parent-child bond will no longer be a natural reality which government is obliged to respect but a legal fiction which the state will define as it sees fit.

Words like husband and wife, mother and father stand for the deepest human relationships and their subversion by a genderless ideology is no small matter. Brendan O'Neill wrote this week:

> Those who say "They're only words, who cares?" clearly don't know their Orwell. The policing of language is very

---

[59] R. Williams, "German incest couple lose rights ruling," *Independent*, 12 April 2012, www.independent.co.uk/news/world/europe/german-incest-couple-lose-rights-ruling-7640247.html

[60] Somerville., "It's all about the children, not selfish adults," op. cit.

often a policing of attitudes, a reengineering of societal values so that they better accord with the elite's view.[61]

We need to revisit our Orwell, and we need to reject Senator Wong's disingenuous words to the Press Club this month that nothing will really change with same-sex 'marriage': that "the sun will still rise; and children will still eat more ice cream than is good for them."[62] That is not what Russian lesbian activist Masha Gessen told the Sydney Writer's Festival in 2012:

> Fighting for gay marriage generally involves lying about what we are going to do with marriage when we get there. Because we lie that the institution of marriage is not going to change. And that is a lie. The institution of marriage is going to change and it should change, and again I don't think it should exist.[63]

We have heard US activist Michelangelo Signorile urge gays "to fight for same-sex marriage and its benefits and then, once granted, redefine the institution of marriage completely."[64] We have read lawyer Paula Ettelbrick's declaration that: "Being queer means pushing the parameters of sex, sexuality and family... and of radically reordering society's view of reality." These are not the words of homosexual people who don't want anything to change, who just want to fit in with the established norms of marriage. No, these are the words of culture warriors who want to take marriage and remake it in their own sexually radical image.

In the gay new world of radically reordered marriage, monogamy is the essential repressive element that has to go. On the same

---

[61] O'Neill, op. cit., n. 53.

[62] "Gay marriage debate: Penny Wong vs Cory Bernardi," op. cit. n. 51.

[63] M. Gessen, interview by Annette Shun Wah, *Radio National,* 11 June 2012, Sydney Writer's Festival 2012, at 6.20min, http://www.abc.net.au/radionational/programs/lifematters/why-get-married/4058506

[64] Michelangelo Signorile, "Bridal wave", *Out*, December 1993, 161.

Sydney Writer's panel as Masha Gessen, Australian gay activist Dennis Altman told us:

> Now I am going to speak now as a gay man: one of the things about gay male culture is that it is not a monogamous culture. All the evidence we have suggests that monogamy is a myth. There are many longstanding gay relationships. There are virtually no longstanding monogamous gay relationships. I happen to think that this is a good thing.[65]

US gay activist Dan Savage agrees, saying gay marriage can at best be "monogamish", not monogamous; open marriage, not faithful marriage "to the exclusion of all others".[66]

Most recently, we have a word coined by a lawyer after this year's US Supreme Court ruling on gay "marriage": "wed-lease" instead of "wedlock". The idea is that marriage should not be a commitment for life, but an agreed term of commitment which expires after, say 5 years, with the option of renewing the 'wed-lease' for another term. Because it's all about love, and marriage should only really last as long as the love lasts. And we are being told that nothing will change.

Conclusion: politics and just discrimination

What, then, is the way forward? How can we live respectfully with our homosexual neighbours and relatives while still protecting the truth about marriage, and defending that triangle of truisms, mother-father-child? Frank Brennan, the former Chair of our National Human Rights Consultation Committee has written:

---

[65] Dennis Altman, interview by Annette Shun Wah, *Radio National,* 11 June 2012, Sydney Writer's Festival 2012, www.abc.net.au/radionational/ programs/lifematters/why-get-married/4058506

[66] M. Oppenheimer, "Married with Infidelities", *The New York Times*, 30 June 2011 www.nytimes.com/2011/07/03/magazine/infidelity-will-keep-us-together.html?_r=0

> I think we can ensure non-discrimination against same-sex couples while at the same time maintaining a commitment to children of future generations being born of and being reared by a father and a mother.[67]

"Non-discrimination against same-sex couples" is exactly what Federal Parliament achieved in 2008, when 85 pieces of legislation were amended by a bipartisan majority, removing discrimination in all areas from tax to superannuation to Medicare to next of kin status.[68]

There is now no unjust discrimination against same-sex couples. A gay couple has full relationship equality with a de facto or married couple – the same legal status and benefits as our former 'first couple' (the Hon. Julia Gillard and Mr Tim Mathieson). And neither couple needs a marriage certificate to achieve this status.

What Frank Brennan calls "commitment to children of future generations" requires that we discriminate, justly, between two quite distinct social projects: the widespread public task of marriage-and-family, and the rare private commitment of gay partnerships. The number of same-sex couples in Australia is indeed very small, only 1% of all couples according to the ABS Australian Social Trends 2013.[69] And only one in a thousand children of couple-households are raised in same-sex households.[70] Only 1.2% of Australian

---

[67] Frank Brennan, "The perils of redefining marriage", 24 November 2010, http://www.eurekastreet.com.au/article.aspx?aeid=24259#.U33yOP1q4uI

[68] P. Osbourne, "Labor to introduce bill legalising gay marriage," *The New Daily*, 26 May 2015, http://thenewdaily.com.au/news/2015/05/26/labor-brings-gay-marriage-laws/

[69] Australian Bureau of Statistics, 2013, "Same-Sex Couples," http://www.abs.gov.au/AUSSTATS/abs@.nsf/Lookup/4102.0Main+Features10July+2013

[70] Australian Bureau of Statistics 2013, "How many same-sex couples have children?" http://www.abs.gov.au/AUSSTATS/abs@.nsf/Lookup/4102.0Main+Features10July+2013#children

adults (1.8% male, 0.6% female) identify as homosexual according to the major 2003 study *Sex in Australia*.[71]

Given these tiny numbers – one in a hundred, one in a thousand – and given that same-sex couples already enjoy the same benefits as any other couple, just what is the terrible injustice that requires marriage and parenting to be redefined for the 99%? There is none. What there is, at the root of this revolution, is an intense psychological craving on the part of the 1% to have society affirm homosexual behaviour as unequivocally normal and right: in our institutions, in our laws, our schools, even – in due course – our churches. Before the relentless rage that demands "equality", nothing less than total acquiescence will suffice.

We cannot acquiesce – not because we want to see our same-sex attracted neighbours continue to suffer psychologically, but because the terms they demand are untrue to nature, unjust to children, and radically damaging to the structures of parenting and kinship.

Even in terms of their genuine suffering, the terms they demand will not resolve their distress. That distress arises more from the intrinsic dissonance of being a male erotically attracted to other males than from the extrinsic structures of society. Above all, it is the injustice inherent in homosexual marriage that must be resisted: so-called 'equality' for homosexual couples cannot be achieved without imposing inequality on others. A law for same-sex 'marriage' means:

> A loss of the right of future children to have both a mother and a father;
>
> A loss of the right of parents to guide the moral education of their children;

---

[71] M.A. Anthony et al, "Sex in Australia: Sexual identity, sexual attraction and sexual experience among a representative sample of adults," *Australian and New Zealand Journal of Public Health* 27, no.2 (2003): 138-45, www. blackwell-synergy.com/doi/abs/10.1111/j.1467-842X.2003.tb00801.x

A loss of the right of conscientious objectors who will be silenced by anti-discrimination law.

No parliament and no court has the authority to legislate a lie about marriage, which predates all societies and all laws. True marriage is given by nature, strengthened by culture, and uniquely empowered to nurture new life. For the sake of the child, it must remain what it is: a man-woman thing.

12

SCIENCE AND THE "MIND OF GOD": A NEW SPRINGTIME FOR THE CHRISTIAN VIEW OF COSMIC HISTORY

Robert Van Gend

ABSTRACT

Since Einstein's encounter with an "illimitable superior intelligence" in the laws of nature, contemporary agnostic scientists like Paul Davies and agnostic philosophers like Antony Flew have also recognised that the universe is imbued with signs of mind, which they call the "Mind of God". Through his scientific work, Davies detects in the cosmos "an ingenuity so astonishing that I cannot accept it merely as brute fact." A famous quantum physicist and Anglican priest, John Polkinghorne has been a leader in the rapprochement of the new physics and old metaphysics, of science and theology. He shows how the scientific picture of the physical world, far from explaining everything away in a materialist fashion, gives a scientist deep reasons for believing the first line of the Christian Creed, that there is an intelligent author of the universe, traces of which can be seen in the laws of nature and read in the language of mathematics. From this position of deism, the second line of the Creed becomes a respectable and valid question. Flew says we must explore "… whether the Divine has revealed itself in human history" because we "cannot limit the possibilities of omnipotence …" What an exciting jolt this could be for our tired, materialist world! An encounter with the "illimitable superior intelligence" would reawaken our culture to transcendence. A return to the first line of the Creed may be the one idea upon which to restore the once-vibrant culture, by anchoring it in the Divine Reason that inspired the Greeks and Christendom.

* * * * *

One important insight I took away from my Campion College liberal arts degree is that ideas have consequences.

In *Understanding the Present: Science and the Soul of Modern Man*, Bryan Appleyard investigates the cultural consequences of the replacement of Aristotelian physics with the mechanical Newtonian physics. The Aristotelian world understood final causes, or purposes, to be part of an explanation of a substance, but in the new science only mechanical causes were of interest. No longer did a planet orbit the sun because of a "transcendent moral order";[1] the planet seeks mechanical equilibrium just like all matter does.

Newton sparked the idea that nature could be completely explained through mechanical causes. The universe was a big machine. Everything in Newton's world was to be explained in terms of matter bumping into or attracting other bits of matter. Laplace, after explaining the fine-tuning of the planets' orbits with only the laws of nature, said of God, "I have no need of that hypothesis."[2] The dazzling mathematical power of science and, later, its impressive technological fruits, would progressively "exclude all possibility of competition, of alternative explanation."[3]

"What must never be forgotten", stresses Appleyard, "is that it was a choice, we adopted a particular perspective, a perspective

---

[1] Bryan Appleyard, *Understanding the Present,* Anchor Books, 1994, 41.
[2] P-S. Laplace, quoted in Augustus de Morgan, *A Budget of Paradoxes*, Open Court Publishing Company, 1915, 2.
[3] Appleyard, op. cit., 44.

which, to Newton, would have been only half the picture. The other half would have been the spirit world..."[4]

The scientific perspective necessarily ignores the world of value, which is outside its sphere of competence. The idea that the scientific perspective gives us the full picture of our world has had consequences for the present culture. The assumption is that nothing in the realm of non-science is real and objective, and all we have is our own subjective experience that we can cut to the shape we like. Everything is the product of blind chance and necessity, according to atheists like Richard Dawkins, and there is no point expecting there to be meaning or objective values in a blind universe.[5] We are disconnected from any reality external to ourselves. We no longer strive after transcendent beauty, goodness and truth, but are subjected to such shabby and accidental artworks as Tracey Emin's bed, which she insists is beautiful to her.[6]

Nietzsche saw with great clarity the cultural situation of modernity. "God is dead", he wrote, "...and we have killed him!"[7] Nietzsche drew the full consequences of the decline of belief in God – if God is acknowledged not to exist, then there are no grounds for traditional morality. It is up to each individual to invent his own morality, his own truth, if he likes, in the cold, Godless universe. "Man", writes the 20th century biologist Jacques Monod in *Chance and Necessity*, "at last knows he is alone in the unfeeling immensity of the universe, out of which he has emerged by chance".[8]

---

[4] Ibid., 43.

[5] Richard Dawkins, *The Blind Watchmaker,* Penguin, 2006.

[6] Transcript of Roger Scruton, *Why Beauty Matters* (BBC Scotland, 2009), available at URL: http://www.facetofaceintercultural.com.au/a-fading-beauty/

[7] Friedrich Nietzsche, *The Gay Science* (1887), Walter Kaufmann ed., Vintage, 1974, 181-2.

[8] Jacques Monod, *Chance and Necessity,* Collins, 1972, quoted in J. Polkinghorne, *Quarks, Chaos & Christianity*, Triangle, 1994, 40.

And so we are left in a desolate, meaningless universe as our home. Is that the last word, or are there ideas out there now that might return the culture to an era when we perceived the universe as "shot through with signs of mind"[9] and meaning?

The former professor of mathematical physics at Cambridge university, John Polkinghorne, who discovered one of the quarks, looks at the same scientific phenomena that led Monod to despair but sees them with different eyes. That is because he, as an ordained Anglican priest, along with a collection of agnostic scientists and philosophers, agrees with physicist Sir James Jeans that "the universe is starting to look much more like a great thought than a great machine."[10] They look at the same physical universe that Monod looked at, but they do not see the same blind chance and necessity at work.

Chance and Necessity

What almost all scientists agree is that in the beginning, the universe was an almost smooth, expanding ball of energy. It was much simpler than the universe is today, which is full of complex systems like galaxies, and the most complicated known systems, us. The early expansion was not completely smooth. There were ripples here and there which meant that there was more matter in some places than others. Where there is more matter, there is more gravitational pull, which attracts more matter. A snowballing process over a billion years formed a universe lumpy with galaxies, which in turn became lumpy with stars.[11] The ripples that led to galaxies and stars rather than a perfectly smooth and uninteresting universe were chance, that is, historical contingency. Gravity was the law that augmented the chance event. This interplay between

---

[9] John Polkinghorne, *Science and Religion in Quest of Truth,* Yale UP, 2011, 73.

[10] James Jeans, *The Mysterious Universe* Penguin Books, 1937, 137.

[11] Polkinghorne, op. cit., n 8, 39-40.

chance and necessity is a characteristic of the evolution of complex systems all throughout cosmic history.

Another case, closer to home, is the biological evolution of complex beings like us. Chance mutations occur from time to time that are rejected or preserved by the process of natural selection. As best we understand, nothing new and complex could develop if these chance mutations did not occur, and nothing new would be preserved if the new genetic information could not be transmitted.

In Polkinghorne's eyes, "chance is the engine of novelty, necessity is the preserver of fruitfulness."[12] Within lawful limits, there is space for novelty in cosmic history, which he thinks is "consonant with the idea that it is the expression of the will of a Creator, subtle, patient, and content to achieve his purposes by the slow unfolding of process inherent in those laws of nature which, in their regularity, are but the pale reflections of his abiding faithfulness."[13] So instead of Monod's nihilistic interpretation of chance and necessity that sees the universe without meaning or purpose, Polkinghorne interprets the interplay between chance and necessity as indicators of the Creator's gift of independence to the world, and of the Creator's faithfulness.

But what justification is there for such an interpretation? Since the 1970s a school of thought has developed among scientists that the "necessity" element, that is, the laws of nature, should not be described by the pejorative word "blind", since the universe's laws seem to be deliberately fine-tuned to support carbon-based life. In this school of thought, ours is a very special universe. Most combinations of laws would create sterile universes. But ours looks fine-tuned to allow for the astonishing complexity of life to emerge. The laws are "tightly knit" – they are related to each other

[12] Ibid., 40.

[13] John Polkinghorne, *One World: The Interaction of Science and Theology* Templeton Press, 2007, 95.

in a delicate balance and set to precise values that make possible the evolution of carbon-based life from the physical fabric of the world, right up to the complexity of self-conscious rational creatures.[14] This includes human beings but would likewise apply to any self-conscious rational creature elsewhere in the cosmos, loosely termed *anthropoi*. This is called the "Anthropic Principle".

To give an example of the tightly knit laws, if the initial expansion of the big bang was too fast, it would quickly become diluted before anything interesting could happen. If it expanded too slowly it would collapse back in on itself before anything interesting could happen. It also needs to expand quite smoothly because large irregularities could cause destructive turbulence, but not too smoothly or stars will not be able to form from irregularities in the distribution of matter.[15]

For stars to be stable, long-burning sources of light and heat that make life on a nearby planet possible, the fundamental forces of gravity and electromagnetism must have a delicate balance. If the balance is slightly off, stars will become too cool to support life or they will overheat and burn out in a few million years, which is too quickly for life to evolve.[16]

The strength of the strong nuclear force, another fundamental force, is critical to the production of carbon inside stars, which is a necessary element in the creation of carbon-based life. Carbon is made when three helium nuclei are joined together. This is impossible to do without a special 'resonance' existing at just the right frequency. To the astonishment of scientists, this resonance does exist at exactly the right frequency, and this is made possible by the fine-tuning of the strength of the strong nuclear force.[17]

---

[14] John Polkinghorne, *Faith, Science and Understanding,* Yale UP, 2000, 85.

[15] Ibid., n 8, 27.

[16] Ibid., 28.

[17] Ibid., 29.

These are just a few of the fine-tuned processes that are critical for life to evolve. John Leslie, in his book *Universes*, uses up several pages listing instances of fine-tuning of which science has become aware.[18]

Polkinghorne says that his colleagues feel "particularly uneasy about the delicate balances required by the anthropic principle", as though it is too much to put down to coincidence.[19] They are challenged by the idea that the interplay of chance and necessity is not blind after all. Polkinghorne does not think that the 'blind' interpretation is the best one. He finds a theistic interpretation most satisfying, where the elements of chance and necessity in cosmic history reflect the twin gifts of freedom and faithfulness that the Creator has given to his creation. Rather than "chance" and "necessity", he prefers to use the terms "happenstance" and "lawful regularity". The lawful regularity is the fine-tuned laws of nature within which a universe can explore the inherent fruitfulness of these laws through the shuffling of happenstance. Within the simple, fine-tuned laws of nature, there is an "astonishing potentiality ... capable of being explored by the processes of chance and necessity."[20] Arthur Peacocke likens the action of chance in the elaboration of complex life to a composition by Bach: "Thus does J.S. Bach create a complex and interlocking harmonious fusion of his seminal material, both through time and at any particular instant ... In this kind of way might the Creator be imagined to unfold the potentialities of the universe which he himself has given it."[21] We need not call chance 'blind'; there is no chance without fine-tuned lawful regularity, and Polkinghorne thinks it is unsatisfactory to explain away this lawful regularity as mere blind randomness.

---

[18] John Leslie, *Universes* Routledge, 1989, 2-6.
[19] Polkinghorne, op. cit. n 13, 94.
[20] Ibid.
[21] Arthur Peacocke, quoted in Polkinghorne, op. cit., 65.

The finely-tuned universe challenges the nihilistic vision of chance and necessity. The only way, says Polkinghorne, that "... a hot soup of elementary particles has become the home of saints and scientists"[22] is because some very delicate initial conditions and balance of laws was met, endowing the simple fundamental laws with astonishing potential. Chance, in this view, is not as blind as it seems.

The agnostic Australian cosmologist Paul Davies is not sure exactly what this all means, but he is sure that it is not meaningless:

> I belong to the group of scientists who do not subscribe to a conventional religion but nevertheless deny that the universe is a purposeless accident. Through my scientific work I have come to believe more and more strongly that the physical universe is put together with an ingenuity so astonishing that I cannot accept it merely as a brute fact.[23]

There is a second insight of the deep rationality of modern science that is a further reason to think that there is more meaning to the universe than meets the eye. As physicist Sir James Jeans said, "the universe begins to look more like a great thought than like a great machine ..."[24]

Signs of Mind

After recognising signs of mind in the universe, Antony Flew, the famous atheist philosopher of the 20th century, wrote a book called *There is a God*:

> I now believe that the universe was brought into existence by an infinite Intelligence. I believe that this universe's

---

[22] Polkinghorne, op. cit., n 8, 39.

[23] Antony Flew, *There is a God: How the World's Most Notorious Atheist Changed His Mind*, HarperCollins, 2007, 16.

[24] Jeans, op. cit., n 10, 137.

intricate laws manifest what scientists have called the Mind of God... Why do I believe this, given that I expounded and defended atheism for more than a half century? The short answer is this: this is the world picture, as I see it, that has emerged from modern science.[25]

Flew echoed the great agnostic Jew, Albert Einstein, who said

Certain it is that a conviction, akin to religious feeling, of the rationality or intelligibility of the world lies behind all scientific work of a higher order ... This firm belief, a belief bound up with deep feeling, in a superior mind that reveals itself in the world of experience, represents my conception of God.[26]

Far from looking like a mindless, purely material universe, our universe is shot through with signs of a rational mind. Both Flew and Einstein were convinced that the Mind of God is the reason for rational character of our universe.[27] The more interesting point, though, is that the rational character of our minds mirrors this rational structure of the universe. Polkinghorne puts it like this: "There is this remarkable congruence between our inward thought and the outward way things are."[28]

First, to the outward way things are.

Modern science has probed the universe from the very largest galaxies to the smallest subatomic particles and quantum fields.

---

[25] Flew, op. cit. n. 23, 88-9.

[26] Albert Einstein, "On Scientific Truth", *Ideas and Opinions*, trans. Sonja Bargmann, Crown Publishers, 1954, 262.

[27] Atheists, pantheists and theists often claim Einstein to be a member of their camp. Flew shows that Einstein expressly denied being an atheist or a pantheist. Einstein did not believe in a personal God, but his God is nevertheless a "superior mind", "illimitable superior spirit" and "superior reasoning force" that is the source of the rationality of the universe (Flew, op. cit. n. 23, 98-101).

[28] Polkinghorne, op. cit. n. 13, 56.

The findings: a universe that is saturated with reason. There are laws that explain the behaviour of the physical world as deep down as we look. Einstein said "Whoever has undergone the intense experience of successful advances in this domain [science] is moved by profound reverence for the rationality made manifest in existence... the grandeur of reason incarnate in existence."[29]

Laws of nature are like "instruction-sets mysteriously imprinted in the very being of all things."[30] They are universal and explain phenomena at every level of the physical world. Even in the unpicturable quantum world, particles and larger objects seem to obey laws. These laws are built into the fabric of the physical stuff. Paul Davies likens them to computer software – the immaterial program that directs the physical universe.[31]

These instruction-sets are not immediately obvious to us. We can all observe that apples fall to the ground. But we cannot observe that the apples fall according to Newton's inverse-square law of gravitation. To observe this we must interrogate nature more deeply, drawing on existing theories – which are expressible in mathematics – about nature's behaviour.

Einstein's Special Theory of Relativity equates matter and energy. The relationship between them is expressed in the mathematical equation $E=mc2$. That means, if we take an object that is stationary, the energy contained in its matter is equal to its mass multiplied by the speed of light squared. Mathematics has an uncanny ability to describe physical laws. Paul Davies suggests that the laws of nature are in code, and the language of the code is mathematics.[32] It is remarkable that the universe's secrets are coded in a language

---

[29] R.A. Varghese, *The Wonder of the World: A Journey from Modern Science to the Mind of God*, Tyr Publishing, 2004, 105.

[30] Ibid., 331.

[31] Paul Davies, *The Mind of God*, Penguin Books, 1993, 84.

[32] Ibid., 79.

that we understand. Einstein said the only incomprehensible thing about the universe is its comprehensibility.[33]

Polkinghorne puts it well:

> We are so familiar with the fact that we can understand the world that most of the time we take it for granted. It is what makes science possible. Yet it could have been otherwise. The universe might have been a disorderly chaos rather than an orderly cosmos. Or it might have had rationality which was inaccessible to us. . . .There is a congruence between our minds and the universe, between the rationality experienced within and the rationality observed without.[34]

Some philosophers seize this idea that our thinking is congruent with the structure of the universe and argue that the laws of nature do not really exist – scientists just use their minds to impose rational patterns on the world. Paul Davies, a scientist, has no time for the idea that the laws are purely human constructions, calling it "arrant nonsense".[35] Polkinghorne thinks it is much more plausible that the scientist does not invent laws but uncovers what really exists:

> The world, though ordered, is strange and subtle. Our powers of rational prevision are pretty myopic and limited by the contingency of the way things are, existing independently of how we think they ought to be.[36]

Another reason to trust this strange affinity between inward thought and the fabric of the universe is that mathematicians and scientists are often convinced of the verisimilitude of a theory

---

[33] Einstein, op. cit. n. 26, 292.

[34] Quoted in A. McGrath, "New Atheism – New Apologetics: The Use of Science in Recent Christian Apologetic Writings," *Science and Christian Belief*, 26, no. 1 (2014): 108.

[35] Flew, *There is a God*, 107.

[36] Polkinghorne, *One World*, 27.

precisely because it is mathematically beautiful. Indeed, Einstein proposed his mathematically beautiful General Theory of Relativity many years before evidence could actually verify it.

Paul Dirac, a distinguished quantum physicist who predicted the existence of antimatter, wrote:

> It is more important to have beauty in one's equations than to have them fit experiment... because the discrepancy may be due to minor features which are not properly taken into account and which will get cleared up with further developments of the theory ...[37]

It really seems like mathematics, the most abstract and logical form of thought we possess, is the key to the nature's secrets. It is written into the fabric of the universe. Paul Dirac said, "God is a mathematician of a very high order and He used advanced mathematics in constructing the universe."[38] So when we do science, we are, in Kepler's words, "thinking God's thoughts after Him."[39]

So not only is the structure of the universe rational, but the structure of our thought is strangely in tune with rational frequency of the universe. It is the reason we can do science at all.

The fact that the physical universe is rationally structured with laws that are written in the intelligible language of mathematics calls for an explanation. Flew thought that the "only viable explanation" of the origin of the laws of nature is the divine Mind.[40] In this he echoed the position of Einstein, who said "the laws of nature manifest the existence of a spirit vastly superior to that of men,

---

[37] Ibid., 55.
[38] Quoted in Varghese, op. cit., n. 29, 106.
[39] Quoted in H.M. Morris, *Men of Science, Men of God*, Master Books, 1982, 12.
[40] Flew, op. cit., n. 23, 121.

and one in the face of which we with our modest powers must feel humble."[41] Flew has joined the position of the great scientists of the past – Copernicus, Galileo, Kepler, Newton, Faraday, Maxwell, Einstein, Planck and Heisenberg – all who believed that the rationality of the universe has its source in God.

Polkinghorne sums up:

> The rational order that science discerns is so beautiful and striking that it is natural to ask why it should be so. It could find an explanation only in a cause itself essentially rational. This would be provided by the Reason of the Creator, which establishes the common ground for the observed rationality of the world and the experienced rationality of our minds, guaranteeing their mutual coherence. This insight gains cumulative force if we widen our view beyond that of science to recognise that we know the world also to contain beauty, moral obligation, and religious experience. These also find their ground in the Creator ...[42]

An Idea with Consequences

This is where the idea of the rationality of the physical universe becomes a really dangerous idea. Surely there is no more dangerous idea than the idea that an "illimitable superior intelligence" is the source of this universe that is "shot through with signs of mind"?[43] It is the agnostic scientists who say it. Once the agnostic scientists start speaking of the Mind of God evident in the mathematical beauty of the cosmos, what is to stop other agnostics, or reverent deists, from discovering that deep rationality in the realm of values that Polkinghorne identified? The Deep Reason in the universe

---

[41] Quoted, ibid., 101.

[42] Polkinghorne, op. cit., n. 13, 94.

[43] Ibid. n. 9, 73.

could apply to more than scientific rationality and extend to the reasonableness of beauty and of moral goodness too.

This insight is respectably multicultural: it is a broadly Deistic, not a specifically Christian, insight. At most it brings the culture back to the first line of the Creed, the recognition of a creative Mind behind all that is. What an idea like this might do to our culture is lift the dead hand of materialism and nihilism, and that will have profound consequences. This idea could re-enchant the cosmos with mind and meaning and revive our tired culture.

And once we acknowledge the first line of the Creed, the second line becomes a more respectable question. As Antony Flew said, what then do we make of claims of revealed religion? The question of whether the Divine has revealed itself in human history remains a valid topic of discussion. You cannot limit the possibilities of omnipotence except to produce the logically impossible. Everything else is open to omnipotence.[44]

Ideas have consequences. The rediscovery by agnostic as well as believing scientists of the idea of Mind underlying the beauty and rationality of our physical world has implications for a renewed sense of meaning, and therefore of purpose and even hope, for our culture.

---

[44] Flew, op. cit., n. 23, 157.

13

RIDICULED REVELATION AND THE FOUNDATIONAL ROLE OF HOLY SCRIPTURE FOR WESTERN CIVILISATION

Benno Zuiddam

ABSTRACT

The world of the early post apostolic fathers was in many ways like ours, that of the post Christian western world of the 21st century. Christianity was a minority religion that faced ridicule and animosity from the world at large and the scientific community in particular. The neo-platonic scholars Celsus and Porphyry launched vehement attacks on the Scriptures, Jesus' incarnation, resurrection and ascension, as well as the character and integrity of the Apostles. Celsus published his "Real Truth" about Christianity and its teachings, while Porphyry wrote a series of books "Against the Christians". In this climate, the early Church reaffirmed its commitment to a Christian worldview that finds its basis in revelation, the voice of God as it was experienced in Sacred Scripture. This is not only reflected by later fathers like Augustine, Hieronymus and Origen, but already at a relatively early stage in the writings of Irenaeus of Lyons and Clement of Alexandria. Their writings show an early and natural acknowledgement of and commitment to the authority of Holy Writ as lively oracles of God. As the early Church was committed to be guided by the voice of God and what she experienced as his perspective on matters eternal and temporal, moral and historical, Christianity ultimately emerged as the dominant religion of the Roman Empire.

* * * * *

1. Propositional Revelation[45] and its Collapse in Western Society

Revelation means that something is shown to us, which we have no means of knowing otherwise. This may be because of a) boundaries in history, b) geographical distance or c) our limited capacity.

Boundaries in history may exist because we did not exist at the time: for instance the doctrine of creation. Or because it concerns the future; like the return of Christ and the Last Judgement. Geographical distance implies that we are limited bodily, restricted to the location where our body finds itself. For instance: we cannot physically go to heaven as the place of God's dwelling. There are also limitations to our mental capacity. Our understanding is too limited to know, let alone comprehend everything. This implies that in certain areas it is unqualified to ascertain truth. In Theology this extends to God's nature and character, more particularly the doctrine of the Trinity or the two natures of Christ (divinity and humanity). To some extent this is true for the assessment of God's character as well, e.g. his love and faithfulness and his moral values in general. For all of these areas of human limitation we rely on outside advice, because we haven't got the ability to test these premises for ourselves.

---

[45] Propositional revelation is used in the patristic sense; namely that revelation is given by God in the form of truths couched in words, or propositions. This should be distinguished from the post Tridentine scholastic positions of Suárez and his followers, which were the subject of extensive critique by Joseph Ratzinger/Benedict XVI. See: Avery Dulles, "Revelation, Scripture, and Tradition," in *Your Word Is Truth: A Project of Evangelicals and Catholics Together*, ed. Colson and Neuhaus, Eerdmans, 2002, 35-58. Cf. D.D. Novatný, *Ens rationes from Suárez to Caramuel: a study in scholasticism of the Baroque*, Fordham University Press, 2013.

At some stage in the history of Western civilisation all Christians used to believe that revelation was propositional: a true premise independent of human recognition for its validity.[1] People also believed that revealed knowledge was as certain as the results of experiential science. But this has dramatically changed during the last two hundred years. A recent Oxford textbook for Theology and Philosophy students summarises this development:

> The traditional Christian view of revelation emphasises the notion that God reveals truths, propositions that human[s] should believe. This traditional view of revelation as propositional in character was questioned by many 20th century theologians. This non propositional view of revelation must be understood in part as an indirect response to historical and critical analysis of the Bible during the 19th and 20th centuries. The liberal theology that developed during this period basically shared the traditional understanding of revelation as propositional in character, but as a result of critical study concluded that the Bible could not be seen as a divinely inspired, infallible book, as many theologians had thought.[2]

This indicates a major shift in worldview, which has also affected our view of God. Instead of a powerful God who managed to transcend his message into human history by means of effective revelation, mankind was left with the impotent god of two world

---

[1] Cf. Thomas Aquinas, *Summa Theologiae*, 1.1. The Church of Rome strongly confirmed the reliability of historic revelation through Sacred Scripture up till Leo XIII (*Providentissimus Deus*, 1893) and Pius X. Cf. Karim Schelkens, *Catholic Theology of Revelation on the Eve of Vatican II: A Redaction History of the Schema De Fontibus Revelationis* (1960-1962), Volume 41 of *Brill's Series in Church History*, Brill, Leiden 2010, 26-7 "Exegesis aimed at 'sensus litteralis as conveying the meaning of the scriptural text as it was intended by its divine author.'" (27)

[2] Cf. C.S. Evans, "Faith and Revelation" In: W. Wainwright ed., *The Oxford Handbook of Philosophy of Religion (Oxford Handbooks series)*, Oxford University Press, 2004, ch. 13.

wars, filtered out of reality by the materialistic world views of the French Revolution and Darwinism. This god, if we had not killed him altogether, Nietzsche's "Wir haben ihn getödtet",[3] only managed to get through some words by means of an otherwise clouded and disturbed wireless connection.

---

[3] Friedrich Nietzsche concluded that mankind had eliminated God from its thinking. One can look for God, but he is nowhere to be found as he was only a manmade construction. After accepting the death of God, people have to take on the high calling of becoming their own god, but without the assistance of knowledge and values. Cf. Die fröhliche Wissenschaft („la gaya scienza"),Verlag von E.W. Fritzsch, Leipzig 1887, 125: "Der tolle Mensch. – Habt ihr nicht von jenem tollen Menschen gehört, der am hellen Vormittage eine Laterne anzündete, auf den Markt lief und unaufhörlich schrie: „Ich suche Gott! Ich suche Gott!" — Da dort gerade Viele von Denen zusammen standen, welche nicht an Gott glaubten, so erregte er ein grosses Gelächter. Ist er denn verloren gegangen? sagte der Eine. Hat er sich verlaufen wie ein Kind? sagte der Andere. Oder hält er sich versteckt? Fürchtet er sich vor uns? Ist er zu Schiff gegangen? ausgewandert? – so schrieen und lachten sie durcheinander. Der tolle Mensch sprang mitten unter sie und durchbohrte sie mit seinen Blicken. „Wohin ist Gott? rief er, ich will es euch sagen! Wir haben ihn getödtet, – ihr und ich! Wir Alle sind seine Mörder! Aber wie haben wir diess gemacht? Wie vermochten wir das Meer auszutrinken? Wer gab uns den Schwamm, um den ganzen Horizont wegzuwischen? Was thaten wir, als wir diese Erde von ihrer Sonne losketteten? Wohin bewegt sie sich nun? Wohin bewegen wir uns? Fort von allen Sonnen? Stürzen wir nicht fortwährend? Und rückwärts, seitwärts, vorwärts, nach allen Seiten? Giebt es noch ein Oben und ein Unten? Irren wir nicht wie durch ein unendliches Nichts? Haucht uns nicht der leere Raum an? Ist es nicht kälter geworden? Kommt nicht immerfort die Nacht und mehr Nacht? Müssen nicht Laternen am Vormittage angezündet werden? Hören wir noch Nichts von dem Lärm der Todtengräber, welche Gott begraben? Riechen wir noch Nichts von der göttlichen Verwesung? – auch Götter verwesen! Gott ist todt! Gott bleibt todt! Und wir haben ihn getödtet! Wie trösten wir uns, die Mörder aller Mörder? Das Heiligste und Mächtigste, was die Welt bisher besass, es ist unter unseren Messern verblutet, — wer wischt diess Blut von uns ab? Mit welchem Wasser könnten wir uns reinigen? Welche Sühnfeiern, welche heiligen Spiele werden wir erfinden müssen? Ist nicht die Grösse dieser That zu gross für uns? Müssen wir nicht selber zu Göttern werden, um nur ihrer würdig zu erscheinen?"

Subsequently cryptographers from the field of Biblical studies were called in and in majority concluded that the connection was so bad that only messages on certain topics could be trusted. The topic of God's expertise, forgiveness continues to be a popular one, as Heinrich Heine said:"Dieu me pardonnera, c'est son métier."[4]

These materialistic philosophies have not only eliminated the God of Christianity, but also radically changed the way society regards the human race, ethical values and personal moral accountability.[5] For many, the human soul has become an illusionary mental construction.[6]

Those who hold the Catholic view from before the paradigm shift, are considered out of touch with scientific realities, as: "critical study concluded that the Bible could not be seen as a divinely inspired, infallible book, as many theologians had thought."

---

[4] The German writer Heinrich Heine (1797-1856), see Alfred Meißner, *Heinrich Heine. Erinnerungen*, Hamburg, Hoffmann und Campe, 1856, 259. A fuller quote (258-9): "Gleich nach seinem Eintreten richtete er an Heine die Frage, wie er mit Gott stehe. Heine erwiederte lächelnd: Seind Sie ruhig! Dieu me pardonnera, cést son metier! So kam die lezte Nacht heran, die Nacht vom 16. Februar."

[5] John Anthony Burgess foreshadowed this brave new world, its dilemma's and the surrogate moral role of the state in *A Clockwork Orange*, Penguin Books Ltd, Harmondsworth 1972.

[6] Cf. Tom Wolfe, "Sorry your Soul has just died," *The Independent*, Sunday, 2 February 1997: "Thereupon, in the year 2006 or 2026, some new Nietzsche will step forward to announce: 'The self is dead' – except that being prone to the poetic, like Nietzsche I, he will probably say: 'The soul is dead.' He will say that he is merely bringing the news, the news of the greatest event of the millennium: 'The soul, that last refuge of values, is dead, because educated people no longer believe it exists.' Unless the assurances of the Wilsons and the Dennetts and the Dawkinses also start rippling out, the lurid carnival that will ensue may make the phrase 'the total eclipse of all values' seem tame."

Amongst these theologians who used to believe that the Bible was a reliable book in all respects were all church fathers.[7] And later doctors of the church, for that matter. This was connected to their firm belief that the author of the Scriptures, and everything in it, was God himself.[8] To their mind, the Father almighty was able to use human writers in such a way that they did not commit any error into writing their sacred task.

This view, which was until fifty years ago the official view of Western Christianity,[9] is articulated by Augustine in one of his letters to Jerome:

> Only to the books of the Scriptures, which are now referred to as canonical, have I learned to offer this respect and honour, as I most firmly believe that none of their authors have erred concerning anything in writing. And if in these

---

[7] Cf. B.A. Zuiddam, "Holy letters and syllables: The function and character of Biblical authority in the second century," *Dutch Reformed Theological J.* XXVIIII.3 (1997), 180-91; "Λόγιον in Biblical Literature and its implications for Christian Scholarship," *Acta Patristica et Byzantina* 19 (2008), 379-94; "Early orthodoxy: the Scriptures in Clement of Alexandria," *Acta Patristica et Byzantina* 21.2 (2010), 257-68. "New perspectives on Irenaeus: Scripture as oracular standard," *Ekklesiastikos Pharos* 93.2 (2011), 288-308.

[8] Cf. Thomas Aquinas, *Summa Theologiae*, 1.1.10: "Quia vero sensus litteralis est quem auctor intendit, auctor autem Sacrae Scripturae Deus est."

[9] Vatican II confirmed the validity of the traditional Christian view on Sacred Scripture and revelation (DV11), cf. *The Catechism of the Catholic Church*, St Pauls, Homebush 1994, 31. But at the same time Dei Verbum effectively created a legitimate position for those who questioned the propositional character of revelation. This was done by restricting the clause "without error," – which formerly applied to all contents of Scripture – to truth which "God wanted to put into sacred writings for the sake of salvation." See: Dogmatic Constitution on Divine Revelation, *Dei Verbum*, Paul VI (1965), chapter 3.5. Online: http://www.vatican.va/archive/hist_councils/ii_vatican_council/documents/vat-ii_const_19651118_dei-verbum_en.html. For the encouragement of private Scripture reading, cf. David Schultenover, *50 Years On: Probing the Riches of Vatican II,* Liturgical Press, Collegeville 2015, 370-80.

writings I stumble on anything which appears against the truth, I do not doubt that either the manuscript is faulty, or that the translator has not caught the meaning of what was said, or that I myself have failed to understand it.[10] (Author's translation)

To Augustine and the early fathers this meant that, unlike other religious books,[11] Scripture did not contain any errors, factually or doctrinally.

Today this view is considered untenable by mainstream theology.

---

[10] Augustinus, Epist. 82 ad Hier. 1.3: Solis eis Scripturarum libris, qui jam canonici appellantur, didici hunc timorem honoremque deferre, ut nullum eorum auctorem scribendo aliquid errasse firmissime credam. Ac si aliquid in eis offendero litteris, quod videatur contrarium veritati, nihil aliud, quam vel mendosum esse codicem, vel interpretem non assequutum esse quod dictum est, vel me minine intellexisse, non ambigam.

[11] Augustinus, Epist. 82 ad Hier. 1.3: Alios autem ita lego, ut quantalibet sanctitate doctrinaque praepolleant, non ideo verum putem, quia ipsa ita senserunt; sed quia mihi vel per illos auctores canonicos, vel per probabili ratione, quod a vero non abhorreat, persuadere potuerunt. Nec te, mi frater, sentire aliud existimo: prorsus, inquam non te arbitror sic legi tuos libros velle, tanquam Prophetarum, vel Apostolorum: de quorum Scriptis, quod omni errore careant, dubitare nefarium est. Absit hoc a pia humilitate et veraci de temetipso cogitatione; qua nisi esses praeditus non utique diceres ... [As to all other writings, in reading them, however great the superiority of the authors to myself in sanctity and learning, I do not accept their teaching as true on the mere ground of the opinion being held by them; but only because they have succeeded in convincing my judgment of its truth either by means of these canonical writings themselves, or by arguments addressed to my reason. I believe, my brother, that this is your own opinion as well as mine. I do not need to say that I do not suppose you to wish your books to be read like those of prophets or of apostles, concerning which it would be wrong to doubt that they are free from error. Far be such arrogance from that humble piety and just estimate of yourself which I know you to have, and without which assuredly you would not have said ...] (Transl. J.G. Cunningham, *Nicene and Post-Nicene Fathers,* First Series, Vol. 1, Master Christian Library, Albany 1997, 679.)

It is ridiculed by scientific celebrities and journalists alike.[12] Our times are not the first to evaluate tenets of traditional Christianity in this way. What we now know as the Catholic view of Holy Scripture, reliable propositional revelation, came under heavy fire in the days of Early Christianity, particularly from the second to the fourth century.

2. Christian propositional revelation ridiculed in the days of the Early Church

Greek scholars charged Christians with gullibly putting their trust in Jewish fables and unreliable Gospel accounts.[13] In the second century, Celsus published his *Real Truth about Christianity and its Teachings*,[14] while some time later Porphyry wrote a series of fifteen books *Against the Christians*.[15]

---

[12] For example, Richard Dawkins, *The God Delusion*, Transworld Publishers, 2006, 284: "Notwithstanding his somewhat dodgy family values, Jesus' ethical teachings were – at least by comparison with the ethical disaster area that is the Old Testament – admirable; but there are other teachings in the New Testament that no good person should support. I refer especially to the central doctrine of Christianity: that of 'atonement' for 'original sin.'"

[13] Cf. B.A. Zuiddam, "Old Critics and Modern Theology," *Dutch Reformed Theological Journal* XXXVI.2 (1995), 256–66.

[14] Henry Chadwick, *Origen: Contra Celsum*, Cambridge University Press, 1980. One century earlier, Th. Keim reconstructed Celsus' book on the basis of materials found with Origen: *Celsus' wahres Wort*, Orell, Zürich 1873. See also J.W. Hargis, *Against the Christians, the rise of early anti-Christian polemic*, Peter Lang, New York 1999. M. Borret, "Celsus: a pagan Perspective on Scripture," In: P.M. Blowers, ed., *The Bible in Greek Christian Antiquity*, UND Press, Notre Dame (Ind) 1997.

[15] Porphyry's criticism of the Scriptures was collected by Adolf von Harnack, *Porphyrius, "Gegen die Christen", 15 Bücher: Zeugnisse, Fragmente und Referate*, Abhandlungen der königlich prüssischen Akademie der Wissenschaften: Jahrgang 1916: philosoph.–hist. Klasse: Nr. 1, Berlin, 1916. Can also be found online at: archive.org/details/HarnackPorphyrius–GegenDieChristen. Porphyrian material is also found with the Church Father Macarius Magnes in his book *Apokritikos* (edn used Fougart, P., *Apokritikos*, Blondel, 1876). English readers

2.1 Moses and the Prophets

They devoted much of their attention to criticiseng the Scriptures. Celsus rejected Christianity's claims that Jesus was the fulfilment of a long tradition of prophecies. "[You Christians] quote prophets as foretelling facts about Jesus' life before they happened, ... but those prophecies could be much better applied to thousands of other people"[16] For Celsus the Old Testament contained many implausible stories, like the barbaric folktale about Lot and his daughters.[17] Jonah's adventures with the big fish were just preposterous fiction; as was Daniel and the lion's den.[18]

It was not by accident that the Greek scientists attacked the prophets Jonah and Daniel in particular. With Porphyry, assaults on Old Testament prophets function as attacks on Christ, because Jesus made direct comparisons between Himself and Jonah (Matt. 12:40).[19] He also saw some of Daniel's prophecies as things yet to be fulfilled (Matt. 24:15).[20]

---

are referred to the edition of Crafer, T.W., McMillan, London, 1919: www.tertullian.org/fathers/macarius_apocriticus.htm. R.J. Hoffmann published an updated translation in Porphyry's *Against the Christians: The Literary Remains*, Prometheus Books, 1994.

[16] Chadwick, op. cit., II.28.

[17] Ibid., IV.45. Cf R. Dawkins, resembles Porphyry's criticism, *The God Delusion*, 172: "If this dysfunctional family was the best Sodom had to offer by way of morals, some might begin to feel a certain sympathy with God and his judicial brimstone." In mainstream theology today the story is generally considered an aetiological myth, an unhistorical folktale to discredit the origin of the nation of the Ammonites. Cf. Van Seters, J., *Prologue to history: the Yahwist as historian in Genesis*, John Knox Press, 1992; Sutskover, T., "Lot and his Daughters (Gen. 19:30-38), further literary and stylistic Examinations," *Hebrew Scriptures* 11:1-11, 2011.

[18] Chadwick, op. cit.,VI.53.

[19] Matt. 12:40.

[20] Matt. 24:15.

Chapters 8-12 of Daniel contain a lot of information that points to a future arrival of the Messiah in the time of Jesus. For this reason Porphyry came up with the idea that the whole book of Daniel was really a fake, produced by a pseudo-graphic author in the second century BC, hundreds of years after Daniel died. It described contemporary events as alleged prophecies.

Hieronymus (better known as Jerome) preserved much of Porphyry's criticism in his Commentary on Daniel.[21] From his prologue:

> Porphyry wrote his twelfth book against the prophecy of Daniel, denying that it was composed by the person to whom it is ascribed in its title, but rather by some individual living in Judaea at the time of the Antiochus who was surnamed Epiphanes.

Today Porphyry's theory in some form is embraced by many, if not all prominent Old Testament scholars.[22] The technical device is called vaticinium ex eventu. This is Latin for a "prediction from the event". For instance, we say that Daniel prophesied about the "abomination that makes desolate" (Dan. 11:31;[23] 12:11[24]). But this

---

[21] Hieronymus, *Commentariorum in Danielem,* Pars I opera exegetica 5, Corpus Christianorum, Series Latina LXXV-A, Brepols, Turnhout 1964.

[22] For a detailed treatment, see: B.A. Zuiddam, "The shock factor of Divine Revelation: a philological approach to Daniel 8 and 9", *Scandinavian J. the Old Testament: An International J. Nordic Theology* 27(2): 247-67, 2013. Since the 1820's OT scholars (Bleek, Von Gall, Wellhausen, etc.) generally opt for a Maccabean date for Daniel, three centuries after its alleged authorship. A.E. Hill and J.H. Walton, *A Survey of the Old Testament,* Zondervan, Grand Rapids, MI, 571, 2009: "It seems that the presuppositional rejection of supernaturalism is often partly responsible for the rejection of a sixth-century date for the book."

[23] Dan. 11:31; Hieronymus, *Commentariorum in Danielem, De antichristo in Dan.xi:30-31,* 921. Jerome translates the end of verse 31 as "et dabunt abominationem et desolationem," but subsequently refers to it in his treatment of the text as "abominationem desolationis".

[24] Daniel 12:11; Hieronymus, *Commentariorum in Danielem, De antichristo in Dan.xii:11-12,* 942-4.

did not happen of course, it was in fact someone laying these words in Daniel's mouth hundreds of years later, when the sanctuary was actually defiled by a Syrian king. The words were only attributed to Daniel to lend them credibility. So Jesus was wrong: it wasn't Daniel and the abomination had already taken place, so it wasn't a prophecy for the future at all (see Hieronymus, Commentary on Matthew, 24:16).[25]

2.2 Life of Jesus: incarnation, passion, resurrection

After the Scriptures of the Old Testament, it was the life of Jesus that came under scrutiny. Celsus and Porphyry denied and discredited Jesus' incarnation, his teachings and his Passion & Resurrection.[26]

To start with Jesus' incarnation – Christ taking on the body of an unborn baby, this was shameful and preposterous in the eyes of the Greek scientists. It was not appropriate for a god to enter this world as a baby.[27] Celsus thought the idea of a conception without visible involvement of a man was borrowed from the Greek myth about the god Zeus changing himself into golden rain to impregnate one of the beauties he fancied.[28] (C.C.I.37). The Virgin Conception was

---

[25] Hieronymus, *Commentatiorum in Matheum 24:16 (Pars I, opera exegetica, corpus Christianorum, Series Latina)*, Brepols, Turnhout 1964, 226-7.

[26] Cf. Chtistopher Hitchens, *God is not great, how Religion poisons everything,* Allen & Unwin, New York 2007, 111: "However, he [Maimonides] fell into the same error as do the Christians, in assuming that the four Gospels were in any sense a historical record. Their multiple authors – none of whom published anything until many decades after the Crucifixion- cannot agree on anything of importance."

[27] The idea of shame culture in Greek antiquity is worked out in E.R. Dodds, *The Greeks and the Irrational*, University of California Press, Berkeley(CA) 2004, 26: "The application to conduct of the terms καλὸν and αἰσχρόν seems also to be typical of a shame-culture. These words denote, not that the act is beneficial or hurtful to the agent, or that it is right or wrong in the eyes of a deity, but that it looks 'handsome' or 'ugly' in the eyes of public opinion.

[28] Chadwick, op, cit., I.37.

just a cleverly devised tale to mask Jesus' illegitimate birth as the result of a liaison between Mary and a Roman soldier. "The mother of Jesus was rejected by the carpenter to whom she was engaged, because she was found guilty of fornication, and had a child of a certain soldier called Panthera" (C.C.I.32).[29]

Not surprisingly for these Neo-Platonist critics, some of the better elements of Jesus' teachings were dependent on Plato – for instance, Jesus' teachings on riches and the parable of the rich man and the needle (Matt. 19:24).[30] Plato taught that it is "impossible for an extraordinary good man to be extraordinarily wealthy" (C.C.VI.16).[31]

But as for Jesus' prophecies and the Gospel portraying him as someone who knew the future; [32]this was all invented by the disciples and Gospel authors. Of course Jesus did not know the future. This was just a tribute in hindsight by his followers, who wanted the world to think about Jesus as a prophet. "Because the disciples couldn't reconcile themselves to the facts, they made up this plan to say that He had known everything before".[33] No, this Jesus was profoundly unsuccessful, attracted low social class people from Galilee and never had a proper job or position in life (C.C.I.62), while his teachings were rejected by anyone who counted in society and religious life at the time.

That in his Passion Jesus took on Himself the sins of the world[34]

---

[29] Ibid., I.32. Apart from possible Roman army reference, *Panthera* translates as "predator of all".

[30] Matt. 19:24.

[31] Chadwick op. cit., VI.16.

[32] Matt. 17:22, 20:18.

[33] Chadwick, op. cit., II.15.

[34] Cf. R. Dawkins, *The God Delusion*, 284: "This teaching, which lies at the heart of New Testament theology, is almost as morally obnoxious as the story of Abraham setting out to barbecue Isaac, which it resembles – and that is

was just a way of his followers making sense of his disgraceful rejection by society. It was attributed and in the mind of the beholder, but the fact of the matter was that Jesus died a cruel and shameful death, and that his life wasn't a success story. Celsus showed himself a real psychologist in explaining away the Resurrection of Jesus. This was a story invented by his disciples, who suffered from severe grief and hallucinations, finding it extremely hard to come to terms with the death of their master.[35] Yes, they may have experienced profound spiritual impressions, but this should not be regarded real in any scientific sense.[36]

For Porphyry the Resurrection stories were part of a cover up. It was easy to allege that Jesus appeared to an inner circle of followers. As these followers of Jesus were biased, who was to say this really happened? If Jesus had really come back from the dead, he should have appeared to Pilate and the Jewish leaders.[37]

2.3 Apostles discredited

Both Celsus and Porphyry went to great length to discredit the Apostles and their teachings. Much of what they wrote in this regard comes under the header "character assassination". Matthew was completely negligent in leaving his responsible job as tax collector on the spot, to follow Jesus.[38] The Apostles were unlearned men,

---

no accident". After firmly rejecting the OT idea of original sin as ridiculous, Dawkins continues to describe the Christian doctrine of atonement, 285: "New Testament theology adds a new injustice, topped off by a new sadomasochism whose viciousness even the Old Testament barely exceeds."

[35] Chadwick, op. cit., II.55.

[36] Ibid., II.61.

[37] Porphyry, *Apokritikos* II.14.

[38] Matt. 9:9. Celsus regarded their master as "a pestilent fellow who told great lies and was guilty of profane acts ... Jesus collected around him a group of tax collectors and boatmen, wicked men, from the lowest level of society", see S. Benko, *Pagan Rome and the early Christians,* Indiana University Press, Bloomington (Ind) 1986, 150.

not even able to recognise normal astronomical phenomena like a sun eclipse.[39] Otherwise the Apostles did not really know their Scriptures properly;: amongst other mistakes, they misapplied prophecies to make them refer to Jesus.

They also wrongly ascribed quotes.[40] As with Jesus' alleged prophetic giftedness, there is a huge difference between what His followers wrote down and what really happened. The book of Acts is a misleading account. The Apostle Peter actually murdered Ananias and his wife Sapphira for their money.[41]

The Apostles' expectancy of a bodily resurrection after this life, also evident from early versions of the Apostles Creed,[42] was incompatible with the worldview of the Greek science of the day. Porphyry said in so many words that this was a ridiculous and unwarranted expectation. To illustrate this, he gives the example of someone who drowns, is eaten by fish, which are, in their turn, consumed by fishermen. These men ultimately die a violent death themselves and are eaten by dogs or wolves, which, in their turn, are devoured by vultures. How can the original body be resurrected as it was part of so many different bodies, Porphyry sneered.[43]

Conclusion

This paper concerned itself with the question: Is the Catholic view on propositional revelation and the Sacred Scriptures a valid one?

---

[39] Matt. 27:45; Hieronymus, *Commentatiorum in Matheum,* 273-4.

[40] Porphyry, op. cit., III.33, cf. Hieronymus "On the beginning of Mark".

[41] Ibid., 3.21, cf. Hieronymus, Ep. 130 ad Demitrius.

[42] For example,, Symbolum Romanum: credo carnis resurrectionem (Rufinus of Aquileia); Πιστευω σαρκος αναστασιν, ζωην αιωνιον (Marcellus of Ancyra); credo in carnis resurrectionem et vitam aeternam (Melchior). Cf. Nicea: Προσδοκῶ ἀνάστασιν νεκρῶν, καὶ ζωὴν τοῦ μέλλοντος αἰῶνος.

[43] Porphyry op. cit., 4.24.

Until roughly 1789 both the Roman Catholic and Protestant branch of Western Christianity united on this issue: "Of course it is!" The acceptance of reliable propositional revelation was a core building block of Western civilisation, foundational for the communio sanctorum. In the words of Christopher Dawson: "Christianity can never ignore history because the Christian revelation is essentially historical and the truths of faith are inseparably connected with historical events."

However, worldview and theology have dramatically changed since. Some might say that Western civilisation has collapsed with the decline of faith in propositional revelation. The theological paradigm has shifted in favour of Celsus and Porphyry: Scripture is riddled with error, possibly only relevant for some moral and metaphysical issues. For the more radical exponents of the Brave New World[44] there almost certainly is no God, not one who makes any practical difference in this world anyway. For the controlling forces of the new paradigm there used to be something like God and an infallible Holy Bible, but only in the minds of the people at the time. And if the new Savages emerging from the remnants of Western Civilisation dare ask: "Why don't you give them these books about God?" The dismissive answer is "For the same reason as we don't give them Othello: they're old; they're about God hundreds of years ago. Not about God now."[45]

---

[44] Cf. D.G. Izzo & K. Kirkpatrick, *Huxley's Brave New World: Essays*, McFarland, Jefferson 2008, 36: "It must stand as an extraordinary coincidence that the religious ceremonies in *Brave New World* employ much of the same vocabulary used by Freud to describe a theory propounded by one of his correspondents (who turned out to be none other than the French writer Romain Rolland): I had sent him my small book that treats religion as an illusion and he answered that he entirely agreed with my judgment upon religion ... The quasi-spiritual rituals of "atonement" in *Brave New World* rely heavily on imagery very close to Freud's here.

[45] Aldous Huxley, *Brave New World*, Vintage, 2007, 157-8.

This brave new world is with us presently. Etsi deus non daretur[46] has become the general principle at all levels of education.

> "Imagine there's no heaven; It's easy if you try
> No hell below us; Above us only sky ..."[47]

Should orthodox Christians surrender to this new paradigm? And be satisfied with a private God illusion for personal purposes? Perhaps compromise with the new paradigm to prevent the ark of Scripture from falling,[48] as one seeks to improve the Church's standing and credibility? I suggest not.

If Celsus and Porphyry were essentially right, then one should opt the honourable way out, and admit that the Church has been following cleverly devised fables[49] for most of its existence.

But if early Christianity was right in its claim that it wasn't, there remains an obligation to the communio sanctorum. If the saints who from their labours rest faced similar rough weather and did not abandon ship, but decided to trust God's revelation and subsequently survived intellectually, then perhaps we should stay on board as well, in faith, serving God with all our mind.[50] As St Paul said: "Guard the good treasure entrusted to you, with the help of the Holy Spirit living in us".[51]

Bonum depositum custodi per Spiritum Sanctum.[52]

---

[46] *Etsi deus non daretur* points to the principle which explain everything from the premise that there is no God. What was considered an exceptional exercise (etsi: even if) has become commonplace and taken on its present meaning.

[47] John Lennon, *Imagine*, from the album *Imagine*, released 11 October 1971, recorded May-June 1971 at Ascot Sound Studios, Ascot Record Plant East, New York.

[48] 2 Samuel 6:1-7; 1 Chronicles 13:9-12.

[49] Cf. 2 Peter 1:16.

[50] Cf. Deuteronomy 6:5; Matthew 22:37.

[51] NRSV, 2 Tim 1:14.

[52] 2Timothy 1:14, Vulgata Clementina.

Colloquium 2016

The Nature of Men and Women – Complementary but Different

Edited by David Daintree

INTRODUCTION TO COLLOQUIUM 2016

David Daintree

That there are fundamental differences between men and women with regard to their physical, as well as emotional and spiritual, characteristics we regard as axiomatic. Yet the dominant mind-set in contemporary society tends to deny or at least underestimate the force of such differences. One of the features of dumbed-down popular controversy is radical oversimplification.

Our 2016 colloquium demanded a higher standard of analysis and sought to explore more deeply and unpack the real and fundamental differences between the sexes, which make them uniquely complementary. This purpose was pursued from the perspective of several key disciplines, including anthropology, family therapy, literature, medicine, philosophy, psychology, religions, sociology and theology.

The Dawson Centre Committee decided on the topic in the preceding year, 2015, when it was becoming clear that the nation was likely to face a choice on whether or not to enshrine same-sex marriage in law. It was also our opinion that the case for the negative was underrepresented in most of the media, and that the level of public debate – on both sides, it should be said – was for the most part shallow and superficial.

Those in favour said it was "all about love" – a very cogent argument at first glance. Those against said it was more about custom and tradition. Theology, Philosophy and Sociology rarely came into the discussion at a popular level, and of course at the popular level the vote will be taken. We felt duty-bound to try to raise the level of the debate.

Most of our speakers (though certainly not all) are strongly in favour of preserving the status quo. And where's the harm in that, when the 'yes' case is being so strongly pushed in the public arena and the label 'homophobic' is being unjustly applied, as a form of abuse, to those who take a different view?

We are in favour of raising the level of debate. Plato put in the mouth of Socrates –

ὁ ... ἀνεξέταστος βίος οὐ βιωτὸς ἀνθρώπῳ

"for human being life is not worth living if it is unexamined".

1

HETEROSEXUALITY AND HUMAN IDENTITY

Shimon Cowen

ABSTRACT

This paper explores from a general theological perspective the concept of the whole human being as one which has its foundation in a committed sexual union (marriage) with a person of the opposite sex. It is explained how, through this relationship one becomes a whole human being, in that one's own being can be completed through the other, by virtue of the complementarity of the sexes. This involves an understanding, in spiritual and material terms, of the distinct character of masculinity and femininity, and how they function as complementaries. The converse, that sexual union with a person of the same sex inhibits and disturbs the stability and wholeness of the individual, is also explored. Whilst this is a contentious issue, it cannot be avoided, especially as it has been made the subject of a national debate. Participation in a heterosexual union is also vital to personal identity through time, the continuity of one's past, present and future through the unique procreative character of the heterosexual union. This too is disturbed by the artificial reproduction requisite for the simulation of reproduction in a same sex union. Finally the union of male and female, as this grants wholeness to the individual, specifically replicates analogous complementary dimensions of the Divine, confirming the human in the imitation of the Divine.

Heterosexuality and (pro)creation

This essay starts from the standpoint of the millennia-long biblical tradition, that the human being was created "in the image of G-d". What this means is that the human soul (which is what was made "in the image of G-d") resonates with Divinely instructed universal ethical principles. This spiritual endowment also makes the human the free and responsible agent of the implementation of the Divine purpose in Creation – namely, to refine the world through a life lived by these ethical principles. Heterosexual unions are alone permitted by this Divine ethics.

Human "heterosexuality" – that is to say, the complementary union of male and female, or masculine and feminine, with its procreative potential – has a metaphorical analogue in the Divine. Religious tradition[1] teaches that G-d Himself employs two kinds of powers to enliven and sustain the creation. One is a transcendental power which enlivens the creation into being in each moment from nothingness (ex nihilo). The second is an immanent, delimiting Divine power which contains and articulates the transcendent G-dly life force in a way that delineates the manifold particularity of creation, and gives each detail its measured vitality. In the mystical tradition these are metaphorically denoted as "masculine" (transcendent) and "feminine" (immanent) powers of G-d.

Human heterosexual reproduction parallels the Divine instruments of creation. The man provides the seed, the "transcendent" possibility, so to speak, of the child. The mother differentiates and articulates the fertilised ovum "immanently" within the womb into a whole human being with its multitude of distinct faculties. So too, after birth, the masculine/feminine division of labour contin-

---

[1] This concept is elaborated at length in the work, *The Gate of Unity and Belief*, by Rabbi Schneur Zalman of Liadi. This work is in fact the second part of his comprehensive work, *Tanya*.

ues: in the nurture of the child, the father is the more remote and abstract sustainer or provider, whilst the mother is the closer and more specific nurturer of the child.[2] Later, in the character- and moral-education of the child, the father models the abstract authority of ethical values, whilst the mother imparts these values with a warmth and application more specifically tuned to the temperament and developmental stage of the individual child. Thus, whether in procreative, nurturing or educative capacities, father and mother combine their distinct masculine and feminine characteristics, in a manner imitative of the Divine in Its complementary "transcendent" and "immanent" powers.[3]

These normative roles of masculinity and femininity are assigned by the Creator to the biological male and female respectively. If, in specific individual cases, physical, psychological or cultural factors have disturbed these potentials of masculinity and femininity in men and women, these are grounds, not for the rejection of these potentials, but for the attempt at their recovery. Homosexual behaviour is not within the Divine law or plan. The homosexual couple cannot themselves procreate, they cannot provide the complementary masculine and feminine dimensions of the nurture and education of the child and even as a unit in itself has a greater inherent instability.[4]

---

[2] Even though the balances in the roles of providing, nurturing and educating supplied by mother and father may change under social and economic conditions, this does not alter the fact of the endowment of father and mother with these unique – distinct and complementary – roles vis-a-vis the child, the value of which should not be lost.

[3] The analogy between "masculine" and "feminine" in the Divine creative powers and in the human procreative unit is not a strict or total one. The engendering role of the father in procreation is not *ex nihilo* – unlike G-d's transcendent engendering power – but from the father's seed.

[4] Male homosexual unions tend to foster promiscuity. The reason for this is that amongst the negative potentials within the male is a stronger promiscuity, and it is the female, which can domesticate and anchor that promiscuity.

Heterosexual procreation and identity: the psychic nexus

A homosexual couple cannot have a child which they can recognise as biologically fully their own. The artificial reproductive techniques upon which they are call use donor gametes (one or both). The child thus "commissioned" conversely also cannot recognise itself as fully biologically their child. Procreation within a heterosexual married unit, on the other hand, does produce a child which they know as wholly theirs, and a child which knows and is raised by its own parents. What difference does this make, if the homosexual loves and rears the commissioned child as best s/he can?

The Bible relates in Genesis:[5] "Therefore a man shall leave his father and mother and cleave to his wife and they shall become one flesh". The "one flesh" which two people, a man and woman, become is their child. This says something very important about identity. The biological parents see their union in their child. That is what they become. Reciprocally, the child understands itself as the product of the union of these people, its parents. The parents know themselves in their child and the child knows itself in its parents.

Consequently, when two males get together in a sexual relationship, there is a significant risk that promiscuity rather than being anchored and contained, can be compounded. The same thing happens in a significant number of lesbian relationships. Amongst the negative potentials of the female is a strong possessiveness, which can be balanced and alleviated by the relative detachedness on the part of the male. In lesbian relationships there is a very high incidence of domestic violence and sexual abuse and this is arguably a case of compounded possessiveness. The same-polarity in both male and female homosexual relationships produces high instability, in contrast with balanced complementarity of male and female. Masculine and feminine cohere optimally within the "whole" married human being as the union of man and wife, as do their counterparts, as powers of G-d, in the spiritual macrocosm. Where homosexual "marriage" has been enacted, the rate of its breakup is higher than amongst heterosexual married couples. See S.D. Cowen, *Homosexuality, Marriage and Society*, Ballarat: Connor Court, 2015, ch. 3.

[5] 2:24.

On this biblical verse – which refers to the becoming one of father and mother in their child – a commentator[6] asks, why this is stated specifically with regard to the human being? Is it not true also of animals – that male and a female mate and from this comes the one flesh of their offspring? The answer he gives points to a subjective and psychological difference. The relationship of parent and offspring ceases to matter to animals beyond the initial phase of nurture. Parent and offspring walk away from each other – at least subjectively and psychologically – forever. With the human being, however, the relationship – the lineage and linkage – of parent and child continues to matter subjectively and psychologically to parent and child, beyond the end of nurture and rearing. Why is this so, psychological terms?

Procreation is the story of a human being's identity through time. My parents, from whose procreation I come, are my past. My relationship (my home) with my spouse (of the opposite sex, with whom I joined to procreate) is my present. My children, which result from my and my spouse's procreation, are my future. The lineage of generations is "my history" through time. The human psyche can grasp this sense of time – or personal history – as an important dimension of one's being.

Now, people in fact do adopt and raise with much love children who are not their biological children. If for some reason, a child cannot or will not be raised by its biological parents, it is certainly meritorious that others step in to care for the child. But this is of value, after the event that a child can or will not be raised by its own parents. It is not a situation, which should be set up in the first instance. Indeed to create children for adoption – to create orphans – as artificial, donor and surrogate reproduction does for homosexual couples does, denies children their full identity: their

---

[6] The commentary *Gur Aryeh* on Genesis 2:24.

psychophysical lineage, with all the deep attachments, to the generations which constitute that lineage.[7] The loss is a deep one. To adopt an orphan is a good deed; to create an orphan is not.

Heterosexual procreation and identity: the spiritual nexus

Still the question arises of a yet deeper basis of the continuity of personal identity through and between biological generations – between grandparents, parents and grandchildren – when each of these generations are discrete bodies. If it doesn't matter to animals, who their parents and offspring are – for after all they are temporally and spatially discrete bodies – why should it matter psychologically to humans? What is this continuous intergenerational identity in humans made of, apart from the sense of time and personal history which humans psychologically have?

As the possessor of knowledge of the Divine and a Divinely sanctioned morality, and as the free moral agent in creation, the human being is entrusted not only to carry out the ethical refinement of the world but also to create further human beings – children – who will continue that task after, and in addition to, them. To this end, there is a need for children not only to be born but also to be nurtured and educated in that moral code and mission. Human reproduction is not simply physical; it is also the generation of offspring as spiritual-ethical agents.

Humanity is thus generally bidden to have children, though there is no obligation upon each and every member of humanity

---

[7] Married heterosexual couples also sometimes use donor gametes in their own IVF procedures. This too raises similar ethical objections. The movement "Tangled Webs" which treats the identity difficulties of children born from donor gametes is well documented in Alana S. Newman, *The Anonymous Us Project: A Story-Collective on 3rd Party Reproduction*, NY: Broadway Publications, 2013.

to procreate.[8] There are also those who marry but are unable to have children, notwithstanding their desire to do so. Indeed, even without bearing children, individuals can carry out a certain kind of spiritual reproduction. Our tradition tells us that "one who teaches his fellow's son [the principles of an ethical life] is considered as having borne him". Our good deeds are also reckoned as "offspring": "The offspring of the righteous are their good deeds". Indeed there have been very great human beings, with immense spiritual legacies, who had no physical children. But we are here speaking of spiritual reproduction through actual children: where children are born, why is it of spiritual importance that the generations be raised by their own biological parents?

In probing the spiritual content of the nexus of biological generations, it cannot be the souls themselves, for people of different generations and in different bodies have different souls. The answer must be that the spiritual "glue" of generations is the common spiritual-ethical legacy – the transmission and continuation of an ethical mission – for which and in which spiritually parents bore, nurtured and educated their children. This is a spiritual "relay" or transmission which travels through the nexus and conduit of biological procreation, nurture and education of the generations.

A famous saying of religious tradition illustrates this: "If one's offspring are alive [that is to say, are active in continuing the moral tradition they received from their parents], so is one [the parent, after one's physical passing considered to be] alive". The essential need and entitlement of children to know and be bound up with their parents (and conversely, the desire of parents for children) is connected with the extension of the common spiritual-ethical life legacy and mission which was the raison d'etre of their procreation. Whether, in fact, parents themselves – or for that matter, the

---

[8] See S.D. Cowen, *The Theory and Practice of Universal Ethics – the Noahide Laws*, NY: Institute for Judaism and Civilization, 2014, 232-4.

children – live up to that mission and legacy in their own lives, it is the enduring, redeemable potential and purpose for which there are successive, begotten generations.

Conclusion

In summary, the continuity of identity between biological generations as extensions of one another backwards and forwards in time is both psychophysical and spiritual. The parent needs the child and the child needs its parents for their own identities. And since the biological matrix of the procreation of the generations is built on heterosexuality, heterosexuality is built into human identity.

What then of persons who experience same-sex attraction? As discussed in my book, *Homosexuality, Marriage and Society*, the sources of homosexual attraction can be temperamental, psychological and cultural. But in all cases, these sources are extraneous to the essential person, the soul, made in the image of G-d, which (however unconscious) knows that homosexuality is not normative and has (whether alone or with the counsel and compassionate help of others) the ability to withstand or transform homosexual impulse. What of persons with hermaphroditism (or "intersex", a mixture of male and female genitalia)? To such persons, who can in no way help their situation, G-d has also commanded laws: the hermaphrodite can serve G-d within the matrix of possibilities granted it by G-d.[9] The individual who feels driven to identify with a gender, other than his or her own biological gender (the "transgender"), will work to overcome that "drive" and will desist from surgical sexual re-assignment,[10] and

---

[9] In universal – Noahide – law, a hermaphrodite is permitted to marry a woman, but not a man.

[10] It is not permissible by biblical law to seek to transition to another sex, since this is in the category of "wounding oneself" and in any case does not change ones born biological status.

strive to carry out his or her Divine imperative and potential as the male or female he or she was biologically born. None of these conditions, challenging and difficult as they may be, can alter the Divine moral normativity of heterosexuality.

Let us say more than this. These people, with all their difficulties, had mothers and fathers. I once heard a homosexual say, "I had my own mother and father, and would not take that away from anyone". Let us pray that these people will, by their efforts and if necessary the help of others, and with G-d's help, themselves also become mothers and fathers, within the procreative bond of heterosexual marriage; that just as they possess a history out of the heterosexual biological matrix, so too they shall have a future out of the same matrix, in children who are wholly – psychophysically and spiritually – their own.

2

CANONICAL CHALLENGES TO CHRISTIAN ANTHROPOLOGY IN TODAY'S WORLD

Mark Podesta

ABSTRACT

The Catholic Church's Code of Canon Law was promulgated in 1983. A revision of the 1917 Code, it was written in the Spirit of Vatican II, addressing social and cultural issues of the time. More than 40 years later, societal and cultural values are changing at a rapid pace, and attempts are being made by Pastors to apply the Code of Canon law to unforeseen pastoral situations. Same sex marriage, adoption, and gender dysmorphia are becoming increasingly acceptable by society. The objective truth of Christian anthropology and the natural meaning of marriage are been challenged by an increasingly tolerant society, media seeking to bring about acceptance, and rapidly changing civil legislation. This paper simply seeks to consider the truths of the faith in a world becoming rapidly hostile, and the lacunae in Canon Law that might need to be addressed, in order that the Church may effectively respond to the challenges of pastoral ministry today, while continuing to be a faithful witness to God's plan in the world.

* * * * *

Marriage Equality and gender-fluidity are major contemporary moral issues. Sexuality and gender are arguably the most important moral issues of our time. Today's contemporary secular beliefs extol the rights of the homosexual person, demanding the same rights to heterosexual couples relating to such areas as marriage and adoption. Twenty years ago, gay-rights groups were known to resist the notion of "gay marriage", seeing the institution of marriage as a patriarchal, heterosexual paradigm, against which some sought to fight. Today, the gay lobby engages in a quest for equality, and the nature of the conversation has changed.

The Church's understanding of homosexuality is obviously incongruous with the contemporary demand for equal recognition of same-sex unions under the title of marriage. Amongst others, Pope Francis has done much to emphasise the dignity and value of the homosexual person. Leaders in the Church need to strive to understand these issues through the eyes of God's intention for humanity.

All human beings long to love and be loved. This longing is imprinted on one's very being; each is created as a being who seeks completion in another. The love one truly longs for is the love of God, satisfied in this life here on earth by unifying with another human being. One of the major problems of the debate today is the loss of literacy of what it is to be a human person. The masses have lost sight of God's plan for humanity; instead humanity seeks freedom: a freedom to choose; a freedom to live one's life as one chooses, or as one is compelled. Freedom: if there is one word that might encapsulate the spirit of the Western world today, freedom would fit the bill. Freedom is a concept which is misunderstood by so many. Freedom is often misunderstood to mean the ability to do what one wants, with no regard for any concept of a natural order – of that which God intended.

As an enlightened and modern society, our world has been deeply infected by Relativism. Pope Benedict XVI strove to address the dangers of Relativism. The thinking is familiar: "As long as I am not hurting anyone else, then I should be able to do what

I want". This line is pursued by the mainstream media and the broadcasting industry, slowly forming the minds of the masses. In the early 1990s, there was a television show that was quite popular, produced in the USA: *Murphy Brown*. It followed the life of a successful single female journalist, after whom the show was named. At that time – the early 1990s – the story line saw the lead character have a baby out of wedlock. This caused an absolute uproar. It was seen as an attack on decency, and "the thin edge of the wedge": fancy portraying a mother having a child out of wedlock! This uproar went right up to the White House, where the Vice President at the time condemned the story line. Now, fast forward some 30 years. The show *Modern Family* presents the reality of the many ways families are composed today, including the inclusion of a same-sex couple raising a child. *Days of Our Lives* recently portrayed a same sex marriage of two young men as a central part of its story line, uniting two dynasties. *The Bold and the Beautiful* has a story line where a man has transitioned into a woman and married the heir to the fortunes of the lead family in the soap opera. These are not side-stories – they are central plots to the shows. Then there are prominent, popular and successful gay celebrities such as Ellen Degeneres, who have achieved much for the homosexual community – acceptance, tolerance, and indeed celebration. Now, of course, same-sex marriage is a reality in the USA, and Australia narrowly avoided the prospect of a plebiscite to inform elected politicians of the mood of the people. Remember, only 30 years ago, there was uproar over a story line wherein a woman had a child out of wedlock. The world has changed so much in such a short period of time. It is less of the case of bracket-creep, and more of the case of bracket-leap!

Returning to the concept of freedom, an often-used example is that of the pianist. Consider someone who cannot play the piano. If that person approaches a piano, sits down, and begins to hit the keys, the piano will make a sound. But it will sound terrible! As an individual, the untrained player has the freedom to hit whichever keys are preferred, but it doesn't make music. However, if that same person were to submit himself or herself to years of diligent lessons, he or she would come to understand the rules surrounding which tones sound assonant when played together, and which tones sound dissonant when played together. He or she would understand the rules of playing the piano, and would become a proficient pianist. Ironically, his or her ability to be truly free to make beautiful music would be based upon an understanding of music and a restriction of which keys he or she could hit at any given moment. That restriction would lead to true freedom. Such an irony! Rules providing freedom!

Freedom and the quest for individual rights – at all costs – can be seen in the Constitution of the United States of America. The world is incredibly influenced by the USA, whether in a financial setting or a moral setting. There's the old saying, when America sneezes, Australia catches a cold. But many Australians are not aware that the Constitution of the Commonwealth of Australia is very different to the Constitution of the United States of America, a country which prides itself on being "the land of the free". The Constitution of the United States of America starts with the rights of the individual, upon which the nation is built. On the other hand, the Constitution of the Commonwealth of Australia does not start with the rights of individuals, rather, it speaks of what Australia is as a nation, and the powers it has to interact with the community: "Whereas America is a state built on the aspirations of individuals with inalienable rights, in Australia the state is the institutional embodiment of sovereignty and power. It exists to preserve community life in a manner that is consonant with personal dignity and individual freedom. This intent, in part, explains the limited explicit freedoms found in the Australian Constitution and its concern, in places, to restrain

Commonwealth power".[1] The Australian Constitution does not begin with a consideration of individuals and their rights. Contrary to common belief, the Australian Constitution does not protect the right to free speech, or any other such rights. Upon reading the Constitution, one will not see any references to freedom of speech. But that doesn't mean that citizens do not have this right. The Australian Constitution considers the citizens of this country as a whole, and it defines the role that the state has in its interaction with its people. Interestingly, the Australian Constitution does not afford the State a freedom from religious interference. On the contrary, Article 116 ensures that religion will be free from interference of the State! This is misunderstood by most, when speaking of the separation of Church and State. The Australian Constitution starts with the protection of the rights of the community, not the rights of individuals. Our Constitution is very different from the Constitution of the USA. This is perhaps why mateship, altruism and a fair go are considered to be the essence of the Australian spirit.

Australia, as much of the Western world, has been infected by this misunderstood pursuit of individual freedom. It is a misunderstanding of the very concept of freedom. It is this misunderstanding of freedom – freedom at all costs – that leads to the American obsession with the right to bear arms. Ironically, it is this right that enabled, at least in part, hate crimes such as the tragic massacre in Orlando, Florida, in early 2016, where 49 people were gunned down as they were gathered together to celebrate their freedom in a gay nightclub. This was a massacre of free individuals that was enabled by one man's right to bear arms. Individual rights need to be balanced with the good of society. The right to freedom needs to be understood in tandem with duties or responsibilities. Today we speak so much of rights but very little of responsibilities. Each person has the responsibility, as a part of God's plan, to see

---

[1] Thomas R. Frame, *Church and State: Australia's Imaginary Wall,* 52-3.

that God's plan is fulfilled in the world. It is only when we have a proper understanding of freedom that one can approach these contemporary debates surrounding sexuality, gender, and rights.

The Catholic Church teaches that:

> God, by his infinite wisdom and love, brings into existence all of reality as a reflection of his goodness. He fashions mankind, male and female, in his own image and likeness. Human beings, therefore, are nothing less than the work of God himself; and in the complementarity of the sexes, they are called to reflect the inner unity of the Creator. They do this in a striking way in their cooperation with him in the transmission of life by a mutual donation of the self to the other.[2]

The Church's teaching on sexuality is fundamentally wound up in the Creation story in the Book of Genesis. Man and woman are created, not equal to each other, but complementary to one another. This is not a discussion of the dignity of the human person: man and woman are created in the image and likeness of God, and thus possess an inherent equality of dignity. Rather, we speak here of a difference in being; a complementarity. Each is created for the other: "a human person is not a sexually undifferentiated entity. On this understanding, a human person is a sexual being ... all of us are either male or female persons, two equal but sexually differentiated and complementary 'words' or images of the Triune God who is asexual".[3]

So we can see that in the coming together of a man and a woman, the two who are sexed (literally 'cut' or 'divided' or 'separated') become one whole just as God is complete. As such, one's sex is not to be dismissed as irrelevant; it is not just a characteristic of

---

[2] *Pastoral Care of Homosexual Persons*, §6.

[3] William E. May, *Sex, Marriage and Chastity* (Chicago: Franciscan Herald Press, 1981), 9.

who we are, like our hair or eye colour, or our height; our sex is a crucial, fundamental part of who we are: "being male or female is not something merely biological. It is not merely biological precisely because the body of a human person is not an instrument or tool of the person, something other than the person, but is rather constitutive of the being of the person and an expression or revelation of the person".[4] Popular culture often proposes that we are spirits trapped in fleshly bodies, and that when we die, we will be free from our bodies – our earthly prisons – and be as free as birds or angels. This is a misunderstanding of the human person. The body and soul are inextricably linked. It is because sex is such a fundamental part of the human person, that one's sex governs the ways in which people interact with one another:

> Sexuality affects all aspects of the human person in the unity of his body and soul. It especially concerns affectivity, the capacity to love and to procreate, and in a more general way the aptitude for forming bonds of communion with others.[5]

Sex plays an important part in the very being of one's existence. To be man is to lack all that it is to be woman; to be woman is to lack all that it is to be man. Men and women have been created in a way that is complementary to one another; when the two combine, the unity provides all that was lacking before. When man and woman combine, the two become one flesh, and are made complete, just as God is complete in Godself. God lacks nothing, it is the human race consisting of 'sexed' beings that is lacking and seeks completion. This is what Pope Saint John Paul II referred to as the Nuptial meaning of the Body.

The primary reason why a man and a woman come together in

---

[4] Ibid., 9.
[5] *Catechism of the Catholic Church*, §2332.

the sexual act, according to God's plan for creation, is to participate in God's creation, by procreating. If the purpose for man and woman coming together in the sexual act is to participate in God's design, then according to Church teaching, the natural extension of this is that to not participate in God's design is flawed; any other form of sexual union would be regarded as unnatural:

> … the church teaches that genital sex acts must be open to the potential for procreation, that procreation is a fundamental, God-given purpose of sexual intercourse, and that any sexual genital expression that excludes the possibility of procreation is unnatural.[6]

This is not limited to homosexual acts, but all sexual acts outside of marriage, including sex before marriage between heterosexual persons. The Catholic Church is not singling out homosexuals. It is evident that Pope Francis has made an effort to reach out to all people. The Catholic Church understands that sex is a gift – a right, and a responsibility – between a man and a woman, in the covenant of marriage, and not outside of it. It teaches: "To choose someone of the same sex for one's sexual activity is to annul the rich symbolism and meaning, not to mention the goals, of the Creator's sexual design. Homosexual activity is not a complementary union, able to transmit life".[7]

The Catholic Church does not teach that to be homosexual is sinful in itself. Rather than being sinful, the Catholic Church considers homosexuality to be a disorder: "Although the particular inclination of the homosexual person is not a sin, it is a more or less strong tendency ordered toward an intrinsic moral evil; thus the inclination itself must be seen as an objective disorder".[8] It is

---

[6] Thomas C. Fox, *Sexuality and Catholicism* (New York: George Braziller, 1995), 134.

[7] *Pastoral Care of Homosexual Persons*, §7.

[8] Ibid., §3.

considered to be a disorder because it is not understood to be in line with the natural order of the complementarity of man and woman. The church does not teach that being homosexual is sinful. Sin is understood to be an act, not a way of being. It teaches that "sin must involve a personal choice and where choice is absent, there can be no sin. Whether the product of inborn characteristics or environment or both, many people believe it is no longer reasonable to see homosexuality, when considered an orientation, as a moral failing".[9] For the Catholic Church, to be homosexual is not sinful; to participate in homosexual acts, or indeed any act outside of marriage, is sinful. The *Catechism of the Catholic Church* says,

> … homosexual acts are intrinsically disordered. They are contrary to the natural law. They close the sexual act to the gift of life. They do not proceed from a genuine affective and sexual complementarity. Under no circumstances can they be approved.[10]

For the Church, homosexuality is a disorder, but not sinful in itself.

The Church asks homosexuals to grow in their awareness of the created order of the world, and the will of God in reserving sexual union to the married state. For the Catholic Church, by being chaste, homosexuals can fully participate in the life of the Church: "they dedicate their lives to understanding the nature of God's personal call to them, they will be able to celebrate the Sacrament of Penance more faithfully and receive the Lord's grace so freely offered there in order to convert their lives more fully to his Way".[11] Every person is called to personal sanctification: "Homosexual persons

---

[9] Fox, op. cit., 131.

[10] *Catechism of the Catholic Church*, §2357.

[11] *Pastoral Care of Homosexual Persons*, §12.

are called to chastity. By the virtues of self-mastery that teach them inner freedom, at times by the support of disinterested friendship, by prayer and sacramental grace, they can and should gradually and resolutely approach Christian perfection".[12] The duty of seeking personal sanctification is not a simple task. Usually, it is easier to simply go with the flow and give in to one's desires. But humans are not simply animals, enslaved by passions. Humans are rational, and can overcome passions. Humans are weak, and often opt for the path of least resistance, or in this case, the path of greatest pleasure. We often hear statements such as: "Everyone wants to love and be loved"; "Why can heterosexuals have their love recognised by the State (and the Church), but homosexual couples cannot?"; "Isn't marriage a right, to be afforded to all?" These statements make a great deal of traction in the community, and on the surface, make sense. The Church teaches that all people, created in God's likeness, are called to perfection. Each person is called to grow in holiness:

> ... a life of chaste celibacy may be the answer. Proposing such a life may seem very far-fetched to someone who has made homosexual behaviour an integral part of life adjustment. But many people who have made heterosexual acts part of their life adjustment have learned to live without genital sexuality, as in the case of widows, divorced persons, and those who have entered religious life after living as adults with no commitment to celibacy or chastity.[13]

Each person makes choices in life, and some of these choices are particularly difficult. Some challenges seem insurmountable. The least the Church can do is offer understanding, encouragement and guidance, rather than hatred, bigotry and misunderstanding.

---

[12] *Catechism of the Catholic Church*, §2359.
[13] Benedict J. Groeschel OFM Cap, *The Courage to be Chaste* (Mahwah: Paulist Press, 1985), 52.

Every person shares the journey of life with every person, and many struggles are shared.

Changes in civil or secular law, recognising same-sex marriage, adoption, and gender-fluidity, will demand a Christian response. This is of particular interest and concern to canon lawyers, who seek to respond to the challenges of today's world in a fashion that is authentic to the teaching of the Church. Consider two men who marry each other and adopt a child, who then present their child for baptism into the Catholic Church. Canon Law prohibits a pastor from refusing the baptism of a child unless there is no chance of a Christian upbringing. Does their pastor refuse to baptise the child? If he goes ahead and agrees to the child's baptism, does he record both men as the parents of the child in his baptismal register? Does he regard both men as parents on the child's school enrolment form? As a representative of the church, if he accepts the reality of their union, does that mean that he is saying that such unions are accepted by the church? What would he do if a 10-year-old girl in the parish school were to publicly declares that she is really a boy and begins the process of transition? Is this acceptable in a church school? Can the government compel the church to accept transitioning children? If a person who was born a man but has legally been recognised to be a woman asks us to change their sex in the baptismal register of their parish, what does the pastor do? Can a person who was born a man but now lives their life as a woman join a convent to be a nun? What if a member of the clergy publicly declares that he is really a woman, and is recognised as such by the state? What of embryos that contain the genetic information of three parents? What of surrogacy? Who are recorded as the parents?

Keeping in mind that Article 116 of the Australian Constitution is supposed to protect the Church from the interference of the State, might the State one day try to force the Church to recognise same-sex marriage? When preparing a heterosexual couple for marriage, a pastor would normally begin by asking if either of them had been married before. Clearly, in the Catholic Church, since a civil divorce has no effect in the Church, if either of them had been married before, they can't enter into a new marriage. What if they've been married to a member of the same sex, and then go on to get divorced? On Church paperwork, their marital status would be regarded as never having been married, but on State paperwork, they'll be regarded as having been divorced! These questions will come up as time goes on. Some may fear that churches will be forced to recognise same-sex marriage – or even conduct same-sex marriages. Emphasis ought to be placed on article 116 of the Constitution, as already discussed, which protects the Church from the interference of the State. For the State to do so would be unconstitutional and ought to be challenged. Perhaps the answer lies in the Catholic Church withdrawing from those institutions that have authorised marriage celebrants recognised by the State. In this scenario, couples would obtain a civil marriage license and then coming to a church for their marriage to be recognised by the Church. A proposed way forward would see the Church claim intellectual ownership of the word 'marriage', and the State use another word.

These questions are not easily answered, so what is the way forward for the Church? While having an obligation to go forward bearing witness to the Truth, this cannot happen as long as semantic barriers endure. At this point, society is incredibly divided: parties are competing in a battle of ideologies, and the victor is often the group with the loudest voice. Shouting at the opposition achieves nothing. It is as though each party is speaking different "languages". This is not engaging in discussion. The media is giving substantial coverage of the pro same-sex marriage cause, while the other side is being silenced. Both sides would do well to engage in a sincere and respectful dialogue.

While changes are not inevitable, as proponents of maintaining the status quo, those within the Church cannot afford to ignore the writing on the wall. It seems that public sentiment, formed by media with a set agenda, as well as a general acceptance of Relativism, has largely decided that is inevitable that same-sex marriage will receive civil recognition in this land. Same-sex marriage – or marriage equality – is held to be a human right. Many people, while not militantly lobbying for same-sex marriage, seem to accept its recognition as a harmless and perhaps long-overdue change. As for the Church – while its fundamental understanding of the human person will not change, it may have to work out ways to respond to these realities that do not fit into its understanding of the human person.

The Church's Code of Canon Law, promulgated in 1983, does not have the ability to answer the pressing social questions of the 21st century. The Code of Canon Law was written in 1983 and is a product of its time. For example, there are canons that refer to the use of social media. In 1983, social media meant the radio, television and newspapers! Facebook, Twitter, Skype, Instagram, Vine, Periscope, emails and the internet in general did not exist. Most Canon Lawyers would agree that a new Code of Canon Law is needed for many reasons, not in the least regarding gender and sexuality. For now, the world is going while its teaching is clear, it lacks the effective structures to assist it in adapting these beliefs to a rapidly-changing world. The role of leaders in the Church, including canonists, is to ensure that the Church, maintaining its steadfast witness to the Truth, is not left behind.

3

"MALE AND FEMALE HE MADE THEM"

Julian Porteous

ABSTRACT

In line with the central theme of this Colloquium, organised by the Dawson Centre for Cultural Studies, this paper explores one of the critical issues of our time – that of the nature of relationship between man and woman. At present we are increasingly confronted by those advocating a radical gender ideology which seeks to eliminate any distinction between the sexes. This paper will explore the Christian understanding of the nature of male and female.

At the outset it is important to say that this is an intellectual exploration of issues related to male and female complementarity and, as such, is respectful of those who experience same sex attraction or gender identity issues.

* * * * *

The Legacy of the Sexual Revolution

The Sexual Revolution has been a very significant cultural movement in our time. Beginning in the 1960s it has been a major factor in a raft of cultural changes in Western societies. We can indeed speak about a revolution in social norms that has significantly changed our society when we think about the wide scale acceptance no-fault divorce, of birth control, of abortion-on-demand, the rise of cohabitation, and the movement advocating legal change to normalise same-sex romantic relationships. It is fair to say that this flood of changes has caught the Church off guard.

This revolution in thinking has promoted the idea that a good and decent society ought to isolate sexual activity from its procreative end and so make it an end in itself without context or intrinsic purpose. We have witnessed this change in attitude so that there is now in the common mind a separation of sexual activity, procreation, and marriage. This is a core idea of the sexual revolution.

Now we are being told that the gender identity of male and female are completely separate from biology and therefore a matter of personal choice. Whether it is relationships, or gender identity, or parenthood, the sexual revolution has adopted the refrain that there's no natural, inherent distinction between men and women. It is all simply a matter of personal choice, of how we see ourselves or how we feel. Anatomy no longer plays a role, and in any case this can be changed by medical procedures and hormone treatment if one desires.

What the Sexual Revolution has done has been to say that we human beings can overwrite nature. The sexual revolution is in the end a rejection of nature and the natural order. And it rests on the assumption that sex, marriage, and family are not based on designed realities, but are concepts that are able to be redefined and reimagined as we see fit.

In recent times the Sexual Revolution has reached a climax in two important areas: in the push for a change in the definition of marriage to incorporate two people of the same sex, and in the pressure for acceptance of fluidity in gender identity.

In this latter issue we are faced with an ideology of gender which takes the idea of gender and combines it with a social constructionist ideology. The view is that even if biological sex is a given, "gender" – one's perception of the self – is a social construct and therefore can be changed. Deconstructing the cultural supports that recognise the differences between men and women has opened the door to the re-definition of marriage to include same-sex unions.

It has also promoted the idea that gender is a fluid reality, and that society should accommodate those who desire one of a number of gender identities. Not only should a person's sense of identity be acknowledged and catered for but everyone should be free to explore a variety of gender identities. Adolescents, in particular, as they move through the phase of finding their identity should be given the opportunity to explore a range of options.

In the name of human rights and in the name of diversity, society is being called upon to change its attitudes towards gender.

This requires a response by Christians and those whose traditions hold to the view that masculinity and femininity are ontologically fixed, , and that marriage is intended to be between people of the opposite sex and naturally open to the generation of new life. However, the claims of those who propose otherwise do need to be seriously examined.[14]

Christians, holding to the dignity of the human person, also need to examine appropriate responses to those who desire to have their same-sex relationship be included in the legal definition of marriage and those who want to change their sexual identity. The in-

---

[14] Christopher Tollefsen writes: "… the consequences of failure to give these questions adequate reflection are clearly grave, both for persons beset with gender confusion, and for a culture struggling to find its footing on matters of sex and marriage." Christopher Tollefsen, "Gender Identity", *Public Discourse*, 14 July 2015. www.thepublicdiscourse.com/2015/07/15308/

dividuals who question their sexual identity and find themselves seeking alternative definitions and expressions of gender need to be respected and loved, but also offered help to find a path to appropriate sexual integrity.

The Christian will have a genuine respect for the person, and at the same time will seek to examine the question from the point of view of Christian anthropology. Simply, the Christian will ask: what is the true nature of the human person? In this we seek the intention of the Creator. We turn for inspiration to the Sacred Scriptures and we draw on the wisdom of the Christian thought over the centuries.

Explaining terms

Firstly, there is a necessity to explain terms. When we speak of "sex" we are speaking of male and female identity. Sex refers to biological differences: chromosomes, hormonal profiles, internal and external sex organs. Gender, on the other hand, identifies the masculine and the feminine. It presents the characteristics of each and describes the way a society or culture delineates its understanding of the masculine or feminine.

An increasing radical gender ideology challenges the idea that sexual identity as male or female is necessarily determined as a biological fact. It claims that what sex means in terms of gender as a 'man' or a 'woman' in society can be changed. The view being promoted is that the person themselves can determine what gender they prefer to express.

In the view of current gender ideology a binary division between 'male' and 'female' is viewed as a system of social and power relations designed to subjugate women as mothers and wives.[1]

---

[1] Dale O'Leary writes: "Radical feminism applied the Marxist theory of class struggle to the relationship between men and women. According to this theory, women were the first oppressed class and men used the biological

The personal and social identity, ascribed at birth on the basis of biological sex, is seen as a social construct which can be changed or rejected entirely.

Gender ideology proposes that gender is, in fact, fluid and does not correspond to a given sex. Gender identity is now not only described as masculine or feminine, but incorporates a number – indeed a growing number – of genders: Facebook provides its users with 58 gender options.

By this account, a rigid binary system forces every person to identify as either as male or female, and punishes people if they are neither, both at once, or something in between or something else entirely. Many are swayed by the apparent logic, or sentiment of the position, especially when combined with the notion of human rights. Simply it is believed that people have the freedom and right to be what they believe or feel they want to be. Certainly, it is now possible for a person to choose to change from the gender role as man or woman to the opposite, through advances in medicine, in particular hormonal treatments and surgical procedures.

From these identities come a range of possible sexual relationships and practices, and, in the view of those accepting this understanding, a variety of sexual practices are justified.

Advances in medicine and technology have also long since

---

sex differences to invent motherhood as the task of women and marriage as a way to secure their power over women. Freedom from this oppression could supposedly be achieved by identifying the ways in which language and culture oppress women and deconstructing the cultural supports for recognition of the differences between men and women. This deconstructing of "gender" is behind the radical feminist war on marriage and motherhood, and their fanatical support for lesbianism and abortion on demand." Dale O'Leary, "Don't say gender when you mean sex," *Crisis*, 1 December 2014. http://www.crisismagazine.com/2014/dont-say-gender-mean-sex

severed the natural link between sexual intimacy and procreation. The contraceptive revolution has changed once and for all the way people view the sexual act. People have the capacity to engage in a range of sexual activities seen as ends in themselves. Sexual expression is now viewed by many solely as an act seeking personal satisfaction.

Modern developments in reproductive technology now enable the generation of new life to be separated from the two parties in a relationship. It is now possible by means of artificial interventions to completely dissociate procreation from sexual intimacy and with this a separation of motherhood and fatherhood from filiation.

However, as Dr Jennifer Roback Morse explained on a recent visit to Hobart, even if modern sexual ideologies resent and seek to transgress the limitations of the human body with contraception, abortion, sex-reassignment surgery, hormones, reproductive technology and sexual license, they will always face "small problems" such as the truth that "sex actually does make babies"; or that "men and women actually are different".

Roback Morse writes: "This is why the Sexual Revolution needs the State. These false premises cannot stand on their own. They must be continually propped up and supported. The ideology needs government coercion, media propaganda, economic restructuring and educational indoctrination to break the connection between sex and babies in the social order and in people's minds."[2]

A process of deconstruction inspired by Marxist structuralist theories has been steadily advanced over recent decades to the extent that it is receiving wide support. The Safe Schools Coalition material is a case in point.

---

[2] Jennifer Roback Morse, "The Sexual Revolution Proves Itself to be a Totalitarian Movement." 30 March 2016. The Blaze. http://www.theblaze.com/contributions/the-sexual-revolution-has-proven-to-be-a-totalitarian-movement/

Sex and Gender

What is the relationship between sex and gender? The biological principle of sex and its cultural expression in gender are not identical but nor are they completely independent of each other. There are in fact three contributing factors at work these are biological sex, psychological sex and social sex.

Biological sex is expressed in genetic or chromosomal sex. Women have XX chromosomes, and men the XY chromosomes. These are set at the moment of fertilisation. This identity established by chromosomal difference in fact affects the entire organism, not only in the internal and external reproductive organs but such things as the functioning of the brain. Each cell in a woman's body is different to each cell in the man's body.

Psychological sex refers to the consciousness of belonging to a determined sex. This identity is formed in the child from the age of 2 or 3. It usually coincides with the biological sex, but very occasionally some will identify with the opposite sex. This is the subject of transgenderism and the moral and physical issues related to gender reassignment, particularly for children.

Sociological sex involves the historico-cultural processes whereby a person is fashioned in their ways of acting as a man or woman.[3] These factors have been very powerful influences in many cultures, but now contemporary ideologies are changing their influence, such that young people are being encouraged to experiment with their sexual identity.

---

[3] "If the radical feminists, post-modern deconstructionists, gender ideologues, sexual utilitarians, and neo-Gnostics were trying to strip away truly oppressive cultural impositions, which kept men and women from being who they truly are (and these certainly do exist), then Christians should join them in this quest. But those pushing "gender" aren't looking for the truth about the human person because they don't believe there is a truth to find. They reject the idea of human nature. Their search is like peeling an onion. They want to remove every layer until there is nothing left." O'Leary, op. cit.

Each person goes through a process during childhood and adolescence in which their sexual identity is clarified. A person usually acquires an understanding of the bio-psychological markers of their own sex in differentiation from the other sex. Thus, they move to a mature sense of their sexual identity, and find their place in the cultural climate in which they live. In a steady and harmonious process of integration all three dimensions coalesce, and the person is secure in their identity.

Recent focus on those who have not been able to reach a position of integrated sexual identity raise important cultural and moral questions. That all people are to be respected is axiomatic, but pressing for active promotion of various alternative sexual identities is problematic particularly among the young who have to navigate a sometimes confusing way in the development of their sexual identity.

Along with developing clarity about one's sexual identity is the question now highlighted in the push for the change in the legal definition of marriage to include couples of the same sex, that of sexual orientation. While over 90% of the population identify as being heterosexually oriented there is a small percentage – around 2.5% – who identify themselves as being homosexually oriented. The causes of this are debated but it is likely influenced by a range of factors which shape the forming of sexual identity during adolescence.

There has been long academic exploration of these issues, particularly in feminist and gender programs at universities. There have been multiple studies and books written. Most of this has been advocating a change in society's attitude to sex and gender. And now the push for actual social change has reached its climax.

A momentum has been in one direction. It is important, even if belated, that a Christian perspective is brought to bear. Does, for example, fluidity in gender identity have accompanying moral dimensions? Can the definition of marriage be changed to accommodate these new understandings?

A Catholic Perspective

In answering these questions I will focus on Catholic thought. Catholic scholars address the question of gender identity by drawing on Sacred Scripture, especially the creation narratives, and the tradition of theological reflection informed by philosophy, a dynamic tradition dating back to apostolic times. If we wish to put a tag on the Catholic understanding we would describe our view as proposing "integral gender complementarity".

I want to focus in particular on the work of two 20th century Catholic thinkers who I believe can provide important insights to address the false understanding of sexual identity and gender that have come to dominate our society. They are Dietrich von Hildebrand (1889-1977) and Edith Stein (1891-1942). Both were converts to the Catholic faith and both studied under the German philosopher, Edmund Husserl, the founder of the school of thought called Phenomenology.

Von Hildebrand wrote on the nature of marriage, writing as a philosopher rather than a theologian. He proposed in his 1929 book, *On Marriage*, that the distinction between 'male' and 'female' is not just biological but it is metaphysical. He argued that marriage involves an I-thou communion formed between two types of spiritual person. He proposed that sexual identity is more profound than its biological or psychological delineation.

Edith Stein was critical of the early stages of the feminist movement. She saw this fledgling movement as actually denying true feminine identity and, as it proposed a unisex identity, she saw it as denying an essential truth about the nature of the human person.

Along with von Hildebrand she maintained that sexual difference is found fundamentally in the soul. She based her thought on Thomistic metaphysics.

Stein, in her *Essays on Women*, explored the nature of femininity as related to the lived experience of motherhood. She saw that the woman receives the world inwardly through the passions. In other words, there was a distinctive way in which a woman lived in the world. By way of contrast she taught that the man receives the world more through the intellect. She understood that the woman embraces the living and personal rather than the objective. She argued that femininity has an ontological basis.

This emerging personalist philosophy which would influence a young priest, Karol Wojtyla, emphasised that each of the persons in a marriage while remaining individual persons, experience marriage as a communion. This communion is achieved because the interpersonal relationship actually results in an integral complementarity. They become a new reality, an ontological reality, as married couple.

In his book, "Love and Responsibility", Wojtyla explores the unique identity of both the man and woman. He writes that marriage is the interpersonal communion which achieves an integration between persons.

Papal teaching

After being elected Pope, Wojtyla began a series of Wednesday audiences in which he outlined what has become popularly known as the "Theology of the Body". In these talks he said that man and woman are two significantly different ways of being persons in the world. He argued that man and woman are equal as human beings and equal as persons, and are intended for the integral complementarity of marriage.

This teaching proposes that masculinity and femininity are not the equivalent of male and female. He argues that masculinity and femininity are a profound sense of one's body. He taught that a woman discovers and fulfils her femininity in motherhood, and a man discovers and fulfils his masculinity in fatherhood.

Pope Francis has spoken out forthrightly on the issue of the complementary nature of masculinity and femininity. In a series of his own Wednesday audiences in 2015 on the theme of the marriage and family, he strongly refuted the foundational tenets of "gender theory" that flow from radical feminism as well as the homosexual political lobby. The differences between men and women are not a matter of "subordination" as feminist and gender theory would have it, but of "communion and generation."

He questioned if gender theory was in fact "an expression of frustration and resignation, that aims to cancel out sexual difference". He added, "Yes, we run the risk of taking a step backwards. Indeed, the removal of difference is the problem, not the solution." He went on in this talk to link a global crisis of faith, of belief in God and Christian teaching as fostering an "incredulity and cynicism," which he saw might explain "the crisis in the alliance between man and woman."

He called for a "rediscovery" of this natural alliance between man and woman. He linked our appreciation of the wonder of natural world, which he expressed so beautifully in *Laudato Si*, with human relationships. He said that "the earth is filled with harmony and trust" because of the alliance between man and woman "lived well." He encouraged intellectuals not to ignore this scheme in their efforts to build a just society.

In his ongoing catechesis on the family, Francis said that within the context of their differences, men and women are equally made "in the image of God." For Pope Francis it is clear that the foundation of Catholic teaching on sexuality is the concept of the natural complementarity between man and woman. He says, "Not only man as such, not only woman as such, but rather man and woman, as a couple, are the image of God. The difference between them is not a question of contrast or subordination, but instead of communion and generation, always in the image and semblance of God."

He goes on to say, "Men and women must instead speak more, listen more, know each other better, value each other more" treating each other "with respect and cooperating in friendship." And it is on this mutually enriching equitable interaction between men and women that families are founded within "a lifelong matrimonial and family union."

Pope Francis has repeatedly warned against the threat of the gender ideology. In 2013, speaking to the Women's Section of the Pontifical Council for the Laity the pope warned against the growth of ideologies that "destroy woman and her vocation." These, he said, promote "a type of emancipation which, in order to occupy spaces taken away from the masculine, abandons the feminine with the precious traits that characterise it." These thoughts are captured in his post-synodal Exhortation on marriage, titled, "The Joy of Love".

Conclusion

This Colloquium provides a means for Christian reflection on the issue of the complementary relationship between man and woman. In the present climate it is important that serious Christian thought be applied to this topic, so that the Church can more effectively engage in the public debate.

Ryan Anderson observes that the two thousand year story of the Christian Church's cultural and intellectual growth is a story of challenges answered. If over the centuries, rigorous debate over the nature of God, of salvation, and of the church were necessary to refine and illuminate the truth of Christianity, "the most pressing heresies – the newest challenges for the church's teaching and mission – centre on the nature of man". He commented,

> These debates, seen from the inside as they are under way, may seem intractable, but in the long run this is how our age will develop a richer anthropology and a richer morality. As we are challenged to defend the truths of human nature – male and female created for each other in marriage – we will discover a deeper reflection on human nature and our fulfilment.[4]

It is my hope and prayer that this Dawson Centre Colloquium will shed light on this topic and will advance our understanding of human nature and the path to human flourishing.

---

[4] Ryan Anderson. *Truth overruled: The future of marriage and religious freedom*. Ch 8. First e-book edition. Regnery Publishing: Washington D.C.

4

GENDER EQUALITY –
AN ISLAMIC PERSPECTIVE

Usman Rana

ABSTRACT

With the help and blessing of the Lord Almighty, I will firstly discuss a few basic aspects regarding Sharia and its implementation which in my view need to be addressed before taking up the questions at hand, questions such as whether Sharia is to be enforced on anyone, what is the purpose of the teachings of Islam, and who is to implement the teachings of Islam. I will also explore the nature of gender equality and ask what examples of equality of the Sexes we find around us, and whether gender equality really does exist.

Secondly I will be discussing the teachings of Islam what Islam actually says and preaches about gender equality.

Thirdly, the main discussion will be around the practical implementation of the teachings of Islam: is Islam's teaching about gender equality practical and suitable for the 21st century what is the inherent philosophy and wisdom of Islam's perspective on gender equality? I will also compare the secular and Islamic approach to the subject.

* * * * *

In today's world perhaps more than ever the question of the role of the different genders is argued and campaigned about. Equal rights are demanded not only by women in society but everyone in

270

the world so much that even countries and nations are demanding equality in the World; some use civilised methods and some who are frustrated and out of arguments use force and bullying tactics to achieve their aims. This paper aims to present an Islamic view about gender equality.

Reality Check

In my humble opinion equality is relative and variable; it depends on the situation and circumstances and at the same time on key principals such as justice which form the bases of society. Equality has to be firmly anchored. For example sensitive information to which the Prime Minister would have access would not be released to an average citizen: though both are citizens of the country and should in theory have same rights, for the sake of the nation the people have surrendered some of their rights to Government for the greater good. If, however, the Prime minister should commit some crime he would be treated the same as a normal citizen. In simple terms to achieve something as a society individuals have to sacrifice and delegate some of their rights to the collective.

Now let's have a closer look at equality matters specific to gender; what examples of equality between man and woman do we find around us?

Ex-President Barack Obama said that a woman who is denied an education is denied equality. This is a reasonable point in theory but there is another side to the picture. In secular society women are too often portrayed as pleasure objects. There is immense pressure on women to pursue 'beauty' and have a 'perfect' figure. Competitions like Miss World contribute. Why not a Mr and Miss World? No man would have a chance. In the Olympics men and woman compete only against their own gender: in recent times during a the Olympics a woman was banned from competing against other

271

women because apparently she was too strong. Recently in New York a man complained about a women-only Swimming Pool on the basis of sexual discrimination. Mankind adopted clothing and dress as signs of civility and culture; it is sad to see that today society is reverting to nakedness in pursuit of what is considered progress.

Feminine charms are always on display even in selling food items or daily necessities such as washing powder. Advertisements require female models, artificially stylish and expensive ways of life are presented as being essential for a woman to realise her dreams. Such a society cannot remain balanced, sober and healthy for long.

According to Islam, woman must be emancipated from exploitation and from playing a role as mere instruments of pleasure; they must have more time to themselves to discharge their responsibilities towards their homes and the future generation of mankind.

The Teachings of Islam

Before we embark on the quest to explore the Islamic view on gender equality I would like to take the opportunity to address a few points which I believe are essential to clarify common misconceptions which often are a great barrier to discovering the true teachings of Islam beyond the stigma and misconceptions often attached to it.

The most famous and important is the implementation of Sharia Law. It is quite understandable why the world at large reacts the way it does on hearing this word, as extremists and radicals over centuries have been very busy imposing it, and even some common Muslims believe that Sharia is to be implemented no matter what and that it is to be implemented everywhere. But Islam only seeks to show the ultimate path to success in any matter it addresses. It is very clear from the Holy Quran that Islam and Sharia is nowhere to be implemented except in one's own Heart and Soul. God Almighty has given every human being the choice either to believe or not to believe, to live life according to Sharia or not, and nobody has the right to force any belief or law on anybody else. Men are allowed only to help each other understand the teachings and wisdom; the choice of following any particular path remains with the individual:

"Whoso does good whether male or female, and is a believer, shall enter Paradise and they shall not be wronged a whit" (The Holy Quran 4:125).

"And they (women) have rights similar to those (of men) over them in equity" (The Holy Quran 2:229).

"And covet not that whereby Allah has made some of you excel others. Men shall have a share of that which they have earned, and women a share of that which they have earned. And ask Allah of His bounty. Surely, Allah has perfect knowledge of all things." (The Holy Quran 4:33).

"Surely, men who submit themselves to God and women who submit themselves to Him, and believing men and believing women, and obedient men and obedient women and truthful men and truthful women, and men steadfast in their faith and steadfast women, and men who are humble and women who are humble, and men who give alms and women who give alms, and men who fast and women who fast, and men who guard their chastity and women who guard their chastity, and men who remember Allah much and women who remember Him – Allah has prepared for all of them forgiveness and a great reward." (The Holy Quran 33:36).

The above verses testify that according to The Holy Quran women stand on the same level as men and that they can attain to all those spiritual heights to which men can attain and enjoy all those political and social rights which men enjoy.

"O ye people! fear your Lord, who created you from a single soul and created therefrom its mate, and from them twain spread many men and women; and fear Allah, in Whose name you appeal to one another, and fear Him particularly respecting ties of relationship. Verily, Allah watches over you." (The Holy Quran 4:2).

The Holy Quran has given the same status to man and woman as it says they are both of the same origin and due to this fact women should not be looked down upon as lower creatures and men and women should respect each other as both are answerable to Allah for their conduct. The Holy Prophet Muhammad used to recite this verse during a marriage ceremony to remind both parties of their duties to each other:

"The pursuit of knowledge is a duty to every Muslim man and woman. I am not leaving a more harmful trial for men than women".

Many other verses of The Holy Quran and Sayings of The Holy Prophet Muhammad can be quoted but I hope the above verses will suffice as a most effective repudiation of the charge that Islam accords a lower status to women though their spheres of activities and their duties are different.

It is this difference in duties of both the sexes that have mistakenly (or perhaps sometimes deliberately) been misunderstood by critics of Islam as implying a lower status for women. The Holy Prophet of Islam told the world that God had especially entrusted to him the task of safeguarding the rights of women. Islam gave women rights that the non-Islamic world has given to women only within the past few hundred years such as the right to inherit property; to own, keep, and manage their own property; to ask and get a divorce in case of ill treatment or abandonment by the husband; the right to remarry; the right to obtain an education.

Islam has proclaimed and enforced the rights of women since approximately the year 600, not because women had to campaign for their rights but because these where granted by God Almighty.

Some of you will surely be thinking about some of the controversial issues which are used by critics and ignorant Muslims alike to malign Islam as these issues can drag a discussion into fruitlessness.

The Practical implication

Let's have a look at the practical implication of the teachings of Islam: how relevant are the teachings of Islam today? "Woman should be taken care of as someone takes care of glass" (saying of The Holy Prophet Muhammad, peace be upon him).

It is a reality that women and children can be overpowered and forced to do acts against their own will but men are unlikely to be made submissive against their will; this is the primary reason why in Islam men have been made guardians. Similarly, some of these very same responsibilities have been delegated to modern governments by which different departments and laws have been created to protect the vulnerable, though with one main difference: Islam's approach is proactive, not waiting for problems to occur then trying to find solutions and punishments as the secular law does. Islam's approach is positive. There are more than 700 commandments of positive things to do in the Holy Quran and a few things not to do. Islam's approach is systematic. It addresses change in the entire society, not just in the individual. Islam realises that good individuals must be placed in a moral and good society so that energies are not spent fighting off evil, but instead are spent in progressing in nearness and communion to God in preparation of the life to come.

The role that women play in Islamic Society is certainly not of concubines in harems nor of a society imprisoned within the four walls of their homes, barred from progress and deprived of the light of knowledge.

The moral, spiritual and economic equality of men and women as ruled by Islam is clearly stated. The specific duties which verses of the Holy Quran address in relation to men or women specifically deal with their physical differences or relate to their different roles and responsibilities in the Family and Social Structure. Men and women have three stages in life, as a daughter or son, as an adult husband or wife, and as a parent mother or father.

Childhood

Let's first have a look what Islam provides for children in terms of equality.

"He who brings up his daughters well and makes no distinction between them and his sons will be close to me in Paradise."

"A man who has three daughters and brings them up and educates them to the best of his capacity shall be entitled to paradise." (sayings of The Holy Prophet Muhammad).

Verses from the Holy Quran could also have been quoted but I hope the above sayings of The Holy Prophet of Islam will suffice to make it clear that both boys and girls have the same rights in Islam. It should also be noted, however, that before the dawn of Islam girls were buried alive in some tribes, or given away as part of inheritance and treated as property. It is very sad and disturbing indeed that even today pre-Islamic behaviour is proudly practiced by some cultures, but let it be very clear that those who behave in this ignorant fashion do so because of their cultural ties and not because of Islam. If they had wholeheartedly embraced Islam they would behave otherwise and no such allegation could have been fairly made against them. An important point in the Holy Quran is that every child is born a Muslim (it should be noted here that

that does not mean that he belongs to the Islamic faith but that the belief in God is innate, embedded in mankind since birth) and the parents make the child what it becomes. It necessarily follows that parents, and the environment of the home and community, and the care and attention (or the lack of such things) shown to a child have consequences. If one plants a tree and does not look after it there is little chance that it will win a gardening award, but if one looks after it, prunes it and waters it its health is assured. Such is the role of Mother and Father as a team. It is also noteworthy that beautiful fruits like apples, grapes and mangos don't grow in deserts, but in specific climates and environments. If the climate and environment of the home is barren or lacks virtue then expect no perfect fruit.

Adult Life

Now let's have a look at adult life. What is the wisdom and reasoning behind Islam's teaching?

"And help one another in righteousness and piety; but help not one another in sin and transgression." (Holy Quran 5:6).

In an Islamic society, men and woman should help each other achieve goodness rather than tempt each other to do the devil's work. This is probably the right place to discuss Islamic wisdom and philosophy behind the injunction for the woman to wear the veil, and the segregation of sexes, as this is the usual basis for allegations that Islam promotes inequality and oppresses women. The first and most important thing to understand is that these commandments are directed to the individual, and that the responsibility to enforce this injunction cannot be delegated to the state. Segregation is a sacrifice that is asked of both women and men, but women particularly for the safeguarding of a moral society. The differences in dress standards and expectations that society has for women and the competitive pressure to cultivate 'beauty' are all exploitative. It is not men who are exploited but women. It is for this reason that Islam has asked Muslim women to make an extraordinary sacrifice, but there should be no external compulsion: women are to embrace it voluntarily and if they chose not to do so no one is allowed to force them.

Traditionally a woman is married for four reasons: (1) wealth, (2) the good name of her family, (3) her beauty and (4) for her good character. The Holy Prophet Muhammad accorded priority only to the last. According to Islam both men and woman are equal in every respect so the foundation of the most important relationship is rightly based not on things which come and go but on things which ought to grow over time – faith and good character.

"And one of His Signs is this, that He has created wives for you from among yourselves that you may find peace of mind in them, and He has put love and tenderness between you. In that surely are Signs for a people who reflect." (The Holy Quran 30:22)

"They are a sort of garment for you and you are a sort of garment for them." (The Holy Quran 2:188).

The purpose of marriage according to Islam is procreation, the attainment of peace of mind, and mutual love and affection. Marriage is also a means of attaining piety and of guarding one's chastity and this can only be achieved when there is mutual and equal trust and treatment in the relationship. One of the verses above says husband and wife are a garment for each other. An important quality of our dress is that it provides protection against hot and cold weather, so in the same way the wife and the husband should stick fast to each other, each serving as a rock of support to the other. The fact that the Holy Quran has used the word "garment" in respect of both the husband and wife clearly demonstrates that they hold equal status; their rights and duties are identical in respect of each other; and both are bound to fulfil their obligations to each other.

One allegation levelled against Islam is that Islam allows men to beat their wives. But how can there be love and respect and tenderness if one is allowed to beat the other? To understand the background one needs to appreciate that in pre-Islamic times Arabs treated woman as property and beating them was the norm. The reality is that the verse which is often quoted actually restricted the scope of this act. Rather than giving them permission to beat their wives, the verse in question commands (1) to admonish the woman, (2) as a second option to separate beds, then (3) as a last resort to chastise them if they are resolute in "disobedience". In my humble opinion "disobedience" here relates to the commandments of God Almighty. If she refuses to discharge the duties which are entrusted to her by Allah her inaction will not only have a effect on the peace of the household but the future generations will be affected as well. If a man practices the first two options I believe the majority of problems will be solved, but those men who jump directly to option three are in violation of Allah's commandments and thus disobedient themselves. It is notable that never did the Holy Prophet Muhammad beat any of his wives. Once a companion of the Holy Prophet Muhammad hit his wife. She came to the Holy Prophet, and complained and asked for divorce for that specific reason. The Holy Prophet granted her divorce. A more recent example is that of the Promised Messiah and Mahdi who was the founder of the Worldwide Ahmadiyya Muslim Community, who like the Holy Prophet of Islam never beat his wife. Having on one occasion addressed his wife in a slightly elevated tone, he later asked God for forgiveness for raising his voice to her.

There is much more that could be said on that point, but it is time to consider another question: how can Islam claim equality between men and woman if men are allowed four wives? The answer to this also lies in the pre-Islamic era. At that time there was no limit to the number of wives a man could have and no responsibilities were attached to marriage. Against this background Islam restricted the maximum number of wives a man could have to four wives and moreover attached a number of responsibilities and rules to marriage where previously men alone held total control. For example Islam does not permit secret and illicit relationships, so if for any reason man wants the company of a woman other than his wife he is bound to marry her and give her the same rights and treatment he gives the first wife. This is a discouragement to immorality, not an encouragement. Surely the fair-minded and unbiased observer would agree that the Islamic approach seems more sensible and better for society then the attitude of secular society which allows men and woman to have secret and illicit relationships, and legalises brothels and strip clubs. It is men who are the beneficiaries of this secular approach and it is women who have been reduced from dignity to the status of objects. The promotion of that sort of immoral behavior, including same sex relationships, and the attitude that whatever is done in secret between four walls has nothing to do with God, is a threat to moral society.

Parenthood

Now let's look at the role of Mother and Father. Does Islam treat both equally?

"Our Lord is He Who gave unto everything its proper form and then guided it to its proper function." (The Holy Quran 20:51)

This is not a question of superiority or inferiority, it is a question of natural capacity and proper function.

In order for any human to become a father or a mother, a child first needs to be born. Regardless of how hard men and woman try by themselves only a woman can become a mother and give birth to a child. Both husband and wife work together as a team. This is the key: both Mother and Father are a team; they both have different roles to play but they both share the responsibility. Think of a cricket team. If the team consisted of only batsmen or only bowlers, what are the chances of their success? They're not going to win the Ashes. Similarly, both parents cannot play the exact same role in the name of equality and expect not to pay a price for it. Brain wave research shows how differently men and woman think and feel and different parts of the brain are affected differentially in the same mental function, hence each of the Parents has a specific kind of influence on the child. According to Islam the father is responsible for the economic affairs of the family, the wife is allowed to work but she has no obligation to share in the expenses; her primary responsibility is the moral training and upbringing of the next generation of mankind. It is also noteworthy that every Prophet who came to mankind was the child of a Mother. What if we had had child care in those days, and the Mother of the Prophet had dropped him in to day care? Would he have learned the same morals as he did learn from his Mother? Today governments spend a lot of resources on schools and education. If we were to spend all the money in the world but had no quality teachers what would the future of mankind be? Once The Holy Prophet Muhammad was asked to whom a man should be kind. "To your mother," he replied. A second time he again said, "to your mother." And when he was asked a third time, again the reply was: "your mother." Only upon being asked a fourth time did he reply: "your father."

"Paradise is at the feet of the mother." (the Holy Prophet Muhammad).

Quite evidently the status of Mothers in Islam is so great that it is the Father who should demand equal rights! Woman's high status is due to the fact that since reaching adulthood she has made enormous sacrifices for society. Women are the greatest teachers of all. Only mothers can instill in their children the habits needed to make this world close to heaven. Mothers are like cool shades.

A father should take care of all the worries his family face and the mother cannot fulfill her role in providing shade if the father does not do his duty.

Conclusion

I have tried to shed some light on Islam's perspective on gender equality. If we consider the different roles and responsibilities that Man and Woman have it should become clear that the equality that the secular West wants is not in the best interest of mankind, but rather in the interest of the few. These few are like a river that does not like its banks to restrict its flow and wants to go on without restraint. When the river breaks its banks it might feel freedom and enjoy it, but apart from its own self-interest it only brings only destruction and suffering. Prosperity for all comes only when the river flows within its banks. In all that I have tried to say my purpose was to elaborate of the truth that Islam seeks to protect the family system and promote a moral and just society. I conclude with this saying of the Holy Prophet Muhammad and leave you all to reflect and draw your own conclusions:

"When you are contemplating a certain course of action reflect first upon its consequences; if they are good persist, if they are bad desist."

I request your prayers Ghulam Masih e Mohammadi.

5

THE ETERNAL NATURE OF GENDER IN LATTER DAY SAINT THEOLOGY AND ITS IMPLICATIONS

Michael Stokes

ABSTRACT

Latter Day Saints believe that gender is an essential characteristic of individual premortal, mortal and eternal identity and purpose. We also believe that marriage between a man and a woman is ordained of God and that marriage and other family relationships can continue in the eternities.

The paper will set out and explain these doctrines and fit them into the overall picture of LDS beliefs on the nature of this life and its relationship with the eternities. it will also consider the implications of these doctrines for the equal but complementary roles of men and women in this life and for major social issues such as whether same sex couples should be able to marry and issues relating to gender identity.

* * * * *

Introduction

In Latter Day Saint (LDS) theology, gender is an essential characteristic of individual premortal, mortal, and eternal identity and purpose,[5] and marriage and family are potentially eternal.

---

[5] *The Family; A proclamation to the World (Proclamation on the Family)*, 1995https://www.lds.org/bc/content/shared/content/images/gospel-library/manual/34190/34190_000_WWC_26-FamProc.pdf>

283

This paper seeks to set out the LDS position on the eternal nature of gender and of family relationships and to consider its implications for current debates about the nature of gender, marriage and the family, especially the same sex marriage debate.

In setting out the LDS position, the paper quotes extensively from LDS scriptures. The Church of Jesus Christ of latter Day Saints accepts four volumes of canonised scripture, the *Bible,* the *Book of Mormon,* the *Doctrine and Covenants* and the *Pearl of Great Price.* As most readers will not be familiar with the latter three volumes, it is necessary to say a little about each. Joseph Smith translated the *Book of Mormon* from gold plates delivered to him by the angel Moroni. The bulk of the book focuses on the history of the Nephites and the Lamanites, who were the descendants of refugees who fled Jerusalem before its destruction by the Babylonians. The highlight of the book is its account of Christ's visit to the Nephites after his resurrection.[1] The *Doctrine and Covenants* consists of revelations which Joseph Smith and later Presidents of the Church have received with respect to Church organisation and some doctrinal matters. The *Pearl of Great Price* contains the Book of Moses, a revelation adding to Genesis, the Book of Abraham, a translation of an ancient document, as well as Joseph Smith's account of the translation and publication of the *Book of Mormon.*[2]

- **The plan of salvation.**

The Plan of Salvation or Plan of Happiness is the title which the LDS Church gives to God's plan for humanity. It deals with the progression of the human spirit through a number of stages leading to a possible state of exaltation or godhood made possible by the power and grace of God. The stages are:

---

[1] *Book of Mormon,* 3 Nephi, chs. 11-29.

[2] All LDS scriptures are available on the church website, lds.org

1. Existence as "an intelligence". God did not create the essence of each person but it existed eternally with God as an intelligence.[3] We know little of the exact nature of these intelligences except that God did not create them. They have no beginning or end and are an eternal aspect of each person.

2. Pre-mortal life as a disembodied spirit. At some point, God converted the eternal intelligences into disembodied spirits. This is a necessary step in the eternal progression of each person. The process makes each person a begotten spirit child of their Heavenly Father,[4] indeed of heavenly parents.[5] The doctrine that we are literally begotten spirit children of our Heavenly Father is based on a literal interpretation of Biblical scriptures such as Romans 8:16 and Hebrews 12:9 as well as revelations received by Joseph Smith, especially in the *Doctrine and Covenants.*[6] The doctrine that we have a Heavenly Mother was revealed to Joseph Smith, and is based on implications from the nature of God and of the LDS doctrine of deification as much as from any particular scripture.[7]

Although it is not clear whether intelligences are gendered, modern revelation makes it clear that disembodied spirits are.[8] Disembodied spirits look like the persons whom they become when they receive a physical body.[9] Disembodied spirits live in the presence of their heavenly parents.[10]

While in the presence of their Heavenly Father, the disembodied

---

[3] *Doctrine and Covenants* 93:29; *Pearl of Great Price* Abraham 3:18.
[4] *Doctrine and Covenants* 76:24.
[5] *Proclamation on the Family,* op. cit.
[6] 6 *Doctrine and Covenants* 76:24.
[7] For more information on the LDS doctrine of a Heavenly Mother, see *Gospel Topics Essays* "Mother in Heaven": www.lds.org/topics/mother-in-heaven?lang=eng&old=true.
[8] *Doctrine and Covenants* 76:24.
[9] *Doctrine and Covenants* 77:2; *Book of Mormon* Ether 2:16.
[10] *Doctrine and Covenants* 138:56.

spirits took part in the great council in heaven, in which they were given the opportunity to endorse the Plan of Salvation, and in particular to accept the need to spend a period in mortality, where they would be separated from their Heavenly Father and would be tested and tried to determine their worthiness for further blessings.[11] Not all Heavenly Father's children accepted the plan and many, led by Lucifer, rebelled and were cast down from heaven.[12] Those spirits who endorsed the plan were given the opportunity to experience mortality.

3. Mortal life. Mortal life is a short period in the context of eternity in which each individual is tested and tried. The conditions of mortality are:

- Each person receives a physical body and becomes subject to physical infirmity, suffering, sickness, and death;
- Each person is separated from God by a veil which leads them to forget their pre-mortal existence and in particular to forget their relationship with their Heavenly Father;[13]
- Each person has agency and is free to choose between good and evil;[14]
- A probationary state in which we are tested and tried, to see if we will be obedient to God's commandments and live by faith not by sight;
- To learn by experience the difference between good and bad, pleasure and pain, joy and misery.[15]
- To learn our utter dependence on God and on his grace for our salvation.

---

[11] *Pearl of Great Price* Abraham 3: 24-5.
[12] Revelation 12: 7-9.
[13] *Book of Mormon* Alma 42: 7-9; Ether 3: 19-20.
[14] Ibid.
[15] Genesis 3:5.

4. The Spirit World. Physical death is the separation of the spirit from the body. After death, the disembodied spirit goes to the spirit world to await the resurrection. The Spirit World is divided into two parts, paradise and the spirit prison. Paradise is:

> ... that part of the spirit world in which the righteous spirits who have departed from this life await the resurrection of the body. It is a condition of happiness and peace.[16]

Although paradise is described as a state of happiness and peace, the dead, even those in paradise, look on their separation from their bodies as bondage.[17]

The Spirit Prison is that part of the Spirit World which houses the unrighteous between death and the resurrection.[18] Alma describes it as a state of outer darkness in which there is weeping, wailing and gnashing of teeth. The wicked bring this state on themselves through their own iniquity,[19] because those who have not repented of their sins in this life must suffer for them.[20]

5. The resurrection and the eternal state of humankind

Every person who has ever lived on this earth will be resurrected, that is their spirits will be reunited eternally with their bodies. After the resurrection, they return to the presence of God for the final judgment.[21] God's love, justice and mercy will amaze us on that day. I noted above that those who have not repented must pay the price for their own sins in the Spirit World. However, their punishment does not continue eternally. On the day of judgment,

---

[16] Bible Dictionary published as an appendix to the LDS edition of the Bible, 742; *Book of Mormon* Alma 40:12.

[17] *Doctrine and Covenants* 138:15-19 and 49-50.

[18] 1 Peter 3: 19-20; *Book of Mormon* Alma 40:13.

[19] *Book of Mormon* Alma 40:13-14.

[20] *Doctrine and Covenants* 19:15-18.

[21] *Book of Mormon* Alma 40:21

all except those guilty of blasphemy against the Holy Ghost, are judged worthy of a Kingdom of Glory. Those who have blasphemed against the Holy Ghost, that is who wilfully deny Christ and assent to his death after receiving a perfect knowledge of him from the Holy Ghost,[22] are never redeemed but are doomed to suffer the wrath of God with the devil and his angels for eternity.[23] All others are redeemed in the Lord's due time, if necessary, after suffering his wrath.[24]

The final destination of resurrected beings, the Kingdom of Glory which is their eternal home, is determined by what they did in mortal life, a time of testing and trial. This does not entail that anyone merits eternal life for all have sinned[25] and are redeemed through the grace of God and the atonement of Christ.[26] But Christ, as our redeemer, is able to determine the conditions of our redemption and requires us to have faith in him, to repent and forsake our sins and to be obedient to his commandments.

There are three degrees or Kingdoms of Glory.[27] The lowest of the Kingdoms of Glory is the Telestial Kingdom. Those who are consigned to this Kingdom are servants of the Most High, but cannot go where God and Christ dwell, worlds without end.[28] Instead, they receive the ministration of the Holy Spirit.[29] These are they who are cast down to hell and suffer the wrath of Almighty God until the fullness of times,[30] when they are redeemed from

---

[22] *Bible Dictionary*, op. cit., n. 18, 626; *Doctrine and Covenants* 76:31-38.

[23] *Doctrine and Covenants*, 76:33 and 36.

[24] Ibid., 76:38.

[25] Romans 3:23.

[26] 1 Corinthians 6:20; Romans 11:6.

[27] 1 Corinthians 15:40; *Doctrine and Covenants* 76:50-112, 88: 20-24.

[28] *Doctrine and Covenants*, 76:112.

[29] Ibid., 76:86.

[30] Ibid., 76:104-7.

the devil in the last resurrection.[31] They include liars, sorcerers, whoremongers and adulterers.[32]

The second of the Kingdoms of Glory is the Terrestial Kingdom. Those consigned to the Terrestial Kingdom do not receive of the fullness of the Father but the presence of the Son[33] and their glory differs from those who receive of that fullness as does the glory of the moon differ from that of the sun.[34] They include the spirits of men kept in the spirit prison whom Christ visited between his death and resurrection and to whom he taught the gospel, and who as a result gained a testimony of Jesus.[35] They also include honourable men who were blinded by the craftiness of men and those who were not valiant in the testimony of Jesus.[36]

The third and highest of the Kingdoms is the Celestial Kingdom. Those who inherit this kingdom are, "… just men made perfect through Jesus the mediator of the new covenant …"[37] All things are theirs and they dwell in the presence of God and Christ forever.[38] Those who attain to the highest degree of glory in the Celestial Kingdom are deified, becoming gods.[39]

- **Gender, marriage and family in the plan of salvation**

Gender is an essential characteristic of individual premortal, mortal, and eternal identity and purpose.[40] The intelligences which

---

[31] *Doctrine and Covenants*, 76: 85.

[32] Ibid., 76:103.

[33] Ibid., 76:76-7.

[34] Ibid., 76:71.

[35] *Doctrine and Covenants*, 76:74.

[36] Ibid., 76:75 and 79.

[37] Ibid., 76:69.

[38] Ibid., 76:59 and 62.

[39] Ibid., s. 131:1-4.

[40] Ibid., n. 1 above.

ultimately become human beings, if not already gendered, become gendered when they progress through spiritual birth to become spirit children of heavenly parents. They are literally spirit sons and daughters of their heavenly parents with spiritual bodies which are the same in appearance as the physical bodies which they will receive when born into mortality.[41] Their gender is an eternal aspect of their being which does not change.

- **Gender, marriage and family in mortality**

Gender, marriage and family are central to our role and purpose while in mortality. God created us male and female and intended that each should complement the other. In both Genesis and the Book of Moses, Adam is described as lacking a "help meet", leading to the creation of Eve.[42] The phrase "help meet" is often used to support the view that women are subordinate "helpers" of men who are ordained by God to be the leaders. However, the Hebrew phrase translated as help meet denotes a helper of great power, a deliverer rather than a subordinate and is most often used in the Old Testament to describe God's relationship to his people.[43] It is not intended to imply that the woman is somehow inferior to the man but that she is his equal in all things.[44] She is the man's deliverer in

---

[41] Text accompanying nn 4-8 above. There are some exceptions to this as one of the trials we may have to endure in mortality is a degree of disability or deformity. Disabilities and deformities are not present in disembodied spirits, not will they be present in our resurrected bodies; *Book of Mormon* Alma 11:43-4.

[42] Genesis, 2:18 and 20; *Pearl of Great Price* Moses, 3:18 and 20.

[43] James M Harper, "A Man … Shall Cleave unto His Wife": Marriage and Family Advice from the Old Testament' *Ensign* January 1990: www.lds. org/ensign/1990/01/a-man-shall-cleave-unto-his-wife-marriage-and-family-advice-from-the-old-testament?lang=eng; "A Suitable Helper" (in Hebrew): http://newlife.id.au/equality-and-gender-issues/a-suitable-helper/

[44] *Proclamation on the Family;* Studylight org, Verse-by verse Bible Commentary Genesis 2:18: www.studylight.org/commentary/genesis/2-18.html.

a couple of ways; she delivers him from that loneliness which is not good and she delivers humanity in that without women, God's plan for humanity would be frustrated.

God's plan requires that each of his spirit children come to earth to receive a physical body. God's first commandment to Adam and Eve in the Garden of Eden was to multiply and replenish the earth.[45] In obeying this commandment, men and women help in furthering God's plan for humanity by providing physical bodies to Heavenly Father's spirit children.[46] It requires a man and a woman to conceive children; neither can do it alone. But God intends that men should do more than play a role in the conception of children; they also have a role in their care and upbringing:

> Husband and wife have a solemn responsibility to love and care for each other and for their children. "Children are an heritage of the Lord" (Psalm 127:3). Parents have a sacred duty to rear their children in love and righteousness, to provide for their physical and spiritual needs, and to teach them to love and serve one another, observe the commandments of God, and be law-abiding citizens wherever they live. Husbands and wives – mothers and fathers – will be held accountable before God for the discharge of these obligations.[47]

God instituted marriage between men and women as equal complementary partners for at least two purposes, firstly to end their solitary state which was not good, and to ensure that they were partners in raising and caring for their children. Adam succinctly describes the ideal of divinely instituted marriage when introduced

---

[45] Genesis 1:28; *Pearl of Great Price* Moses, 2:28; *Proclamation on the Family,* op. cit., n. 1.

[46] *Proclamation on the Family* op. cit., n.1; *Gospel Principles* ch 36: www.lds.org/manual/gospel-principles/chapter-36-the-family-can-be-eternal?lang=eng.

[47] *Proclamation on the Family,* op. cit.,. n. 1.

to Eve: "Therefore shall a man leave his father and his mother and shall cleave unto his wife: and they shall be one flesh."[48]

Adam's statement emphasises that marriage unifies the husband and wife – they become one flesh – and that no other human relationship, not even that with their parents, takes precedence over it.

2.2 The eternal nature of gender, marriage and family

LDS doctrine teaches that gender and families continue in the eternities. Marriage may do so if the parties enter into the new and everlasting covenant of marriage, which incorporates all other covenants and commandments, and are true to that covenant. When Jesus appeared to the apostles and others after the resurrection, there is no suggestion that he was not a man, that he was no longer gendered. Many passages in the scriptures revealed to Joseph Smith make it clear that he remains a man. Perhaps the clearest are passages found in *Doctrine and Covenants* section 130 which make it clear that the Father and Son have bodies of flesh and bones[49] and that when the Saviour appears in his Second Coming, "… we shall see that he is a man like ourselves."[50]

The *Proclamation on the Family* emphasises that gender is an eternal aspect of every person's identity. This would appear to be the case regardless of the Kingdom of Glory which that person inherits and whether or not they have entered into the New and Everlasting Covenant of Marriage.

Families also continue in the eternities. Malachi describes how before the great and dreadful day of the Lord (the second coming), Elijah will come and turn the heart of the fathers to the children and the heart of the children to their fathers.[51] If this did not happen,

---

[48] Genesis 2:24; *Pearl of Great Price* Moses, 3:24.
[49] *Doctrine and Covenants,* 130:22.
[50] Ibid., 130:1.
[51] Malachi 4:6.

the earth would be smitten with a curse when the Saviour comes.[52] Joseph Fielding Smith, President of the Church from 1970-72, explained that Elijah came to restore the sealing power, the power given to prophets to bind on earth and in heaven:

> Elijah came to restore to the earth, by conferring on mortal prophets duly commissioned of the Lord, the fullness of the power of Priesthood. This Priesthood holds the keys of binding and sealing on earth and in heaven of all the ordinances and principles pertaining to the salvation of man, that they may thus become valid in the celestial kingdom of God …[53]

In New Testament times, Peter received the sealing power from Elijah on the Mount of Transfiguration,[54] but the power was later lost. Elijah restored it to Joseph Smith in the Kirtland temple on 3 April 1836.[55] The sealing power enables families to be sealed for eternity, so that family ties survive beyond the grave.[56] There are two sealing ordinances performed in LDS temples, husbands to wives and parents to children. The object is weld the human race together in one grand family with Adam at the head:

> We are taught in the gospel of Jesus Christ that the family organisation will be, so far as celestial exaltation is concerned, one that is complete, an organisation linked from father and mother and children of one generation to

---

[52] Ibid.

[53] *Teachings of Presidents of the Church – Joseph Fielding Smith* (Church of Jesus Christ of Latter Day Saints 2013) chapter 17, "The Sealing Power and the Temple" 218-9, < www.lds.org/manual/teachings-of-presidents-of-the-church-joseph-fielding-smith/chapter-17-sealing-power-and-temple >. On the general nature of the sealing power, a power given to the Lord's prophets to bind on earth and in heaven, see *Doctrine and Covenants* 128:8-9.

[54] Matt 16:19, 17:1-13; Mark 9:2-13; Luke 9:28-36.

[55] *Doctrine and Covenants*, 110:13-16.

[56] Ibid., 132:19.

the father and mother and children of the next generation, and thus expanding and spreading out down to the end of time.

There must be a welding, a joining together of the generations from the days of Adam to the end of time. Families will be joined and linked together, parents to children, children to parents, one generation to another, until we shall be joined together in one great grand family with our father Adam at the head, where the Lord placed him.[57]

- **Eternal marriage and deification**

Not only can marriage be eternal, but it is necessary for deification or godhood. The aim of Heavenly Father's plan for humanity is to enable people to attain to godhood.[58] To do this, a person must enter the new and everlasting covenant of marriage[59] and abide in that covenant, that is live according to its terms.[60] The first requirement of this covenant is that a man and a woman are sealed as husband and wife for time and all eternity. No single person of either gender can attain to godhood. As the terms of that covenant incorporate all other covenants which a person can enter into with God, including the baptismal covenant, the oath and covenant of the priesthood and other temple covenants, it requires a person to keep all God's commandments.

The requirement that to be deified, men and women must enter the new and everlasting covenant of marriage does not limit deification to members of the Church of Jesus Christ of Latter Day Saints. Latter Day Saints perform proxy eternal marriages in their

---

[57] Joseph Fielding Smith, n. 55 above, 224-5.

[58] *Pearl of Great Price,* Moses, 1:39; Romans 8:13-19; *Doctrine and Covenants* 76:54-60.

[59] *Doctrine and Covenants,* 131:1-4.

[60] Ibid., section 132:19.

temples for the dead so that the blessings of deification may be extended to the dead who are worthy to receive them. Eventually, eternal marriage will be performed for every person who ever lived and is worthy to receive its blessings. Even people who for any reason had no opportunity to marry in this life, including those who died as children, will be given the opportunity to enter into eternal marriage and thus attain godhood.[61] Any other result is inconsistent with the justice of God. Besides, if the sealing ordinances were not performed for the dead, humanity could not be united in one grand family with Adam at its head.[62]

3. The implications of the eternal nature of gender, marriage and family

The Church's position with respect to the eternal nature of gender, marriage and family has important implications for individuals and also for the Church's position on public policy relating to gender, marriage and family.

3.1 Implications for individuals

Gender, marriage and family are eternal and sacred in that they play a crucial role in God's plan for humanity and are essential for deification. As gender, marriage and family are eternal and sacred, individual decisions with respect to them should be taken from an eternal perspective. To ignore their eternal aspect is short-sighted because it can lead to the loss of eternal blessings, especially the blessings associated with deification. Maintaining an eternal perspective can require tough choices when its demands conflict with our desires and appear to deny us happiness in the here and now. For that reason, it is almost impossible for a person to maintain such a perspective without trusting in God and his goodness and in the promised blessings attached to the eternal marriage covenant.

---

[61] Joseph fielding Smith op. cit., n. 55, 197-8.

[62] Ibid., n. 59.

Because God intends that marriage is to be eternal, husbands and wives are under a duty to honour their marriage vows with complete fidelity. Any departure may threaten the marriage and hence the possibility of deification, especially for the party in breach of the marriage vow. As God intends that relations between parents and children are also to be eternal, they are equally sacred. As children can only be sealed to their parents if their parents are sealed to each other in the new and everlasting covenant of marriage and as children benefit from living in a stable loving family, parents owe a similar obligation to their children to honour their marriage vows with complete fidelity.[63]

Sexual relations are also sacred. We do not know whether sexual relations will continue in the eternities, although we do know that a deified couple will have eternal increase, that is they will share in the divine creative power and will have spirit children throughout the eternities.[64] However, because sexual relations enable humans to share in God's creative power in mortality by providing physical bodies to God's spirit children, they play an essential role in the divine plan and hence are sacred and are only to be exercised between husband and wife within marriage:

> We further declare that God has commanded that the sacred powers of procreation are to be employed only between man and woman, lawfully wedded as husband and wife.[65]

Hence, sexual relations between an unmarried couple, whether of different sexes or of the same sex are wrong for the same reason; they violate God's command that only married couples are to engage in sexual relations. Adultery is a greater sin than sex between an unmarried couple because it not only violates God's command

---

[63] *Proclamation on the Family.*
[64] *Doctrine and Covenants* 132:19.
[65] *Proclamation on the Family,* n. 1.

that sex is limited to married couples but also violates the sacred marriage covenant and threatens the stability of an existing family.

Church policy is to encourage individuals who are attracted to persons of the same sex not to engage in sexual relations with persons of the same sex. Feeling same sex attraction is not a sin nor is identifying as gay or lesbian.[66] Hence if persons who feel same sex attraction do not have sexual relations with persons of the same sex, they may hold Church callings and temple recommends.[67]

It may appear to be lacking in compassion to require individuals who are attracted to the same sex to abstain from sex with them, as that may require them to abstain from sex completely. That may be the case from a worldly perspective because popular culture encourages people to indulge rather than control their appetites, especially their sexual appetites. The world teaches that failure to express ourselves sexually leads to frustration and misery. However, the Church, along with many other religions, teaches that the way to true happiness is to control our appetites and places strict limits on sexual behaviour in order to ensure true happiness in this world and the next. The Church encourages members to encourage and offer love and all possible support to those who are gay or lesbian and who do not want to give in to same sex attraction.[68]

3.2 Public policy implications of the eternal nature of gender, marriage and family

As they are eternal and sacred, the nature and role of gender, marriage and family is determined by divine law rather than by

---

[66] "Same Sex Attraction" topics.lds.org

[67] *Handbook 2 : Administering the Church* Chapter 21 – Selected Church Policies and Guidelines, par 21.4.7: www.lds.org/handbook/handbook-2-administering-the-church/selected-church-policies/21.4.12?lang=eng#214. A calling is a position in a Church organisation. A temple recommend indicates a member's worthiness to enter the temple and take part in temple ordinances.
[68] *Gospel Topics* "Same Sex Attraction": www.lds.org/topics/same-sex-attraction?lang=eng&old=true.

human desires, customs and practices. God has fixed the nature of gender, marriage and family for eternal purposes and human practices cannot change that. Human laws and practices may sanction departures from the divine model to take into account human weaknesses and failings, to protect children whatever the nature of the household in which they are raised and to ensure equal access to justice for all. However, human laws and practices are not binding eternally,[69] especially where they depart from divine standards.

Christ himself gave an example of human law making concessions to human weakness when explaining the divine law of marriage. He told his audience that Moses permitted divorce because of the hardness of their hearts.[70] However, Christ pointed out that it was not always so and that from a divine perspective, a person who marries a divorcee commits adultery.[71] The Church does not enforce the divine standard today, allowing divorcees to hold temple recommends and many leadership positions.

Justice may also require that human law recognise relationships which do not comply with divine standards. The law traditionally treated sexual relationships outside marriage as illegal, although not criminal, and refused to recognise or enforce arrangements with respect to property, maintenance and other related matters between parties who were in a de facto relationship. In the 20th century, the law adopted a more tolerant attitude towards stable de facto relationships.[72] Today, relationships in which the parties live together and form a household, whether or not there is a sexual component to those relationships, may be registered. Whether or

---

[69] *Doctrine and Covenants* 132:13-14, 18.
[70] Matt. 19:3-9; Mark 10:2-12.
[71] Ibid.
[72] *Ashton v Pratt* [2012] NSWSC 3.

not they are registered, the law views their breakdown as similar to the breakdown of a marriage. The Commonwealth *Family Law Act* now extends the powers of the Family Court with respect to property, finances, and maintenance and custody of children to the breakdown of all de facto relationships, whether heterosexual or same sex.[73]

In my opinion, the LDS Church's views on the eternal nature of marriage and the family do not entail that it is necessarily opposed to legislation such as the Relationship Acts or the de facto relationship provisions of the *Family Law Act.* Although they may extend recognition to sexual relationships which from the Church's standpoint are immoral, they are not necessarily wrong for that reason. It may be better to recognise such relationships and to give legal protection to the parties to them than for the law to act as if they did not exist. To do the latter may cause injustice and hardship to one of the parties if the relationship breaks down, a wrong which the State may commit and which is separate from the immorality of the relationship.

It may be that treating the breakdown of de facto relationships in the same away as a marriage lowers the status of marriage, making it in the eyes of the law only one possible type of significant relationship among many. From the point of view of the LDS Church, that is not desirable. However, there is nothing in LDS teachings which require a committed Latter Day Saint to support this view or to oppose legislation such as the Relationship Acts.

However, the Church does not support same sex marriage because it teaches that God has defined marriage as the union of a man and a woman. If that is the case, the state does not have

---

[73] *Family Law Act 1975* (Com) Part VIIIAB – Financial Matters Relating to De Facto Relationships.

the power to change the nature of marriage.[74] This may cause problems for the Church. If same sex marriage were legalised and if all marriage celebrants were denied the right to refuse to perform same sex marriages, church officials who now perform marriages as one of their official functions would have to surrender that right. They could not, as a representative of the Church, perform a marriage which the Church did not recognise as a marriage and which violated Church teachings.

The effect of this would be to separate religious and civil marriage so that a person who wanted to have a religious marriage or to be sealed to their spouse would need to go through two ceremonies, a civil and a religious marriage. Both would be necessary because with few exceptions a couple cannot be sealed without being married according to the law of the land.

Conclusion

The Church of Jesus Christ of Latter Day Saints teaches that gender, marriage and family are eternal or potentially eternal. These teachings are best understood in the context of the Church's teachings about the nature of God the Father as an exalted man with a physical body and about the possibility of deification, which is only available to married couples who have been sealed for eternity as husband and wife.

The teachings have implications both for our personal lives and for public policy. They emphasise the sanctity of marriage and the family and the wrongfulness of any sexual relations outside marriage, encouraging husbands and wives to honour their marriage

---

[74] *Handbook 2: Administering the Church* Chapter 21 – Selected Church Policies and Guidelines, par 21.4.10 "Same Gender Marriages": www. lds.org/handbook/handbook-2-administering-the-church/selected-church-policies/21.4.12?lang=eng#214

vows with complete fidelity. In the area of public policy, they have led the Church to oppose same sex marriage. If same sex marriage were legalised and if marriage celebrants were required to perform them, church officers would no longer be able to perform civil weddings as representatives of the church. To do so would violate fundamental Church teachings. As a result, those who wanted a religious marriage, in particular those who wanted to be sealed for time and eternity, would need to perform two marriages, a civil marriage and the temple sealing.

6

JOHN MILBANK ON SEXUAL DIFFERENCE AND THE ONTOLOGY OF PEACE

Brendan Triffett

ABSTRACT

Is it possible for man and woman to be brought into harmony, and still be genuinely man and woman? Is it possible for the two to be peacefully united even in their mutual difference? As long as the mystery of man and woman is interpreted according to a Marxist narrative, in which the man as such is the oppressor and the woman as such is the oppressed, there cannot be harmony between the sexes. For implicit in the Marxist-feminist narrative (not to mention certain reactions against feminism) is a particular interpretation of being, a particular understanding of reality as a whole, which understanding is an ontology of conflict. On this view, the self-expression and fulfilment of the man is in conflict with the self-expression and fulfilment of the woman. From the perspective of the woman, the man cannot be trusted. The deepest inclinations in a man, when allowed to grow and express themselves according to their inner law, impinge upon the deepest inclinations in a woman, and eventually obliterate them. Now an ontology of peace (this is the term of Anglican theologian John Milbank) thinks the relation between man and woman quite differently. On this view, true masculinity does not impinge on femininity, but actually opens a space in which a woman is released to be a woman. True femininity does not impinge on masculinity, but actually opens a space in which a man is released to be a man. In this paper (1) I apply Milbank's ontology of peace to the difference between the sexes along these lines, (2) use Milbank's work to critique the Marxist-feminist narrative of strife and (3) explain the significance of Milbank's claim that sexual difference cannot be fully comprehended in some "essentialist" fashion—that it can only be discerned, narrated, and lived.

* * * * *

This paper proceeds in three stages. First, I give a brief explanation of John Milbank's notion of the "ontology of peace". For Milbank, Nietzsche's philosophy of the will-to-power is an "ontology of strife". By contrast, Christianity understands the Triune God – and therefore Reality as such – to be infinite peace and harmony. Second, I elaborate on Milbank's ontology of peace with a brief philosophical investigation into the meaning of shared space. In order to apply the notion of shared space to the difference between the sexes, I turn to the Christian understanding of Adam and Eve in the Garden of Eden. Finally, I offer some brief remarks and raise a few questions about the possibility of same-sex marriage.

The Will-to-Power versus the Ontology of Peace

In the Gospel of John (10:10), Jesus says: "I have come that they may have life, and have it to the full."[75] One might ask, what does the fullness of life look like? What form must one's life take if it is to be an abundant life? Christians will of course look to the life of Jesus for the answer. But in order to bring out an important contrast, I am going to turn first to an influential German philosopher of the late 19th century. For Friedrich Nietzsche, abundant life is the will-to-power expressed in all its fullness. By the will-to-power he means the force of life asserting its presence and flowing over into expression and self-expansion. The will-to-power is an essentially

---

[75] NIV.

303

blind and reckless vital force that rises up and exerts itself in the world. The will-to-power stirs in the depths of each of us. Nietzsche recommends that we release this vital power into full expression. In order to be "true" to our nature, we must leave behind all ethical principles and social conventions, since these repress the raw potentialities inherent in nature. We must do away with the constraining norms of truth, goodness and beauty and celebrate the raw dynamism of life, the dark and formless will-to-power. We are to let nature express itself as it would, unconstrained by form, *logos* or convention. The calculating, reasonable ego must give way to the unpredictable and irrational movements of life itself. For fundamentally, life is nothing but sheer power – it is essentially irrational, heartless, formless, meaningless.[1]

Nietzsche, then, recommends that we affirm existence in all of its nihilistic brutality. The *Übermenschen* – the supermen who live life "beyond good and evil"[2] – will enjoy life *without measure*. By that he means first, that life is ultimately chaotic, formless and meaningless, and second, that living an abundant life means not pretending that life has any organising form or higher meaning or final purpose. Life simply *is*; the will-to-power simply exerts itself as it does. Since there is no higher purpose, it is more honest if we simply give ourselves over to the sheer play of natural forces, the stark and brutal expression of will-to-power. Let me give two illustrations. We see the Homeric brutality of this nihilistic view of life expressed in the popular HBO television series, *Game of Thrones*.

---

1 See, for example, John Milbank, *Theology and Social Theory: Beyond Secular Reason,* 2nd ed. (Oxford: Blackwell 2006), §10. For alternative readings of Nietzsche and the "will-to-power" see R. Lanier Anderson, "Friedrich Nietzsche", *The Stanford Encyclopedia of Philosophy* (Summer 2017 Edition), Edward N. Zalta (ed.), forthcoming URL = https://plato. stanford.edu/archives/sum2017/entries/nietzsche/, §6.1.
2 Friedrich Nietzsche, *Beyond Good and Evil*, Walter Kaufmann (trans.) (New York: Vintage, 1966).

And each year at Dark MOFO, the Hobart City Council joins with Nietzsche (to some extent) in commending a nihilistic celebration of chaos, a Dionysian descent into the dark and irrational.

The Christian view of abundant life is of course quite different. According to this world view, the fullness of life is the divine life lived in the Trinity. Life is *not* meaningless, for it is intrinsically oriented toward a loving communion of persons. Life is *not* irrational, since it includes the divine Logos. Life is not formless, for the absolute expression of life is the infinite harmony and perfect order of the Trinity. As Orthodox theologian David Bentley Hart points out, in the Christian understanding of Being the infinite is not *without* form as it was for the ancient Greeks, but rather *coincides* with form.[3] Divine being occurs as Trinity, and the Trinity is perfect harmony, order, meaning and love. God is Truth, Goodness and Beauty.

Recall that Nietzsche *opposes* the fullness of life to the constraining measure of form. Recall also his recommendation that we live life unconstrained by the measures of form, unfettered by truth, goodness or beauty. But as the contemporary Anglo-Catholic theologian John Milbank explains, the Christian understanding of life does not oppose life to form at all. For on the Christian view, there is no such thing as sheer life without direction, sheer will-to-power without form. On the contrary, *there are certain ontological norms that things have to abide by in any order to have life at all.* There are universal laws of being, and beings must participate in these laws in order to have being. A thing has life and power to the extent that it is measured by unity and truth, goodness and beauty. God himself is life without limit, but *not* life without measure.

I began this section by asking what the fullness of life looks

---

[3] David Bentley Hart, *The Beauty of the Infinite: The Aesthetics of Christian Truth* (Grand Rapids, MI: William B. Eerdmans, 2003), 178-86.

like. What form must one's life take if it is to be an abundant life? The Christian answer to this question is that an abundant life will necessarily take a Trinitarian form – it will reflect and participate in the harmony lived out by the three divine persons from all eternity.[4] There can be no such a thing as an abundant life without truth, goodness and beauty. A full release of the power of being takes the form of love and communion. An amoral display of sheer power, then, is not a more generous expression of life, as Nietzsche claimed, but is rather a *diminishing* of life. On Nietzsche's view, the full plenitude of life is life without measure, which is to say, life beyond form, meaning and order. On the Christian view, by contrast, the full plenitude of life is life found *in* form, meaning and order. On Nietzsche's view, conflict is an inevitable expression of life, since life in itself is sheer will-to-power. Violence is not a lesser expression of being when compared with peace and harmony. On the Christian view, by contrast, the gathering of things together into a meaningful and harmonious order is what life in its fullness looks like. Violence does not have a foothold in the deep structure of reality. It is not an inevitable expression of life. It is rather an accidental intrusion into reality, a distortion and lessening of being. Such, at least, is the Augustinian understanding of being which John Milbank puts forward as the authentically Christian one.[5]

---

[4] The notion of "participation" is central to the theology of John Milbank. For an explanation and further references see Brendan Peter Triffett, "*Processio* and the Place of Ontic Being: John Milbank and James K.A. Smith on Participation" in *The Heythrop Journal* (57), 900-16.

[5] "Christianity, however, recognizes no original violence. It construes the infinite not as chaos, but as a harmonic peace which is yet beyond the circumscribing power of any totalizing reason. Peace no longer depends upon the reduction to the self-identical, but is the sociality of harmonious difference. Violence, by contrast, is always a secondary willed intrusion upon this possible infinite order (which is actual for God). Such a Christian logic is not deconstructible by modern secular reason; rather, it is Christianity which exposes the non-necessity of supposing, like the Nietzscheans, that difference, non-totalisation and indeterminancy [sic] of meaning necessarily imply arbitrariness and violence. To

This understanding of being is what Milbank calls *the ontology of peace*.[6] In the following, I apply Milbank's ontology of peace to the difference between the sexes.[7]

Shared Space and the Difference Between the Sexes

We modern tends to imagine that each individual thing, and each individual person, simply expresses its *own* individual force, its *own* individual life, its *own* individual tendencies, its *own* individual nature. But according to Milbank, this view of things reads violence into the heart of reality. Suppose that the deepest inclination of every individual is simply to exert itself in the world – to express its own will-to-power. In that case, there is no possibility of genuine harmony between things, nor genuine peace between persons. Each individual being must struggle against other individual beings; many individuals must fight over the same space to exist. It is a metaphysical zero-sum game: if one individual gains the right to express itself in a particular space, then other individuals lose that right. At the social level, this conflictual dynamic is typically played out in collective terms: to the extent that one identity group (say, women) wins the right to express itself more fully in a certain arena, the opposing group (in this case, the sum of all men) loses that right. Marxist theories read culture and history in these conflictual terms.

Inspired by Milbank, I would say that what underlies this Marxist, conflictual view of reality is the notion of an *unshareable space* (here I'm using the word "space" in a broad, analogous

---

suppose that they do is merely to subscribe to a particular encoding of reality. Christianity, by contrast, is the coding of transcendental difference as peace." John Milbank, *Theology and Social Theory*, 5-6.

[6] Ibid., §12.

[7] For Milbank's own thoughts on sexual difference, see his *Being Reconciled: Ontology and Pardon* (London & New York: Routledge, 2003), 205-9.

sense, not just the literal, physical sense). When it is applied to the difference between the sexes, the notion of unshareable space is expressed more or less as follows: "Either we women are able to be here, to speak and express ourselves in this space, or you men are able to be here, to speak and express yourselves in this space. But it is impossible for both our identity group and your identity group to enjoy the same space at the same time. And we now declare that your allotted time in this unshareable space is now up. It's our time now, thank you very much." The alternative view, which amounts to the *ontology of peace*, is to understand that spaces are *shareable*.

So what do I mean by the "sharing" of space? Let me explain what I mean by returning to the beginning – to the first chapters of Genesis.[8] Adam and Eve lived in the very same Garden of Eden. They shared the same perfect place of dwelling. But that does not mean that there was Adam's territory over here, and Eve's territory over there. Rather, *there was equal sharing without competition and without division*. There are three parts to this idea. In the first place, there was *equal sharing* – Adam and Eve were given equal dignity as human beings, equal dominion over creation, equal freedom to enjoy all the non-forbidden fruits of the garden, equal right to enjoy the whole of their common paradise. Second, there was *no competition*. The vocation of Adam and the vocation of Eve were different. Before the Fall, the role that Adam played in the created order did not compete with the role that Eve played in the created order. It was not as if Adam and Eve found themselves competing over the same resources, or over the same position or status. Adam's dominion as a man, and Eve's dominion as a woman, were in no way in conflict. They did

---

[8] Chapters 1 and 2. While there are strong theological reasons for believing in the historical existence of Adam and Eve, my argument doesn't require this.

not even have to compromise. For compromise only arises where the needs and wants of one come into conflict with the needs and wants of the other. But before the Fall this was never the case – the trajectory of Adam's vocation, and the trajectory of Eve's vocation, were perfectly complementary. It was not as if Eve had to say "Okay Adam. Mondays, Tuesdays, Wednesdays and half of Thursdays will be your days. On those days, whenever your happiness comes into conflict with my happiness, or whenever your role in the Garden comes into conflict with my role, I will give way to you. All of the other times, you give way to me." Nor did Eve have to say, "Okay Adam. How about you have that half of the Garden, and I have this half of the Garden. You can have all of that space to yourself. You can be completely happy and fulfilled that way—your needs and wants won't conflict with mine. That can be your individual domain for your flourishing, and this will be my individual domain for my flourishing. (And by the way, I suggest we split the Garden just here, so I get this particular tree)."

My point is that the *sharing* of space that I've been talking about is not like this – it is not a *division* of space. Nor is it the common use of the same space at different times. Sharing space, in my sense, is rather this: living fully in the same space at the same time, in such a way that one person's living in that space is actually *enhanced* by the other person's living in that space. What this means, if we return to creation story, is that Adam is given his freedom to live in the garden fully *only at the point of Eve's creation.* Before that point, his dwelling in the Garden is existentially incomplete. He is lonely, in need of a companion.[9] Eve does not arrive in Adam's world as a threat. With the creation of Eve, it is not as if Adam is somehow robbed of his free reign, or diminished in his capacity

---

[9] Genesis 2:18-24.

to enjoy his world. Rather, Adam's dominion in the Garden only properly begins once he rules there *with* Eve. His kingship is incomplete without Eve's queenship. The same point can also be made in terms of *meaning*. Perhaps Adam was able to name the animals without Eve beside him. Even so, there was a sense in which the world he inhabited lacked meaning. We all intuitively grasp this point. A world that is not shared with another is a world that lacks meaning.[10] The world is only really *given* to us once it is given to *two of us at once.* "I wish you were here" is what one lover writes to another when visiting some new place as a tourist.

Let me summarise the points made above. The Garden of Eden is God's gift to Adam. The same Garden is also God's gift to Eve. But to say that the Garden is "also" God's gift for Eve is not say that it is a gift for Eve in some lesser, qualified sense. Nor is the Garden split into two separate domains, one for Adam, the other for Eve. The same Garden in its entirety – the same domain – is given for the enjoyment of both. Moreover, Adam's enjoyment of the Garden and Eve's enjoyment of the Garden are *inseparable.* Like acts of marital intimacy, full enjoyment by one cannot be separated from full enjoyment by the other. Further, the same Garden in its entirety is given for the freedom and dominion of both. Adam's dominion over material creation and Eve's dominion over material creation are inseparable. This is analogous to the sharing of sovereignty between God the Father and God the Son. The reign of God the Father is inseparable from the reign of Christ. (There are limitations to the analogy, but it still serves to illustrate my point).

In short, Adam and Eve inhabited the very same space but in

---

[10] I should acknowledge the philosophical influence of Jean-Luc Nancy and Francis Jacques here, and the theological influence of St. John Paul II and the *Communio* School.

different and complementary ways. That creation is a gift to Adam is inseparable from the fact that the same creation is equally a gift to Eve, albeit differently. That the world is intelligible to Adam is inseparable from the fact the same world is also intelligible to Eve, albeit differently. In sum, Adam and Eve can only receive the world *together*, can only make sense of the world *together*, can only be free in their world *together*, and can only rule in their world *together*. This is a law written in the order of creation, and grounded in being itself.

Closing Thoughts

Let me close with a few provocative thoughts.

Is it possible for two kings to occupy the very same throne at the same time? The answer is no, for one and the same domain cannot be ruled in the same way by two persons at once. A certain domain is either the domain of this man who is therefore king, or this other man who is therefore king, but surely it cannot be the domain of both at once – at least not in the same way, with the same mode of ruling. The same can be said in respect to the idea of two queens occupying the same throne. There is only space for one king in each kingdom, and one queen in each kingdom (or queendom), and even for one king and one queen in each kingdom (for king and queen do not rule in precisely the same way when they rule together – otherwise they could not rule *together*). But there cannot be room for more than one of each. This follows from the very nature of sovereignty.

Analogously, it is not possible for one and the same (immediate) family unit to function with two people assuming the role *of the father* at the same time – or with two people assuming the role *of the mother* at the same time.

Perhaps it is inappropriate to imply that the father should

rule as the "king" of the household, or to imply that the mother should be "queen" over her children. I will leave that point aside here – except to say that it is absurd to claim that parents should not have any authority over their children, at least when the children are young.[11] My point is not about ruling and hierarchy *per se*. My claim is simply that the mother and the father occupy – and therefore open – the family space in distinct ways, just because they have distinct functional and symbol roles in the family unit. The "masculine" mode of parenting and the "feminine" mode of parenting are quite distinct (which does not mean that men and women cannot perform the same practical tasks).

In short, man and woman are ideally suited for harmonising together with their children in a single family unit, just because man and woman are designed to *occupy the same parental space differently*. If things go according to the divine plan, then, man and woman in their sexual difference are uniquely able to occupy the *entirety of the same parental space, but without competition*.

At this point in time, I cannot see how *both* members of a homosexual couple could occupy the same parental space *wholly and fully*, in relation to the *same child or children*, without either (i) being in conflict with each other by attempting to occupy the same space in the same way or (ii) differentiating themselves more or less along "traditional" gender lines. In the first scenario, the two adults are unable to occupy the same parental space wholly and fully after all.[12] The second scenario, then, appears to be the only one that is (or at least approaches being) possible. If

---

[11] It would seem that a purely egalitarian style of parenting is impossible. Suppose that a (caring and present) parent disavows all parental authority over his/her children. In this very act, the parent is already exerting an authoritative influence on the children.

[12] This is also true when the members of the household effectively form a single parent family 'unit' with a second adult added on the (out)side with no parental role.

that is true, then the homosexual parenting couple only works to the extent that it emulates what it is not – namely, a heterosexual parenting couple. It is hard to see how this does not imply that heterosexual coupling is the ideal and norm when it comes to parenting.

7

POPE FRANCIS'S VISION OF GENDER

Richard Umbers

ABSTRACT

Pope Francis believes that the differences between male and female are not just a matter of social convention, but that men and women truly need each other in order to understand themselves:

> The differences between men and women are not of the order of opposition or subordination, but rather communion and generation, always as the image and semblance of God.

This talk will explore how in Pope Francis' vision of the family, recognition of the radical equality that exists between the sexes does not entail uniformity.

> Might we say that the greatest mission of two people in love is to help one another become, respectively, more a man and more a woman? (*Amoris Laetitia* 221)

* * * * *

The thinking that underpins the Pope's restatement of traditional Catholic teaching is the preference he gives to the poor and simple as a locus for theological interpretation. This so called teologia del pueblo, one of a family of liberation theologies to have emerged from Latin America, looks to the practices and piety of the common people free from the bourgeois concerns of the learned and clever who are often the proponents of ideological colonisation. Think of the pressure brought to bear by rich world governments on the poor ones with regards to "reproductive rights" or *"LGBTQI"* issues.

The ultimate praxis is the *lex orandi*. Catholic Faithful have always distinguished men from women in the way that they have celebrated certain sacraments. We are not just speaking of certain cultural practices as still evidenced in some countries today, where men and women will sit on separate sides of the Church. We have godfathers and godmothers. Marriage is between a man and a woman. Not only holy orders but even the office of acolyte is reserved to men.

In *Evangelii Gaudium* 103-104 the Pope refers to certain essentialist features of women – what is often referred to as the feminine genius – whilst at the same time taking into account that only men may be priests:[13]

> 103. The Church acknowledges the indispensable contribution which women make to society through the sensitivity, intuition and other distinctive skill sets which they, more than men, tend to possess. I think, for example, of the special concern which women show to others, which finds a particular, even if not exclusive, expression in motherhood.[14]

> 104. … The reservation of the priesthood to males, as a sign of Christ the Spouse who gives himself in the Eucharist, is not a question open to discussion.[15]

Feminists rail against these teachings as the institutionalisation of patriarchy and hetero-sexism to the detriment of women and homosexuals. What may seem like common sense to many ordinary people is simply a mask for historical forces that have served to oppress certain groups and the sooner we are brought

---

[13] Pope Francis, *Evangelii Gaudium* (The Holy See, 2013), 103-4.

[14] Ibid., 103.

[15] Ibid., 104.

to the realisation that this is the case the better chance we have to make socially advantageous changes.

Specifically, where Marx might speak of capital and the alienation of the working class, in feminism we have the unmasking of the binary labeling of male or female, and gender essentialism – this is a man's job, that is women's work – for the oppressing class to get what they value. How? Men value love. By controlling the structures surrounding love, men seek to exploit women's erotic and caring powers, their life force, without giving back to women in the same measure. Women are thereby systematically impoverished in the socio-sexual stakes. Men are seen as independent but women are seen as dependent – on men. Indeed, the very abilities and values of women are held to have originated from men. The authority of men is upheld on the basis of quashing the worth and excellence of women. Men can hold back but women come to depend on one man for love and will settle for exploitative conditions in order to obtain that love. Just as a capitalist is vulnerable to a workers' strike, however, so a man can be seen to be ultimately vulnerable when a woman withdraws her love and erotic affection. A woke woman doth a woke man make. But does it lead to real change on the part of men or simply strategic lip service so they can still get what they want as per the old ways? This is the war men and women have been fighting since Genesis 3.

The new way of seeing what it means to be sexually human is best illustrated with Tumblr's Genderbread person:

According to the *Stanford Encyclopaedia of Philosophy*, the distinction between sex and gender can be traced to the work of psychologist Robert Stoller (1968) in order to explain why some people felt that they were "trapped in the wrong bodies". He began using the terms "sex" to pick out biological traits and "gender" to pick out the amount of femininity and masculinity a person exhibited. This Cartesian dualism allowed Stoller to explain the phenomenon of transsexuality: transsexuals' sex and gender simply don't match. Feminists can agree with him that gender is socially constructed but they cannot agree on how.

Second wave feminists like Janice Raymond struggled with the trans aspects of gender as a potential time bomb for feminism:

> ... is individual gender suffering relieved at the price of role conformity and the perpetuation of role stereotypes on a social level? In changing sex, does the transsexual encourage a sexist society whose continued existence depends upon the perpetuation of these roles and stereotypes? These and similar questions are seldom raised in transsexual therapy at present.[1] (Technology on the Social and Ethical Aspects of Transsexual Surgery)

Eminent queer theorist Judith Butler dismisses these claims as the prejudice of Terfs:

> I think that it is incumbent on all of us to get rid of these approaches – they are painful, unnecessary, and destructive. Raymond sets herself up as the judge of what transsexuality is and is not, and we are already in a kind of moral prison as we read her work. What is much more important than any of these behaviorist or "moral" approaches are all the stories, poems, and testimonies, the theoretical and political works, that document the struggle to achieve embodied self-determination for individuals and for groups. What we need are poems that interrogate the world of pronouns, open up possibilities of language and life; forms of politics that support and encourage self-affirmation. And what we need is a political and joyous alternative to the behaviorist discourse, the Christian

---

[1] Janice Raymond, *Technology on the Social and Ethical Aspects of Transsexual Surgery* (Massachusetts, 1980).

discourse on evil or sin, and the convergence of the two in forms of gender policing that tyrannical and destructive.[2]

For Butler, gender is performative and sex itself is a socialised and normative term. "I see no problem with women having a penis, and men having a vagina."[3] The doctor is taking a normative step when she names the baby a boy or a girl. The recognition of a spectrum of gender along a continuum is a transgression of the binary construct and as such should be promoted in opposition to the cis-police who are stigmatising highly suicidal people as sinners, criminals or diseased folk. It is the individual person concerned who is best able to determine how he, she or xe identifies and that should be respected.

Perhaps an alternative image to the genderbread person could be that of liquorice allsorts. You can have butch trans women, femme trans men, transitioning agender and non-binary. The reductio ad absurdum of such thinking has been left for all to see, however, if you should care to YouTube "60 different genders".

Pope Francis is aware of these disputes and will go out of his way to treat homosexuals and transsexuals with affection and respect. Nevertheless, when it comes to the teachings of the Church on these matters he doubles down on the male/female distinction and considers the elimination of these differences a failure.

Eradicating male and female identities does nothing to solve the problem of unfair or disrespectful treatment based on people's gender. In a General Audience on the Family Pope Francis said that:

> Getting rid of the difference is the problem, not the solu-
> tion, … I wonder if so-called gender theory may not also
> be an expression of frustration and resignation that aims

[2] Judith Butler, http://transadvocate.com/gender-performance-the-transadvocate-inteviews-judith-butler_n_13652.htm
[3] Ibid.

to erase sexual differentiation because it no longer knows how to come to terms with it".[4]

With gender theory, which argues that male and female characteristics are largely malleable social constructs, he said, *"we risk going backward."*[5]

In Chapter 2 of *Amoris Laetitia* he is even more specific:

56. Yet another challenge is posed by the various forms of an ideology of gender that "denies the difference and reciprocity in nature of a man and a woman and envisages a society without sexual differences, thereby eliminating the anthropological basis of the family. This ideology leads to educational programs and legislative enactments that promote a personal identity and emotional intimacy radically separated from the biological difference between male and female. Consequently, human identity becomes the choice of the individual, one which can also change over time". It is a source of concern that some ideologies of this sort, which seek to respond to what are at times understandable aspirations, manage to assert themselves as absolute and unquestionable, even dictating how children should be raised. It needs to be emphasised that "biological sex and the socio-cultural role of sex (gender) can be distinguished but not separated." On the other hand, "the technological revolution in the field of human procreation has introduced the ability to manipulate the reproductive act, making it independent of the sexual relationship between a man and a woman. In this way, human life and parenthood have become modular and separable realities, subject mainly "to the wishes of individuals or couples". It is one thing to be understanding of human weakness and the complexities of life, and another to accept ideologies

---

[4] Pope Francis – General Audience (15 April 2016, St. Peter's Square).
[5] Ibid.

that attempt to sunder what are inseparable aspects of reality. Let us not fall into the sin of trying to replace the Creator. We are creatures, and not omnipotent. Creation is prior to us and must be received as a gift. At the same time, we are called to protect our humanity, and this means, in the first place, accepting it and respecting it as it was created."[6]

Pope Francis' encyclical on creation – *Laudato Si* – is a paean to respect for God's handiwork and links the problems that beset the environment, the poor and man himself when that order is disrupted.

This does not mean the Pope is not open to further discussion. It does mean that the discussion will take place along certain lines. In paragraph 221 of *Evangelii Gaudium* Pope Francis sets forth four specific principles which serve as "primary and fundamental parameters of reference for interpreting and evaluating social phenomena".[7]

1. Time is greater than space.

Accepting and seeing creation as a gift to respect, including our bodies, (Laudato Si 155), calls for a recognition of the tension between fullness and limitation. This is apparent in Chapter 9 of *Amoris Laetitia* with regard to the patience spouses should bear with each other – perfection is only to be found in heaven! Taking an embodied perspective of our position in space also means realising that we are on a journey to perfection within time. We need to be patient, to be accepting of our bodies, and in the interaction of a family made up of women and men, to build up habits and virtue in the anticipation of a fulfilment that can only be reached in heaven.

---

[6] Pope Francis – *Amoris Laetitia*, Chapter 2, (2016, The Holy See), 56.

[7] Pope Francis – General Audience, (15 April 2016, St. Peter's Square).

The right way to solve the problems and conflicts in male-female relations is to have men and women "talk to each other more, listen to each other more, know each other better, care more for each other".[8] Conflict arises between the sexes because of a loss of faith in God the Father. Separated from God-given reality our discourse falls into rhetoric and the manipulation of truth. Secular discourse spatialises time within a hermeneutic of technology and immediate desire rather than love and gift. Therein we see the trend to certain biological solutions of near infinite malleability to accord to one's own interior impulse without recourse to an objective judgment on that choice.

2. Realities are greater than ideas

The pope writes, "It is dangerous to dwell in the realm of words alone, of images and rhetoric."[9] We need to attend to the revelation of the mind of God in nature (and in scripture) as the measure for reality and, pace Protagoras, reality is the measure for our minds. The way we interpret our bodies must be in reference to God's design. It is here that we can look to some of the latest work in Feminism which has taken a turn back to nature and the challenging of anticategorical assumptions.

Lena Gunnarsson is a Marxist Feminist from Sweden who has taken Butler to task for stigmatising the category of 'women'. If we are to hold that men and women are of equal ability and worth then we are implying a stable ontological reality.

Says Gunnarsson:

> This ontological tension is at the heart of the feminist project and cannot coherently be made sense of without a notion of natural necessity, of a "natural ontological order" on which any society must base itself and whose inherent

---

[8] Pope Francis – General Audience, (15 April 2016, St. Peter's Square).
[9] Pope Francis, *Evangelii Gaudium,* (The Holy See, 2013), 231.

structure and constraints will cause human suffering and unfreedom unless accommodated.[10]

Nature may evolve but it remains fairly stable. If the feminist project is to be taken seriously then the metaphysical commitments that biological sex brings with it must be dealt with rather than strategically deferred. "Although women and men are more than women and men" – there are a range of complex relations and forces that position a person – "they are still women and men."[11]

Butler is wrong to have addressed ontology in epistemological terms. To say that we only know about sex through culturally constructed systems does not mean that there is no such thing as sex or that sex is a fiction. Neither is transgression a good for its own sake – not all transgression liberates and not all kinds of stability are oppressive.

It does not take much of a leap from here to begin discussion on the importance of the family.

3. Unity prevails over conflict

If everyone should be treated with dignity, how can we make the very vulnerable – and here we think especially of transsexuals – feel included? By sensitively dealing with conflict head on, the Pope exhorts us to establish communion amid disagreement. Pope Paul VI's *Ecclesiam Suam* provides us with a model for dialogue. That means not speaking from 'on high' but rather listening actively, recognising the person, and attending to the evidence and arguments.

Butler is certainly onto something when she says that:

---

[10] Lena Gunnarsson, "The Dominant and its Constitutive Other: Feminist Theorizations of Love, Power and Gendered Selves", *Journal of Critical Realism* (Volume 15, 2016), Issue 1.

[11] Lena Gunnarsson, "A Defense of the Category Women Feminist Theory", 12 (1): 23-47 (2011), 33.

> We do not have to agree upon the "origins" of that sense of self to agree that it is ethically obligatory to support and recognise sexed and gendered modes of being that are crucial to a person's well-being … [some trans people] have a strong sense of self bound up with their genders, so to get rid of gender would be to shatter their self-hood.[12]

One can't knock down if there is to be no building back up. Once again this is an argument in favour of marital and family stability for the raising of children with a proper sense of identity. It is incumbent upon families to also reach out with hospitality to people who have houses but find themselves homeless.

4. The whole is greater than the part

Synergy does not mean eradicating differences but consists, rather, in seeking to make a place for everyone in the manner of a polyhedron. Our deepest identity is the one that Christ has won for us as children of God. This is the category that intersects with any other we might care to name: sinner, saint, XX, XY, XXY … In Christ we are all children of God in whom there is no more male or female, Jew or Greek, slave or free. All of us have a white stone awaiting us with our own name written on it if we are faithful and are prepared to wash our vestments in the blood of the lamb. In heaven there is no marrying not giving in marriage except for the marriage of the lamb. And it is in the Mass that we remember this glorious future when God will be all in all.

The Church herself is a family where, as Archbishop Fisher puts it, "Everyone is invited and everyone is held to the same high standard."[13]

---

[12] Judith Butler, http://transadvocate.com/gender-performance-the-transadvocate-inter views-judith-butler_n_13652.htm

[13] Anthony Fisher OP, *Archbishop's Order of Malta Defence of the Faith Lecture* (2015, Sydney).

8

GLTG: WHAT'S OUR PROBLEM?

Haydn Walters

ABSTRACT

This paper will attempt to outline the scale of these conditions and their biological and social relevance in human and community terms. From this objective perspective Prof Walters will try and rationalise his own attitudes to the questions that emerge and to try and offer some advice on what Christian institutional responses could look like.

* * * * *

Are men and women different? Well, obviously! At least physically!

But how different are they really, especially psychologically, emotionally and psycho-sexually, taking into account the physical characteristics imposed by the Y chromosome in men and its lack in women, and perhaps also the societal/nurturing expectations imposed on this underlying template?

That`s much more difficult to answer, and human beings are hugely variable even when well within the range of "normal"; remembering that most biological traits are normally distributed in the population in a "bell-curve", and although for many traits this curve will be different and displaced apart for men and women, there will almost always be overlap to a greater or lesser extent. In terms of these complex and "softer" domains it is easy to recognise and describe the extremes: the hyper-feminine woman or the hyper-manly man, with perhaps a fair bit of narcissism and neurosis on the one hand and tendencies to anger and violence at the other. Both rather sociopathic. Most of us of course are somewhere in between, with a mix of both classic male and female traits emotionally and psychologically, and indeed importantly for relationship, in terms of sex-drive. Each of us has a quite unique personal balance bundle and profile of these.

This complexity and enigma, is largely reflected in modern neurobiology research using functional MRI. In response to stimuli the brains response does have "typical" male and female appearances, but again archetypes are only seen at the small minority extremes, and most individuals are such a mix that their gender cannot be discriminated on this basis alone.

Does any of this really matter? Perhaps not, and this biological approach may not be a good starting point for this discussion. Because when all is said and done, and taking into account such real variation in personal traits and responses to visual/ auditory stimuli in the lab, the vast majority of men and women know with certainty whether they are male or female, men or women, and in addition are in fact unequivocally and stably heterosexual. The theory and speculation about day-to-day "gender-fluidity" is just "false truth" to use a current neologism, and merely the wishful thinking of trendy pseudo-liberal greenie-leftie neo-Marxist social re-engineers who haunt this societal and (pseudo-)academic debate. Given the endless vagaries of biological settings, there may well be someone out there in the world who truly fits this coming-and-going "gender-fluidity" model, rather than being a poser-exhibitionist fake, but if so he/she exists, then it will only be as a very rare human variant indeed. Notably, this almost completely fixed gender identity applies as much to homosexuals as much it does to heterosexual.

Transgenderism and gender dysmorphism are quite different entities; they are rare in fact in spite of the publicity, and involve fixed ideation of belonging to the non-biological gender. In children it can resolve by teen-year, and even more rarely does it occur de-novo in adult, but it is not a short term "fluid" fluctuating condition.

The numbers game ... and why it is important?

Recently in *Eureka Street* (ES), the on-line Jesuit magazine (which I enjoy reading in spite of its frequent and irritating PC), there was an article focused on demands to increase the representation of homosexual personalities on TV from the current 3%. It wasn't clear to me how that figure was arrived at, but I am happy to accept it (because I think it's spot on). The thesis of the article was that this representation should be a least 10% to better reflect the numbers of gays in the community. Although not stated in this article, this argument could be, and I suspect already is being, made about every other public office, paid or unpaid. This is classic inward-looking, victimhood "identity politics", for which hard numbers and solidarity within tribe are very important; one really needs to feel part of at least a significant minority to be in this game. Developing coalitions of vaguely related types is also part of it, thus the expandable LGBTG labels.

So, the numbers game here is very important. This is what I wrote for my notes for the talk to the Dawson Centre Colloquium back in mid 2016, after a reasonably lengthy review of the scientific literature: "The oft-quoted 10% figure comes from the essentially non-scientific data of Masters and Johnson in the 1970s, and old studies about any same-sex feelings or events up to adolescence. However, the literature has moved on and is markedly improved. There are now many surveys of stable homosexual orientation in adult life and the answer is always <3%, anywhere in the world. Bisexuals are less common at less than 0.5%, usually in persons regarding themselves as heterosexual, and more than that mainly in places where sexes don't mix, essentially (reluctant) prison experiences; and I am tempted to say English Public Schools! Transgender etc is very exceptional i.e. one in many thousands or tens of thousands. Numbers don't erase the need for individual respect, but they are in danger of being grossly manipulated in the current politicisation of matters "queer"".

Since then, in response to the article in ES I mentioned above, there was this more erudite and expansive piece from a more public health literature perspective by David van Gend (2.12.16), which trumps me, and is worth quoting verbatim: "The major study by Latrobe, "Sex in Australia: Sexual identity, sexual attraction and sexual experience among a representative sample of adults", was published in the Australian and New Zealand Journal of Public Health in 2003. It found that 97.5% of Australians identify as heterosexual. The number who identify as homosexual is 1.2% (being 1.6% for men, 0.8% for women). Bisexuality adds another 1.2%, giving a total same-or-both-sex identification of 2.4% among Australian adults. Overseas, the official figure for the US is 1.6% and for the UK is 1.1%. The US National Health Interview Survey for 2013 reports "96.6% of adults identified as straight, 1.6% identified as gay or lesbian, and 0.7% identified as bisexual. The UK Office for National Statistics found a slightly lower number in 2014, with 1.1% of adults identifying as gay or lesbian; bisexual adults took the total figure to 1.6%. A claim of 10% can only be concocted through the sort of false figures for intersex used by Safe Schools (a 100-times exaggeration) and no doubt counting 'transgender' rates for young people prior to puberty (when 70-90% of these young people leave their transgender identity behind)." QED.

To get to even 2-3% of the adult population, one needs to lump together what are in fact quite different sexuality phenotypes. But if we accept for argument's sake that the concept of a consolidated LGBTG entity is legitimate, then it is certainly small. Indeed, biologically-speaking, this is outside 2 standard deviations of the normal range (5-95% of the population distribution). I want to avoid any suggestion of using pejorative terms for what a group of this size could be labelled biologically, but what I can say, really as an important introduction to the next section, is that it also cannot reasonably be regarded as a "normal variant" in biological terms, which might indeed be the case if the larger total adult number were true.

What agendas are running?

My thoughts on this were stimulated by a *Tablet* piece "From the Archive", on 20 February 2016, containing a historic commentary first published in the edition of 19 February 1966, on the Bill then in the UK Parliament lifting legal sanctions against male homosexual acts between consenting adults in private.

Much of the article would now seem, at least to me, rather old-fashioned and out of touch. But it made one very far-sighted and telling point pretty relevant to today: "As soon as these activities cease to be illegal, we must expect a movement to make them socially respectable ...". There does seem to me to be a great deal of truth in that, in so much as what was intended as a means of liberating a relatively small number of individuals from unreasonable and punitive intrusion into their private sexual lives, and resulting social humiliation and disgrace, has become one vehicle for the neo-Marxist inner-city elite to attack traditional normative moral and aesthetic attitudes; just for the sake of attacking established society using whatever the available cause in hand. This has almost inevitably lead to the current attack on conventional marriage, in many ways merely "using" the homosexual community as a convenient weapon to openly attack another major traditional institution, and deliberately one inextricably linked to the stability of family and of child rearing, both held in contempt by this anarchistic but very influential fringe.

On the other hand, it seems to me that something that was missing in the Tablet assessment of 50 years ago, was this: the changes to the Law at that time have allowed us as a society to move away from focus on "mere acts" (though I personally consider the very idea of the act of buggery as at least unhygienic and actually all round pretty unappealing, but as a literally unadulterated monogamous heterosexual I suppose that I would say that; indeed, as the man said, who am I to judge!), and has allowed gay people to be honest about themselves to the rest of us, and much more importantly to be accepted into a full and creative part of society, as themselves, as respected human beings. That for me is something really important, but t the same time does not pretend homosexuality is somehow biologically "normal" for human beings. Definitionally, from the numbers alone, it just ain't.

What might be sensible community and Church responses?
Individuals should not be defined by their sexuality, but by their humanity, though it is two-way street; if LGBTG individuals are being freely invited to become full, respected members of the secular and also Church communities, then that has to be under the rules that apply to all of us, with no special pleading within a framework of made-up rights from the specious rule book of "identity politics".

Recognise that individuals are not "choosing" to be gay, lesbian or transgender; stuff just happens! We don't understand much about it all, but it is not a lifestyle choice and it cannot be "cured".

The issue of Marriage "Rights" for all, irrespective of sexual orientation or gender(s) of the couple, I find a difficult one, mainly because I don't think that the depth of the Church's thinking on marriage has developed as it should have done over the past 50 years; handicapped I believe by a neurotic fixation on technologies of family planning, mainly I believe because of being over-obsessed about potential loss of face rather than emphasising the common good and the centrality of conscience, experience and good-judgement of those directly "carrying the baby" (as it were). But that being as it may, the strongest argument from "tradition" here is the right of all child-citizens, if at all possible, to be nurtured by their own mother and father, together in long term commitment. This works extraordinary well, and is our DNA. For the State, as guardian of the common good, to endorse policy settings which encourage any other format of child rearing, essentially declaring anything goes, and in the absence of evidence of long-term lack-of-harm, seems to me to be a dereliction of this duty of care. That of course is not to say that other modes of parenting will not be needed in extremis, indeed will need state support, but always to be seen as second best.

I have spent a lot of time discussing "the numbers", because the Church/society has a lot of cards to play here: remembering that the pressure for change comes from highly questionable sources only nominally on behalf of what are very small minorities in the community. Such small minorities should be encouraged to fully join in, but only as everyday citizens or Church members, leaving any baggage around their sexuality at the door. No special favours unless as individuals there are proven real legacy problems (as perhaps we all my have), but no prejudice either. Mutual respect has to be the core rule.

Disproportionate time and energy seems to have been spent especially on the area of juvenile transgender/gender dysphoria. Again, the starting point should be that in reality a true and lasting case is a very rare event; the hype that has been generated relates yet again to socially-destructive neo-Marxist agendas to manipulate society's genuine concern for distressed young people, so as to undermine accepted norms of boy/girl differentiation. This takes practical form in disrupting such common-place concepts as normal gender-based use of toilets! These anarchists, I strongly suspect, don't really care about this in itself, or indeed much about the individuals concerned, but they are happy to manipulate tragic personal circumstances cynically just to destroy certainty in all established norms and authority figures. So, what's the reality?... the average school will need to deal with any transgender issue only every few years, and even more rarely for an individual who is so unhappy (dysphoric) about their biological gender that they would be considered for surgical and endocrine transition to the phenotypically opposite sex. The school should make no special concessions or arrangements for any individual until they have been fully assessed over considerable time, by teams of expert paediatricians and psychiatrists, who are prepared to attest that there is sufficient concern about clinical depression and especially potential self-harm that special arrangement really do need to be made. It should be up to the school to discuss with parents and health professionals what these might be, e.g. potential use of more private staff facilities, and allowing cross-dressing of school uniform. Classmates will need counselling about need the to continue decent respectful interactions, maintaining friendship and avoidance of bullying. However, the idea that ALL and every school toilet facility should be routinely gender-neutral, "just in case", is evidently ludicrous. Similarly, the Safe-School initiative implies that gender issues are a major source of bullying in schools is just foolish. No doubt bullying is a big school problem, but sexuality as a cause must be a very small percent of this in totality, and focusing on this once more says more about the authors' underlying agenda than the needs of schools, their students and encouraging respect for everyone.

I have deliberately said little about the rare incidence of adult-onset gender dysphoria (transgender), because each case will be an unique mix of complex psych-social-sexual history, frequently involving personal experience of child abuse and substantial psychiatric morbidity. Unfortunately, "transitioning" to the opposite gender (most usually male to female) will not likely do much for their unhappiness and major risk of self-harm. The outcome for adolescents who undergo gender transition is probably a bit better, but not much; at least 50% will remain unsatisfied about themselves. This is all a very messy and unsatisfactory area of medicine, but we should recognise that most of what is done to try and help is in good faith. I don't think that grandstanding about he evils if transition surgery, for example, are very helpful, as sad as it is.

In all of these diverse areas of sexuality "going awry", societal and Church attitudes need to be caring, respectful, supportive, and non-judgemental, but also realistic about human weakness, and recognising the likely unhappiness and distress of the individual and family involved in their lives. There is huge amount of psychiatric and psychological morbidity ongoing in these groups, which have not much been helped by "liberation". If there is ever a place for "Christian mercy" then this is it. However, there should be no place for de-peronalising identity politics, whether generated by the LGBTG "industry" itself, neo-Marxist trouble makers, or indeed conservative churchmen.

9

"THE MARRIAGE OF THE LAMB HAS COME, AND HIS BRIDE HAS MADE HERSELF READY": THE PRIMARY NUPTIAL EXEMPLAR

Christine Wood

As we know there has been much heated debate throughout the Western world about the redefinition of marriage. The USA and most of Western Europe has expanded the definition of marriage to legally recognise homosexual relationships alongside heterosexual marriage. Much of the opposition to this redefinition is founded upon the Judeo-Christian Tradition that God's original plan for marriage was that one man and one woman would enter into an exclusive union of life-giving love for the term of their natural life. It is an impossible task to argue that this vision for marriage has been the norm for all civilised cultures throughout history for there have been a number of cultures that have recognised polygamy, including within the ancestry of the Israelite Patriarchal period.

Christians often attempt to propose arguments for one man, one woman marriage within the public square from the standpoint of reason alone. In other words, they assert that God's plan for marriage is something knowable from reason alone because it is part of the natural order. Hence, they enter into dialogue with their revisionist interlocutors, leaving faith and divine revelation aside. These Christians often intentionally exclude divine revelation from their conversations with unbelievers because they seek the common ground of basic human reason.

The problem with this approach, however, is that it can underestimate the power of sin in distorting one's ability to reason properly. Sin in the individual and within society can cause intellectual blindness, or at the very least a sort of intellectual myopia. This condition of the human person, affected by sin, is the reason why much of the Catholic intellectual Tradition has asserted the necessity of divine revelation. In revealing himself and the mysteries of his plan of salvation, God not only revealed truths beyond access to human reason, but also naturally knowable truths. The great Dominican philosopher and theologian, St. Thomas Aquinas (1225-74), comments:

> Even as regards those truths about God which human reason could have discovered, it was necessary that man should be taught by a divine revelation; because the truth about God such as reason could discover, would only be known by a few, and that after a long time, and with the admixture of many errors.[1]

For the purpose of this paper, I will assert that the complementarity of male and female in marriage, as well as the exclusivity and life-long faithfulness of the spouses, are truths that could be known to some extent by reason alone, but are also truths that divine revelation teaches so that all people can come to know them with certainty and ease.

Looking to divine revelation, then, St. Paul writes to the Ephesian church, exhorting wives to obey or submit to their

---

[1] *Summa theologiae*, I, q. 1, a. 1, co. The passage continues: "Whereas man's whole salvation, which is in God, depends upon the knowledge of this truth. Therefore, in order that the salvation of men might be brought about more fitly and more surely, it was necessary that they should be taught divine truths by divine revelation. It was therefore necessary that besides philosophical science built up by reason, there should be a sacred science learned through revelation."

husbands (Eph 5:22). Such a notion can be abhorrent to modern-day sensibilities about the equality of men and women. But often it is misunderstand, for we need only read on to find Paul's extreme demands of husbands: "Husbands, love your wives, as Christ loved the church and gave himself up for her" (5:25).[2] Much ink has been spilt on the debate about whether Paul's exhortation is applicable to Christians today in light of what many would say is his misogynistic view of women. But I think such a question misses the point of Paul's argument. Without the Old Testament background, we cannot understand the Apostle's statements. The clue to his vision of marriage is found in his conclusion:

> "For this reason a man shall leave his father and mother and be joined to his wife, and the two shall become one flesh." This is a great mystery, and I mean in reference to Christ and the Church (Eph 5:31-32).

Paul references here the second creation narrative in the Old Testament, in which the woman, Eve, is formed from the side of Adam, then she is brought to him and they are united in marriage. This is the climax of the creation narrative. But we note that Paul interprets this passage as actually having reference to Christ and the Church. In other words, Adam and Eve were the proto-type of the ante-type, which is Christ and the Church. The prototype must give way when the reality has come. The fullness of the reality of God's plan for marriage is to be found in Christ's nuptial union with his bride, the Church. We can study the creation account to see God's original plan for marriage, but the complete picture

---

[2] All biblical references are taken from the *Revised Standard Version Catholic Edition*, copyright © 1965, 1966, a division of Christian Education of the National Council of the Churches of Christ in the United States of America.

of this plan only unfolds in the *Totus Christus,* that is, in Jesus Christ united to his Church in a nuptial union.[3]

In order to understand the nuptial reality of Christ and the Church we must look to God's revelation in the Old Testament, for as St Augustine says, "The New Testament lies hidden in the Old, and the Old is made manifest in the New."[4] Or to use Christ's words, "Do not think that I have come to abolish the law and the prophets; I have come not to abolish them but to fulfil them" (Matt 5:17).

Where then shall we start? Due to constraints on this length of this paper, I will skip over an analysis of the creation accounts in Genesis 1 and 2. The only thing to take note of there is that in Genesis 1 both man and woman were made in God's image, and they were to be fruitful and multiply (Gen 1:26-28). Genesis 2 tells us that Eve was formed from the side of Adam, then the two were joined together in a one-flesh union of holy wedlock as the pinnacle of creation (Gen 2:21-25).

My entry point for this paper is the formation of Israel as a nation at Mt. Sinai under the leadership of Moses. It was there that God swore a covenant with Israel to be their God, and they would be his people. A selection of passages from the prophetic literature show that the prophets understood the Mosaic covenant in terms of a divine wedding between God and Israel. The prophets reveal

---

[3] A number of Christian writers throughout the centuries describe the relationship of Christ to his Church as a corporate person or as the *totus Christus,* for example St. Augustine in his *Homilies on the First Letter of St John,* 1.2 (*PL* 35: 1979): "'the Word was made flesh, and dwelt in us.' To that flesh the Church is joined, and so there is made the whole Christ [*Christus totus*], Head and body." See also his *Homilies on the Gospel of John,* XXI.8 (*PL* 35, 1568), for a discussion of the union of Christ and his Church. St. Gregory the Great writes, "Our redeemer has shown himself to be one person [*unam personam*] with the holy Church whom he has taken to himself" (*Moralia in Job, præf.,* 14, *PL* 75, 525A).

[4] St. Augustine of Hippo, *Quaestiones in heptateuchum,* 2.73 (*PL* 34, 623).

that despite Israel's unfaithfulness to the covenant, God promises to re-woo and re-wed her in a new and everlasting covenant. Turning to the New Testament, I will briefly mention the nuptial imagery in the narrative of Jesus and the Samaritan woman in John 4, and the parable of the "sons of the bride-chamber" in Mark 2. Here we will discover the ultimate purpose of the Incarnation and Redemption of Jesus Christ: the nuptial union of the divine Bridegroom to his People, Israel.

It may seem surprising that Jesus enters into this nuptial union in his passion and death on the Cross. Christians renew the climax of this union in the Eucharistic celebration where the divine Bridegroom gives his flesh and blood to his bride in an act of life-giving love. This is why the Book of Revelation gives the liturgical exclamation: "The marriage of the Lamb has come, and his Bride has made herself ready" (Rev 19:7). Although this is the title of this paper, I will not be speaking directly about the Eucharistic celebration, nor the Book of Revelation; rather, I hope to provide a reflection on some of the background to the nuptial meaning contained therein. And finally, I will outline some points for reflection that connect directly with the topic of this colloquium.

Mosaic Covenant and the Prophetic Testimony: God Weds Israel at Sinai

Most of us are familiar with the story of Israel's miraculous Exodus from Egyptian slavery and subsequent journey to Mt. Sinai where she entered into covenant with the LORD God and received God's commandments. Most of us get caught up in how Israel violated the covenant through the worship of the golden calf. But do we realise that the prophetic figures of Israel in the eighth century BC onwards considered the Sinai event to be nothing less than a *divine wedding*?

From the perspective of prophets like Hosea, Isaiah, and Ezekiel, the Mosaic covenant established between God and Israel at Sinai, was the foundation of Israel's status as a nation, and the reason Israel initially received the Promised Land and was thrown into exile.

Covenants were very important in the ancient world for uniting individuals and whole peoples together.[5] What is unique in Israel's history is that the LORD God swore a covenant with the people of Israel to be their God, and they his people. This covenant formed a permanent sacred kinship bond between God and Israel. But there were covenant conditions: if Israel obeyed the commandments of God, she would be blessed. In fact, God says to Israel in Exodus 19:

> [I]f you will obey my voice and keep my covenant, you shall be my own possession among all peoples; for all the earth is mine, and you shall be to me a kingdom of priests and a holy nation (Exod 19:5-6).

But if she disobeyed God's commandments, thus violating the covenant, Israel would trigger the covenant curses and would be exiled from the Promised Land. In Deuteronomy 30, Moses lays before the Israelites two paths on which to travel:

> See, I have set before you this day life and good, death and evil. If you obey the commandments of the LORD your God which I command you this day, by loving the LORD your God, by walking in his ways, and by keeping his commandments and his statutes and his ordinances, then you shall live and multiply, and the LORD your God will bless you in the land which you are entering to take possession of it. *But if your heart turns away, and you will not hear, but are drawn away to worship other gods and*

---

[5] Cf. D.J. McCarthy, *Old Testament Covenant: A Survey of Current Opinion* (Oxford: Blackwell, 1973).

serve them, I declare to you this day, that you shall perish; you shall not live long in the land which you are going over the Jordan to enter and possess (Deut 30:15-18).

What stands out here is Moses' warning about worshiping other gods and the consequent exile from the land. Centuries later, the prophets saw the reason for the conquest of Israel by the Assyrians and Babylonians, and Israel's subsequent exile from the land, to be found in Israel's unfaithfulness to the Mosaic covenant. Israel had begun to worship other gods. What is so striking is the prophetic description of this *idolatry* as equivalent to *spiritual adultery*, for the prophets considered the Mosaic covenant to be a divine marriage between the LORD God and Israel. Biblical scholar, Brant Pitre, writes: "From the perspective of the prophets, who saw the covenant between God and Israel as a divine marriage, the worship of other gods was not just a transgression of divine law, but an act of *spiritual adultery*."[6]

Hosea

The prophet Hosea, who prophesied to the northern kingdom of Israel before it was destroyed by the Assyrians in 722 BC, was commanded by God to take a wife of harlotry. This was to be a symbolic action to demonstrate to the Israelites what they were doing to God through their violation of the Mosaic covenant. Gomer is unfaithful to her husband, Hosea, and has three children to other men. One child is named *Jezreel*, which is Hebrew for "judgment," while another child is named *Not Pitied*[7] – indicating God will not show pity to sinful Israel – while the third child is called, *Not My People*[8] (literally: "I am not I AM to you") – indicating how radical Israel's sinfulness has divided her from the LORD God (Hos 1:4-

---

[6] Brant Pitre, *Jesus the Bridegroom: The Greatest Love Story Ever Told,* (New York: Crown Publishing, 2014), 15. [Emphasis in the original].

[7] Heb.: *Lo-ruhamah.*

[8] Heb.: *Lo-ammi.*

9).[9] Each of these children are symbolic of the consequences of Israel's unfaithfulness to the Mosaic covenant through her worship of other gods. Judgment has come upon Israel for she has triggered the covenant curses. Destruction is coming unless she repents and returns to her divine Bridegroom.

What is interesting for our purposes in Hosea is God's poetic promise of restoration in which, as in former times, he will re-woo Israel in the wilderness where he will enter once again into a nuptial covenant with her:

> Therefore, behold, I will allure her, and bring her into the *wilderness*, and speak tenderly to her ...
>
> And there she shall answer as in the *days of her youth*, as at the time when she came out of the *land of Egypt*.
>
> "And in that day, says the LORD, you will call me, '*My husband*,' and no longer will you call me, 'My Ba'al.' For I will remove the names of the *Ba'als* from her mouth, and they shall be mentioned by name no more. And I will make for you a *covenant* on that day with the beasts of the field, the birds of the air, and the creeping things of the ground; and I will abolish the bow, the sword, and war from the land; and I will make you lie down in safety. *And I will espouse you for ever; I will espouse you in righteousness and in justice, in steadfast love, and in mercy. I will espouse you in faithfulness; and you shall know the LORD* (Hos 2:14-20).

We see here language that is evocative, not only of creation, but more importantly of the Sinai covenant and Israel's Exodus experience.[10] Hosea perceives the covenant at Sinai to have been

---

[9] Cf. J.A. Dearman, *The Book of Hosea: The New International Commentary of the Old Testament* (Grand Rapids, MI: Eerdmans, 2010), 101-2, 119-31.

[10] Cf. R.C. Ortlund Jr., *God's Unfaithful Wife: A Biblical Theology of Spiritual Adultery* (Downers Grove IL: InterVarsity Press, 1996), 66-72; F. I. Andersen and D.N. Freedman, *Hosea*, vol. 24 in *The Anchor Bible* (Garden City, NY: Doubleday, 1980), 262-9.

a *spiritual espousal* of God and Israel. Since Israel has been unfaithful to the covenant, a restoration is required. At a future time, therefore, God will swear a new covenant with Israel in which the *nuptial vows* will bespeak enduring faithfulness and righteousness. Once again, Israel will become God's bride.

Ezekiel

The prophet Ezekiel prophesied to the southern kingdom of Judah during the Babylonian captivity a couple of centuries after Hosea. By this time only the southern kingdom of Judah remained since the Assyrians had destroyed and taken into exile the people of the northern kingdom of Israel in 722 BC. Like Hosea, Ezekiel also uses nuptial imagery to express Judah's covenant identity.[11] In chapters 16 and 23 of the Book of Ezekiel we find two accounts of Jerusalem's origins and sordid history. Jerusalem is the capital city of the kingdom of Judah, and is thus representative of the whole of Judah. If we look simply at chapter 16 we see Jerusalem described in her infancy as a Canaanite city before her elevation by King David to be the capital of Israel. Jerusalem is described as a newborn child who is unloved and cast off to die of exposure. But the LORD God passes by and takes care of her, raising her to maidenhood when he betroths himself to her (16:8). The LORD bestows upon his beloved spouse all kinds of gifts – the finest jewels and embroidered gowns and linens, fine flour, honey and oil. Jerusalem was exceedingly beautiful, and was recognised as such among the nations. But Jerusalem trusted in her own beauty,

---

[11] Cf. Ortlund, *God's Unfaithful Wife,* 101-17; R.B. Chisholm, *Handbook on the Prophets* (Grand Rapids, Michigan: Baker Academic, 2009), 250-2; A. Cody, *Ezekiel,* vol. 11 in *Old Testament Message: A Biblical Theological Commentary* (Wilmington, Del.: M. Glazier, 1984), 74-9; D.I. Block, *The Book of Ezekiel,* Chapters 1-14: *The New International Commentary of the Old Testament* (Grand Rapids, MI: Eerdmans, 1997), 459-503.

not recognising that all her gifts came from the LORD, that she was nothing apart from her incorporation into Israel's marital covenant to her divine Bridegroom. She fell into spiritual harlotry by chasing after other nations and worshiping their gods. She gave the gifts the LORD had given her to these idols. It is interesting that the gifts were all items to be used in Israel's temple liturgy – embroidered linens, jewels, fine flour, honey and oil. Rather than putting them to the purpose of worshiping the LORD God, the divine Bridegroom, Jerusalem chose to use them in the idolatrous worship of false gods.

Ezekiel employs graphic metaphors, having overtones of sexual infidelity and even revealing the sin of child sacrifice, in order to describe Jerusalem's covenant violation:

> You also took your fair jewels of my gold and of my silver, which I had given you, and made for yourself images of men, and with them played the harlot; and you took your embroidered garments to cover them, and set my oil and my incense before them…. And you took your sons and your daughters, whom you had borne to me, and these you sacrificed to them to be devoured (Ezek 16:17-18, 20).
>
> Adulterous wife, who receives strangers instead of her husband! (Ezek 16:32)
>
> [Your] shame was laid bare and your nakedness uncovered in your harlotries with your lovers (Ezek 16:36).

Not only do we see here the sin of idolatry described as spiritual adultery, but we also see that Jerusalem's spiritual adultery leads her to offer her own children in sacrifice to false gods. Children, who were to be considered the fruit of Israel's covenant relationship with the LORD God, are sacrificed on idolatrous altars to "other lovers." What a great distortion of the reality of the nuptial union formed at Sinai!

At times, Ezekiel beckons Jerusalem to recall her origins in her *youth*, hoping she will return to the LORD:

> And in all your abominations and your harlotries you did not remember the *days of your youth*, when you were naked and bare, weltering in your blood (Ezek 16:22).

But all hope it not lost. After destruction comes, God promises to restore the fortunes of Israel (Ezek 16:53) for he remembers the covenant he swore with her in the beginning:

> I will deal with you as you have done, who have despised the oath in breaking the *covenant*, yet I will remember my *covenant* with you in the *days of your youth*, and I *will* establish with you an *everlasting covenant*.... I *will* establish my *covenant* with you, and you shall know that I am the LORD (Ezek 16:59-60, 62).

This passage from Ezekiel 16 looks in a twofold direction: back to David making Jerusalem Israel's capital city and hence incorporating her into the Sinai covenant, which is described in terms of nuptial imagery, and forward to a future time where God will establish an everlasting covenant with Jerusalem (embodying all Israel), in which she will be a faithful spouse to him. This was the expectation of the Jewish people for the Messianic age: the divine Bridegroom would once again enter into a nuptial union with Israel through an everlasting covenant which will cover the shame of Israel's former unfaithfulness.

Christ the Divine Bridegroom

We skip ahead now to the first century AD, in which Jesus Christ, a Jew born in Bethlehem and crucified in Jerusalem, claims all sorts of divine prerogatives. Throughout his public ministry, the identity of Jesus is a source of bafflement to the Jews, and even to his own disciples.[12] Some think him to be the Messiah, while others suspect him to be Jeremiah, Elijah, or one of the other prophets.[13] The Temple authorities, the scribes, and Pharisees are scandalised by Jesus' claims and seek to destroy him.[14]

One of the most underestimated claims Jesus makes is to be the divine Bridegroom. Although there are numerous references to nuptial imagery in the words and deeds of Christ, for our purposes I will simply mention two: (1) the nuptial imagery in the narrative of Jesus' encounter with the Samaritan woman found in John 4; and (2) Jesus' parable of the "sons of the bride-chamber" in Mark 2:19-20, and its relation to Jesus' crucifixion and death.

Encounter with the Samaritan Woman

In John 4 the gospel writer presents us with the narrative of Jesus' encounter with a Samaritan woman. Jesus goes to a Samaritan town in the noon-day heat, meets a woman at a well, and asks her for a drink. The woman is astonished that he speaks with her, for "the Jews have no dealings with Samaritans" (Jn 4:9). Nuptial imagery is woven throughout this passage.[15] For instance, the patriarchs often met their wives at wells.[16] Jesus is here at "Jacob's well" (Jn 4:6) and he begins to woo the woman into a spiritual betrothal. They enter into a dialogue about "living water" – a term bearing a double-meaning, with nuptial overtones from the Old Testament.[17]

---

[12] Cf. Jn 6:42; 7:27-28, 41-42; 52; 8:14; 9:29.

[13] Cf. Matt 16:14, 16.

[14] Cf. Mk 3:6; 11:18; Matt 12:14; 27:20; Jn 5:18; 7:1; 10:31; 11:49-53.

[15] F. Martin and W.M. Wright IV, *The Gospel of John: Catholic Commentary on Sacred* Scripture (Grand Rapids, MI: Baker, 2015), 85-8; Brendan Byrne, *Life Abounding: A Reading of John's Gospel* (Collegeville, MN: Liturgical Press, 2014), 78-90.

[16] For example, see Isaac and Rebekah (Gen 24), Jacob and Rachel (Gen 29), and Moses and Zipporah (Exod 2:15-22).

[17] For example, Jer 2:13 and 17:13 refers to God as source of living water, while in Songs 4:15 the bridegroom describes his bride as "a garden fountain,

The woman misunderstands Jesus' meaning, so he turns the discourse to the topic of the woman's husband:

> Jesus said to her, "Go, call your husband, and come here." The woman answered him, "I have no husband." Jesus said to her, "You are right in saying, 'I have no husband'; for you have had five husbands, and he whom you now have is not your husband; this you said truly" (Jn 4:16-18).

The context of the passage supports Jesus' assertion, which the woman does not deny, that she has had five husbands and the man she is now with is not her husband.[18] On the surface the meaning is clear: she is a woman of ill-repute having numerous husbands and now living in an illicit sexual relationship. But on a deeper spiritual level the woman may embody the historical state of the Samaritan people. The Samaritans were not pure-blooded Israelites, for centuries earlier the Assyrian conquerors had resettled five foreign tribes with their foreign gods in that area and these tribes had intermarried with the remnant Israelites.[19] This brought the introduction of a syncretistic religion in which the Samaritan people not only worshiped the LORD God but also foreign deities. Their religion was not the pure form of religion God desired through the Mosaic covenant. These foreign deities were foreign "ba'als" meaning "lord,"

---

a well of living water." Zech 14:8 predicts that "living water will flow out of Jerusalem" and this is connected with all of Judah becoming holy as the temple itself (14:20-21). Jerusalem is often spoken of as the LORD's bride (Isa 54:1, 5-7, 11-12; 62:1, 3-5; Ezek 16:1, 8; Rev 21:2, 9-10).

[18] C. Keener, *The Gospel of John* (Grand Rapids, MI: Baker, 2003), 605-8.

[19] Cf. 2 Kgs 17:24 which speaks of the king of Assyria settling peoples from five foreign nations in the land of Samaria. They brought their own deities (Heb.: "ba'als"), setting them up on the altars of the Samaritans (2 Kgs 17:29-34). These foreign peoples worshipped their own gods alongside the LORD God. The Samaritans of Jesus' day were descendants of people who had intermarried with these five foreign peoples and had worshiped their gods. Keener disagrees with this allegorical reading of Jn 4:18 (*Gospel of John*, 606).

"master" or "husband."[20] Hence, Samaria had five husbands, yet the one present now, Jesus, was not her husband. The covenant language and imagery is very clear in this passage. Samaria had fallen into spiritual adultery through covenant idolatry. Jesus was reaching out to the Samaritan people through meeting this woman and calling her into a spiritual betrothal with himself, the divine Bridegroom.

This passage alludes to prophecies found in Hosea, Ezekiel, and elsewhere, in which the LORD God promises, in the latter days, to re-woo and re-wed Israel, as in former times in the Sinai wilderness. Jesus is appropriating to himself the role of the divine Bridegroom reaching out to the scattered tribes of Israel, to gather them to himself in order to enter into a *divine wedding*.

Parable of the Sons of the Bride-chamber

One of the most perplexing parables of Jesus is the one he gives in response to the question about why John the Baptist's disciples fast while the disciples of Jesus do not fast (Mk 2:18).[21] The parable reveals Jesus' implicit claim to be the divine Bridegroom.[22] Jesus responds:

> Can the sons of the bride-chamber[23] fast while the bride-groom is with them? As long as they have the bridegroom with them, they cannot fast. The days will come, when the

[20] Cf. M. O'Connor, "Judges," in *The New Jerome Biblical Commentary,* ed. R.E. Brown, J.A. Fitzmyer, and R.E. Murphy (London: Geoffrey Chapman, 1989), 8:19; S. Hahn, ed., *The Catholic Bible Dictionary* (New York, Doubleday, 2009), 84.

[21] Parallel passages are found in Matt 9:14-17 and Lk 5:33-38.

[22] M. Healy, *The Gospel of Mark: Catholic Commentary on Sacred* Scripture (Grand Rapids, MI: Baker, 2008), 62.

[23] The Greek *huioi tou nymphōnos* is often translated simply as "wedding guests," although a more literal translation would be "sons of the bridegroom" or "sons of the bride-chamber." The RSVCE edition has "wedding guests" but I have substituted this for "sons of the bride-chamber" to emphasise the nuptial imagery.

bridegroom is taken away from them, and then they will
fast in that day (Mk 2:19-20).

Jesus makes an analogy between himself and his disciples, and
the bridegroom and the sons of the bride-chamber in an ancient
Jewish wedding celebration. The point Jesus makes is that his
disciples do not fast because he, the bridegroom is still with them.
But when his marriage occurs, he will be taken away, and his
disciples will then fast. Ancient Jewish wedding celebrations were
particularly festive occasions, with seven days of feasting among
family and friends, followed by the nuptials on the seventh day.

Although the phrase "sons of the bride-chamber" occurs
nowhere in the Old Testament, it arises several times in Rabbinic
literature within the discussion over whether the bridegroom and
his attendants were bound by certain religious practices.[24] In
this context, the sons of the bride-chamber are the friends of the
bridegroom who prepare his bridal-chamber and attend him at the
wedding. The Rabbinic tradition indicates that during wedding
celebrations the bridegroom and the sons of the bride-chamber,
are exempt from observing certain religious practices like the daily
"standing prayer." The implication of this parable, then, is that if
Jesus' disciples were to fast while he were with them, they would
be denying Jesus to be the Bridegroom.

The parable says the "sons of the bride-chamber" will fast
when the bridegroom is taken away. On the last day of an ancient
Jewish wedding, the bridegroom would depart from his family and
friends to enter his bridal-chamber where he would consummate
his marriage with his bride. It was on that day that the bridegroom
would be separated from his friends to be joined to his bride; and
as a result, the sons of the bride-chamber would mourn the loss of
their friend. Jesus, as the Bridegroom, seems to indicate that this

---

[24] Brant Pitre, op. cit., 88. Pitre quotes the Babylonian Talmud, *Sukkah* 25b–
26a, as evidence from Rabbinic literature.

day would be his crucifixion and death, for it is on that day that he will be taken from his disciples and they will fast and mourn.

Jesus offers us a curious notion: his nuptial consummation with his bride occurs at his death. It seems strange to connect a brutal crucifixion and death with the festivities of a nuptial union, and yet there are connections between Jewish weddings and the cultic practices of the Jewish people.[25] In particular, the Jewish bridal-chamber was designed to replicate ancient Israel's Tabernacle, which was the site of the enduring presence of God and the Ark of the Covenant as Israel wandered through the wilderness. The priest entered the Tabernacle to offer sacrifice to renew the Mosaic covenant with God. Hence the people understood the Tabernacle to be the place of the consummation of the marriage of God to Israel through the blood of the covenant. Brant Pitre, observes:

> Just as God was united to his bride, Israel, through the covenant sacrifice in the Tabernacle of Moses, so too the Jewish bridegroom was united to his bride in the miniature tabernacle of the bride chamber, in a permanent and loving marriage "covenant" (Malachi 2:14). The same is true of the Bridegroom Messiah. When the time comes for his wedding day on the cross, Jesus "decks himself as a priest" (1 QIsaiaha 61:10) in order to offer the nuptial sacrifice of his own flesh and blood, through which God will be united to his people in a new and everlasting covenant.[26]

Hence, Jesus fulfils the marital union of the LORD God and Israel as he consummates his marriage to his bride, the Church, through the offering of his flesh and blood on the cross. The gospels offer supporting evidence that Jesus' passion and crucifixion are his wedding day. For instance, in ancient Jewish weddings the bridegroom would wear a crown, indicating he was "king for a day."

---

[25] For a fuller explanation of these aspects see Pitre, *Jesus the Bridegroom*, 82-114.

[26] Pitre, op. cit., 108-9.

To identify the bridegroom you would look for the one wearing the crown. A Jewish bridegroom would also customarily be dressed as a priest. Hence, we was a "priest for a day."

These customs relate to Jesus' passion and crucifixion. The gospel writers tell us that when the soldiers of the praetorium mocked Jesus, they vested him in royal-coloured garments, placing a crown of thorns on his head, and hailing him "king of the Jews" (Jn 19:1-5). Jesus was acclaimed a King, but unlike the custom of ancient Jewish weddings, Jesus was not "king for a day," but will ascend an everlasting throne upon his resurrection (Acts 2:33; 5:31).

After being mocked, the soldiers dressed Jesus in his own garment, which is described as a seamless tunic, woven from top to bottom (Jn 19:23-24). The gospel writer notes that the soldiers cast lots for his clothing for they did not wish to tear it. This is evocative of the high-priest who would have worn a seamless tunic on that same day in order to sacrifice the Passover lamb in the Temple. It was unlawful for this priestly garment to be torn. There is a clear twofold connection here: (1) Jesus is dressed as a priest, just as the high-priest enters the temple to sacrifice the Passover lamb; (2) and Jesus is dressed as a bridegroom approaching his bridal-chamber.

These few Gospel passages point to Jesus' fulfilment of the Messianic prophecies of the Old Testament in which the LORD God would wed himself again to Israel in a new and everlasting covenant.

Points of Reflection

I have laid down some of the aspects of what St. Paul calls the *mysterion magna* – the great sacrament – in bringing to light Jesus' role as divine Bridegroom. Of course, we can trace the "one man-one woman" model of marriage back to the creation narrative in Genesis 2, but according to Paul's insight this was merely the prefigurement of the divine plan in which God would wed himself to his people in and through Christ. How then does this relate to human marriage and the complementarity of man and woman? I can draw four points from the testimony of divine revelation regarding marriage:

(1) Marriage requires the *complementarity* of male and female: both the marriage of Adam and Eve, and the marriage between Christ and his Church are set within the parameters of male-female complementarity. The prophets describe the marriage covenant between the LORD God and Israel at Sinai in the language that speaks of male-female complementarity even though the LORD is *per se* genderless.[27] Whenever the New Testament writers speak of the Church's relationship to Christ as Bridegroom, the Church

---

[27] From the historicist's point of view, the basis for the complementarity of male and female in marriage in the Judeo-Christian Scriptures is historically- and culturally-conditioned, and hence not necessarily relevant for informing modern culture of the nature of marriage. This perspective would argue that God's revelation of his relationship with Israel, and later Christ's relationship with the Church, is couched in male-female images because this was the language and imagery to which the ancient peoples were accustomed. Anything outside these parameters would not be understood by Israel or first-century Christians. In response to this position, I would argue that Israel was surrounded by peoples who bore relationships to their own local deities, none of which relationships were ever considered to be elevated to a nuptial covenant. The fact that Israel's relationship to the LORD God was revealed to be a nuptial covenant was unique in the Ancient Near East. Hence, the assertion that divine revelation always assumes pre-conceived notions of reality in the recipients of that revelation falls short of the actual situation of ancient Israel and first-century Christianity. Divine revelation often brings something new and unexpected, although never in contradiction to creation. It is worth questioning then how much divine revelation regarding the complementarity of male and female in the marriage of Adam and Eve, and later in the covenant between the LORD and Israel, informed the consciousness of Israel in determining its concept of marriage to include the complementarity of male and female. Often the direction of influence is considered to be one way: Israel's own cultural norms moulding divine revelation, and not vice versa. The historicist's position requires critical assessment.

is always referred to in the feminine gender, even though members of the Church are both male and female. St. Paul and the Book of Revelation describe the Church as Christ's bride (Eph 5:32; Rev 19:7, 21:2, 9; 22:17). Interestingly, in the Catholic Tradition, the icon of the Church is embodied in Mary, the Mother of Jesus, who is both virgin and mother. The Book of Revelation also describes the Church as the woman who gives birth to a male child who would rule the nations – a reference to Jesus Christ -, and to other offspring who keep the commandments of God and bear testimony to Jesus (Rev 12:5, 17).

(2) Marriage requires the *mutual reciprocity* of spouses in their total gift of self to each other: marriage requires the otherness of the recipient in order for the gift to be given and mutually reciprocated. Christ desires communion with humanity and he achieves this through his Church. In turn the Church offers herself completely to her divine Bridegroom. We see this for instance most fully in the total self-offering of the martyrs who surrender their lives in an act of love for Christ. In human marriage, spouses are called to surrender their whole lives – their desires, their comforts, their preferences, their energies, their finances, and even their fertility – to their spouses. This mutual self-gift in marriage results in the two becoming one flesh. Previously two separate lives, become one life lived in unity.

(3) Marriage requires the *exclusivity* of the spouses: just as the LORD God was jealous of Israel's other lovers (false gods), so too human marriage requires spouses to exclude other persons from their self-gift to their chosen spouse. Christ gives himself completely to his Church, at the exclusion of other potential spouses. This means that all who come to union with Christ must do so through the Church. On the flip side, the Church gives herself to none other than Christ himself. Just as ancient Israel found herself in violation of the covenant when she fell into idolatrous worship

of false gods, the Church must avoid this error for she cannot falter in her faithfulness to her divine Spouse at the exclusion of all others. Once someone enters into a marital covenant, swearing an oath to give oneself faithfully to the other, this excludes all others from the intimacy of this covenant relationship.[28] The exclusivity of marriage protects the marriage covenant and sets the spouses free to give themselves completely to one another without interference from those outside the covenant bond.

(4) Marriage requires *fecundity* or openness to life: the fruit of the mutual self-giving of spouses cannot remain within themselves alone, but rather must be outward looking. Just as the LORD's covenant union with Israel was intended to bring mercy and grace to the other nations, so too the fruit of human marriage is ordered toward the gift of children, and hospitality towards others, among other things. We see this modelled in the union of Christ and the Church insofar as whenever this union is renewed in the Eucharistic celebration, the faithful go out to evangelise the world. They take Christ into the world, proclaiming the Word of Life, and bringing people to Jesus Christ and into union with his Bride. When the Church forgets to evangelise, she forgets the fruitfulness of marriage. Likewise when members of the Church neglect the fruitfulness of marriage, they neglect to evangelise.

In conclusion, I have attempted to argue that the exemplar of marriage is the nuptial union of Christ and the Church, as prefigured in the Mosaic covenant in which God wed Himself to Israel. Marriage is a covenant, not merely a contract. The modern

---

[28] Scott Hahn, *Catholic Bible Dictionary*, 170: "When both parties swear the covenant oath, a 'kinship' (or 'parity') covenant is formed. This covenant type is labelled 'kinship' because the familial nature of the covenant-bond is at the forefront of the relationship, rather than the subordination of one of the parties to the other. The mutual swearing of the oath indicates that both parties accept responsibility for keeping the covenant obligations, resulting in an equal, or at least reciprocal, relationship between the two."

world must recall this truth if it is going to embrace the reality of marriage. If we consider marriage merely as a contract we focus on the exchange of goods and services, and even focus either on the rights inherent in marriage, or the rights legally conferred upon entering marriage. A mercantile and dehumanising view of marriage arises. The Judeo-Christian view of marriage, on the other hand, traces its roots back to ancient biblical history, conceiving marriage as a covenant in which spouses give their whole selves to each other. Such self-donation requires *self-control* and *self-possession*, both of which our modern culture does not foster. The model for this *self-donation* is seen in the LORD God's covenant faithfulness to Israel in the Old Testament, and then we see the *mutual self-donation* in Christ's nuptial union with his bride, the Church. This union is founded upon a total, faithful, and life-giving love. This is the "great mystery," the "great sacrament," of which St. Paul speaks, and which we seek to emulate in our marriage covenants.

10

MARRIAGE: THE CONCEPT OF HUSBAND AND WIFE, FATHER AND MOTHER

Sophie York

How and why humankind found this a great idea. (And why it still does!)

* * * * *

Marriage is important to any stable society, and it is revered as a strong foundational unit in a Judeo-Christian society.

I will talk about three points.

1. Marriage in history and in Australia
2. What Marriage Alliance is
3. Some ways in which we can best defend marriage

1. Marriage in history and in Australia

Marriage in the history of the world came about as a sensible arrangement for the survival of the human race. It has been around in every culture, since time immemorial.

A man and a woman would bond together and form a family.

The commitment and ongoing protection offered by the man, the actual bearing of the children by the woman, and the *raising together*, was a remarkably natural and sensible feat by humankind, and that would explain why it has endured.

Marriage makes sense biologically, philosophically and theologically.

Biologically needs no explanation – there is no child created without a mother and father. Philosophically – it reflects the natural-law-based human right to marry and procreate.

Theologically – a few samples:

"… at the beginning of creation God made them male and female."

"Be fruitful and multiply." (Genesis 1:28)

"For this reason a man will leave his father and mother and be united to his wife, and the two will become one flesh.' So they are no longer two, but one flesh.

"Therefore what God has joined together, let no one separate." (Mark 10.6-9)

These are rather profound and unassailable statements, one would have thought:

It is not only a traditional societal ritual, it is a sacrament in many world religions.

Marriage is cross-cultural, timeless, and pre-dates registration by the machinery of state.

Throughout history, there have been numerous marriages for reasons of great love and a desire to form a family with the other person.

Because of the important nature of marriage, people have also sought to use it for all sorts of strategic purposes – to bring influential families together, to end wars between nations, to improve social position, to gain access to wealth and title. There have been arranged marriages. There have been dowries attached. At times, politicians have introduced a racial bar, restricting marriages between races. And then such anti-miscegenation law has been lifted, correctly – as it should never have been imposed. Rights and obligations in relation to property ownership, debt, succession, expectations of spouses, and with respect to children, have varied across cultures. Most cultures have acknowledged adultery as a violation of the bond of marriage.

Always, the institution of marriage has been understood as being between the opposite sex.

This fact has been respected in cultures internationally, even where there was tolerance of homosexuality such as ancient Greece and Rome and until recently, this fact was respected in modern Western civilised culture.

The right of men and women to marry and found a family is recognised in the Universal Declaration of Human Rights at Article 16, which also recognises that the family is the natural and fundamental group unit of society and is entitled to protection by society and the state.

In Australia, the Commonwealth power to make laws with respect to marriage is found in section 51 (xxi) of the Constitution, an Act which took effect on 1 January 1901.

As the various Australian colonies were established, each passed its own marriage laws providing for State recognition of marriages between one man and one woman.

So the Commonwealth got the "Marriage" power in 1901, and used it when it passed the Matrimonial Causes Act 1959, and the Commonwealth Marriage Act of 1961.

Marriage is currently governed by this Act, and in it "marriage" is defined as "the union of a man and a woman, to the exclusion of all others, voluntarily entered into, for life".

This was the common law definition btw, and it was spelt out formally in the Marriage Act via amendment in 2004. (It didn't need to be spelt out before – as people the world over knew what marriage was!)

In short, the law codified what human culture had already defined.

The Parliament does not, and never has "bestowed" the right to marriage. The human right of a man and woman to marry and procreate *pre-dates* such machinery of government, which *recognises* the right – offering protection by way of an administrative framework for it – in law. It is clearly a public good, that the government ought not undermine.

Certain unions are not marriages – such as between a man and a man, or a woman and a woman.

Even if solemnised overseas, these combinations are not to be recognised as marriage in Australia.

Bigamy, polygamy, polyandry, incest, and marrying a child are also not permitted.

In October 2013, same-sex marriage was legalised in the ACT. The ACT legislation was, however, struck down by the High Court for being constitutionally invalid. [Citation: The Commonwealth v Australian Capital Territory [2013] HCA 55 (12 December 2013)]

Basically – the High Court found that the Commonwealth covered the field of marriage, as per the Constitution, so the states and territories could not.

Rather fascinatingly, "Marriage" was found to mean in s 51(xxi) of the Constitution, (by High Court Chief Justice French and his brethren judges in a joint judgment), as including a marriage between persons of the same sex, despite the word marriage never having that meaning at the time of the Constitution being formed, and furthermore, in 1901 homosexuality was a crime! [He could also have read Quick and Garran's definitive Annotated Constitution, published in 1901, which gives clear guidance on what marriage means.]

Normally, a change to the Constitution is subject to the stricture in s 128 which says "This Constitution shall not be altered except in the following manner ..." and includes the mechanism for a Referendum.

I've read it, and *nowhere* does it say: "... the Constitution may be changed by judges giving new meanings to key words."

Importantly, and arguably, if, in the future same-sex marriage is allowed by Federal law in the future, if challenged it could be struck down as unconstitutional, if it goes before judges who are learned, impartial, and faithful to their interpretive duty.

A plebiscite is the next best thing, if we are denied a referendum, and the government has indicated it will mimic a referendum in all aspects, but it is not binding on politicians, and the change-seeker doesn't require a win in the majority of states, and if voting is not compulsory. The Prime Minister of the Day decides on the question, and this may induce in the public a loss of confidence in objectivity, as the current Prime Minster has declared publicly that he is pro-same-sex marriage.

If the Coalition wins on 2 July, Australians will be turning up to vote in a plebiscite at a not-yet-nominated future date to decide whether marriage in Australia ought to remain between one man and one woman, or change to being between two adult consenting people who are not related.

If Labor wins, legislation for SSM will be enacted in its first 100 days in office. Bill Shorten has promised no safeguards. At *The Guardian's* "Why Knot" marriage equality talk in Sydney, he said Labor would not support any religious exemptions to amendments to the Marriage Act which would allow same-sex marriage. He said "We don't need to water down anti-discrimination law to keep some people happy."[1]

---

[1] The Coalition won government by one seat, and put up The Plebiscite Bill which passed the House of Reps on Thursday 20 Oct 2016, 76-67 votes.

The closest he has come to indicating that he might protect rights and freedoms was only what he said (in a non-binding comment on the campaign trail in May 2016), "We are not interested in telling religious organisations how to run their faith-based organisations".

Letting the issue go to the people by the Coalition was decided by a majority vote in the Coalition party-room on 11 August 2015, which sensibly determined that a matter relating to our social infrastructure or of such sensitive and emotive nature should be decided by the people, who then live with the outcome.

It is not reported whether the nature of this would be via referendum (which some reasonably argue is the only way to alter the meaning of the word "marriage" in the Constitution) or plebiscite, but since this meeting, the office of Prime Minister changed hands on 14 September 2015, as it did four times in five years, and the current Prime Minister (Malcolm Turnbull) – sworn in the next day – in order to keep the Coalition intact, signed an agreement in writing with the Nationals that he would give the people of Australia a plebiscite on the issue.

This means that the Yes/No case must be aired and debated, for the public to vote from an informed perspective on any legislative change.

It then went to the Senate where our politicians quietly exterminated it, depriving Australians of both the ability to be adequately informed – and to have a voice – on whether Marriage should be re-defined in our nation.

The extermination of the Plebiscite was done *late at night* in the Senate, on the Monday night of the US election – Mon 7 Nov 2016, in a week they knew all eyes were on the US election: voting took place the next day in the US.

The voters in the *US election* startled the world by basically saying "We have had enough of political-class skulduggery, and we are fed up with paying people in public life who rob us of our voice".

And yet that was the ***exact double-trick*** played, in relation to the *Oz* Plebiscite – no coverage, and no voice. The irony of it all is lost on many of our pollies, unfortunately.

The good news is: the people's push-back is underway, across the West!

For practical purposes, good-faith acknowledgement of this requirement will take the form of equal government funding for each side of the argument, with a factual, apolitical presentation of the issues, plus an impartial question on the actual ballot paper, and a date to suit most of the general public, amongst other things.

So that's the legal definition of marriage sorted.

Culturally and socially, a married man and woman are known in Australia as *husband and wife,* and if they have children they are known also as the *mother and father.*

In 2009 the Australian government introduced reforms amending 85 Commonwealth laws to eliminate discrimination against same-sex couples in a wide range of areas. The reforms came two pieces of legislation [The Same-Sex Relationships (Equal Treatment in Commonwealth Laws-General Law Reform) Act 2008 and the Same-Sex Relationships (Equal Treatment in Commonwealth Laws-Superannuation) Act 2008.

These laws removed any differences for same-sex couples in:

- Taxation
- Inheritance
- Superannuation
- Health Insurance
- Social Security
- Aged care and child support
- Immigration
- Citizenship
- Veterans' Affairs

So people can rest assured that there is not discrimination in Australian law against gay people.

We are talking about whether or not ***marriage*** should be *re-*

defined, **not** whether there is discrimination against gay people. The laws have been changed to *remove* discriminatory treatment.

Marriage is a particular thing.

Blurring the two issues – of discrimination and marriage re-definition – is what the same-sex marriage outfit called "Australian Marriage Equality" has attempted to do, and it is not correct.

Some of the same-sex marriage advocates frame SSM as "a human right". They argue that equality means there should be no difference in treatment.

The history of discrimination law has found consistently that to treat people the same where there are demonstrable differences, is discrimination. So, for example, were the government to *require* gays to get married, *that* would be discriminatory. You could argue persuasively on the body of Western anti-discrimination law and philosophy, that their combination is different, and they are thus entitled to be treated differently.

To treat "unlike" as "like" is discriminatory. So, for example, in sport, there are different requirements of women than men, recognising that women have different physiques and strength. This is reflected in shorter tennis tournaments, for example. In the workplace, women cannot be required to carry the same weight in kilograms as men. They are permitted to take time off work prior to, as well as after, delivering a baby. Mushrooming prayer spaces for Islamic adherents recognise that they are different in their daily religious requirements, and to say "there are no prayer spaces for anyone" would not recognise these differences.

Marriage is a particular thing, one man and one woman, based upon their complementarity. It is the fact of opposite sex which makes it a marriage. And it is only the combining of male and female that is possibly procreative.

Currently, some states have some form of couple registration.

The ACT provides same-sex couples with the right to access a civil union. Under the federal law, these unions are treated as de facto unions.

2. What Marriage Alliance is

Marriage Alliance is an independent, apolitical, grassroots organisation, which was launched on 2 August 2015. It has of course attracted support from all persuasions since then.

Our aim is to preserve the current definition of marriage which has served Australian society and its children well.

We are also about providing a voice for all sections of the society – a hub, if you like, for different voices. So, for different migrant groups, the Indigenous people, Jewish and Christian religions, other religions, and for people who may not fall into any of these categories *but who simply think marriage should remain between a man and a woman.* We also have some gay supporters, who treasured having a married mother and father, think other children should have that as well, and so do not support SSM.

The media were invited to our launch but only the ABC and SBS attended.

We booked paid television ads with all the channels. You may have seen the ad – it had a drawing of an ice-berg, with the words "Same-sex marriage" above the water-line and a ship heading towards it that looks like the Titanic. Beneath the waterline are things like children's rights, parental rights and so forth.

The Ad simply makes the point that *there's more to the issue than we think.*

The ads were passed by the commercial standards regulator CAD. They were booked and paid for.

Channel 7 and 10 at the last minute pulled them, with no formal reason given.

Channel 9 and Foxtel ran them.

It goes without saying – but I will say it for emphasis – a free press should certainly not be engaging in suppressing an issue which ought to be the subject of analysis and review.

Our former Human Rights Commissioner, Tim Wilson, observed there are real religious freedom issues in relation to the introduction of same sex marriage. This is correct, but too narrow. There are many other rights affected also.

The clash of the new proposed definition with other freedoms, warrants careful consideration. This is one of the matters the "Marriage Alliance" advertisement highlights. It was one of the concerns addressed by the 4 minority judges in the *Obergefell case* in the USA.

Television stations should not be preventing one interest group from paying to raise issues for consideration about marriage – particularly where the free press has *failed to do so itself*.

This is censorship.

Freedom of speech in Australia is robust enough that this kind of obstruction of dialogue should be viewed as unacceptable. It would trigger serious concern in most Australians who became aware of it.

Paul Barry on the ABC, to his enormous credit, noted all this and exposed it on *Media Watch*. He said: "Whatever happened to freedom of speech? And was the ad really so offensive? . . . All pretty mild, surely? ... The ad in fact makes hardly any claims at all and in my opinion to say it's inviting hate is ridiculous."

And he is correct.

On 17 September 2015 the Australian Communications and Media Authority, following two complaints, determined that the advertisement was *not* in breach of the television codes of practice. ACMA also found that the TV commercial gave additional context by suggesting that people visit the Marriage Alliance website.

One thing *no* media outlet has made any mention of, is that in August 2015, a Bark petition was signed by 47 Indigenous tribal leaders, saying that marriage is sacred, and it is an affront to their ancient culture to seek to redefine it. It was presented to the Parliament. No coverage was given of this despite it occurring, despite the community also taking out a large ad in the Australian newspaper.

So how did we end up at this stage – where people could even allege that running an ad saying there was *more to an issue*, about a contemplated change in Federal legislation, was offensive?

The same-sex marriage advocates, led mostly by Australian Marriage Equality (AME) has cleverly framed the debate in terms of the civil rights' struggles of America.

Advocates say not allowing gay marriage is "like condoning slavery".

They label anyone who disagrees as *bigoted* and *homophobic,* and *talking hate-speech.*

This has caused great distress to many Black Americans, who see the gay marriage drive as completely different, and who also often hold Natural marriage in high regard.

The worst case where this was exemplified was in Washington DC at Gallaudet University, where a deaf, black-American woman academic – Angela McGaskill – was suspended from her job after she signed a petition simply arguing that the issue of same-sex marriage should be *debated,* before a vote. Her job was Chief *Diversity* Officer at the University.

This leads me to the most important issue being examined by Marriage Alliance.

We have discovered that same-sex marriage is not being introduced overseas simply to allow a relative handful of gay couples to get married. *It is being introduced under draconian conditions for the rest of society.* It is affecting basic human rights of –

Freedom of speech and opinion,

freedom of religion and conscience,

Freedom of trade,

Parental rights,

Children's rights; and

Rights to privacy.

Yet these are rights acknowledged internationally.

For example:

- Article 18 Universal Declaration of Human Rights (UDHR): Everyone has the right to freedom of Thought, Conscience and Religion.

- Article 30 (UDHR) : Nobody, [i.e. not an individual, not the state, not the SSM lobby], is permitted to destroy those freedoms!

- Article 7 Convention on the Rights of the Child: A child has the right to know and be cared for by his/her parents as far as possible and the state [i.e. nation's government] must respect these rights.

- Article 18 (4) International Covenant on Civil and Political Rights (ICCPR): States undertake to respect the liberty of parents to ensure the religious and moral education of their children in conformity with their own convictions.

Canada legalised gay marriage in 2005.

Dawn Stefanowicz, author of *Out From Under – The impact of homosexual parenting*, who was raised by a gay father, now dead from AIDS. She visited Australia earlier this year to describe the Canadian situation, where people are being litigated against in business for not wishing to participate in gay marriages, parents have found their rights curtailed when it came to what their own children are exposed to educationally,[2] and so on.

From Ireland, we learned of the famous Asher's bakery case[3] where a bakery could not, in conscience, provide a cake for a gay activist event, a cake which would be sent out in a big box under their business label. They were sued and fined, and it was very distressing for all concerned. (And yet in Australia, when Jimmy Barnes and John Farnham didn't want to have their music played at a Reclaim Australia rally, by people who had bought their music, this was regarded as reasonable.)

In Oregon, USA, in the Sweetcakes by Melissa case,[4] a family-run cake-shop was closed down [due to financial & emotional strain] resulting from the litigation.

In the USA an Asian couple who were photographers & who did not do gay weddings, were sued and they closed their business.[5] An elderly lady florist in the US was also sued.[6]

---

[2] See for example: *ET v Hamilton-Wentworth District School Board*, 2016 ONSC 7313.

[3] *Gareth Lee v Ashers Baking Co Ltd and Colin McArthur and Karen McArthur*, 19 May 2015.

[4] In the Matter of MELISSA and AARON KLEIN dba Sweetcakes by Melissa Case Nos. 44-14 & 45-14 Final Order of Commissioner Brad Avakian Issued 3 July 2015.

[5] Chris and Nang Mai, URLoved Photography.com 2014

[6] *State of Washington v Arlene's Flowers*; *Ingersoll v Arlene's Flowers* 19 Dec 2014. The Alliance Defending Freedom petitioned the Washington Supreme Court to take up Barronelle's case, and, in March 2016, the court agreed. It is still on foot, and Mrs Stutzman is now a public speaker for freedom of conscience.

Remember those words – husband and wife, mother and father?

In Spain, reportedly, these words cannot be used on official forms anymore. It's "Progenitor 1", and "Progenitor 2".

In Canada, a university (Trinity Western) is currently fighting for accreditation for its law students when they graduate, in order that they may be able to practise as legal practitioners, because one of the University's covenants requires that students refrain from sex on campus, unless they are married – and marriage is regarded as being between a husband & wife.[7]

In Australia, as we all know, Catholic Archbishop Julian Porteous the subject of a complaint to Tasmania's Anti-Discrimination Commission by Hobart transgender activist and Greens' candidate Martine Delaney, that Archbishop Porteous and the Catholic Bishops Conference breached the Tasmanian Anti-Discrimination Act by circulating a booklet to the parents of Catholic school students called "Don't Mess with Marriage".

I've read it. It contains standard Catholic teaching on the issue of marriage, is respectful towards gay people and was produced in a context where the Archbishop has a duty to inform his flock. Importantly, the booklet also alerted readers to the litigation overseas – a topic which has not been emphasised in the Australian media and yet needs to be, for an informed decision to be made by the public.

What the case highlighted, before it was strategically dumped, is that if same-sex marriage is legalised, the rights of religious schools to have their own employment and enrolment policies, and

---

[7] *Trinity Western University v. Law Society of British Columbia*, 2015 BCSC 2326, 392 D.L.R. (4th) 722) (TWU was successful in *BC Ct of Appeal); The Nova Scotia Barristers' Society v. Trinity Western University*, 2016 NSCA 59 (TWU was successful in Nova Scotia Ct of Appeal); *Trinity Western University v. The Law Society of Upper Canada*, 2016 ONCA 518 (TWU lost in Ct of Appeal in July 2016).

create their *own* curriculum content based on their own teaching on marriage, could well be compromised.

This is NOT the strait-jacketed Australia *anyone* wants!

We cannot ignore the overseas cases, they have happened.

And there are many other instances overseas, *which simply do not get to court*. Many people simply cannot afford to fight the claims.

There is no respect being shown for people's freedom of religion, freedom of conscience, freedom of trade, nor right to privacy on the issue.

We have already had the CEO of a major airline, saying basically that you cannot fly or bank in Australia if you're not comfortable with same-sex marriage – forcing people at commercial gun-point to agree with it.

How can employees of the airlines or banks then feel free to hold a differing opinion? Do they have to remain silent on the issue? Can they keep their *privacy*? Will they be *penalised* if they get found out?

We don't force doctors to do euthanasia or abortions. We don't force butchers to sell halal meat, we don't require Jewish restaurants to sell pork. And yet *all the indicators are* that on *this* particular issue, it will be – participate or be sued, or perhaps face a tribunal.

There's another aspect as well, which should sound a warning to our government.

Katy Faust, who recently visited from America and was on Qa-ndA, was raised by two lesbians. She is now a children's rights activist. She pointed to much research including a submission to the Supreme Court in the *Obergefell v. Hodges*[8] case by the Ameri-

---

[8] *James Obergefell et al, Petitioners v. Richard Hodges Director, Ohio Dept of Health et al 576 US_ (2015)*

can College of Pediatricians[9] which says that children should have a right to their mother and father. *Thousands of doctors* who are treating children physically and mentally *every day* support the College's conclusion as to this being the *best* for children.

With two men "marrying" and procuring/raising children, mothers are airbrushed out of the picture. With 2 women – fathers are. At a time when there are strong moves to correct gender imbalance and put women on Boards, the proposal here is that they be shoved aside in what is the most important role of all – that of mothering.

This is an attack on what is distinctive about womanhood/ manhood. To say that a marriage between a man and a woman is *the same as* a man and a man is to utterly repudiate the woman's full personhood. A mother is so important to a child that it has been written about for centuries. Art is devoted to it. Fields of medicine have examined it – and *the effects of deprivation of it*. The mother who carries her baby in her body, she may breastfeed that baby, she will nurture and devote her energies and no matter what happens to that child, she will always be the mother, a *phenomenally important person*. Sons have role models in their fathers, daughters their mothers. And also – sons and daughters love and learn from the opposite sex parent. There is so much material on the importance of this. Both are influenced in their understanding of the opposite sex, by how the mother and father relate to *each other* – and it influences their relationships late in life.

What is going on here is a denying of truth – and therefore a denial of the most fundamental human needs, created by such human *distinctiveness, in each sex.*

With two men, there is no womb. And yet little discussion is being had with the Australian people about how the babies are going to be provided to these couples, post legalisation.

---

[9] www.acpeds.org/about-us

At present, there are very few children available for adoption at all throughout Australia. The adoption laws vary from state to state. {The NSW law permitting gay adoption was deviously passed with little publicity in the State Parliament by 2 votes during the 17 days in 2010 when all eyes were on Canberra to see which way the Independents would go, to form a Federal government.}

At present altruistic surrogacy is permitted in Australia, for married or de facto heterosexual couples in NT, WA and SA, and elsewhere for same-sex couples also. Commercial surrogacy is not permitted at all, for any couples.

There are good reasons for this. There is a global movement against it, in that it commodifies women. Kajsa Ekis Ekman, a Swedish Journalist, examines this in her book "Bought and Being Bought" where she equates commercial surrogacy to prostitution.

All states and territories already recognise female co-mothers as the birth parents of children conceived through in vitro fertilisation or artificial insemination.

The Australian Constitution at s 51 (xxii) mentions parental rights, but parental rights and children's rights are in a state of flux at present in Australia.

They will only get more blurry if Same-sex Marriage is legalised.

For example, if two men cannot conceive, they can provide sperm, but they need an egg, and they need a womb for it to be carried in for nine months. These two requirements could be provided by two different women. And I won't analyse today mitochondrial donation, where a baby is produced with the DNA of two opposite-sex biological parents, as well as some DNA from a third healthy donor.

The rights of the parents and the child in this Brave New World, are mind-boggling.

From current trends, and overseas examples, it is highly likely that if same-sex marriage was introduced in Australia, children would have very few – if ANY rights protected at all – in relation to having any knowledge of, or entitlement to contact with, their biological parents. And yet we know that accurate identity, heredity and health all matter, and that even happily adopted children often seek this information. The Birth Certificates of children in same-sex legalised countries have had the parents' names changed on the Birth Certificate depending upon whom the parent's latest relationship is with.

As far as children's education goes, already there are signs that children will be taught at school not simply where babies come from, but homosexual and bisexual sex techniques. Parents will not be allowed to object.

The Orwellian, falsely-named "Safe Schools" Coalition Project has given a taste of things to come. It includes such "gems" as a reference describing gay sex as "the ultimate sex". It includes exercises where the children must imagine they have no genitals, and Martians arrive and decide their gender. It also includes exercises where children sit down as they agree with awkward PC questions, and the only children left standing are likely to be those children who are from migrant or traditional faith-based backgrounds, ironically painting them as targets. It also encourages gay sex experimentation at a time in life when young people often hero-worship role models of the same gender – a normal part of growing up – so the program is *sexualising what is non-sexual* – running the risk of confusing them for now, and embittering them later in life.

Some of the "Safe Schools" material could be accurately described as "Millstone" material.

Undoubtedly we all want gay students to feel comfortable at school. The priority of a school ought to be to teach the three Rs, in a safe learning environment for all.

But the program ignores the topmost reasons for bullying, such as ethnicity and body image, and desires to make teachers assist a tiny, fringe group of students who might want to transition gender, some of whom take hormone blockers as part of the process and cross-dress, and in the process the authors are recommending sacrificing the privacy, modesty and safety of *many other students*.

It creates an unhealthy self-absorption, in that it unrealistically requires everyone else to adapt to their unusual predilections, even down to insisting that all people at the school, including teachers and principal, must check with the student *which pronouns* may be used in relation to students who could be transitioning gender one day – but who also may change their minds the next.

And so too the "Early Start" Programme, designed for toddlers and pre-schoolers. This program teaches toddlers cross-dressing and to feel comfortable in the toilets of the opposite-sex. At best, it is a travesty, in that it rolls back the efforts of program such as the Bravehearts program and "Stranger Danger" teaching, which over the last two decades has taught children to NOT go along with odd behaviour, but to say "No" and to report it. At worst, it can be characterised as paedophiliac grooming.

Labor announced on Saturday 11 June 2016 that it would establish a taxpayer-funded, full-time LGBTI Anti-Discrimination Commissioner within the Human Rights Commission.

Because there is now NO discrimination in Australian law against same-sex attracted people and couples, this powerful government commissioner will have nothing to do except pursue court cases against Australians who disagree with same-sex marriage and "Safe Schools" and Early Start programs. Most people will find this stressful & many will not be able to afford to defend such cases.

To join the dots: there **is** a connection between such sexual-anarchy-brainwashing in schools, and politics. The method is to deviously hook up *primal human passions* to *Marxist politics*, and also make people feel bad about the past, so then they will *embrace* this new zeitgeist.

It seems that the same-marriage move towards State-sanctioned fatherlessness and motherlessness, is going to end in tears.

Like the Stolen Generation, The Forced Adoptions… poor policy & ill-thought-out law ends in Formal Apologies and suits against government.

We also have some groups like Beyond Blue recklessly shaping a horrible narrative so that if any gay person doesn't get their way on this SSM issue, they could feel justified in feeling suicidal. Instead of suggesting reasonable expectations based on the history and nature of marriage, BB is ironically (given its charter) "setting them up" for sadness. Gary Johns recently wrote in the Australian that, on the evidence, the opposite is true – the suicide rates have *not* gone down in Canada, after legalisation of gay marriage, as you could have expected, if the two matters were related.

3. Some ways in which we can best defend marriage

Marriage has served Australia well, and its children, and it will continue to do so.

It does not need to be re-defined. And we do not need the societal fall-out witnessed overseas.

As of 28 April 2016, according to Wikipedia, fifteen countries permit it nationally:

> Argentina, Belgium, Brazil, Canada, Columbia, France, Iceland, Ireland, Luxembourg, Norway, Portugal, South Africa, Spain, Sweden and Uruguay; and in about five others, there is partial permission, with sub-jurisdictions or

parts of Denmark, Mexico, the Netherlands, New Zealand, the United Kingdom and the United States, allowing same-sex couples to marry.

So at the time of writing this paper, about 20 countries do, and 176 countries DON'T.

Introduction of same-sex marriage laws has varied by method but overwhelmingly, the template for its introduction has been this: gay rights groups have gradually won over members of the Parliament or Congress to their cause, getting them to trade their votes in favour of it, for other issues that may matter more to them.

It has required a collaboration of manipulated Parliamentarians, judiciary who have abandoned normal judicial process, biased Media, and it has mostly been in defiance of the wishes of the general population.{When I say biased media, I mean "frightened", as a number of outlets have been afraid to publish any views in dissent.}

Of the 20 countries, the vast majority are affluent Western nations. This is revealing, as it is a symptom of how the culture of the West has been affected.

The general method has been to introduce it swiftly, shunt it through Parliament, and Not allow the matter to go to an informed population.

If Australia gets to holds a plebiscite on the issue it will *one of only a few nations to do so*.

Croatia held a referendum in 2013 which amended the constitution to define marriage as being a union between a man and a woman 65% voted *yes to lock this into the Constitution, and lock out SSM*.[10]

---

[10] https://en.wikipedia.org/wiki/Croatian_constitutional_referendum,_2013-cite_note-BBC-1https://en.wikipedia.org/wiki/Croatian_constitutional_referendum,_2013-cite_note-BBC-1

In 2015, Slovenia held a referendum and by a majority of votes rejected a Bill allowing same-sex marriage.

In Ireland in 2015 there was a referendum with a different result. The result in favour of SSM was approx 62%. But only 60% of the population voted at all. So a yes to SSM, but only from 34% of the actual voting population.

There are many factors which may have influenced the success of the vote. The "Yes" vote was well-financed, some Irish people may have felt that having to vote for something as obvious as marriage, was not something that merited a vote.

Interestingly, the Irish Federal General election shortly afterwards saw the same-sex supporting President lose so many seats that he was almost unable to form government.

According to some, what should happen in AUSTRALIA is that there ought to be a *referendum* on defining the word marriage in the Constitution, since it is highly arguable that the High Court made an ultra vires definition of marriage. Judges interpret law but it must be a reasonable interpretation, not an invention. It was simply not within his power to change the meaning of the Constitution, as has happened, in effect.

Same-sex marriage in Canada was originally legalised in a slice-by-slice method which was a result of court cases in which judges in provinces ruled that existing bans on same-sex marriage unconstitutional for purported "equality" reasons.

Then the *Civil Marriage Act* was introduced in the Canadian Federal Parliament and passed in 2005.

You will be interested to know that under Canadian law they have a "living tree" doctrine of constitutional interpretation, that says that a constitution is organic and must be read in a broad and progressive manner so as to adapt it to the changing times.

In France, according to BBC, people in favour of natural marriage between a man and a woman have vastly outnumbered supporters of same-sex marriage at public demonstrations. Up to 800,000 people gathered in Paris in January 2013 for a rally against same-sex marriage. It included religious leaders, atheists, and even gays who support marriage between a man & a woman.

It didn't matter what the people felt.

President François Hollande and the French Prime Minister, Jean-Marc Ayrault, successfully introduced a law which after 18 May 2013, granted same-sex couples the right to marry and jointly adopt children. European socialism overrode Democracy.

A challenge to the bill was immediately filed with the Constitutional Council by opposing MPs. They cited insufficient consultation with religious leaders, incompatibility with the Convention on the Rights of the Child, and the passage of the bill without NO referendum put to the people.

The Court effectively ignored them – and ruled the law was constitutional. The judiciary over-rode democracy.

Meanwhile, a ruling of the European Court of Human Rights (ECtHR) published on 10 June 2016 in the case of *Chapin and Charpentier v. France*[11] (known in France as the *"mariage de Bègles"*) the Court unanimously found Reserving marriage to a man and a woman is NOT discriminatory. It found that Article 12 (right to marry), taken together with Article 14 (prohibition of discrimination), and Article 8 (right to respect for private and family life), taken together with Article 14, were not violated.

Marriage is a unique combination.

The US Supreme Court in *Obergefell v. Hodges* in 2015 year ruled in favour of same-sex marriage. They overruled some 30

---

[11] *Chapin and Charpentier v. France* (no. 40183/07).

or so states which democratically had decided to uphold the traditional one man-one woman definition of marriage. It was not based on any constitutional basis, just the personal opinion of five unelected judges. I urge you to read the judgment of Chief Justice Roberts. He said basically "Whom do we think we are?"

And Justice Scalia said in effect: You may not care one way or another on *this* issue, but you might care who rules you.[12]

It is worth reading Alito's and Thomas' dissenting judgments also. (Clarence Thomas is an African American on the Court – he supports natural marriage).

The US Supreme Court made a similar major error in the past, in Dred Scott[13] when they approved slavery, on a fashionable interpretation of property rights, contrary to the natural law of humans having a right to be free. It was only resolved via a bloody civil war in the USA.

Within weeks of the bizarre Obergefell judgment, Kody Brown and his 4 wives were suing to have their polygamous relationship recognised in Nevada, and so is Nathan Collier and his two wives in Montana. They claim that restricting marriage to two persons is discriminatory, when marriage is nothing other than "it's all about Love".

Same-sex marriage advocates in Australia should be strongly reassuring us how *our* rights will be protected. *They* are the advocates for change. How will it benefit our society?

If you want to build a building in Australia, you have to provide an environmental impact statement. It has to show benefit and where there's problems arising, how these will be addressed.

---

[12] "It is of overwhelming importance, however, who it is that rules me." Justice Scalia per *Obergefell v. Hodges* 576 U.S. (2015)].

[13] *Dred Scott v. Sandford*, 60 U.S. 393 (1857).

Where is the social impact statement, for this monumental change proposed for our social infrastructure?

They are pretending change will be minimal, just the changing of a word! When the overseas experience is that this is *false*. It is much more than that, and it is causing misery. It has given people a weapon against others, to force them to endorse their world view.

They are offering no safeguards. Why would we ever agree to changing the definition of marriage?

The first person to be gaoled over this issue was last year in America. A district judge ordered Kentucky county clerk Kim Davis to gaol for six days in jail for contempt, for defying his orders to issue same-sex marriage licenses – *against her conscience.*

Pope Francis on his 2015 visit to America, met with Kim, thanked her for her courage and told her to "Stay strong."

The gaoling is a warning that religious freedom is now not guaranteed, where same-sex marriage is concerned, even in America – the Land of the Free.

Australia, clearly, must learn from the ruthlessness shown overseas – and carve its own path.

11

WOMAN TAUGHT ONCE, AND RUINED ALL:

SOUTHERN AFRICAN PERSPECTIVES ON NEW TESTAMENT APARTHEID BETWEEN THE SEXES IN 1 TIMOTHY 2:11-15

Benno Zuiddam

ABSTRACT

An overview of contemporary approaches by Southern African scholars indicates that 1Timothy 2:11-15 has patriarchal overtones which are irreconcilable with socio-political agendas that aim at a greater leadership involvement of women in church or society. A philological examination of 1Timothy 2:11-15 brings similarities in argument to light with Matthew 19:4-6, emphasising the non-cultural basis for the separate roles for women and men that the author of 1 Timothy envisages.

An examination of the textual context shows that this 'Apartheid' between the sexes is not abusive, but aims at an environment that is respectful towards women and in harmony with the purposes of humanity's Creator God. To preserve the integrity of the text and its message, either a traditional or a 'wild life' solution is preferable, where 1Timothy 2:11-15 is allowed to function in the context of its own habitat and world view.

* * * * *

Distinction between the sexes

Until the 20th century the social order and philosophy of the Western world reflected a clear distinction between the sexes.[1] This was considered to be a natural order. This was generally agreed on, whether one consulted Plato, Aristotle, Plutarch, St. Paul or even Immanuel Kant. Christianity has interpreted passages like 1 Timothy 2:11-15 in a patriarchal way for most of its existence. Women's exclusion from authority and teaching in the early church on the basis of this passage is well documented: "Teaching and any form of public speech is reprehensible and shameful".[2]

Chrysostom (Homily 9 on 1 Timothy)[3] is representative when he writes:

If it be asked, what has this to do with women of the present day? It shows that the male sex enjoyed the higher honour. Man was first formed; and elsewhere he shows their superiority. Neither was the man created for the woman, but the woman for the man. Why then does he say this? He wishes the man to have the pre-eminence in every way ...

[1] Uwe Krebs, "Geschlechterspezifik und Interdisziplinarität. Methodologisch-theoretische Anmerkungen", *Anthropologischer Anzeiger*, 63/3(2005), 294.
[2] Korinna Zamfir, "Women Teaching – Spiritually Washing the Feet of the Saints? The Early Christian Reception of 1 Timothy 2:11-12", Annali di Storia dell'Esegesi 32/2(2015), 377. Some argue that in the early Church a surprising number of women may have occupied positions of formal leadership. This is sometimes based on the premise that masculine descriptions in the NT equally apply to women. For instance Uke E. Eisen, *Women officeholders in early Christianity: epigraphical and literary studies*. Translated by L.M. Maloney (Collegeville: Liturgical Press, 2000), 5-6. However, patristic sources suggest that women's ordination and public teaching in situations of mixed company was only advanced in Gnostic and heretical sects, e.g. Irenaeus, *Adversus Haereses*, 1, 13, 2; Tertullian, *De Praescrip. Haeretic.* 41, 5; Firmilian of Caesarea, in Cyprian, Epist. 75; Origen, Fragmentum in 1 Cor. (74); Epiphanius, Panarion 49, 2-3; 78, 23; 79, 2-4. Didascalia Apostolorum (15); Constitutiones Apostolicae, 3.6,1-2; 9,3-4; Chrysostom, De Sacerdotio 2,2.
[3] John Chrysostom, *Homilies on Galatians, Ephesians, Philippians, Colossians, Thessalonians, Timothy, Titus, And Philemon* (Albany: Ages Software, 1997), 893.

The woman taught once, and ruined all. On this account therefore he says, let her not teach.[4]

Thomas Aquinas[5] writes on the basis of this text that "woman is in a state of subjection: wherefore she can have no spiritual jurisdiction, since the Philosopher also says (Ethic. viii) that it is a corruption of public life when the government comes into the hands of a woman. Consequently a woman has neither the key of order nor the key of jurisdiction. Nevertheless a certain use of the keys is allowed to women, such as the right to correct other women who are under them, on account of the danger that might threaten if men were to dwell under the same roof."[6] Thomas allows for women to teach privately (cf. Priscilla in Acts and the women on resurrection morning), or to baptise in circumstances of emergency, but a woman may not teach publicly in church.

---

[4] Chrysostom, In epistulam ii ad Timotheum, homiliae 1-10 (Athens: Τμήμα Πολιτισμικής Τεχνολογίας και Επικοινωνίας, 2006), 35-36: Τί οὖν ταῦτα πρὸς τὰς νῦν; Ναὶ, φησί· τῆς πλείονος ἀπέλαυσε τιμῆς τὸ τῶν ἀνδρῶν γένος· πρῶτον ἐπλάσθη. Ἀλλαχοῦ δὲ καὶ τὸ μεῖζον ἔδειξεν, οὕτω λέγων· Οὐ γὰρ ἐπλάσθη ὁ ἀνὴρ διὰ τὴν γυναῖκα, ἀλλ' ἡ γυνὴ διὰ τὸν ἄνδρα. Τί οὖν τοῦτο λέγει; Πολλαχόθεν βουλόμενος τὸν ἄνδρα πρωτεύειν ... Ἐδίδαξεν ἅπαξ ἡ γυνὴ, καὶ πάντα κατέστρεψε· διὰ τοῦτό φησι, Μὴ διδασκέτω.

[5] Thomas Aquinas, Summa Theologica Volume 6 supplement (Albany: Ages Software, 1997), 166-7.

[6] Thomas Aquinas, Supplement to Summa Part 3, QXIX,3; "ad quartum dicendum quod mulier, secundum Apostolum, est in statu subiectionis, et ideo non potest havere aliquam spiritualem iurisdictionem: quia etiam secundum Philosophum, in VIII Ethic, corruption ubanitatis est quando ad mulierem dominium pervenit. Unde mulier non habet neque clavem ordinis neque clavem iurisdictionis. Sed committitur mulieri aliquis usus clavium: sicut habere correctionem in subditas mulieres, propter periculum quod imminere posset si viri mulieribus cohabitarent." See Aquinas, Opera Omnia, Tomus duodecimus, Tertia Pars Summae Theologiae (Roma: S.C. de Propaganda Fide, 1906), 39. Aquinas seems to refer to Aristotle's Nicomachean Ethics 8.5 where government by men is the rule, and women only take on authority in matters feminine if it is delegated, or temporarily out of necessity.

This patriarchal reading of 1Timothy remained consistent in the church, well into the 20th century. In the meantime society had changed. The French revolution of 1789 was the effective start of morality being defined from and by humanity, on the basis of a rights philosophy. It took another two centuries for male politicians to realise that equal socio-political rights for women were desirable on that basis. But this was effectively secured after the suffragette movement of the early 20th century and the aftermath of two world wars, and the sexual revolution of the 1960s and birth prevention liberating women to play a more dominating role in the public workforce. Since the United Nations adopted these and related causes, most Western governments have opted for a "politically correct" philosophy. Consequently, during the last fifty years or so, there has been substantial socio-political pressure in most western societies to abandon non-conformist views. It should therefore come as no surprise that theologians reflect the convictions, pressures and ideologies of their times and have increasingly experienced unease in dealing with what they consider to be "patriarchal teachings" in holy writ.[7] A feeling of embarrassment seems to prevail regarding the traditional interpretation of these passages in the history of the church. This essay will concentrate on one such passage, 1Timothy 2, verses 11-15. I will first show how this embarrassment has become vocal in post-colonial Southern Africa in the 21st century, and then subsequently focus on the philology and theology of this passage.

Southern African perspectives

Southern Africa is worth an inventory, as the African continent at grass roots level still carries many elements of a traditional

---

[7] Cf. A.E. Swart and C.F.C. Coetzee, "Die skrifbeskouing van feministiese teoloë, in die besonder dié van Fiorenza, Brenner en Van Dijk-Hemmes – beoordeel in die lig van die gereformeerde teologie", In die Skriflig/In Luce Verbi 47/1(2013), 1-9.

society,[8] although this is not necessarily reflected by the post-colonial Western democratic political system: together with English as official language the two lasting contributions of Colonialism to this region. The African continent traditionally has a male dominated hierarchical social structure, which sits well with the orthodox views on "differentiation between the sexes", seemingly advocated by 1 Timothy. It is therefore interesting to ascertain whether traditional African role-models are encouraged or opposed by educational leaders at Southern African universities. Do research articles on 1 Timothy 2 seek to confirm or overthrow traditional models of separate roles for the sexes? Was the apostle Paul[9] right or outdated? Are male theologians concerned with this topic at all, or if so in what way? Or is it mainly women taking up a cause against oppression doing away with the traditional understanding of the text? Or are there also those who seek relevance and validity of patriarchal teachings in a contemporary context of male domination and abuse?

Natal University's Gerald West was one of the first Southern African theologians to write about this passage in the 21st century. True to the continent he uses terms that are normally reserved for a context of lions and wildlife reserves.[10] He considers 1 Timo-

---

[8] Cf. A. van Niekerk, *Saam in Afrika* (Kaapstad: Tafelberg, 1992), 41-7.

[9] Early Christian witness to attribute this epistle to St. Paul is as old as Polycarp of Smyrna. See K. Berding, "Polycarp of Smyrna's View of the Authorship of 1 and 2 Timothy", *Vigiliae Christianae* 53/4 (1999), 360: "There is a marked tendency in Polycarp's letter to the Philippians to cluster Pauline citations and allusions in the three passages in which he mentions the name of Paul. This indicates that Polycarp (consciously or unconsciously) considered the references to be Pauline. In addition, the first cluster contains a phrase from 1 Tim 6:10 followed by one from 1 Tim 6:7. The second cluster contains a phrase from 2 Tim 4:10. The most plausible conclusion which can be drawn is that Polycarp considered these also to be Pauline".

[10] Gerald West, "Taming texts of terror: Reading (against) the gender grain of 1 Timothy", *Scriptura* 86 (2004), 160-73.

thy a "text of terror" that needs to be tamed. In the end, West is pessimistic about the possibility of taming this particular lion. He concludes:

> There are no easy answers here. Texts like 1 Timothy 2:8-15 are not easily tamed. Margaret Atwood's harrowing tale of a possible future world in which bits of the Bible are used to ensure that women are only saved (literally) through childbirth (1 Timothy 2:15) and in which this text's other clauses are used to legislate that women should "learn in silence with all subjection" is a chilling reminder of just how difficult it is to tame this text.

West hopes for an "enabling voice of God" that will help to overcome the disabling dimensions of this text and its interpretations. He is profoundly embarrassed with its contents and suggests that perhaps the voice of God will appear through human action: "We must take up each and every opportunity we get to contest and destabilise – in the public realm of our communities and churches – the interpretations we have inherited and which continue to do so much damage.[11]

UNISA theologian Maretha Jacobs[12] shares West's embarrassment. While she emphasises the historical-cultural context of 1 Timothy 2:9-15 for the interpretation of this passage, this is ultimately insufficient to 'redeem' the text for our times. Jacobs acknowledges the influence of this passage in the history of the church, but largely evaluates its effect in a negative way. She 'exposes' the patriarchal roots of the cultures in which this text was interpreted for the greatest part of its existence. According to Jacobs, people taking this passage seriously "closely cohered with the view of the Bible as an authoritative book and answer book". She argues that, in order to

---

[11] Ibid, 172.

[12] Martha M. Jacobs, "On 1 Timothy 2:9-15: why still interpret 'irredeemable' biblical texts?", *Scriptura* 88 (2005), 85-100.

deal with issues pertaining to women and other contemporary matters "in a more meaningful and humane way", a different view of the Bible and a different view of our relation to our Christian past is necessary. Jacobs regards the Timothy passage as an irredeemable text, which at best confronts the reader with the dark side of his religious roots:

> Why remember, when reminiscences are all but pleasant? To find out where we have come from, we have said. To identify the human, historical reasons which brought us where we are. Confronting and struggling through our Christian past can for women often be demoralising. For it reveals the darker side of the Bible and its ongoing interpretations, for contemporary people, the side which was and is often still rendered invisible by the unholy piety which characterises so much of biblical interpretation, especially in a church context. At times this rouses acute anger. However, if the exposure of the "malemad(e)ness" of this past could lead to arguing and disagreeing with our sources and their patriarchal authors, this confrontation can become a therapeutic exercise, a turning-point and thereby a starting-point for going ahead in a very different way. Together with those males who have also left the patriarchal dispensation behind or never really felt fully at home within it.[13]

Elna Mouton and Ellen van Wolde,[14] writing for Stellenbosch University's theological journal, have a similar approach but a different solution. They struggle to make sense of the utterances regarding women in 2:8-15, and particularly the explanation in 2:13-15, from a Western 21st century perspective. In the end they argue

---

[13] Ibid., 98-9.
[14] Elna Mouton and Ellen van Wolde, "New Life from a pastoral Text of Terror? Gender Perspectives on God and Humanity in 1 Timothy 2", *Scriptura* 111 (2012), 583-601.

that 1 Tim 2:8-15 is a context-specific appropriation of the creation story rather than a universal statement on the relationship between women and men:

> We therefore suggest that 1 Timothy 2 be regarded as re-sembling the dynamic processes through which the early faith communities wrestled to understand the will of God for their particular time, while using available language and metaphors from their contexts.[15]

In other words, its usefulness is primarily dated, at best flowing from a concern with the integrity of the Christian gospel within the larger Greco-Roman society at the time. They rightly conclude that attempts to find an allegorical solution (e.g. Kenneth Waters)[16] do not really solve the problem:

> There is, however, no guarantee that such rhetoric would have produced a counter-cultural interpretation of Genesis 2-3. Allegory as sense-making of the past in view of the (patriarchal) present runs the risk of endorsing a hierarchi-cal interpretation of the creation story similar to that of a literal reading. The reason for this is that both the trans-formative potential and risk of metaphor lies in its refer-ence. If the 'new' in its reference is not recognisable to an audience, it will not shock or surprise, but (unwittingly) support the status quo.[17]

In short, allegory offers no solution, but would have only con-tributed to the patriarchal cause in the context of the first century.

Mouton and Van Wolde therefore argue that for today only two alternatives are open. The first option is to "boldly read" 1 Timothy

---

[15] Ibid., 596.

[16] Kenneth L. Waters, "Saved through Childbearing: Virtues as Children in 1 Timothy 2:11-15", *Journal of Biblical Literature*, 123/4(2004), 703-35.

[17] Mouton and Van Wolde, op. cit., 594.

2:8-15 against its patriarchal grain and history of reception, in other words, deliberately interpret the passage against its original intent and context. This might, according to the authors allow the text "to speak afresh in its full (con)textuality" to readers with opposing views today. This is not even a radical reinterpretation, but using a text against its meaning. This may be "bold", but it is questionable from a scholarly and moral perspective.

Their second option is along the lines of Jacobs, namely to acknowledge that the passage is irredeemable for the modern reader. Rather than to try and interpret a text against its obvious meaning, confirmed by two millennia of church history, one may prefer to regard this passage (or at least some aspects of it) "as irretrievably patriarchal and 'violent' without saving it theologically, yet allowing it to function as a mirror for on-going discussions on human dignity and the integrity of creation".[18]

Another perspective comes from Zimbabwe. While the previous scholars are white theologians, Francis Machingura is a black African man who as a member of a faculty of Education is mainly interested in the negative impact of Paul's injunctions in 1 Timothy 2 on the fight against HIV and sexually transmitted diseases. "We feel that it is our call to interrogate masculine readings of biblical texts like 1 Timothy 2: 11 and urge women to speak up and be heard in challenging such readings. The call must involve all weaker groups of society, particularly women, the disabled and children facing HIV and AIDS."[19] Machingura reflects the 'bold' voice of Mouton and van Woude. He is not so much interested in the message of the text. If necessary the passage must be made to read something

---

[18] Ibid., 597.
[19] Francis Machingura, "A woman should learn in quietness and full submission (1 Timothy 2: 11): Empowering Women in the Fight against Masculine Readings of Biblical Texts and a Chauvinistic African Culture in the Face of HIV and AIDS", *Studies in World Christianity* 19/3 (2013), 244.

completely different than what it says. He feels that African society uses 1 Timothy in an unhelpful way:

> In most cases, when women want to express their feelings, biblical texts (like 1 Timothy 2:11-12) purporting to be "inspired words" of God are invoked to silence women. Yet it is clear that, even though the Bible is the "word of God", it is also the "word of men" which arose in a religiously, economically, politically and culturally defined environment that favoured and gave all the power to men to control the health and reproductive systems of women.[20]

Machingura suggests that humanity is the legislative authority for its own religion. For all intents and purposes the message of 1 Timothy 2 should not be treated as valid for 21st century Africa:

> It is our plea and our call that biblical texts such as 1 Timothy 2:11-12 that sound chauvinistic must be read and exegetically analysed in their context rather than being foisted literally on contemporary women. Biblical texts that appear to promote patriarchy at the expense of women must be re-read and re-examined in a liberative way so as to benefit every member of society.[21]

In Machingura's post-modern approach, exegesis should not be based on the text of Scripture, but on what readers today consider to be helpful, or not. He desperately wants women to be leaders in church and society. If the Bible does not say the 'right' thing to that cause, the church should change it or disarm the passages in Scripture that are perceived to stand in the way. Machingura's call, though motivated by concern for a dire situation he seeks to combat, runs the risk of pressuring scholars into becoming ventriloquists for socio-political causes.

---

[20] Ibid., 245.
[21] Ibid., 248.

A text based approach from a theological rather than an educational perspective suggests that 1Timothy 2 intends to have implications for both church services[22] and society in general. NWU Potchefstroom theologian Douw Breed concludes:

> From research into the line of thinking in 1 Timothy 2, it has emerged that in this passage Paul addresses the worthy conduct of men and women, according to God's will, conduct that will lead to the salvation of men and to knowledge of the truth. This suggests that it is more likely that Paul addresses in 1Timothy 2 the conduct of men and women in normal life or in marriage, than their respective behaviour in worship.[23]

Breed's overall conclusion regarding 1Timothy 2:8-15 is that St. Paul gives prescriptive rules of conduct in married life.[24]

This brief overview of perspectives suggests that regardless of sex, race or orthodoxy African theologians are pessimistic about the possibility to 'redeem' 1Timothy 2 for anti-patriarchal causes. None of the Southern African scholars mentioned interprets this passage in the traditional way (Chrysostom & Aquinas). Only Breed's exegesis leaves room for traditional African values.

---

[22] Cf. Mark M. Yarbrough, *Paul's Utilization of Preformed Traditions in 1 Timothy, An evaluation of the Apostle's literary, rhetorical, and theological tactics* (London: T&T Clark, 2009), 87.

[23] Douw G. Breed, "Die voorskrifte in 1 Timoteus 2:8-15 soos geïnterpreteer vanuit die breër tekstuele konteks van 1 Timoteus", *In die Skriflig* 40/4(2006), 614. Translation by author from Afrikaans original: "Uit die ondersoek na die gedagtestruktuur van 1 Timoteüs 2, het dit geblyk dat Paulus in die gedeelte oor die waardige optrede van mans en vroue in ooreenstemming met God se wil handel – optrede wat tot redding van mense en tot kennis van die waarheid sal lei. Daaruit kan afgelei word dat dit meer waarskynlik is dat Paulus in 1 Timoteus 2 oor die gedrag van mans en vroue in die gewone lewe of in die huwelik handel, as oor hulle optrede in die erediens."

[24] Ibid., 615.

Philology confirms patriarchal meaning

These Southern African perspectives are also reflected in scholarship elsewhere. Perhaps most clearly by Larry Kreitzer who summarises:

> We see a brief indication of this when we turn to the passage in 1Timothy 2:13- 14. There the assumption of Adam as the first historical man underlies the author's point, but 'Adam' begins to take on an additional meaning as well. We see this in the way that the writer delivers his instruction concerning the submission of women to men and bases it upon the Genesis account of the creation of woman from man. Adam and Eve are called into service as historical, and normative, examples of how men and women should interrelate. However, here an additional problem surfaces by the way in which 'Adam' and 'Eve' are used in a manner which betrays a male-centred culture. In short, the story presented in 1 Timothy smacks of the worst kind of chauvinism. The author has interpreted the Genesis stories in such a way as to support his understanding of the natural hierarchy between the sexes.[25]

Even a reinterpretation of the Timothy passage is attempted, the results are unconvincing. At best it justifies a possible adjustment of elements of the text, but it does not warrant a proclamation that the overall picture has changed.

Jamin Hübner,[26] for instance, attempts a reinterpretation based on the Greek verb for exercising authority in 1Timothy 2:12: διδάσκειν δὲ γυναικὶ οὐκ ἐπιτρέπω οὐδὲ αὐθεντεῖν ἀνδρός, ἀλλ᾽ εἶναι ἐν ἡσυξίᾳ ("I permit no woman to teach or to have author-

---

[25] Larry Kreitzer, "Adam as Analogy: Help or Hindrance?", *New Blackfriars* 70/828 (1989), 278.

[26] Jamin Hübner, "Translating αὐθεντέω (authenteō) in 1Timothy 2:12", *Priscilla Papers* 29/2(2012), 16-26.

ity over a man; she is to keep silent"). Hübner argues against "exercising authority" as translation and insists on a negative or 'pejorative' interpretation. Admittedly, this is how the King James version translates αὐθεντεῖν, "to usurp authority", probably following the Vulgate: *docere autem mulieri non permitto, neque dominari in virum, sed esse in silentio*. If "dominari" was considered to be a proper Latin rendering in days when both Latin and Koine Greek were still spoken as native languages, it is likely to be at least a possible translation. Still, it must be mentioned that one of the best classical Greek authorities firmly insists on "to have full power or authority over" as translation for αὐθεντέω and takes care to specifically refer to 1 Timothy 2:12 as example.[27] Bauer and Aland take a similar approach with "herrschen".[28] Collins takes it in a profoundly positive meaning, as he believes that in Greco-Roman society authority was not so much about obedience, but about knowing one's place in the greater whole.[29] Without observance of one's distinct place, society would be negatively affected.

Note however, that even when one allows a negative thrust for αὐθεντεῖν, it is very hard to argue the same for διδάσκειν. In the Latin Vulgate translation "teaching" is not regarded in a negative way and neither is it in the English KJV. Even if the text were only directed against women unlawfully usurping authority over men, this would not change the fact that the Timothy passage is far from 'gender' neutral. There is no evidence in this otherwise cohesively

---

[27] H.G. Liddell and R.A. Scott, *Greek-English lexicon*, with a revised supplement (Oxford: Clarendon Press, 1996), 275.

[28] W. Bauer, K. Aland and B. Aland, *Wörterbuch zum Neuen Testament. 6., völlig neu bearbeitete Auflage* (Berlin: Walter De Gruyter, 1988), 242.

[29] Raymond F. Collins, *1 & 2 Timothy and Titus: A Commentary* (Louisville: John Knox press, 2002), 69.

structured epistle[30] that there are any lawful ways in which wives can exercise authority over their husbands. Or, 'women' over 'men in general', as Gordon Fee points out that 'women', in this context, is used without the definite article, implying or suggesting a broader context than merely wives and marriage.[31] This also weakens Breed's thesis that was discussed earlier.[32]

Köstenberger's rule for positive parallel structures applies,[33] as in this particular case Hübner requires "teaching" to be a parallel negative entity. For his anti-patriarchal interpretation to work. he wants the passage to argue against women doing bad teaching and against women abusing authority to lead others into sin. Which could be as easily said of men, and eureka, arguably the perfect gender neutral solution. Woman doing proper teaching of man and woman exercising authority over man (as long as she does not tempt them into sin like Eve did), would then be quite all right.

Still, this is a rather desperate intellectual exercise. At micro level with a sentence read in isolation from the passage and the rest of the epistle and its context, it seems to work. But is this convincing? No, the apostolic motivation from Genesis that follows the prohibition in verse 12 is as definite as it is general. This is not a pronouncement against a few dominating busybodies, but one that concerns womanhood in general. The fact of the matter is that

---

[30] See J.T. Reed, "Cohesive ties in 1 Timothy: in Defense of the Epistle's Unity", *Neotestamentica* 26/1(1992), 146.

[31] Gordon D. Fee, *1 & 2 Timothy, Titus. Understanding the Bible Commentary Series* (Grand Rapids: Baker, 1988), 73.

[32] See Douw G. Breed, "Die voorskrifte in 1 Timoteus 2:8-15 soos geïnterpreteer vanuit die breër tekstuele konteks van 1 Timoteus", *In die Skriflig* 40/4(2006), 597-616.

[33] See Andreas J. Köstenberger and Thomas R. Schreiner, *Women in the Church: An Analysis and Application of 1 Timothy 2:9-15.* 2d ed. (Grand Rapids: Baker, 2005), 53-84.

the apostle argues against all teaching by women in church.[34] If anything, it is this very teaching of men by women in Christian congregations that the author of 1Timothy considers "unsuitable domineering behaviour" and "usurping authority". Heinz-Werner Neudorfer explains that the concepts of teaching and taking up authority are closely related. Teaching in mixed company implies taking up authority over men, and it is exactly this, what the apostle prohibits: "Der Lehrer stellt nicht nur sein Denkvermögen aus, sondern er gebietet. Die lehrende Frau geböte also dem Mann, und dazu gibt Paulus ihr Erlaubnis nicht".[35]

---

[34] In the early Church Paul's command that women should not teach in the congregations, also applied to prophecy (1 Cor 11). Origen argued that the prophesying of women both in Old and New Testament was of a private nature and did not involve public teaching or taking up authority over men, Fragmenta ex commentariis in epistulam i ad Corinthios (74 xiv 34-35): Ὡς γὰρ πάντων λεγόντων καὶ δυναμένων λέγειν, ἐὰν ἀποκάλυψις αὐτοῖς γένηται, φησὶν Αἱ γυναῖκες ἐν ταῖς ἐκκλησίαις σιγάτωσαν. ταύτης δὲ τῆς ἐντολῆς οὐκ ἦσαν οἱ τῶν γυναικῶν μαθηταί, οἱ μαθητευθέντες Πρισκίλλῃ καὶ Μαξιμίλλῃ, οὐ Χριστοῦ τοῦ ἀνδρὸς τῆς νύμφης. ἀλλ᾽ ὅμως εὐγνωμονῶμεν καὶ πρὸς τὰ πιθανὰ ἐκείνων ἀπαντῶντες. τέσσαρές φασι θυγατέρες ἦσαν Φιλίππου τοῦ εὐαγγελιστοῦ καὶ προεφήτευον. εἰ δὲ προεφήτευον, τί ἄτοπόν ἐστι καὶ τὰς ἡμετέρας, ὡς φασὶν ἐκεῖνοι, προφήτιδας προφητεύειν; ταῦτα δὲ λύσομεν. πρῶτον μὲν λέγοντες ὅτι Αἱ ἡμέτεραι προεφήτευον, δείξατε τὰ σημεῖα τῆς προφητείας ἐν αὐταῖς· δεύτερον δὲ Εἰ καὶ προεφήτευον αἱ θυγατέρες Φιλίππου, ἀλλ᾽ οὐκ ἐν ταῖς ἐκκλησίαις ἔλεγον· οὐ γὰρ ἔχομεν τοῦτο ἐν ταῖς Πράξεσι τῶν Ἀποστόλων. ἀλλ᾽ οὐδ᾽ ἐν τῇ παλαιᾷ· Δεββώρα μεμαρτύρηται προφῆτις εἶναι, λαβοῦα δὲ Μαριὰμ ἡ ἀδελφὴ Ἀαρὼν τὸ τύμπανον ἐξῆρχε τῶν γυναικῶν. ἀλλ᾽ οὐκ ἂν εὕροις ὅτι Δεββῶρα ἐδημηγόρησεν εἰς τὸν λαὸν ὥσπερ Ἱερεμίας καὶ Ἡσαίας· οὐκ ἂν εὕροις ὅτι Ὀλδὰ προφῆτις οὖσα ἐλάλησετῷ λαῷ ἀλλ᾽ ἑνί τινι ἐλθόντι πρὸς αὐτήν. ἀλλὰ καὶ ἐν τῷ εὐαγγελίῳ ἀνα γέγραπται Ἄννα προφῆτι, θυγάτηρ Φανουήλ, ἐκ φυλῆ Ἀήρ· ἀλλ᾽ οὐκ ἐν ἐκκλησίᾳ ἐλάλησεν. ἵνα οὖν καὶ δοθῇ ἐκ σημείου προφητικοῦ εἶναι προφῆτις γυνή, ἀλλ᾽ οὐκ ἐπιτρέπεται ταύτῃ λαλεῖν ἐν ἐκκλησίᾳ. ὅτε ἐλάλησε Μαριὰμ ἡ προ φῆτις ἄρχουσα ἦν τινων γυναικῶν· αἰσχρὸν γὰρ γυναικὶ λαλεῖν ἐν ἐκκλησίᾳ, καὶ διδάκειν δὲ γυναικὶ οὐκ ἐπιτρέπω ἁπλῶς ἀλλ᾽ οὐδὲ αὐθεντεῖν ἀνδρό.

[35] Heinz-Werner Neudorfer, *Der erste Brief des Paulus an Timotheus* (Wuppertal: Brockhaus, 2004), 130.

That this passage hardly lends itself for a non-patriarchal reinterpretation is also clear from the specific road to redemption that
Paul recommends for women. He does not suggest proper teaching
and non-domineering ways of taking authority. His answer could
be argued to be feminism's worst nightmare: "she will be saved
through childbearing" (σωθήσεται δὲ διὰ τῆς τεκνογονίας) and that
only if she continues to aspire to faith, love and purity in all modesty. Waters argued for "Childbearing" in 1 Tim 2:15 as a metaphor for "virtuesbearing",[36] but at a philological level his translation "All women and men must give birth to and continue in faith,
love, holiness, and temperance in order to be saved"[37] lacks support
in the textual context or the reception and history of this passage.
And as Mouton and van der Wolde already pointed out, this hardly
helps the cause against a patriarchal reading, because this metaphor
would only reinforce existing traditionalist conditions.

But taken literally in context, this is "childbearing salvation" is
the final patriarchal sting, as it shows that according to the author
of 1Timothy, a woman will be saved in her very relation to her husband. Admittedly, this phrase can also be translated as "But she will
be kept safe through <the ordeal of> childbearing",[38] but this would
only intensify the patriarchal nature of this passage. The condition-
al clause causes that a woman's survival of childbirth now becomes
dependent on her faith, love, purity and overall modesty. From a
feminine perspective this would make the passage worse, not better. It is the equivalent of "Don't forget that lots of women die in
childbirth and you might be next". It also emphasises that physical

---

[36] Waters, op. cit., 734.

[37] Ibid., 735.

[38] See Moyer Hubbard, "Kept safe through childbearing: maternal mortality,
justification by faith, and the social setting of 1Timothy 2:15", *Journal Evangelical Theological Society* 55/4 (2012), 743-62; cf. S. Fuhrmann, "Saved
by childbirth: struggling ideologies, the female body and a placing of 1 Tim
2:15a", *Neotestamentica* 44/1(2010), 31-46.

union with a husband might be deadly, but that a woman may still survive all real and present dangers if she has enough faith. This message spoken in a society where at least one out of ten women died in childbirth is rather nightmarish. If a woman doesn't survive the consequences a bodily relationship with a man, one may infer it is due to her lack of faith, love, purity or modesty. Only a 21st century male theologian could come up with a solution that carries these implications.

Perhaps the most significant for this debate, is the fact that the structure of the apostle's argument for the silence and submission of women is built on non-cultural factors.

11 Let a woman learn in silence[39] with full submission. 12 I permit no woman to teach or to have authority over a man; she is to keep silent. 13 For Adam was formed first, then Eve; 14 and Adam was not deceived, but the woman was deceived and became a transgressor. 15 Yet she will be saved through childbearing, provided they continue in faith and love and holiness, with modesty. (1Tim2:11-15, NRSV).[40]

To warrant his silencing of women in church, the apostle takes his readers back to the prehistorical creation events that are revealed in Genesis. For Paul these have repercussions for all time. In his apostolic teaching it is decisive that in God's role model or

---

[39] Paul's view is not unlike that of Aristotle who says that it is a special attribute of women to be silent but of men to command, quoting a poet who insists: γυναικὶ κόσμον ἡ σιγὴ φέρει; freely translated as "silence is a woman's glory" (Politics I.V). See Aristotle, *Politics*. Loeb Classical Library 264 (Cambridge: Harvard University Press, 1944), 64-5.

[40] 1Tim2 (NA28): 11Γυνὴ ἐν ἡσυχίᾳ μανθανέτω ἐν πάσῃ ὑποταγῇ· 12διδάσκειν δὲ γυναικὶ οὐκ ἐπιτρέπω οὐδὲ αὐθεντεῖν ἀνδρός, ἀλλ' εἶναι ἐν ἡσυχίᾳ. 13Ἀδὰμ γὰρ πρῶτος ἐπλάσθη, εἶτα Εὔα. 14καὶ Ἀδὰμ οὐκ ἠπατήθη, ἡ δὲ γυνὴ ἐξαπατηθεῖσα ἐν παραβάσει γέγονεν· 15σωθήσεται δὲ διὰ τῆς τεκνογονίας, ἐὰν μείνωσιν ἐν πίστει καὶ ἀγάπῃ καὶ ἁγιασμῷ μετὰ σωφροσύνης·

prototype, man was created first and woman only subsequently as a help for man (Gen 2:20). In Paul's view, the distinct places of the sexes in the congregation of Ephesus, or wherever for that matter, should be naturally modeled after this same authority structure.

After pointing to God's creation purposes and the order of creation, Paul moves on to mankind's fall into sin (Gen. 3). The historical events leading up to the fall with God's subsequent curse are a second reason to warrant the silencing of women in church and to prevent them from usurping authority over men. 'Woman' (ἡ δὲ γυνὴ: generic use, not 'Eve') took the initiative in humanity's disobedience against God and actively took prohibited fruit from the tree of knowledge of good and evil. She also gave to her husband, who ate as well. While Adam was ultimately responsible and accountable as head of woman, it is clear that 'the weaker sex' took the active role in ruining humanity's relationship with its Creator.

Significantly, there is a parallel for this creation-based differentiation between the sexes in the Gospels. The Lord Jesus provides a similar pattern of argument in his view of marriage. Particularly Mark's Gospel places these teachings within a context of little children and Jesus' protective concern and welcoming attitude towards them. Although not as a sandwich, similar emphasis is also found in the parallel passage in Matthew. While not outspoken, the structure of the narratives suggests that Jesus teachings on marriage and divorce were also with wider family life and the vulnerability of children in mind. In the Gospels these teachings are not argued on the basis of culture or general humanistic values, but Jesus states that he derives his view from God's revelation about the historical creation of mankind. This is particularly clear in Matthews' Gospel, where Jesus specifically refers to a written record of revelation (Matt 19:4-6):

> 4 "Haven't you read," he replied, "that at the beginning the Creator 'made them male and female,'5 and said, 'For

> this reason a man will leave his father and mother and be
> united to his wife, and the two will become one flesh'?
> 6 So they are no longer two, but one flesh. Therefore what
> God has joined together, let no one separate."

Like the author of 1 Timothy, Jesus points to the record of God's revelation in Scripture as the source and authority for his views. Like Paul he also takes this creation account as historical and with enduring effects. Therefore these events in the Genesis narrative are taken as normative, even though there were no humans present or able to observe and record. In that sense the creation stories are prehistoric, and Jesus and Paul take God's (and Moses') Word for it. This makes their views entirely reliant on the reliability of God's revelation in Scripture.

Jesus' line of reasoning in Matthew is very similar to the argument in 1 Timothy 2:11-15. Paul's reasons for insisting on public submission of women, in church or elsewhere, are not cultural but historical:

1) His first argument points to God's purpose in creating woman originally as a support for man, Genesis 2:20-25 (NRSV):

> 20 The man gave names to all cattle, and to the birds of the
> air, and to every animal of the field; but for the man there
> was not found a helper as his partner. 21 So the Lord God
> caused a deep sleep to fall upon the man, and he slept; then
> he took one of his ribs and closed up its place with flesh.
> 22 And the rib that the Lord God had taken from the man
> he made into a woman and brought her to the man. 23 Then
> the man said, "This at last is bone of my bones and flesh of
> my flesh; this one shall be called Woman, for out of Man
> this one was taken." 24 Therefore a man leaves his father
> and his mother and clings to his wife, and they become one
> flesh. 25 And the man and his wife were both naked, and
> were not ashamed.

The NRSV introduces the word "partner," but this suggestion of equality is not found in the Hebrew or the LXX, which both read "an help meet for him" (cf. KJV).

2) Also Paul's second argument is founded outside temporary cultural circumstances: the role of the woman in humanity's original rebellion and God's subsequent curse on creation, which would historically be overcome by the continuation of life, Genesis 3:15-16 (NRSV):

> 15 "I will put enmity between you and the woman, and between your offspring and hers; he will strike your head, and you will strike his heel." 16 To the woman he said, "I will greatly increase your pangs in childbearing; in pain you shall bring forth children, yet your desire shall be for your husband, and he shall rule over you."

So although the cultural Greco-Roman context may have played a role of some sort, and may have helped Paul and his readers (including Jews with similar views) to embrace these views more readily, it does not feature in the apostle's argument. Had Paul motivated the submission and silence of women on the basis of not giving offence to others; that would have been a different scenario entirely. However, he does not. Paul's argument lies in God creation purposes and the historical events leading to the post-Fall condition of this present world. Exegetical options for any other than patriarchal use of this passage are rather limited.

This being said, it is also important to put the question whether Paul's patriarchal teachings in 1Timothy 2:11-15 automatically equals a call for discrimination of women, exposing them to health risks and all sorts of abuse? The short answer to this is "no", and the long answer has been given by others already.[41] Within the con-

---

[41] E.g. P.H.R. van Houwelingen, "Macht, onmacht en volmacht in 1 Timoteüs 2:8-15", *HTS Teologiese Studies/Theological Studies* 68/1(2012), 1-9.

text of Paul's world view, it is the main thrust of this pastoral letter that all Christian conduct, especially by male leaders, should be marked by "love, in faith, in purity" (1Tim 4:12). He explains this at the very start of his epistle: "But the aim of such instruction is love that comes from a pure heart, a good conscience, and sincere faith" (1Tim 1:5). In a practical way this is expressed in man's respectful attitude to women. Timothy is enjoined by Paul to speak to "to older women as mothers, to younger women as sisters—with absolute purity" (1Tim 5:2). The care for widows is especially encouraged: "And whoever does not provide for relatives, and especially for family members, has denied the faith and is worse than an unbeliever" (1Tim 5:8).

This shows that while the apostle's teaching calls for distinct roles for women and men, this is not in any way aimed at promoting a situation of an abusive male leadership. The very opposite is called for: a safe environment for women, dominated by love, social care and sexual purity.

Conclusion: a way forward?

An overview of approaches of 1Timothy 2:11-15 by 21st century scholars from Southern Africa has shown that none defend traditional African values on that basis of this passage, or at all. Instead nearly all contemporary contributions are vocal in their support for socio-political agenda's that aims at a greater leadership involvement of women in church or society. At the same time all theologians concerned are pessimistic that 1Timothy 2:11-15 lends itself for that purpose. However, attempts to 'redeem' this passage have been shown to fail at a linguistic or theological level. A philological examination of 1Timothy 2:11-15 indicates that this failure is largely due to the non-cultural arguments which are employed by the author of this epistle, who points to God's revelation about a pre-historical creation order and fall of mankind into sin as basis for the separate roles for women and men that he advocates. It is also clear that, in the context of St. Paul's world view, these distinctions are not perceived discriminatory in the 21st century sense. His admonitions are directed at women taking God's intended place, as all men and women are pieces of this jigsaw puzzle of a fallen world. One may not agree with 1Timothy's perspective, but its attitude towards women is one of concern and the greatest respect.

As a result there seem only two viable ways forward to come to terms with this passage in a 21st century situation, in or out of Africa:

1) A traditional solution. This approach adopts 1Timothy's view of history and revelation and prefers the traditional interpretation of the Church and the cultural heritage of the African continent over and against the prevailing Western socio-political pressures of the 21st century. This is not a popular solution, but it carries textual weight and scholarly integrity.

2) The "wildlife solution". A realisation that failures to 'redeem' this passage were not caused by a want of trying or lack of scholarship, leaves the alternative of preferring the socio-political paradigm over and against the teachings of 1Timothy. Rather than to try and tame an African lion, and using Scriptural primary source against its message and context, the preferred course would be to leave the "text of terror" in his natural habitat. Lions belong to the African Savanna.

www.ingramcontent.com/pod-product-compliance
Lightning Source LLC
Chambersburg PA
CBHW030634270326
41929CB00007B/71